SCHOENBERG
AND HIS WORLD

D1557172

SCHOENBERG AND HIS WORLD

EDITED BY WALTER FRISCH

PRINCETON UNIVERSITY PRESS
PRINCETON, NEW JERSEY

Copyright © 1999 by Princeton University Press

For permissions information see p. xi

Published by Princeton University Press, 41 William Street,
Princeton, New Jersey 08540
In the United Kingdom: Princeton University Press,
Chichester, West Sussex

All Rights Reserved

Library of Congress Cataloging-in-Publication Data

Schoenberg and his world / edited by Walter Frisch.
p. cm. — (Bard Music Festival series)
Includes bibliographical references p. and index.
Contents: Essays—Arnold Schönberg (1912)—Arnold Schoenberg speaks—
Schoenberg and America.
ISBN 0-691-04860-6 (cl : alk. paper).—ISBN 0-691-04861-4 (pb : alk. paper)
1. Schoenberg, Arnold, 1874–1951. I. Frisch, Walter. II. Series.
ML410.S283S36 1999 780'.92—dc21 99-31792 CIP

This publication has been produced by the Bard College Publications Office:
Ginger Shore, Director
Juliet Meyers, Art Director

This book has been composed in Baskerville
by Juliet Meyers

Music typeset by Don Giller

The paper used in this publication meets the minimum requirements of
ANSI/NISO Z39.48-1992 (R1997) (*Permanence of Paper*)

http://pup.princeton.edu

Printed in the United States of America

1 3 5 7 9 10 8 6 4 2

1 3 5 7 9 10 8 6 4 2
(Pbk.)

Designed by Juliet Meyers

Contents

Contents

PART IV
SCHOENBERG AND AMERICA
Selected and Introduced by Sabine Feisst

Schoenberg on America: Articles, Speeches, Commentary

American Composers on Schoenberg

Preface and Acknowledgments

Schoenberg made clear that he wanted to be appreciated and remembered primarily as a composer. But almost fifty years after his death, and as the twentieth century draws rapidly to a close, it is the diversity of Schoenberg's talents and accomplishments that seems to attract the most interest. Analytical studies of his music still appear with regularity. But a heavily theoretical and work-immanent focus, characteristic especially of the first two decades after his death, has given way to—or is more often enriched by—considerations of Schoenberg's activities as teacher, performer, commentator, music theorist, painter, and Jewish thinker-activist. It has become increasingly apparent that all of these facets are integral to Schoenberg's personal and artistic identity.

Schoenberg and His World takes a multi-pronged approach to the daunting task of capturing this protean figure between two covers. The volume opens with a chronology of Schoenberg's life and works, prepared by Marilyn McCoy from the most current biographical and historical information. The six essays in Part I project something of the diversity (and frequent revisionism) of recent perspectives on Schoenberg. Leon Botstein suggests that Schoenberg's music altered the conventional relations between audience and composer by eliminating a psychological and more "comfortable" style of listening, and by substituting for it an appreciation that was to be based on ethical and cultural considerations. Drawing on important primary sources not previously treated, Severine Neff demonstrates how the apparent lack of a system in Schoenberg's theoretical writings, often seen as a limitation, is in fact a direct result (and virtue) of his compositional thinking and personality. In a study of Schoenberg's later Berlin period that focuses on the composition and reception of the often-neglected (or misunderstood) Six Pieces for Male Chorus, Op. 35, of 1929–30, Joseph Auner demonstrates that despite his image as an elite and isolated artist, Schoenberg was in fact deeply engaged in public, societal issues as both composer and performer.

Rudolf Stephan, in a classic essay first published in 1978 and translated here for the first time, probes aspects of Schoenberg's profound relationship to the music of J. S. Bach, as manifested not only in his own compositions, transcriptions, and statements, but also in his revealing annotations on an analysis by Heinrich Schenker. Reinhold Brinkmann's account of the Chamber Symphony, Op. 9, which appeared originally in German in 1977, reveals how extensively this key work of Schoenberg's early period is embedded in, and reflective of, the turn-of-the-century Viennese crisis of subjectivity. Finally, J. Peter Burkholder shows that even in his most apparently radical atonal and twelve-tone works, Schoenberg seeks to recreate, out of a "reactionary" impulse but in new terms, the abstract compositional principles of traditional Austro-German music.

The extensive documentary portions of *Schoenberg and His World* (Parts II–IV) reveal Schoenberg at three successive locales and stages of his career: Vienna in the first two decades of the century; Berlin in the later 1920s and early 1930s; and the United States, after 1933. Part II presents a complete translation, by Barbara Z. Schoenberg, of the earliest book devoted to Schoenberg, a collection of essays by pupils and admirers presented to the composer in 1912, a period when (although temporarily resident in Berlin) he was most closely associated with Viennese musical life and culture. Part III presents lively and revealing accounts from newspapers, compiled by Joseph Auner, of Schoenberg's public lectures and interviews in Berlin in the period 1926–33, when he occupied one of the most prestigious chairs of musical composition in Europe, at the Prussian Academy of the Arts.

Part IV of *Schoenberg and His World*, assembled and introduced by Sabine Feisst, offers the richest documentary picture available to date on the final eighteen years of Schoenberg's life, which were spent in the United States. Contrary to received opinion, these selections show that Schoenberg was closely involved with, and widely recognized within, the musical life of his adopted country. We learn how he took an interest in American musical culture well before he arrived here, and how he participated in it eagerly after he settled here. Also included in this segment of the volume are writings by important American critics and composers that make clear how much interest, respect, and informed commentary were generated by Schoenberg's arrival and presence.

Many different colleagues and friends have helped bring this volume into being. For assistance with aspects of translation from German, I am extremely grateful to Willi Goetschel, Ulrich Krämer, and Robert Snarrenberg. Two scholars represented in the volume,

Joseph Auner and Sabine Feisst, were generous with their knowledge and time far beyond their own contributions. Wayne Shoaf and Jerry McBride, former archivists at the Arnold Schoenberg Institute in Los Angeles, were responsive to all queries. Wayne's encylopedic knowledge of Schoenberg proved especially valuable throughout the preparation of the volume. The archivist of the new Arnold Schönberg Center in Vienna, Therese Muxeneder, has been helpful and wonderfully prompt in providing materials for publication. As always, Lawrence Schoenberg, was generous with permissions for access to and reproduction of materials. I am extremely grateful to my research assistant at Columbia, Mark Burford, for his efficient and technologically adept work. To Paul De Angelis, Ginger Shore, Juliet Meyers, the editorial/production team at Bard College, I owe my thanks for making the publication process remarkably smooth and anxiety-free.

• • •

The images of Schoenberg's paintings are reproduced with the permission of Artists Rights Society, New York, and Verwertungsgesellschaft Bildender Künstler, Vienna. The essays by Reinhold Brinkmann and Rudolf Stephan appear here in translation with the authors' permission. The measures of Schoenberg's Fourth String Quartet, Op. 37, appearing in J. Peter Burkholder's essay are reprinted with permission from G. Schirmer, Inc. The measures of Schoenberg's *Erwartung*, Op. 2, no. 1; "Das schöne Beet," Op. 15, no. 10; and Piano Suite, Op. 25, appearing in Burkholder's essay are reprinted with permission from Belmont Music Publishers. The text of *Arnold Schoenberg* (Part II) was originally published in German in 1912 by Piper Verlag in Munich. It appears here in translation with the permission of Lawrence Schoenberg. The articles, speeches, and commentaries in Part IV, "Schoenberg on America" are reprinted with permission from Lawrence Schoenberg. Nicolas Slonimsky's article "American Composers on Schoenberg," in Part IV, originally appeared in the *Boston Transcript* in 1933, and appears here with the permission of Electra Yourke Slonimsky. Lou Harrison's article is reprinted with the author's permission. The article by Roger Sessions is reprinted with the permission of Elizabeth Sessions. Henry Cowell's article is reprinted with permission from Richard Teitelbaum. The musical examples from Schoenberg's Op. 35 appearing in Joseph Auner's essay are reprinted with permission from Boosey & Hawkes, Inc.

A Schoenberg Chronology

MARILYN McCOY

Year	Life	Works
1874	Arnold Schoenberg[1] born on September 13 in Vienna. Eldest child of Jewish parents Samuel (1838–89) and Pauline Schönberg (1848–1921).	
1876	Birth of sister, Ottilie (1876–1954).	
1880	Enters elementary school.	
1882	Birth of brother, Heinrich (1822–1941). Begins to learn violin.	
1883		First attempts at composition, mostly violin duets.
1885	Enters secondary school (Realschule). Meets Oskar Adler (1875–1955), who teaches him music theory and becomes close friend. Teaches himself cello and begins playing chamber music with friends.	Begins composing marches, polkas, and other modest works.
1889	Father, Samuel Schönberg, dies.	
1890	Leaves school without completing diploma to help support his family. Starts work as bank clerk.	
1891 or 1892	Becomes friends with David Josef Bach (1874–1947), who shares his interests in poetry, philosophy, and music.	
1893	Plays cello in amateur orchestra, Polyhymnia, conducted by	Wins a composition prize for his song "Schilflied," one of at least

---

[1] Throughout this chronology, titles of Schoenberg's compositions are shown in uppercase letters, and the spelling of his name is the one he adopted after his departure from Germany.

Alexander von Zemlinsky (1871–1942). Zemlinsky becomes Schoenberg's first composition teacher. Spends time in cafés engaged in passionate discussion with friends.

twenty-eight songs composed before the publication of Op. 1, TWO SONGS.

1894

Composes THREE PIANO PIECES.

1895 Gives up his job at bank. Decides to devote himself completely to music. Begins to conduct choruses of factory workers.

1896

Composes SIX PIECES FOR PIANO FOUR HANDS, SERENADE FOR SMALL ORCHESTRA, and a number of songs.

1897 Earns money doing orchestrations and piano-vocal scores of other composers' works.

Begins to compose in "expanded" tonality. Composition and premiere of STRING QUARTET IN D MAJOR in Vienna. Composition of Dehmel settings "MÄDCHENFRÜHLING" and "NICHT DOCH!"

1898 Converts to Protestantism.

Composition of TWO SONGS, Op. 1 (Levetzow). Attempts a symphonic poem, FRÜHLINGSTOD (Death of spring).

1899 Conducts men's chorus in Heiligenstadt, near Vienna.

Composition of FOUR SONGS, Op. 2 (Dehmel, Schlaf), and string sextet, VERKLÄRTE NACHT (TRANSFIGURED NIGHT), Op. 4. Begins SIX SONGS, Op. 3 (*Des Knaben Wunderhorn*, Keller, Dehmel, Jacobsen, Lingg).

1900 Working several jobs to support himself and family: conducts worker choruses, orchestrates operettas. Meets Alma Schindler (1879–1964), who will later marry Gustav Mahler (1860–1911).

Begins work on GURRELIEDER (Jacobsen). Premieres in Vienna of Op. 1, Op. 2, and Op. 3, no. 6.

1901 Marries Mathilde von Zemlinsky (1877–1923), sister of Alexander, his teacher. Moves to Berlin.

Composes eight cabaret songs, the *BRETTL-LIEDER*. Finishes drafting GURRELIEDER, but does not

Works as conductor and arranger at Ernst von Wolzogen's (1855–1934) Buntes Theater, a cabaret.

complete the orchestration until 1911.

1902 Birth of daughter Gertrud (1902–47). Orchestrates operettas for extra money. Meets Richard Strauss (1864–1949), who recommends him for teaching job at Stern Conservatory.

Begins symphonic poem PELLEAS UND MELISANDE, Op. 5. Breaks off work on GURRELIEDER. Premiere of VERKLÄRTE NACHT in Vienna.

1903 Meets and begins correspondence with Ferruccio Busoni (1866–1924). Signs contract with first publisher, Verlag Dreililien in Berlin. Returns to Vienna. Strauss's support helps him win Liszt Stipend. Teaches harmony and counterpoint at private school, Schwarzwaldschule, in suburbs of Vienna. Egon Wellesz (1885–1974), Heinrich Jalowetz (1882–1946), and others study composition privately with Schoenberg.

Completes PELLEAS UND MELISANDE and SIX SONGS, Op. 3. Begins EIGHT SONGS, Op. 6 (Hart, Dehmel, Remer, Conradi, Keller, Mackay, Aram, Nietzsche); and SIX ORCHESTRAL SONGS, Op. 8 (Hart, *Des Knaben Wunderhorn*, Petrarch). Opp. 1–2 published by Verlag Dreililien.

1904 Meets Gustav Mahler. With Zemlinsky, founds Vereinigung schaffender Tonkünstler (Society of creative composers); Mahler chosen as honorary president. Alban Berg (1885–1935), Anton Webern (1883–1945), and Erwin Stein (1885–1958) become private composition students.

Completes SIX ORCHESTRAL SONGS, Op. 8. Begins FIRST STRING QUARTET IN D MINOR, Op. 7.

1905 Architect Adolf Loos (1870–1933) secretly finances many early concerts of Schoenberg's works; later on they become friends.

Completes FIRST STRING QUARTET and EIGHT SONGS, Op. 6. Conducts premiere of PELLEAS UND MELISANDE in Vienna. Begins, but does not complete, EIN STELLDICHEIN (A Rendezvous), a piano quintet.

1906 Birth of son Georg (1906–74).

Composition of FIRST CHAMBER SYMPHONY, Op. 9. Begins work on SECOND CHAMBER SYMPHONY, Op. 38, which is not completed until 1939.

1907 Begins to experiment with painting. Befriends painter Richard Gerstl (1883–1908).

Composes chorus *FRIEDE AUF ERDEN* (Peace on earth), Op. 13, and TWO BALLADS FOR VOICE AND PIANO, Op. 12 (Ammann, V. Klemperer). Begins SECOND STRING QUARTET, Op. 10, and TWO SONGS, Op. 14 (George, Henckell). Premieres of FIRST STRING QUARTET and FIRST CHAMBER SYMPHONY in Vienna cause scandal; Mahler comes to Schoenberg's defense.

1908 Marital crisis: Mathilde briefly abandons Schoenberg and her two children to live with Gerstl. She soon returns to Schoenberg, but Gerstl commits suicide. First concert of music by Schoenberg's students.

Begins to compose in more dissonant, free atonal style. Completes SECOND STRING QUARTET; its premiere in Vienna causes the greatest scandal to date. Also completes TWO SONGS, Op. 14. Begins song cycle *DAS BUCH DER HÄNGENDEN GÄRTEN* (The book of the hanging gardens), Op. 15 (George), and Rilke setting "AM STRANDE" (On the shore).

1909 Seriously devotes himself to writing and publishes "About Music Criticism," the first of many articles. Experiments with invention of a typewriter for music notation. Signs contract with Universal Edition, Vienna, and begins long relationship with its director Emil Hertzka (1869–1932). Busoni irritates Schoenberg with "arrangement" of Piano Piece, Op. 11, no. 2, but they remain friends.

Completes *BUCH DER HÄNGENDEN GÄRTEN*. Composes three masterworks at great speed—THREE PIANO PIECES, Op. 11; one-act monodrama, *ERWARTUNG* (Expectation), Op. 17 (Pappenheim); and FIVE ORCHESTRAL PIECES, Op. 16.

1910 First exhibition of Schoenberg's paintings at Galerie Heller, Vienna, supplemented by concerts of his music. Lectures on music theory and teaches composition at the Royal Academy of Music in Vienna. Begins *Harmonielehre* (*Theory of Harmony*). Successful performance of *PELLEAS UND MELISANDE* in Berlin.

Premiere of THREE PIANO PIECES, Op. 11, and *BUCH DER HÄNGENDEN GÄRTEN* in Vienna. Composes THREE LITTLE PIECES FOR CHAMBER ORCHESTRA; third one remains a fragment. Begins one-act opera *DIE GLÜCKLICHE HAND* (The hand of fate), Op. 18, to his own text.

1911 Begins correspondence with painter Wassily Kandinsky (1866–1944). Three of Schoenberg's paintings are exhibited at Kandinsky's "Blue Rider" exhibit; article by Schoenberg will appear in *Blue Rider Almanac*. Moves back to Berlin in fall, because of poor financial situation and anti-Semitism; begins teaching at Stern Conservatory. Finishes writing *Harmonielehre*, dedicated to memory of Mahler, who died this year. Meets Otto Klemperer (1885–1973) and Hermann Scherchen (1891–1966), who will both premiere Schoenberg works.

Completes the *GURRELIEDER* after a ten-year hiatus. Composition and Vienna premiere of SIX LITTLE PIANO PIECES, Op. 19. Also composes the vocal chamber work *HERZGEWÄCHSE* (Heart's flowering), Op. 20 (Maeterlinck, trans. Ammer and Oppeln-Bronikowski).

1912 Teaches composition in Berlin; Edward Steuermann (1892–1964) and Edward Clark (1888–1962) become students. Students present him with essays in his honor in *Arnold Schönberg*, first book about him (Piper Verlag). Conducts *PELLEAS UND MELISANDE* in Prague, Amsterdam, and St. Petersburg. Gives lecture about Mahler in Prague and Berlin. Tours with *PIERROT LUNAIRE* through Germany and Austria.

Composes and conducts premiere of *PIERROT LUNAIRE*, Op. 21 (Giraud, trans. Hartleben), in Berlin. First Berlin performance of SIX LITTLE PIANO PIECES, Op. 19, and *HERZGEWÄCHSE*. Arranges three Schubert songs and Beethoven's *Adelaide* songs, Op. 46, for voice and orchestra. Premiere of FIVE ORCHESTRAL PIECES in London, conducted by Sir Henry Wood (1869–1944).

1913 Schoenberg is awarded the first Mahler Stipend.

Completes *DIE GLÜCKLICHE HAND*. Begins FOUR ORCHESTRAL SONGS, Op. 22 (Dowson, trans. George; Rilke). Premiere of *GURRELIEDER* in Vienna, conducted by Franz Schreker (1878–1934), is Schoenberg's biggest success to date. But scandal again ensues during a Vienna performance of works by Mahler, Zemlinsky, Webern, Berg, and Schoenberg. First American performance: FIVE ORCHESTRAL PIECES in Chicago with Frederick Stock (1872–1942) and the Chicago Symphony Orchestra.

1914 World War I begins. Conducts FIVE ORCHESTRAL PIECES in London and Amsterdam, *GURRELIEDER* in Leipzig.

Premiere of three of the SIX ORCHESTRAL SONGS, Op. 8, in Prague. Sketches a scherzo, part

Begins keeping a "cloud diary" to predict the outcome of war.

of a projected symphony, which has a theme using all twelve notes of the chromatic scale.

1915 Conducts Beethoven's Ninth Symphony in Vienna. Moves back to Vienna. Volunteers for Austrian army in December.

Begins text of an oratorio, DIE JAKOBSLEITER (Jacob's ladder).

1916 With requests of friends and help from Béla Bartók (1881–1945), Schoenberg is discharged from army as medically unfit.

Completes FOUR ORCHESTRAL SONGS, Op. 22. Resumes work on JAKOBSLEITER. Inspired by his war experience, composes a march for chamber orchestra, DIE EISERNE BRIGADE (The iron brigade).

1917 Recalled to Austrian army, but discharged permanently because of health problems. Egon Schiele (1890–1917) paints Schoenberg's portrait.

Finishes text and begins music for JAKOBSLEITER, in which he starts to experiment with serial techniques of composition.

1918 World War I ends. Starts new composition seminar at the Schwarzwaldschule. Moves to Mödling in outer suburbs of Vienna. Conducts ten public rehearsals of FIRST CHAMBER SYMPHONY in Vienna. Founds Verein für musikalische Privataufführungen (Society for private musical performances) with Erwin Ratz (1898–1973) and others.

1919 Hanns Eisler (1898–1962), Rudolf Kolisch (1896–1978), and Karl Rankl (1898–1968) join Schoenberg's composition class. Speaks at symposium in honor of Loos. Josef Matthias Hauer composes the twelve-tone work *Nomos*.

1920 Extended visits to Netherlands. Attends first Mahler Festival in Amsterdam in summer; named first president of the International Mahler Society. Concert tour to Netherlands in fall and winter; gives composition lessons. Maurice Ravel (1875–1937) and Alfredo

Begins FIVE PIANO PIECES, Op. 23, and SERENADE, Op. 24. Further experimentation with serial techniques.

Casella (1883–1947) perform at
Verein concert in Vienna.

1921 Returns to Vienna in spring. With
various assistants, arranges works
by Busoni, Mahler, Reger, and
Johann Strauss for Verein per-
ormances until its last regular
concert in December. Conducts
GURRELIEDER in Amsterdam;
Zemlinsky conducts GURRELIEDER
in Prague. Suffers anti-Semitic
prejudice during a vacation in
Mattsee, near Salzburg. Death of
mother Pauline. Publication of
Schoenberg biography by Egon
Wellesz.

Completes formulation of
twelve-tone method. Begins
PIANO SUITE, Op. 25. Though
all movements of opp. 23 and
24 are composed according to
serial procedures, only 5th
mvt. of Op. 23 and 4th mvt. of
Op. 24 are based on a twelve-
tone row. Op. 25 is
Schoenberg's first completely
twelve-tone work.

1922 Conducts PIERROT LUNAIRE in
Prague. GURRELIEDER performed in
Duisburg, PIERROT given in
Switzerland and Netherlands.
Meets Darius Milhaud
(1892–1974) and Francis Poulenc
(1899–1963); corresponds with
Edgard Varèse (1883–1965).

Breaks off work on JAKOBSLEITER;
the work remains unfinished.
Composition and world premiere of Schoenberg's orchestral arrangements of two Bach
chorale preludes, "SCHMÜCKE
DICH, O LIEBE SEELE" and "KOMM,
GOTT, SCHÖPFER, HEILIGER GEIST,"
in New York with Josef
Stransky (1872-1936) and New
York Philharmonic; this was
the first world premiere of a
Schoenberg work in America.

1923 Breaks off relations with
Kandinsky because of anti-Semitic
tendencies of Bauhaus group.
Conducts concert of his own
works in Copenhagen. His wife,
Mathilde Schönberg, dies.
Roberto Gerhard (1896–1970)
becomes student. American premiere of PIERROT. Correspondence
with Joseph Matthias Hauer
(1883–1959), who also is experimenting with serial composition,
and who will later claim that he
invented twelve-tone method
before Schoenberg. Begins planning a Zionist play, *Der biblische
Weg* (The Biblical way).

Returns to composing in traditional forms, including variations and dances. Finishes FIVE
PIANO PIECES, Op. 23; SERENADE,
Op. 24; and PIANO SUITE, Op.
25. Begins WIND QUINTET, Op.
26.

1924 PIERROT concert tour in Italy,
where he meets Giacomo Puccini

Finishes WIND QUINTET, Op. 26;
its premiere is directed by

(1858–1924) and other Italian composers. Special concerts and publications arranged in honor of Schoenberg's 50th birthday. In August, marries Gertrud Kolisch (1898–1967), sister of student, Rudolf Kolisch. Paul Stefan (1879–1943) biography of Schoenberg published. Oskar Kokoschka (1886–1980) paints Schoenberg's portrait. Performance of PIERROT in Paris. Begins planning his autobiography.

Schoenberg's son-in-law, Felix Greissle (1894–1982). Begins SUITE FOR PIANO, WOODWINDS, AND STRINGS, Op. 29. Conducts the premiere of SERENADE, Op. 24, in Donaueschingen. Premiere of ERWARTUNG in Prague, conducted by Zemlinsky. Premiere of DIE GLÜCKLICHE HAND in Vienna, conducted by Fritz Stiedry (1883–1968).

1925   In Italy on honeymoon, meets Casella and Gian-Francesco Malipiero (1882–1973). Conducts SERENADE, Op. 24, at the Festival of International Society of New Music in Venice. Igor Stravinsky (1882–1971) also attends the festival, but the two composers apparently do not meet. Upon death of Busoni, called to be professor of master classes in composition at the Prussian Academy of the Arts in Berlin. Begins to formulate *Der musikalische Gedanke und seine Darstellung* (The musical idea and its representation), an ambitious, ultimately unfinished theoretical treatise about his compositional aesthetic. PIERROT and FIRST CHAMBER SYMPHONY performed in Barcelona.

Composes FOUR PIECES FOR MIXED CHORUS, Op. 27 (Schoenberg, Bethge). Begins THREE SATIRES FOR MIXED CHORUS, Op. 28 (Schoenberg).

1926   Moves to Berlin. Students Roberto Gerhard, Winfried Zillig (1905–63), Josef Rufer (1893–1985), and his first American pupil, Adolph Weiss (1891–1971), follow him there; Walter Goehr (1903–60) joins composition class. Visits Vienna in fall. Named honorary member of Academy of Santa Cecilia in Rome. Makes detailed outline for *Der biblische Weg*.

Finishes THREE SATIRES FOR MIXED CHORUS and SUITE, Op. 29. Begins VARIATIONS FOR ORCHESTRA, Op. 31.

1927   Conducts radio performance of PELLEAS UND MELISANDE in Berlin. Writing text, designing sets, and composing fragmentary incidental music for *Der biblische Weg*; the work, published posthumously, has never been performed. Makes peace with Kandinsky. Festival of Schoenberg's works in Paris. Also conducts in Spain. Becomes enthusiastic tennis player. Marc Blitzstein (1905–1964) becomes Schoenberg's student.

Composition and Vienna premiere of THIRD STRING QUARTET, Op. 30, commissioned by the American patron Elizabeth Sprague Coolidge (1864–1953). Premiere of SUITE, Op. 29, in Paris, Schoenberg conducting.

1928   Conducts GURRELIEDER in London. Concert tour of Switzerland. Performance of DIE GLÜCKLICHE HAND in Breslau. Spends summer on French Riviera; because of health problems, takes six-month leave from Berlin.

Finishes VARIATIONS FOR ORCHESTRA, which is premiered under Wilhelm Furtwängler (1886–1954) in Berlin. Arranges PRELUDE AND FUGUE IN E♭ MAJOR BY J. S. BACH for orchestra. Preparing libretto for opera MOSES UND ARON. Begins THREE FOLKSONGS FOR MIXED CHORUS, one-act comic opera VON HEUTE AUF MORGEN (From today until tomorrow), Op. 32 (text by Gertrud Schoenberg); and PIANO PIECE, Op. 33a.

1929   Resumes teaching in Berlin.

Finishes THREE FOLKSONGS FOR MIXED CHORUS, VON HEUTE AUF MORGEN, and PIANO PIECE, Op. 33a. Begins BEGLEITUNGSMUSIK ZU EINER LICHTSPIELSZENE (ACCOMPANIMENT TO A FILM SCENE), Op. 34, and SIX PIECES FOR MALE CHORUS, Op. 35 (Schoenberg). Arranges FOUR GERMAN FOLKSONGS for chorus and piano. Premiere of arrangement of BACH PRELUDE AND FUGUE IN E♭, Webern conducting.

1930   Performances of *ERWARTUNG* and *DIE GLÜCKLICHE HAND* at Kroll Opera in Berlin under Klemperer. Correspondence with Thomas Mann (1875–1955).

Finishes *BEGLEITUNGSMUSIK*; Hans Rosbaud (1895–1962) conducts its radio premiere in April with the Südwestfunk Symphony Orchestra in Frankfurt, and Klemperer conducts its "official" premiere in November in Berlin. Also completes SIX PIECES FOR MALE CHORUS, Op. 35. Premiere of

VON HEUTE AUF MORGEN in
Frankfurt. Begins composing
music for *MOSES UND ARON*.

1931   Because of poor health, moves to
Territet, Switzerland, then
Barcelona for an extended period
after conducting *ERWARTUNG* for
BBC in London.

Working on *MOSES UND ARON*.
Composes PIANO PIECE, Op.
33b, his last published work
for piano.

1932   Birth of daughter Nuria. Returns
to Berlin in June. Meets and
befriends Henry Cowell
(1897–1965). Berlin performance
of SECOND STRING QUARTET by
Kolisch Quartet in Berlin is last
performance of a Schoenberg
work in that city until after World
War II.

Finishes second act of *MOSES UND
ARON*; the third act remains
unfinished. Premiere of FOUR
ORCHESTRAL SONGS, Op. 22, in
Frankfurt under Rosbaud.
Begins CONCERTO FOR CELLO AND
ORCHESTRA AFTER A HARPSICHORD
CONCERTO BY G.M. MONN, a work
for which Schoenberg had composed a continuo part twenty
years earlier; he dedicates the
work to Pablo Casals (1876–
1973), who had championed
his music in Spain.

1933   Rise of Nazism in Europe.
After government takeover by
Hitler and the Nazis, Schoenberg
leaves Berlin in May; he will never
return to Europe. Nazis expel him
from Academy and freeze many of
his bank accounts. He and his
family spend summer in France.
Before Schoenberg, his wife, and
daughter Nuria depart via luxury
liner for New York in October, he
re-converts to Judaism in Paris in
the presence of Marc Chagall
(1889–1985) and others. After
conversion, changes spelling of
name to "oe" and stops using old
Gothic script. At first they settle in
Boston, where he teaches at
Malkin Conservatory; he also
travels by train to New York to
give private lessons.

Completes MONN CELLO
CONCERTO. Composes CONCERTO
FOR STRING QUARTET AND
ORCHESTRA AFTER THE CONCERTO
GROSSO IN G MINOR BY G. F.
HANDEL, and THREE SONGS, Op.
48 (Haringer).

1934   Conducts *PELLEAS UND MELISANDE* in
Boston. Lectures at University of
Chicago, Princeton, and on radio;
Chicago Symphony performs
FIRST CHAMBER SYMPHONY. Spends
summer in Chautauqua, New

Composes SUITE FOR STRING
ORCHESTRA, first work written in
U.S. Begins VIOLIN CONCERTO,
Op. 36. HANDEL CONCERTO pre-
miered in Prague.

York. Moves from Boston to Hollywood, California, because of health problems. Writes and lectures about plight of the Jews. Meets the physicist Albert Einstein (1879–1955).

1935	Health and financial circumstances improve. Teaches summer composition seminar at the University of Southern California in Los Angeles. Also gives private composition lessons to Hollywood composers and others; John Cage (1912–92), Gerald Strang (1908–83), Oscar Levant (1906–72), Alfred Newman (1900–70), David Raksin (b. 1912), and Leonard Stein (b. 1916) are among his students. Conducts concert of his own music in San Francisco. His old friend Klemperer conducts the Los Angeles Philharmonic in *VERKLÄRTE NACHT*, arranged for string orchestra. Meets Charlie Chaplin (1889– 1977). Considers, then rejects, request to compose music for film *The Good Earth*, but makes many sketches. Death of Alban Berg.	Continues work on VIOLIN CONCERTO. Arranges FIRST CHAMBER SYMPHONY for orchestra, numbering it Op. 9b. Premiere of SUITE FOR STRING ORCHESTRA under Klemperer in Los Angeles. Premiere of MONN CONCERTO by Emanuel Feuermann (1902–42) in London.
1936	Appointed Professor of Music at University of California, Los Angeles (UCLA). Moves to final residence in Brentwood Park, West Los Angeles, where he lives until his death. Befriends George Gershwin (1898–1937). Dika Newlin (b. 1923) becomes Schoenberg's student.	Completes VIOLIN CONCERTO, Op. 36. Composes FOURTH STRING QUARTET, Op. 37, commissioned by Elizabeth Sprague Coolidge.
1937	Kolisch Quartet performs all four string quartets at UCLA and completes first recording of the works under Schoenberg's artistic direction, produced by his student Alfred Newman. Birth of son Ronald. Begins writing *Fundamentals of Composition*.	Arranges BRAHMS'S PIANO QUARTET IN G MINOR, Op. 25, for orchestra. Premiere of FOURTH STRING QUARTET by Kolisch Quartet in Los Angeles.
1938	Anschluss of Austria into Third Reich. Teaching privately and at	Composition and premiere of *KOL NIDRE*, Op. 39, in Los

UCLA; Leon Kirchner (b. 1919) is one of his students. Conducts concert of his own music in San Diego. Schoenberg's oldest daughter from his first marriage, Gertrud, and her husband Felix Greissle flee Austria and immigrate to U.S. with Schoenberg's assistance. Schoenberg's music targeted in exhibit of "Entartete Kunst" (Degenerate Art) in Düsseldorf. Zemlinsky immigrates to New York.

Angeles, Schoenberg conducting. Premiere of Schoenberg's BRAHMS arrangement in Los Angeles under Klemperer.

1939 World War II begins. Many friends and relatives, including cousin Arthur, sent to concentration camps. Speaks at convention of Music Teachers National Association in Kansas City.

Completes SECOND CHAMBER SYMPHONY, Op. 38, begun in 1906.

1940 Conducts and records PIERROT LUNAIRE, with Erika Stiedry-Wagner, for Columbia. Also conducts PIERROT in New York. Reunion with his daughter Gertrud in New York. Schoenberg's old friend Alma Mahler and her third husband, the dramatist Franz Werfel (1890–1945), move to Beverly Hills and rejoin his social circle.

Premiere of SECOND CHAMBER SYMPHONY under Stiedry in New York. Premiere of VIOLIN CONCERTO in Philadelphia, with Louis Krasner (1903–95) as soloist; Leopold Stokowski (1882–1977) conducts.

1941 Arnold, Gertrud, and Nuria Schoenberg become U.S. citizens on April 11. Birth of son Lawrence. Death of brother Heinrich. Gives lecture, "Composition with Twelve Tones," at UCLA. Continues his attempts to help friends and relatives immigrate to U.S.

Composes VARIATIONS ON A RECITATIVE FOR ORGAN, Op. 40.

1942 Compiles *Models for Beginners in Composition*. Pianist, sometime movie actor, and former Schoenberg student Oscar Levant commissions Schoenberg to write a piano piece for him, but withdraws when Schoenberg presents him with the ambitious and costly PIANO CONCERTO, Op. 42; another

Composition of ODE TO NAPOLEON BUONAPARTE, Op. 41 (Byron), and PIANO CONCERTO, Op. 42.

Schoenberg student, Henry Clay
Shriver (1917–94) steps in as
patron. Death of Zemlinsky.
Antony Tudor (1908–87) choreo-
graphs ballet, *Pillar of Fire*, to
VERKLÄRTE NACHT, which premiered
at the Metropolitan Opera House
in New York. Playwright Bertolt
Brecht (1898–1956) and Hanns
Eisler attend Schoenberg's composition courses at UCLA and
join his social circle. Leonard
Stein becomes Schoenberg's
teaching assistant.

1943 Befriends Thomas Mann, another
member of emigré community
in Los Angeles. Lou Harrison
(b. 1917) begins studying composition with Schoenberg.

Composes THEME AND VARIATIONS
for Wind Orchestra (Op. 43)
and for Orchestra (Op. 43b).

1944 Health deteriorates. Forced
retirement at age 70 from
professorship at UCLA. His
pension is small (averaging $40
a month), and he must continue
giving private lessons to support
his family. Considers emigrating
to other countries. Too ill to compose, but plans autobiography.
Many concerts given in honor
of 70th birthday.

After a long hiatus, begins
working on JAKOBSLEITER again.
Premiere of the PIANO
CONCERTO, Op. 42, in New York,
with former student Edward
Steuermann, piano, and
Stokowski conducting.
Premiere of THEME AND
VARIATIONS FOR ORCHESTRA,
Op. 43b, in Boston under
Koussevitsky. Premiere of ODE
TO NAPOLEON BUONAPARTE in New
York under Artur Rodzinski
(1892–1958). Premiere of
VARIATIONS ON A RECITATIVE FOR
ORGAN by Carl Weinrich
(1904–91) in New York.

1945 World War II ends. Applies for a
Guggenheim Fellowship to finish
JAKOBSLEITER, MOSES UND ARON, and
other planned theoretical books;
his application is rejected. Death
of Anton Webern.

The composer Nathaniel
Shilkret (1895–1982) commis-
sions Schoenberg, Milhaud,
Stravinsky, and three other com-
posers to contribute a move-
ment to a work entitled GENESIS
SUITE; Schoenberg composes the
first movement, PRELUDE FOR
ORCHESTRA AND MIXED CHORUS,
Op. 44. Premieres in Los
Angeles under Werner Janssen
(1899–1990).

1946 Lectures at University of Chicago. City of Vienna invites Schoenberg to visit, but he does not make trip. Appointed Honorary President of International Society for Contemporary Music. Resumes contact with friends and relatives in Europe, and sends many CARE packages to them. Suffers severe heart attack and nearly dies on August 2, an experience he composes into STRING TRIO, Op. 45. Princeton University grants honorary doctorate, which is not conferred because Schoenberg cannot attend ceremony.

Composition of STRING TRIO, Op. 45. Premiere of THEME AND VARIATIONS for Wind Orchestra in New York by Goldman Band.

1947 Receives $1000 Award of Merit for Distinguished Achievement from National Institute of Arts and Letters. Compiles *Structural Functions of Harmony*. Consults with H. H. Stuckenschmidt (1901–88) and Josef Rufer (1893–1985) about books on his life and music. Concerts of Schoenberg's music given in Paris and Genoa. Works performed at Darmstadt Festival. Health improves. Death of eldest daughter from first marriage, Gertrud.

Composition of *A SURVIVOR FROM WARSAW*, Op. 46 (Schoenberg), commissioned by the Serge Koussevitzky Foundation in New York. Premiere of STRING TRIO in Cambridge, Mass.

1948 Schoenberg's music played at New Music festivals in Darmstadt, Leipzig, and Venice. Max Deutsch (1892–1982) conducts radio performance of FIVE ORCHESTRAL PIECES for French and Swiss radio; Dimitri Mitropoulos (1896–1960) conducts same work in New York. Dispute with Mann about parallels between Schoenberg and Adrian Leverkühn, the hero of Mann's novel *Dr. Faustus*; Mann adds prefatory note to book.

Premiere of *A SURVIVOR FROM WARSAW* in Albuquerque, New Mexico, under Kurt Frederick (1907–98). Composes THREE FOLK SONGS FOR MIXED CHORUS, Op. 49, new settings of tunes he had arranged in 1929.

1949 Poor health prevents Schoenberg from attending European festivities in honor of 75th birthday. Named an honorary citizen of

Composition of choral work *DREIMAL TAUSEND JAHRE* (Three times a thousand years), Op. 50a (Runes). Composition of

Vienna. Gives lecture, "My
Evolution," at UCLA, which is
recorded.

PHANTASY FOR VIOLIN WITH PIANO
ACCOMPANIMENT, Op. 47,
premiered in Los Angeles by
Adolf Koldofsky (1905–51)
and Leonard Stein.

1950 After many years and several
rejected translators, Schoenberg's
collection of essays, *Style and Idea*, is
published; some are translated by
former student Dika Newlin. The
book will appear in a new
expanded edition in 1975, edited
by Leonard Stein. Writes texts
entitled *Modern Psalms*, later setting
one of them to music. Sells original
manuscripts of VERKLÄRTE NACHT,
PIERROT LUNAIRE, and SECOND STRING
QUARTET to Library of Congress.
Steuermann plays Schoenberg's
complete piano works in
Pittsburgh. All four string quartets
performed at the Juilliard School
of Music.

Composition of choral works
DE PROFUNDIS (Psalm 130), Op.
50b, and MODERNER PSALM NR. 1,
Op. 50c (Schoenberg); the latter remains incomplete.

1951 Named honorary president of
Israeli Academy of Music in
Jerusalem. Donates his correspon-
dence to Library of Congress.
GURRELIEDER performed in
Cinncinati under Thor Johnson
(1913–75). Dies at home on
July 13.

Premiere of the Golden Calf
Scene from MOSES UND ARON in
Darmstadt under Scherchen.

1974 Schoenberg's ashes buried at
Zentralfriedhof in Vienna on
June 6.

PART I
ESSAYS

·

Schoenberg and the Audience: Modernism, Music, and Politics in the Twentieth Century

LEON BOTSTEIN

I. Polemical Preliminaries

These festival weeks have had nothing to do with music. Schoenberg's followers have overdone it. What the consequence of the absolute domination by dodecaphony will be . . . is that in ten years, I am convinced, no one will talk about the twelve-tone system.

—G.F. Malipiero, June 1932[1]

It seems that the last twenty years of eclecticism in contemporary music may have finally undone what "Schoenberg's followers" have "overdone" for nearly half a century. It is now respectable and even fashionable to concede that perhaps audiences have been right all along. Abstract, inaccessible, unfriendly, harsh, hard to follow, dense, even boring are still the adjectives applied by most concert-goers to Arnold Schoenberg's music. The twentieth-century composer, once most highly respected by generations of academics, whose music and theoretical writings reveal a daunting intellect and capacity for analysis, and whose own legendary contempt for others became routinized posthumously among those who specialized in his defense, now appears entirely vulnerable.[2] With a slight edge of delight, critics are increasingly able to declare—along with Malipiero, and only superficially in imitation of Boulez, decades later—that Schoenberg is "dead."

Although thinking and writing about Schoenberg remain valued academic pursuits, to the public beyond academic circles Schoenberg, except for a few early works, commands little spontaneous affection, and at best a grudging respect.[3] If his music is as great as he and his disciples claimed, why does it remain so difficult, so merely intellectual for so many; why after three quarters of a century are essays in the genre of Alban Berg's 1924 classic "Why is Schoenberg's Music so Difficult to Understand?" still appropriate?

Five basic factors currently stand in way of a sympathetic reconsideration of Schoenberg. First and foremost is the success of the so-called "post-modern." With the collapse of the perceived tyranny of those who viewed Schoenberg as the true prophet of new music, voices have emerged (some of them repentant former adherents to the cause) who actually relish the slaughter of the main sacred cow.[4] From 1945 until the early 1980s, the accepted wisdom among composers and scholars echoed Ernst Křenek's closing comments at the Second International Schoenberg Conference in Vienna in 1984: Schoenberg and the Second Viennese School had altered musical thinking forever. No composer in the future would be able to circumvent Schoenberg and his influence, even if he was to write minimalist and tonal music. Just fifteen years later most successful younger contemporary composers appear to have paid little or no attention to Schoenberg.[5] This has altered the paradigm of the history of twentieth century music that held sway into the mid-1970s, in which Schoenberg played the central role.

Second is the accumulated weight of sustained historical reevaluation. Those who question how modern Schoenberg really was challenge a facile equivalence between the terms "modernist" or "avant-garde" and the twentieth century. Perhaps, they seem to say, modernism in the sense of Schoenberg and his school refers merely to one limited historical period and group within the twentieth century. Or there is the line of argument first put forth decades ago independently by Pierre Boulez and Elliott Carter questioning how far Schoenberg had really traveled from a dependency on late nineteenth-century musical models. Were not Webern, Varèse, Ives, Messiaen, and even Stravinsky equally innovative and significant?[6] This differentiation within modernism sought to help emancipate post-World War II composition from too exclusive a bias in favor of Schoenberg. A divergent view of the century and modernity emerges from these types of revisionism, one in which Schoenberg holds merely one place of prominence among many. Schoenberg may have been less a radical conservative and more a radical reactionary, one who carried Wagner's belief in a progressive imperative for music to an absurd extreme into an age in which history would no longer matter.[7]

By refusing to see Schoenberg as the pivotal figure in the history of twentieth-century music, these revisionists create a third factor: they detach Schoenberg's music and its aesthetic and historical valuation from the social and political projects to which it was once inextricably linked. During the 1920s, Hanns Eisler, who retained an unqualified admiration for Schoenberg, his teacher, was among the first in Schoenberg's circle to speculate independently about the function of new music in modernity.[8] Schoenberg's modernism consistently offended its audience. If that audience had been merely made up of smug owners of capital and their bourgeois apologists, there might have seemed something redeemingly "progressive" about Schoenberg's brand of modernism. But the failure of Schoenberg's modernism to gain any audience beyond its own elite of admirers—however constituted—revealed just how hollow were his supporters' appeals to historical necessity or a Platonic belief system that legislated a normative ideal of musical thought and form and therefore a typology of proper listening. [9]

Since Schoenberg's brand of innovation as well as his Jewish identity became the focus of anti-Semitic right-wing politics early in the 1920s and later the object of Nazi persecution in the 1930s, the dissonances between the progressive in politics and the modernist in music were left unresolved. The alliance between the two went largely unquestioned for decades, even well after 1945. In the context of Cold War politics, Eisler's challenge to Schoenberg and his school from the left could be discredited as "Stalinist" and reactionary, while Schoenberg's brand of modernism continued, until the late 1960s, to appear as a non-subversive but forward-looking contemporary line of defense of individuality and freedom against uniformity and tyranny within the "free world."

Adorno's analysis of Schoenberg and his influence created a powerful critical and philosophical framework that buttressed Schoenberg's post-war influence, particularly in academic circles.[10] According to this line of interpretation, modernism in music of the sort audible in Webern and in the work of the younger composers supported at Darmstadt and Donaueschingen in the 1950s and 1960s eloquently confronted the corrupting influences represented in the West by commercialism and mass society, the very ills that had helped fascism succeed.

With the receding prestige of socialist and progressive politics in the early 1980s, the growing critique of the liberal welfare state in

England and America and ultimately the collapse of Communism and and fall of the Berlin Wall, the critique of capitalist culture and society put forward by Adorno and other Frankfurt School contemporaries, particularly Herbert Marcuse, became less attractive in the West to new generations of young people. Schoenberg and his notions of musical modernism were gradually detached from a plausible justifying political and historical logic locating them on the side of freedom and anti-fascism, and therefore of the angels.

While the later twentieth century heirs of the left have largely rejected modernism in favor of popular musical culture as an important dimension of political resistance, neo-conservatives have taken their own peculiar revenge on Schoenberg. Some have risen to Schoenberg's defense, citing his work and legacy as a bulwark against the collapse of cultural standards after the mid-1960s. Other neo-conservatives, however, have delighted in the idea that the largely liberal and left-wing post-war academic community's "emperor had no clothes" after all.[11]

The fourth factor working against Schoenberg is the reemergence of an empirical and principled set of arguments prevalent at the turn of the century that defend tonality (or something very much like it) as natural and objective.[12] According to this argument, which makes an appeal to normative philosophy, psychology, and physics, certain ways of organizing sound and time in music correspond to facts and laws of nature. In the early twentieth century, Schoenberg found himself on the side of those who argued against the idea that the Western system of harmony was privileged and rooted in nature, rendering tonality normative and objective. The sophisticated revival of the idea of a "natural" music has been fueled partly by linguistic theory (e.g. Chomsky and generative grammar), language philosophy (from the late Wittgenstein on) and the analysis of syntax.

Theorists as disparate in their approaches as Boretz and Epstein have suggested that when we look carefully at music as a reflexive system of communication we need to explain rather than dismiss the failure of any music to gain response, engage listeners or be easily preserved in memory. Perhaps it is not tonality that is natural. But the need for particularly evident patterns in music: repetition, focal points, continuities, tensions, resolutions and regularity—the accumulation of classes of events that can be processed and associated readily by the brain—may be universal. Schoenberg's modernism may lack these requirements because of an inherent conflict between the way we are as humans and the way twelve-tone music is organized. The wide dissemination (or to put it more plainly, the popularity) of a form of music need not be considered a sign of vulgarity, ignorance or concession to corrupt fashion or style. Populist politics and high theory have now merged: Schoenberg's brand of modernism, particularly in its twelve-tone phase, becomes a failed experiment that cannot intersect effectively with wider human experience cognitively and therefore either aesthetically or politically.

The fifth and final barrier to a sympathetic rehearing of Schoenberg today is ironically the difficulty we have in transcending the accumulated traditional rhetoric of criticism and defense surrounding the question of Schoenberg. Schoenberg and his disciples in the 1920s can be compared properly to the circle around the poet Stefan George, to whose work Schoenberg turned at a pivotal moment when the composer took a decisive step away from tonality.[13] But the most apt comparison is with Richard Wagner. Not only did they both have disciples and demand uncommon degrees of loyalty from their followers, but Wagner and Schoenberg invented and institutionalized a rhetoric of self-defense and description. They both brilliantly placed themselves within music history and connected their work to past and future. Institutions designed to preserve and defend the Schoenberg legacy were created, first in Los Angeles, then in Vienna.[14] Schools of composition and criticism that developed after 1945 relied heavily on Schoenberg's analysis of compositional methods, his views on form and structure, and his readings of Mozart and Brahms. To generations of Schoenberg admirers, followers and scholars, any departure from this self-constituted (or auto-poetic) code of discourse of defense and description was tantamount to ignorance or betrayal.

Schoenberg's philosophy of music and his logic of self-estimation have cast a decisive shadow over music theory and musicology in this century. Whether it is the concept of "idea" (as opposed to "style"), the "Grundgestalt," "developing variation," the "emancipation of the dissonance" or the relation of music and text, the way Schoenberg thought and wrote about music and its meaning has had perhaps more influence in the arenas of performance practice and critical approaches to music in this century than his own music has had on the writing of new music. At the end of this century, almost fifty years after Schoenberg's death, it is in part the institutionalized charisma of Schoenberg the teacher and theorist that retards a new appreciation of his music. Perhaps if we successfully challenge the rhetoric of Schoenberg and his most ardent posthumous defenders, we will be able to open up new avenues of access to his music.

II. Music and Psychology

TO MUSIC

Music: breath of statues. Perhaps:
stillness of paintings. You language where languages
end. You time,
placed vertically on the course of hearts that expire.

Feelings . . . for whom? O you the transformation
of feelings . . . into what?—: into audible landscape.
You stranger: music. You heartspace
grown out of us. Innermost thing of ours,
which, exceeding us, forces us out, —
sacred farewell:
when the inner surrounds us
as the most practiced distance, as the other side
of the air:
pure,
like a giant,
no longer livable.
　　　　　—R. M. Rilke, Munich, January 11–12, 1918[15]

　　　In 1926 the Polish composer Karol Szymanowski completed a draft of an essay on contemporary music. It was not published in his lifetime and appeared first in 1958 (see Appendix, p. 47).[16] In it, Szymanowski argues that Schoenberg alone represents a true break with the past; Schoenberg was the only one to "cross the Rubicon" into modernity. Szymanowski understands Debussy, Stravinsky and Strauss as tied to pre-war traditions. At the same time Szymanowski remains entirely aware of the extent to which Schoenberg is not just a European but distinctly a German. He clearly identifies Schoenberg with a tradition of German composition and sees him as the heir to Wagner: the composer who represents the future of German music. Szymanowski echoes Berg's 1924 conclusion that Schoenberg would "predominate in German music for the next fifty years."[17] Yet Szymanowski accepts the universal consequences of Schoenberg's achievement. He is unstinting in his praise and admiration for Schoenberg's philosophical vocabulary and rhetoric of self-assessment. The essay is curious in part because Szymanowski—unlike Stravinsky and Copland later on in the 1960s—

never sought to emulate Schoenberg in his own approach to composition by experimenting with twelve-tone composition.[18]

What struck Szymanowski was Schoenberg's remarkable sojourn from Wagnerism to a new modernism. No other composer had worked so well in the pre-World War I expressionist idiom and yet had shown the courage to break away. The decisive step was the explicit severing of a long tradition of parallelism between musical form and structure and "direct psychological truth." Schoenberg put forward a notion of absolute music that cut against the traditions of emotional response and attachment to music so eloquently witnessed by Rilke's 1918 poem. Yet Szymanowski remained ambivalent about this. On the one hand, the "natural" development of music required that music somehow become finally independent, in the twentieth century, of reality and life, and reverse the exaggerated emotionalism of romanticism. Szymanowski shared a Hanslick-like prejudice about the inherently "absolute" non-representational character of music. On the other hand, he realized the power of an historical achievement, beginning in the nineteenth century and culminating with expressionism, in which the "horizontal" dimension of music became gradually influenced by the vertical, creating an "enriched" sound world which, metaphorically speaking, ran parallel with the "lyrics of direct life reality." Music became "rooted in life's psychological rhythm," just as Rilke suggests in his response to hearing music. Extended tonality and extreme chromaticism, strengthened by the expanded palette of orchestral sound, made the Rilke-like parallelism between feeling and sound irresistable.

Schoenberg brought this historical process to completion and ultimately abandoned the residual framework of the "horizontal"; the "vertical" dimension of music was placed in the foreground. He rendered the "vertical" in music absolute. Gone were issues of "mood" and "color" or even the contrast between the static and the dynamic highlighted by modulation. The "absolute vertical" found a value in itself, not as a function of musical "expression." This led to "the essential atomism" of Schoenberg's modernism, by which Szymanowski means the twelve-tone compositional breakthrough of the 1920s. Szymanowski's essay ends abruptly, incomplete, with praise for Schoenberg's ethical authenticity and seriousness as well as a reference to the consequences of the opening up of a "limitless domain" in which truth became subjective and relative. Schoenberg had created a space in which everything seemed now permissible.

Crucial to the contemporary and posthumous defense of Schoenberg and the modernist tradition linked to his innovations from the 1920s has been an explicit and implicit assent to his critique of the traditions and character of how audiences listened, followed and understood music. An audience that was truly musically literate, which thought purely musically i.e. could grasp music without any refuge in psychological allegory, either of narrative or mood—such an audience could truly appreciate the music of Schoenberg and his followers. As Schoenberg himself pointed out, his greatest success as a composer derived from his capacity, in his pre-twelve-tone music, to facilitate with great originality and inventiveness the listener's capacity to listen allegorically and through the use of allusion, without refuge in illustration or representation. Furthermore, as Szymanowski observed, the extension of tonality and the virtuosity in the use of modulation displayed by Schoenberg in *Gurrelieder*, for example, expanded the utility of music as a framework—independent of the text—for internal psychological reflection on the part of the listener. But then Schoenberg stopped himself and history short, interrupting the continuity of these traditions. (A typical pictorial representation of the sort of listening common at the end of the nineteenth century is the 1895 painting by the English painter Francis Dicksee [1853–1928], entitled *A Reverie*, reproduced in figure 1.)

Figure 1: Francis Dicksee, *A Reverie*

One can locate the cause for the widespread contemporary and posthumous perception that Schoenberg was the creator of a unique radical modernism in precisely this interruption, the self-conscious break with the parallelism between music and life (and therefore language) as expressed in the expectations of generations of European composers and audiences. By creating a new mode of pitch relationship and therefore a new basis for constructing the basic cells or thematic elements for works of music, Schoenberg in the 1920s explicitly attacked the dominant habit of listening within nineteenth-century musical culture, rendering it irrelevant and useless. With the fundamental abandonment of tonality, music lost its connection to the Rilke-like internal psychological dialogue conducted by the individual and therefore, as Szymanowski suggests, its evident connection to life. The aesthetic dimension had been emancipated from the psychologically instrumental. But the question remained: into what and for what?[19]

It is well to remember that many of Schoenberg's earliest and most ardent defenders and advocates were young listeners who sought a new and different inspiration from music; they were not professional musicians or critics. Consider for example the fascinating fragment by Arnold Zweig from 1913 entitled "A Quartet Movement by Schoenberg."[20] In this short prose work Schoenberg emerges as the prophetic and triumphant outsider who has arrived to rescue Europe through art exactly one hundred years after Napoleon's defeat at the battle of Leipzig in 1813. The story takes place in 1913. An Eastern European Jew is on his way to Palestine. After travelling through Berlin he visits his brother in Leipzig The young man, the protagonist, is both impressed and revolted by the middle-class opulence and self-satisfaction evident in the architecture and the people he encounters in Leipzig. In Leipzig the sound of the Saxon dialect reminds him of the French and of Napoleon. The reunion with his brother is unsatisfactory. He becomes bored.

He wanders into a concert without seeing what is on the program. It is a quartet concert. The first work is by Haydn and the young man is lost in a quite typical reverie. He dreams of nature and the simple pleasures of life. A pre-modern idyllic world appears before his eyes. After enthusiastic applause the quartet plays the next work. The audience is stunned; it does not know how to react. But the young man is transported. He is inspired: he senses through the music the power of modernity, the city, and of science and progress. He also senses the alienation of the modern individual. He perceives the extent to which an excessive optimism about modernity prevalent within the audience has gone awry. A nameless artist, the composer of this new music, reveals through sounds the contradictions of modernity and truth-fully celebrates the possibilities of cultural renewal.[21] Aesthetic inno-vation and ethical truth merge in the music.

Although the audience is at a loss, the young man leaves the con-cert hall suddenly seized by doubt about his own plans to leave Europe for the more primitive and yet-to-be-realized new social order of Palestine. As he wanders about on his way to the train station to resume his journey, he sees a poster and notices the name of the com-poser whose music he has just heard: Arnold Schoenberg, a fellow Jew. Although he proceeds with his plans, he senses that he must ultimately return to Europe to take on the cause of the rebirth of European culture along the path set forth by Schoenberg. Schoenberg's music has awakened the young man to the idea that he has not exhausted his identity as a European. A sense of homeless-ness, triggered by the pogroms in the East he is fleeing, has been assuaged by the music. The possibilities for a cultural and political future, for internal personal are rekindled, forcing him to reconsider his Zionism, his life's plan and his sense of self. The story ends with the hero repeating the words "O return, o return."

It is more than likely that the music Zweig had in mind was either Schoenberg's Op. 7 or Op. 10, both of which were performed in Berlin in 1912 and 1913, the year the fragment was written.[22] Zweig therefore implicitly refers to at least two works which created a great uproar in Schoenberg's career and helped established his reputation as a radical. (At issue, therefore, is not *Verklärte Nacht* or *Gurrelieder*.) Although the music Zweig alludes to is not the same repertoire Szymanowski discusses, Schoenberg's break with the past was well underway in Opp. 9 and 10. Op. 7, however, possessed a "very defi-nite but private program."[23] Nevertheless, Szymanowski's 1926 con-struct of Schoenberg's project can be applied to Op. 7, Op. 9, and Op. 10. Despite the presence of poetic texts, Schoenberg's first decisive breaks with habits of listening based on psychological parallelism between musical space and time and real life sensibilities, particularly the internal clock of reflection, took place before the invention of twelve-tone composition, particularly in Op. 9.

Zweig's account is all the more remarkable for its political over-tones. Indeed, as the story develops Schoenberg functions for the young man as modernity's Napoleon: the new-world historical hero from humble origins. Napoleon was a hero to most Jews because of his role in their emancipation. The image of the Jewish composer as a new Napoleon redeeming the possibilities of European culture in the name of freedom, ethical progress, and enlightened modernity, fits quite closely to Schoenberg's own self-assessment before his stunning and disillusioning encounter with anti-Semitism in the 1920s.[24] Zweig and Schoenberg also implicitly agree in their critique of the pre-World War I audience. Zweig gives us a picture of an uncomprehending group of affluent middle-class Europeans, suffused with culture, who delighted only in the familiar. There is however no description of booing or hissing, as took place in Vienna. Zweig's account of his fellow audience members is critical but not entirely dismissive (the experience after all raises his hopes about the use of art as an instrument of cultural and social renewal). One comes away from the fragment with a sense that confronting the public with a radical new art may in fact set in motion a social and political transformation.

Leaving aside the many implications imbedded in Zweig's strange story, it is curious that Zweig's protagonist's habit of listening did not change with the music. He listened to Schoenberg the way he listened to Haydn. Indeed, one way to understand what was going on in concert halls between the years 1909 and 1913 at performances of Schoenberg's music—events that attracted furious response and intensive critical attention—is to concentrate on one consistent thread within the notion of psychological listening shared by Zweig's protagonist, his audience, and one which is implicit in Szymanowski's analysis: the act of listening with the visual imagination. Rilke confirms the pervasive attachment to music as inspiring of a species of sight; music is the breathing statue, the stillness of paintings, the audible landscape.

The visual imagery inspired by the idea of music at the turn of the century, particularly in light of Schoenberg's own brief career as a painter and his life-long engagement with the connection between the musical and the visual, merits close historical scrutiny. What changes in Zweig's story is the substance and character of that which is visualized or imagined through music. It is in turn the perceived failure of this mode of listening to music that drove Schoenberg, after World War I, to the complete break with expressionism, a break whose courage so impressed Szymanowski.

The predominance of visualization by the listener in the presence of music led to the popularization of idealized iconographies during the second half of the nineteenth century—visual representations of the essence and nature of music. These were regularly displayed in the context of public music-making, particularly through architecture and design. One such example, with which Schoenberg and all his immediate Viennese contemporaries would have been familiar—was the curtain displayed at the performances of tragic opera at the Imperial Opera House in Vienna. A constant reminder was placed before the audience of the parallels between the visual and the musical. Architecture and iconography were used to embody musical expectations and habits of listening. Even in Zweig's fragment, the narrative moves effortlessly from the description of architecture to the account of how music was heard. The painterly and architectural realizations of the character and nature of music prevalent in the late nineteenth century, and with which Schoenberg grew up, tell us much about the values and expectations of the audience.

Carl Rahl (1812–1865) designed the Vienna Opera curtain (commissioned by the opera house's architects) for tragic opera.[25] Rahl was highly respected as the leading forerunner of Hans Makart within the Viennese school of historical painting. The centerpiece of the curtain was an allegorical composition entitled *The Triumph of Harmony* (figure 2). First and foremost in it is the striking, albeit cliché-ridden, link between the idea of harmony and classical architecture and mythology.[26] Rahl's composition is exactly symmetrical. At the center is a tempieto. In it is a throne on which king and queen are seated. The king's right foot marks the exact midpoint; below it is an

Figure 2: Carl Rahl, *The Triumph of Harmony*

altar with fire. All human emotions, from sorrow to contemplation and from fear to hope are embodied by figures arrayed around the altar and the throne. Truth and power are firmly rooted, stabilizing the widest range of human experience. The governing control of harmony is rendered concrete. Beneath and above this massive representation of the triumph of harmony over the wide-ranging intensities of human expression are somewhat smaller rectangular panels (figures 3 and 4) depicting the effect of song on human beings. Music, cast once more in the iconography of classical antiquity, is present in the singer, who, in turn, inspired by the unseen heavens, guides human emotion and reflection on the ship of time and through the stages of life. But it is harmony, not melody, which dominates the sense of truth in music. Melody (the horizontal) is subordinated in the curtain design, as is the idea of music with words.

Figure 3: Panel from Rahl, *The Triumph of Harmony*

Figure 4: Panel from Rahl, *The Triumph of Harmony*

Although truth in the triumph of harmony is elevated to normative status by the prestigious garb of antiquity in Rahl's tapestry, the connection between music and emotion is left ambiguous. Music (i.e. harmony and melody) does not function as an instrument of illustration or representation. The nature of music's special power to inspire the individual's emotion is left unseen. Only its effect is depicted. Music per se, divorced from its programmatic function (i.e. even in opera in its pre-Wagnerian construct, since Rahl's composition predates Wagner's influence in Vienna) provides the opportunity and perhaps the illusion of individuality of response. In a cultural context in which uniformity, fueled in part by the scale and mechanization explicit in modernity, is understood as a threat, music becomes a resistant vehicle of personal emotion and self-realization. Music's popularity and the allegiance to what Szymanowski characterized as the psychological parallels were rooted in a Rahl-like conception of its essence: the capacity of the act of listening to music to reaffirm the authenticity of individuality in a manner that implied a fundamental reconciliation of the idea of an objective order with subjective differentiation. It is this prevalent illusion of the facite reconciliation of the contradictions spun by musical conventions that Schoenberg explicitly sought to challenge. Music appeared autonomous in that it was not descriptive of emotion, but yet it was a pure unseen instrument of human experience, adaptable by each person, founded on eternally valid rules.

At every performance of serious opera throughout Schoenberg's years in Vienna and therefore throughout Mahler's reign, audiences were reminded of this idealization: not of any particular style of music but of the essential character of all music. The prestige accorded to a system of music-making that ensured comprehensibility through the use of a stable harmonic system in which all human emotions could be channeled and expressed, cannot be underestimated. Represented in this manner, music reinforced an internalized belief system that went far beyond the realm of the aesthetic. When the audiences heard for example Op. 9 and Op. 10 in Vienna, the violent reaction that what they were hearing was not music, and that whatever it was was somehow socially and morally destructive, cannot be written off as a case of superficial philistinism. The audience had lost a fundamental reaffirmation of its own worth and individuality, cast within a cherished shared ritual of culture.

Viennese audiences were not inherently reactionary, ignorant or hostile to the new, as has often been argued. As Karl Kraus understood, the Viennese were all too eager for the new and the modern.[27] *Jugendstil* and the Secession (as well as their literary counterparts) enjoyed quick and easy acclaim in Vienna. Even Mahler's new productions designed by Alfred Roller were eagerly embraced, despite the reservations of some critics.[28] In the years 1907 to 1913, the old and the new in art and architecture lived comfortably side-by-side in the lives of the affluent middle class audience for the arts. The most successful operetta composer of the age and an admirer of Schoenberg (of whom Schoenberg in turn thought well) was Franz Lehár.[29] If one looks at the way Lehár furnished his 1909 Viennese apartment one notices a seamless integration of Secession design, *Jugendstil,* and late nineteenth-century furniture and painting (figure 5).[30] Historicism and certain dimensions of modernism in design merge very comfortably. Functional, streamlined chairs and a more Spartan approach to ornament and space stand side-by-side with the elaborate gilded furniture and old-fashioned realist paintings and sculpture.

Figure 5: Apartment of Franz Lehár in Vienna

Josef Frank, the distinguished Viennese architect, would complain in the 1920s that radical modernism in the design of spaces for living frequently defied the psychological needs of human beings.[31] Architects and designers, including Josef Hoffmann and later Le Corbusier (and sometimes Adolf Loos, despite himself) would insist that everything in a space had to be new, coherent and of a piece, down to the tableware. Modern architecture required the discarding of eclectic artifacts and items accumulated naturally over generations. When Frank participated in the design of workers' housing in Vienna in the late 1920s and early 1930s, he argued for simple white-walled functional interiors which permitted individuals to decorate their homes with all the aesthetically inconsistent and seemingly contradictory clutter that mirrored their own life and family experience. To be psychologically at home meant rendering modernist domestic architecture in its interior spaces neutral, so that the occupant could individualize the space and not be ruled by the tyranny of a purist modernist ideology of aesthetic design and consistency.

Why then did a musical audience otherwise receptive to new directions in art, architecture and literature react particularly violently to Schoenberg as early as 1908? It would be simplistic to describe even the Viennese critics as incompetent and excessively conservative. Consider for example the repeated appeals by J. P. Gotthard, the Viennese composer and conductor (1839–1919). He wrote the summaries of the Viennese musical season for the *Wiener Almanach,* an annual journal on the Viennese scene in literature, art and public life. In 1911, commenting on the year gone by, he wrote:

> Apart from a few exceptions, the programs of most performances in the 1911 season brought us things long known to us. This fact, when we consider the rigid conservatism of our performers, will not surprise anybody. The refusal to bring anything new on the part of performing artists is in step with music publishers who cannot be moved to publish works which do not already, in advance, promise successful sales. On the one hand we have the worship of Secessionist outbursts, and on the other hand we have the evaluation of the new from a purely commercial standpoint. Nowhere is there the prospect for a truly artistic-idealistic approach! In view of such a situation, what shall the young among the real composers do in order to realize their ideas so that they gain the chance to be taken seriously artistically? Neither in Vienna nor in the German empire does the Viennese composer find recognition and support. Indolence and cowardice hide behind the common excuse of having a surplus of manuscripts for many years to come! Dance music elevated to operetta dominates the day, and the rest is satisfied by the cabaret arts of the couplet poets and composers of the twentieth century.[32]

It is not clear what Gotthard understood as a "real" (i.e. legitimately artistic) composer within the realm of the new; the phrase "Secessionist outbursts" may refer to Schoenberg. But it is not too speculative to assume that Gotthard's audience expected in music the moral equivalent of the Secession—a kind of new music whose style and character could live side-by-side comfortably with the old, just as in the furnishings in Lehár's apartment. To some extent the music of Mahler played this role. Richard Strauss's music always did. Artistic music was considered "ideal" proportionately to its capacity to generate not so much moods, as images and a personalized inner narrative of some sort. Opponents of Strauss well into the Nazi era thought of his music as too "nervous" and "neurotic"; it was too effective as narrative and all too stimulating. It was decried as decadent (as opposed to degenerate).[33] The radical condensation of form in Schoenberg's Op. 9 and the strangeness of the instrumentation (in contrast to, for example, the 1916 *Kammersymphonie* of Franz Schreker) totally frustrated an audience accustomed to using musical time psychologically.[34]

For Schoenberg the essence of the classical tradition had nothing to do with Rahl's imagery regarding the triumph of harmony. Music was not only autonomous in a cognitive sense but unstable (except perhaps in memory) and dynamic in its essence; it was not really susceptible to an architectural allegory. To Schoenberg the late nineteenth-century critics and audiences in fact never really understood classical compositional traditions and the classical heritage in music. Their allegiance to the transposition of music into classical architecture was emblematic of this fact. This explains why Schoenberg allied himself less with the artists associated with Mahler (e.g. Klimt, Moser, and Roller) and more with the radical expressionist group (Kokoschka and Schiele). They were the first to challenge the technical illusions of realism and representation in painting. But the difference between modernism in painting (with the exception of Kandinsky and his followers in non-objectivism), and music, was Schoenberg's search for an autonomous temporal structure clearly emancipated from the psychological-linguistic-visual nexus between sound and listener.[35] By abandoning repetition and the security of tonality as a memory-signpost and frame-of-reference for the listener, by pursuing instead immediate and radical thematic transformation, Schoenberg created a musical space which seemed unlivable and unusable.

From his beginnings in Op. 7 and particularly Op. 9, Schoenberg ultimately arrived at more than a revival of Hanslick's notion of absolute music. Hanslick's formalism merely argued that music should not be subordinated to or organized on the basis of the emotional, the visual, and the literary. He never believed that the hearing of music would be stripped of all possibilities for supplemental psychologizing within the framework of musical time constructed musically—that is to say, without personalized references to verbal narration, pictures, or the expression of emotion. Hanslick's point was not that great music could not mean something to the listener in a form other than the purely musical. He admired Schumann, whose connection to the literary within the musical was overtly central to his music. Rather Hanslick felt that the inevitable extra-musical meanings were at best coincidental and supplemental, and should not serve as the basis upon which one writes music, defines its content, or judges the nature of its unique beauty. Implicit in this argument was that if music was well-composed without reference to the logic of the extra-musical, it probably worked better and in a more lasting manner over time in its subordinate and perhaps vulgar role as psychological backdrop.[36]

In the rejection of the established psychological connections between listener and music, Schoenberg nonetheless sought to create music that itself might generate a different but equally powerful form of attachment. In this sense Adorno properly understood the radical implications of the twelve-tone strategy; it forced a critical and searching encounter with the present, through music. It did not provide an affirmative aesthetic, shielding the listener from a serious internal dialogue concerning the tensions between ordinary life in the modern world and the individual imagination.

In order to contextualize this conflict with inherited patterns of listening, one can consider comparisons to reading habits and literature. *Der Stechlin* (1897), the last novel of Theodor Fontane (1819–98), the greatest German exponent of the novel prior to Thomas Mann, is an experiment in slowing down and distorting time, particularly for the reader. Following in the path of Adalbert Stifter's 1857 *Der Nachsommer,* Fontane adds the extensive use of dialogue in concert with description to create a novel without much action or plot, whose pace, through the use of language, undercuts the illusions of realism. Fontane makes easy reading difficult in order to generate critical distance. The clock of reading does not seem to run magically parallel to that of life experience (as, for example, in Balzac); rather the act of reading subverts and interrupts expectations, creating a new sense of time and space. The reader can then penetrate conventions and opinions as they appear imbedded not only in daily experience and the time of daily life, but in ordinary language. The next step beyond Fontane can be found in Joyce and Musil.

The intervention by Schoenberg represented the conscious desire to write music that presents intentional difficulties for the listener. The obstacles to staying with the music parallel contemporaneous experiments in prose writing and poetry. In prose fiction the radical instruments against the fiction of realism were repetition and the static. In Schoenberg, the means he employed prior to 1909 were compression and constant alteration; the ultimate rejection of parallelisms then took place in the 1920s.[37]

If, in fact, it was Schoenberg's ambition to shatter the foundations of musical expectation on the part of the listener by breaking the capacity to listen psychologically—to abandon, as Szymanowski suggests, an explicit psychologism in music—then it is clear from contemporary critical reaction that he succeeded well before the 1920s. Zweig's protagonist, after all, responded at best to general impressions and only to the contrasts with Haydn that the new music created. But he got a good deal of the message. Turning a negative contrast into a positive attribute in some general way was not Schoenberg's project. By 1907 he had embarked, albeit haltingly, on an effort to create a new kind of modernism that implied a new kind of cultural order. Part of the ambition was to suggest a world in which the alienated and homeless individual—in both the psychological and political meanings of these modifiers—could find a place. Art became part of a project of cultural and ethical restoration, not an act of aestheticist withdrawal, which explains Schoenberg's affinity to Karl Kraus.

This project gained particular urgency after World War I. Schoenberg's desire to break with the past and invent a new system was fueled by the post-war sense of chaos which in turn inspired both a kind of optimism and confidence as well as the panic, anger and reaction against the new articulated by Hans Pfitzner. Owing to the catastrophe brought on by the past, it appeared to many artists that something wholly new and free of the tragic and comic pretensions of late nineteenth-century culture had to be put into place. However, before ascribing too much to the social or political impetus behind Schoenberg's radicalism, it is well to reflect on more local reasons for Schoenberg's evolution after 1907 away from expressionism, and particularly from alliances between musical continuities and the workings of the psyche and the visual imagination.

The effort to free music from its ties to the inherited psychological and visual patterns of listening that culminated in the 1920s germinated in Schoenberg's mind for at least fifteen years. He always identified Op. 9 as pivotal in his development. One context for the composition of Op. 9 was, as Gotthard suggested in 1911, the oppressively overwhelming success enjoyed by operetta.[38] One thinks particularly of Leo Fall's *Die Dollarprinzessin,* which opened in 1907. Schoenberg was fond of operetta and Webern, his student, earned money conducting this particular hit among others. 1907 also saw the premiere of *Ein Walzertraum* by Schoenberg's friend Oscar Straus. Schoenberg, as we know, earned money helping to orchestrate operettas. His affection for this art form coexisted with ambivalence, since the operetta was the most powerful demonstration of the consequences of the old models of musical continuity. An audience that reveled in operetta proabably liked to hear good light music for the wrong reasons. The operetta's reductive psychology of pessimistic escapism and superficial lightheartedness itself became a source of resistance against seriousness in art, particularly as operetta grew to dominate an entire musical culture.[39] While Schoenberg struggled in a musical culture awash with operetta, a decisive trauma shook his personal life: his wife's affair with Gerstl, her flight from home, Webern's intervention, his wife's return, her subsequent unhappiness and ultimately Gerstl's suicide in 1908.[40]

These events forced a fundamental internal reevaluation in Schoenberg's mind about music and its function. Unease and ambivalence remained. Schoenberg completed and wrote works in which the psychological use of music became more exaggerated, as the second part of *Gurrelieder* and *Erwartung* indicate. He painted in a manner and with images that placed the subjective experience and the internal state of mind entirely in the foreground. In a reverse of Rilke's observation, one can hear the sound and breathing of Schoenberg's paintings from these years. But the making of art in the old way gradually appeared dishonest, since it was insufficient to allay Schoenberg's internal sense of homelessness. Subjective expression through the use of an old, late-romantic aesthetic framework tied to conventional psychological parallelisms provided no relief to the sense of loneliness, a word Schoenberg would use in his rhetoric of self description.[41] This concept is distinct from solitude, implying a state of mind not dissimilar to that of Zweig's protagonist. By 1908 Schoenberg's loneliness had become both personal and political, both private and public.

The emancipation of music through a new framework of order seemed to suggest themselves not only as necessary to an adequately post-war "modern" art, but as the possible ethos of a new community based on reason and ethical truth. The ideal suggested by Carl Rahl's tapestry was not so much rejected as appropriated. Order was not replaced by disorder; neither was the classical replaced by the modern. Rather, the classical was re-invented. Harmony was supplanted. The discontinuity between past and present involved discarding all the accumulated late nineteenth-century attachments to the particular symbolisms in Rahl's tapestry, that mirrored the expectations of the audience. Schoenberg became indeed what Zweig's protagonist dreamed he would be: the creator of a new art, emblematic of a new modern European world where the sense of homelessness could be purged. Schoenberg's post-1933 enthusiasm for an idealized Zionist state was analogous to his adherence to the twelve-tone system: they were equally disciplined expressions of an imperative to replace the continuities derived from the late nineteenth century with new ones, to jettison that which had brought him so much personal and professional unhappiness.[42]

III. The Composer and his Public

As is well known, the Vienna premieres of Op. 7 and Op. 9 in 1907 and Op. 10 in 1908 (particularly the 1908 concert) occasioned an intense scandal and outcry among critics in Vienna.[43] There was a physical scuffle at Bösendorfer Hall. In the span of two years Schoenberg defined the terms of the debate about the modern in music. That controversy only intensified in 1910, when Op. 11 and Op. 15 were performed at a concert, and Op. 10 was repeated. It reached a climax with the scandal concert of 1913, in which applause and intermissions were excluded. A cursory survey of the critics' observations reveals the topography of objections that would stick to Schoenberg and his music: Schoenberg was an *enfant terrible* who intentionally outraged the public in order to draw attention to himself; his music was calculated, even mechanically devised, with neither melody nor sonority; it was essentially formless, and not so much music as the sound mirror of the "psychic illness" of the age.[44]

By the mid-1920s in Berlin the essentials of the Viennese critical pre-war vocabulary had been translated into a fourth, surprisingly widespread direction. A line of reasoning left largely implicit in the leading Viennese press had become explicit: the abstract and calculating dimension in Schoenberg's music was little more than a Jewish gambit, another vindication of Wagner's assertion that Jews were incapable of genuine creativity.[45] Since most of the leading critics in pre-war Vienna were themselves Jews (e.g. Hirschfeld, Karpath, Korngold, and Kalbeck) this line of reasoning cannot be equated with the anti-Semitism that later evolved into the Nazi propaganda of the 1930s, even if it is classified under the questionable historical rubric of so-called Jewish self-hatred. The conflict between Schoenberg and his Viennese critics of Jewish origin (as well as those in Berlin later on) was rather an intra-ethnic debate regarding political security, cultural identity and assimilation. The critique of Schoenberg in a key passage from a 1907 review in the respected journal *Die Zeit*—usually a progressive organ of opinion—illustrates the argument that no real malady rested not so much with the composer and his ambitions but rather with the audience. In former times, the critic noted, one would have shouted down the sort of music Schoenberg was writing. But now "there is an anxiety . . . an inner insecurity."[46] The contemporary audience doubted its own judgment; it was not sure that perhaps it was not missing something legitimate. Audiences listened dutifully to the new because they were not secure in their own standard of taste. Had the audience become paralyzed and therefore unable to damn openly something that was simply no good?

At stake for the Viennese Jews and the Jewish critics (most of them highly assimilated and no longer active participants in the official Jewish community) was precisely the issue that faced Zweig's protagonist and Schoenberg himself. Viennese music journalists in the years between 1907 and 1914 saw themselves as not only arbiters of taste, but as protectors of the public. Since an extraordinarily high percentage of the concert-going audience in Vienna was Jewish, Schoenberg's music could be seen as a direct challenge from one Jew to another regarding the security of Jewish assimilation acquired and maintained through an allegiance to the dominant habits of European culture. In the years between 1907 and 1913 in Vienna both anti-Semitism and Zionism—the Jewish Question—were at the center of politics and the discussion of culture as politics. [47] Many Jewish members of the audience were themselves emigrants to Vienna and at best first-generation natives. Schoenberg understood that the post-Wagnerian approach to music, including its massive sonorities and formal strategies (e.g., Bruckner) created a psychological euphoria in the audience that was not merely private and personal. Music as mere expressionism and suggestive of mood had political consequences, particularly in the context of the codification of nationalist schools of music and cultural rhetorics of identity outside of German-speaking Europe, particularly in Russia, Hungary, and the Czech provinces of the Empire. Late nineteenth-century musical composition assisted in heightening the way culture intersected with race thinking, nationalist constructs of history and ethnic mythology. This was equally true for German-speaking Europe. The operatic and orchestral music of Humperdinck, Strauss, Weingartner (*Orestes*, 1902), Schillings (*Ingwelde*, 1894, and *Oresteia*, 1900), Hausegger (*Barbarossa*, 1900) and Pfitzner (*Von deutscher Seele*, 1922) was all too often celebratory of the mythic German, or the Greek as German, or the Gothic as German. Post-Romantic large-scale composition was easily appropriated by nationalist politics. Ideals of ethnic authenticity and anti-Semitism created an uncomfortable contradiction to the Jewish audience's enthusiasm for late nineteenth century romanticism.

A new art of music that established music's autonomy was not therefore an "art for art's sake" project. The creation of a cultural system in music with alternative political consequences, perhaps more universalistic, required among other things a turn to smaller forms and smaller ensembles. Modernism needed to erect a barrier against nationalism using the very same public cultural instruments of social formation, and in the case of Jews, of assimilation. German and European music after 1918 had to promise a firmer and certainly less self-deceptive cultural antidote for a nationalism in which Jews were either marginalized or excluded.

After 1914, and particularly in the 1920s, the critics' approach to Schoenberg, including rabid anti-Semitic attacks, became more tied to generically general notions of a post-war crisis in the world concerning modern life and culture. With the appearance of the first twelve-tone works some criticism became more respectful, but rarely more sympathetic. Oscar Bie, for example, made an unfavorable but polite comparison between Bartók and Schoenberg. Bie unwittingly confirms the idea that Bartók had no need to invent artificially; he could reach back into the cultural roots of his homeland and find natural sources of originality. Bie's unfavorable comparison hides an implicit agreement with the view of the Jew as inferior, foreign, and without genuine roots in Europe. What Schoenberg lacked was sensuality, something Bartók possessed in abundance. The Jew was thrown back purely on the intellect, and therefore on supposedly abstract and artificial invention. Schoenberg's music was a "document of the intellect and of the idea with an abruptness—severing all connections with the past." The modern, assimilated Jew had no natural alternative "past" to fall back on.[48]

Leopold Schmidt, the enthusiastic proponent of Strauss, wrote in a response to a post-war performance of *Gurrelieder* that with his new music Schoenberg had unfortunately left his "natural impulses" behind. Drawing a contrast between Schoenberg's present work and *Gurrelieder*, Schmidt implies that Schoenberg's work had deteriorated into sophistries, artistic abstinence and a "doctrinaire fixation on the new." In response to Op. 16 Schmidt accused Schoenberg of the attempted "dissolution of music." [49]

Critics both for and against Schoenberg after 1914 frequently share a common ground. Hans Kleemann in an article on "Futuristic Music" accuses Schoenberg of "acoustic games" and an "abstract, intellectually devised way of music-making devoid of imagination."

He explicitly picks up the pre-war theme that Schoenberg is preying on the audience's gullibility.[50] Adolf Weissmann concedes that Schoenberg, following the path of late Beethoven, is searching for a complete restructuring of music. Weissmann is not sure that something "positive" can emerge, but is certain that the effort is ethically on a par with the reforms of Wagner.[51] Weissmann is equally confident that Schoenberg's project is uniquely Jewish.[52] Paul Bekker sides with Schoenberg, but with considerable emotional restraint, defending Schoenberg as operating in a historical context in transition, bereft of a useful compass for standards and values; at least Schoenberg shows courage and maturity.[53]

Within this barrage of criticism the defense crafted by Schoenberg and his supporters—casting Schoenberg as the restorer of the purely musical and therefore pre-Romantic classical values—was ineffective. If one were only able to throw away the crutches of psychological listening, the defenders say, and respond to music on music's own unique terms, one would see that Schoenberg is not a radical after all. What makes Schoenberg's music great are exactly the attributes we locate in Bach, Mozart, and Beethoven: the inspired command of compositional procedures essential to a refined sense of form and unique to the dynamic realization of musical ideas.

The tradition of reception which has identified Schoenberg as a radical conservative or a conservative revolutionary derives from this species of the contemporaneous defense of Schoenberg. Twelve-tone composition was proclaimed to be no more abstract than the classical system—it was merely a fresh approach to an old problem. Schoenberg, accepting the Wagnerian progressive imperative that the artist must respond to the contemporary moment, saw twelve-tone composition as what the great pre-Wagnerian masters might have done in the same historical circumstances. Schoenberg became therefore a kind of updated Brahms: a conservative as progressive. The music written with twelve tones needed to be judged by the same aesthetic criteria by which one judged Brahms and Beethoven.[54]

The flaw in this post-1920 appeal to a novel concept of neoclassicism lay not in its aesthetic premises. Rather, this appeal attempted to circumvent the decisive moment of history, the one discussed by Szymanowski, leaving unanswered the political challenge of late nineteenth-century, post-Wagnerian cultural nationalism in music. The era whose authority was invoked on behalf of Schoenberg was prenationalist, and therefore irrelevant as a cultural symbol. By preaching a more authentic and valid characterization of musical classicism, Schoenberg and his defenders also challenged the widespread late nineteenth-century appropriation of Haydn, Mozart, and Beethoven as uniquely German figures in a post-Wagnerian nationalist sense. Schoenberg's 1933 refuge in the example of Brahms constituted the most convincing and reassuring appeal to history. Brahms, as even Szymanowski realized, had been a solitary figure, unsympathetic and out of step with Wagnerian nationalist politics. He had not been an anti-Semite. A north-German Protestant, Brahms had lived in Vienna and found himself somewhat homeless in the racialist and radical nationalist politics of the 1890s, as revealed by his failed and naïve effort to convince Dvořák to move to Vienna.[55]

The allure of late romanticism had been ultimately, as Schoenberg himself argued, a deceptively easy way to reach a wide and not necessarily well-educated mass audience.[56] Its consequences were ultimately disastrous, both aesthetically and politically. Wagner and his successors deluded the late nineteenth-century audience and its early twentieth-century successor into believing that by listening psychologically, by following and adding stories and visual impressions, one was actually thinking musically. The audience was rendered capable of understanding Mozart, Beethoven, and even Brahms the way they should be understood by applying the model of Wagner's music.

Hidden in the press reports, both those before 1914 and those before 1933, is the fact that some significant segment of the audience either liked what they heard or was not outraged. Schoenberg's own defense, and that of Berg, made the assumption that printed critical journalistic rhetoric actually reflected audience attitudes. Implied was a dissatisfaction with the musical competence of both the audience and the critics. But beyond this point of view Schoenberg and his defenders failed to question the validity of their own historical narrative. Were the classical models so energetically praised and analyzed by Schoenberg truly examples of self-consciously formalist music? Why was the imposition of a narrative or visual fantasy onto an instrumental work by Mozart, Beethoven or Brahms historically false, inappropriate, or in conflict with the intentions of the composer? Did the kind of puritan habits of listening so energetically propagated and wished for by the Society for Private Performances in the 1920s ever exist? We know from the use of specific keys by Mozart, the hidden existence of extra-musical narratives in Beethoven's instrumental music, and the biographical context and philosophical intentions of Brahms, that the kind of pure musical listening so desperately desired by the organizers of the Society and implicit in its manifesto may never have existed.[57]

The call by Schoenberg and his defenders for a new musical elite that could truly appreciate the classical masters and therefore modern music— for a public separated from its journalistic masters— was not so much a call for a cultural restoration or a return to a vanished classical era as it was a radical and novel fundamentalism about the nature of music and its public function. In this peculiar way Schoenberg followed directly in the path of Wagner's schemes for educational reform as characterized and understood by Eberhard Preussner in 1935. In Preussner's view, the intent of Wagnerian reform was to raise the level of musical culture in an urban capitalist and industrial world by restoring an active amateurism. Schoenberg and Wagner are allied in their implicit critique of what Preussner viewed as the consequences of high capitalism and commercialization. Preussner's ultimate solution was fascist politics and conservative aesthetics, whereas Schoenberg's modernism legitimately allied itself with Adorno's critique of modern culture and its doubts about the virtues of commercial music.[58]

Let us return for a moment to Zweig's enthusiastic hearer in Berlin. Much of Schoenberg's audience in Berlin was made up of Jews. Music, as in Vienna, had been a primary instrument of assimilation. Like Karl Kraus, Schoenberg had come to revile the self-delusion of most urban Jews who assumed that the mere acquisition of wealth and culture was a sufficient basis for a sense of security. The unease identified by critics within the audience was not merely an insecurity of judgment. It mirrored an insecurity of belonging and identity in Weimar society. As Schoenberg's own sojourn back to self-professed Jewish identity indicates, the Jew's cultural experience of hearing music tied in directly with issues of membership in European culture and society. The radical surface of Schoenberg's music cut through the legacy of complacency, security and self-satisfaction. It challenged the premises of the audience's fragile sense of place.

It is as if Schoenberg's post-1920s modernism was a coded language alerting the Jews in the audience to the growing danger and instability inherent in their situation. Anti-Semitism, a key element to Viennese politics circa 1907, had become a major aspect of the political discourse in Germany during the 1920s. The late Romantic conventions of Wagner and post-Wagner composers needed to be attacked because, in the large-scale and grandiose orchestral music of Strauss for example, there lurked, as Szymanowski recognized, a Wagnerian ideal of the quintessentially Germanic: a blood-and-soil aesthetic of rootedness and collective spirituality that was ultimately appropriated by fascism.

Mahler's mix of success and disappointment in Vienna, and Schoenberg's lingering ambivalence toward's Mahler's music were part of a prescient instinct on Schoenberg's part. Zweig's protagonist was right: the aesthetic credo of a new Europe in which the Jew could truly belong could not be derived from Wagnerian aesthetics. A truly modern, ethically and aesthetically refined, logical system of expression was needed, one that mirrored the ideals and possibilities of the future. Aesthetics could prefigure a different political and social world. In this sense it is wrong to consider Schoenberg's gradual turn back to Judaism and form of Zionism as irrelevant to his late works for instruments.[59] The power of the work from the 1930s, beginning with *Moses und Aron* and ending with the very latest pieces, derives from the synthesis of aesthetic and political radicalism. This explains Schoenberg's remarkable and eloquent enthusiasm at the end of his life for the possibilities of musical culture in the new Jewish state.[60]

• • •

From our vantage point at the end of the century there appear to be two ways to rehear Schoenberg's work with sympathy. First, we must discard the traditional rhetoric of criticism and defense. Second, we must penetrate beyond the point at which Symanowski stopped: at Schoenberg's commitment to sever the link between psychology and music. From 1907 on, Schoenberg's modernism contained a vision of music as a means of cultural renewal and ultimately as a dimension of political utopianism cloaked in a Stefan George-like aestheticism. In Schoenberg the spiritual and the rational merged and confronted the individual's self-conscious struggle with modernity. Schoenberg's initial focus had been Europe, especially German-speaking Europe. He shifted his gaze by the late 1920s and envisaged a new society in which political membership for the Jew could be realized, a society in which reason flourished in both culture and art. The beneficiary of this new society would be the emancipated, diaspora Jew, previously cut off from stable membership in any European nation. Schoenberg thus repeated the pattern of recognition and response experienced by Theodor Herzl in 1897.

Like Bartók, Szymanowski was not a Jew. Like Bartók, he had an unchallenged connection to a folk heritage, which he could use as a basis for innovation.[61] Despite his sympathy for Schoenberg, Szymanowski never understood the extent to which Schoenberg was not German. Nor did he understand Schoenberg the Jew as intimately as the Jewish critics who hated his music. They were angry because they heard Schoenberg's challenge to their status as European cosmopolitans. With no recourse to a pre-modern, landed national folk or cultural tradition, Schoenberg, like Herzl, tried to reassert the rational in the new. Schoenberg appealed to the spirit of Mozart and Haydn, the Enlightenment and the classicism of the eighteenth century. Schoenberg at first assumed, as did Zweig's hero, that if reason and art could be combined in a new language detached from allusions to mythology and ethnicity (as evident in Wagner's work), then a new universalistic basis for society and culture might be created in the aftermath of World War I. In such a context, the Jew would be secure. Initially Schoenberg believed that post-war Germany might hold out that promise. He never took America seriously, but turned his attention, after 1933, to the possibilities in Palestine and Israel. In this peculiar sense, Schoenberg's modernism was like Herzl's vision of the new Jewish State: a displaced European utopia for Jews, and a fantastically poignant and carefully constructed expression of a secure and rooted political future without anti-Semitism.

Schoenberg's music after 1909 and particularly after 1920 is therefore profoundly psychological and emotional in its communicative structure. It derives from pressing human necessities, without lapsing into representation or illustration.[62] The Jewish element in Schoenberg's modernism has little to do with the allegations of dryness and artificiality put forward by anti-Semites. There was, however, something Jewish about Schoenberg's modernism, as Adolf Weissmann suspected. But it was something that neither Szymanowski nor Strauss could understand. Bartók could stick with tonality because in the politics of the 1920s his reconciliation of pre-modern rural music with modernism meant forging a connection with a rediscovered national past in which he had legitimacy, and located in a specific region. We too rarely connect Schoenberg's invention of twelve-tone composition with nationalism. His finest contemporaries, from Stravinsky to Janáček[63] and Bartók, had their own authentic folk roots to fall back on as a source of originality and modernist renewal. What did the assimilated German Jew have to fall back on? By inventing a system, modeled in its own way on Viennese classicism, Schoenberg sought to transmute a German national heritage—the pre-Wagnerian German tradition, seen as the universal in music—adequately into the twentieth century. In this way Schoenberg sought to dominate the musical world the way Wagner had, but in a manner in which all Jews—particularly assimilated, cultured Jews with no easy access back to traditional Judaism—could partake as equals.[64]

There was nothing unnatural or artificial about twelve-tone music or Schoenberg's modernism in the 1920s—it sprung from the existential condition of European Jewry before 1933. Like the inter-war protagonists of Esperanto, Schoenberg sought to fashion a new, valid universal modernist art in which both reason and emotion could be communicated and to which no social class, religion or ethnic group had claims of priority or higher status. In the wake of the collapse of this dream he used his modernist method with searing emotion to critique the past and support the idea of a new political utopia—in *Kol Nidre*, the *Ode to Napoleon*, as well as in the String Trio, Op. 45, and the Fantasy, Op. 47.

The angry audiences and critics of yesteryear are gone. In the contemporary world the particular issues that inspired Schoenberg have become largely moot. There is now an opportunity to embrace Schoenberg's music with the appropriate kinds of psychological listening it demands and rewards. We need to be inspired by the intense utopian emotionalism of Schoenberg's modernism and by his unsentimental and subtle imagination and vision—communicated through music—of future cultural and human possibilities.

APPENDIX
Excerpt from "W sprawie 'muzyki współczesnej',"
(On the question of "contemporary music")
by Karol Szymanowski

It is understandable that after the epoch of the absolute reign of Wagner, a battle of ideas articulated in part by his prominent successors was rekindled again. (We are omitting here intentionally the solitary figure of Johannes Brahms who stood aside from the battle. His art—notwithstanding its absolute value—has played hardly any role in the evolution of recent music).

During the final pre-war years, among the factions with divergent opinions and growing protests against the might of the creator of Nibelungen, given the dread of oncoming thunderstorms, there was an inevitable crisis of ideas. The necessity for a basic internal reordering was finally felt. Characteristically, this feeling was supported by the awakening of interest in the musical modernism of other nations, mainly France and Russia.

Under such circumstances, within major conflicts and battles for even the right to express an opinion, emerged slowly the fame of the most amazing composer in contemporary Germany, Arnold Schoenberg.

Here we arrive at the nucleus of the problem. Schoenberg is indeed the only one in the group of the still-living excellent colleagues representing pre-war modernism in music who not only transformed the cataclysms of the horrible war that shook Central Europe, but survived as a banner, an emblem, a representative of ideas which were to lead German music out of its pre-war suffocating atmosphere toward new achievements and conquests. He is, according to the prevalent German opinion, the long awaited builder of the aerial bridges leading to the road toward the future.

His name, along with the name of Stravinsky, is a symbol, a symbol of revolutionary modernism in music.

It is worthwhile to reflect on the psychology of this phenomenon.

It is necessary to use maximum thoughtfulness and objectivity when voicing criticism of Schoenberg. His enormous creative energy, his fanatic belief in his own mission, his unshaken loyalty to ideas—all aspects of this extraordinary personality demand respect.

A laconic superficial dismissal of the artist whose achievements tipped the scales of contemporary music—is out of the question.

The internal reconstruction of the basic means of expression found its deepest meaning in Schoenberg. He aimed somewhat *centrifugally* away from the ideal nucleus, toward absolute re-evaluation of formal elements of music, toward entirely new basic foundations.

Most puzzling is the fact that Schoenberg used the post-Wagnerian epigonism as a point of departure, as confirmed eloquently by *Gurrelieder*, with its undeniable romantic elements.

We notice step-by-step how a musical dynamic, heading by necessity to relaxation, and the organic cohesion of form, give way characteristically to extra-musical contents. These mysterious connections—developed through Wagner, German romanticism and also the secure traditionalism of a well-founded culture, are the only points of departure for any critical appraisal of Schoenberg's work. This is all in spite of the paradox that today the traditional culture has deviated far from its natural sources.

Let's consider the separate ways in which formal musical elements gradually developed depending on ideological foundations. Musical romanticism, predominant in Germany, was the epoch of breakthrough. The "horizontal" style of the classics, which implied in principle the construction of pure musical "form," changed gradually to a "vertical" style. This happened under the influence of the "dramatization" of the content, connecting music with the direct psychological truth. For completely understandable reasons a more differentiated and enriched *harmony* became the starting point for the romantic style of music.

Increasingly music was saturated with the lyrics of direct life, a reality rooted in life's psychological rhythms which was, strictly speaking, formally framed by the rhythms of a *living word* with all its arbitrary improvisations and emotional paths. These rhythms diverted music from its natural ways of development. The strong bonds of rhythm—the external skeleton which make the proportions of separate parts of a musical work understandable—loosened gradually—whereas the vertical, harmonic sounds emerged into the foreground as cornerstones, landmarks, creating arbitrary points of support (in a formal sense) and a general background for music saturated with lyrics. Besides, in an abstract sense, harmony created a gratifying frame for the so-called "mood" (*horribile dictu*), the formal "nothing." Musical dynamics were set aside for the benefit of the dynamics of "emotions," leading to a new feeling of "color" in music and therefore in essence a *static* notion. Harmony, deriving from formal principles, followed its own motion as long as the concept of *modulation* was possible. With the increasing differentiation of the separate elements of harmony (simultaneous sound) the moment arrived when dissonant harmony created a *chord* as a *value in itself*, a chord coming from nowhere and going nowhere, an *unresolved dissonance*—and an absolute vertical simultaneous sound. In the history of this chord Tristan's chromaticism was the breaking point. It underwent further evolution in the works of prominent composers in the post-Wagnerian era (mainly Strauss, Mahler, etc.).

However, this chord was used by these composers as an expression of conflict, as a "mood"—never as a *formal absolute value*. It was a derivative, a departure, a wandering. But by its very existence the possibility of a true road leading to the goal remained. The concept of an absolute vertical sound as a *value in itself*, not as a function of musical "expression," became the transition to the essential atomism.

Arnold Schoenberg crossed the Rubicon. He separated the lines from the past forever with a complete sense of responsibility. With the realization of this idealization through his decision, he found himself in the limitless domain of all possibilities in which—to quote Nietzsche—*"Nichts ist wahr, alles ist erlaubt."*

It is important to realize the seriousness and the consequences of this step.

NOTES

1. Quoted in Anna Maria Morazzoni, "Der Schönberg-Kreis und Italien. Die Polemik gegen Casellas Aufsatz über 'Scarlattiana,'" in *Bericht über den 2. Kongreß der Internationalen Schönberg-Gesellschaft: Die Wiener Schule in der Musikgeschichte des 20. Jahrhunderts,* ed. Rudolf Stephan and Sigrid Wiesmann, (Vienna, 1986), p. 80, n. 13. I would like to thank Paul De Angelis, Irene Zedlacher, and Karen Painter for their advice and assistance with the essay. Prof. Painter, Joseph Auner, and Klaus Kropfinger kindly made archival materials available to me. The translations are the author's, with the exception of those from the Polish, which are a collaboration with Dr. Anne Botstein.

2. See Norbert Linke, "Die Nachwirkungen Schönbergs in der Gegenwart—Auswertung einer Umfrage," in *Bericht über den 3. Kongreß der Internationalen Schönberg-Gesellschaft: Arnold Schönberg—Neuerer der Musik,* ed. Rudolf Stephan and Sigrid Wiesmann (Vienna, 1996), pp. 40–56; Alex Ross, "Schoenberg, Anyone?" *The New Yorker* (8 March 1999): 84–86; and David Schiff, "A New Measure for Heroes in Music's Valhalla," *The New York Times,* Sunday Arts and Leisure Section (28 February 1999). See also Walter B. Bailey "Changing Views of Schoenberg" in *The Arnold Schoenberg Companion,* ed. Walter B. Bailey (Westport, Conn., 1998), pp. 3–10.

3. Much to Schoenberg's annoyance, only *Verklärte Nacht* from 1899 seemed to have entered the repertoire and become popular by the 1930s. As a result of the Mahler craze of the past several decades, *Gurrelieder* has found a new following, vindicating its enormous success at the premiere in Vienna in 1913.

4. Schoenberg has been retrospectively judged as the "false" messiah. During the past decade William Thomson, Martin Vogel, and Joseph Swain have all argued with varying degrees of resentment against Schoenberg's innovations, rejecting the idea that he defined and set the proper course for musical modernism, particularly in the 1920s, with twelve-tone composition. See William Thomson, *Schoenberg's Error* (Philadelphia, 1993); Martin Vogel, *Schönberg und die Folgen. Die Irrwege der Neuen Musik,* vol. 1 (Bonn, 1984) and vol. 2 (Bonn 1997); Joseph P. Swain, *Musical Languages* (New York and London, 1997), esp. pp. 119–40.

5. Certainly not in the sense that that even the first generation of post-modernists did (e.g., Górecki, Penderecki, Del Tredici, Glass, and Rochberg). See Křenek, "Schlusswort," in *2. Kongreß der Internationalen Schönberg-Gesellschaft,* p. 285.

6. See Pierre Boulez, "Schoenberg is Dead," in Boulez, *Notes of an Apprenticeship*, trans. Herbert Weinstock (New York, 1968), pp. 268–76; and on Carter's views see David Schiff "Redefining Boundaries. Carter as Symphonist," *Musical Times* 139 (1998): 10.

7. See Heinrich Helge Hatteson, *Emanzipation durch Aneigung. Untersuchungen zu den frühen Streichquartetten Arnold Schönbergs* (Kassel, 1990), pp. 1–7.

8. See Jürgen Schebera, *Eisler. Eine Biographie in Texten, Bildern und Dokumenten* (Mainz, 1998), esp. pp. 23–33.

9. Copland and Blitzstein (who studied with Schoenberg in Berlin) had similar misgivings in the 1930s about the incongruity of an assumed coherence between progressive politics and musical modernism, and not only in Schoenberg's version of it. The modern in music that challenged inherited expectations about musical beauty and comprehensibility tied to the use of tonality appeared more aristocratic than democratic. See Aaron Copland and Vivian Perlis, *Copland. 1900 through 1942* (New York, 1984), pp. 226–30 and p. 237. David Josef Bach, Schoenberg's old friend and a socialist, had similar doubts well before the First World War.

10. See Theodor W. Adorno, "Schönberg und der Fortschritt," in Adorno, *Philosophie der Neuen Musik* (Frankfurt/Main, 1978), pp. 36–126; It is remarkable how high the prestige of Schoenberg and his post-war following was. This can be gleaned from the library of the pianist Claudio Arrau, who did not play contemporary music but who followed carefully and admired the radical modernism of the 1950s and 1960s. See also Joseph Horowitz, *Conversations with Arrau* (New York, 1982), p. 118.

11. See for example Samuel Lipman's essay "Schoenberg's Survival" (originally published in *Commentary*) in *Music after Modernism* (New York, 1979), pp. 31–47.

12. See David Epstein, *Shaping Time. Music, the Brain, and Performance* (New York, 1995); Benjamin Boretz, "Sketch of a New Musical System (Meta-Variations, Part II), *Perspectives of New Music* 8/2 (1970): 49–111; Swain, *Musical Languages*. Also see Leonard Bernstein's Norton Lectures at Harvard published as *The Unanswered Question* (Cambridge, 1976).

13. See Albrecht Dümling, "Public Loneliness: Atonality and the Crisis of Subjectivity in Schoenberg's Opus 15," in *Schönberg & Kandinsky. An Historic Encounter*, ed. Konrad Boehmer, (Amsterdam, 1997), pp. 101–38, esp. 124–36. The sociologist Max Weber took particular aim at George and the aestheticist isolationist position in the immediate post-war years. Weber was also suspicious of cults of personality and tightly drawn circles of disciples on the grounds of their inherent tension with intellectual freedom and the ethics of responsibility in a democracy—a criticism that might aptly be applied to Schoenberg and his defenders. See the historic speeches of 1919 entitled "Wissenschaft als Beruf" and "Politik als Beruf."

14. At the Los Angeles Schoenberg conference in 1991 honoring Leonard Stein one could detect remnants of something not unlike the attitiude of Wagnerians at Bayreuth after the master's death. The *Journal of the Arnold Schoenberg Institute* had its parallel in the *Bayreuther Blätter*. The Los Angeles Institute's mission and that of the Vienna Arnold Schönberg Center, both with their faithful recreations of the study in Brentwood and the close cooperation if not control by more than one generation of family descendants, have a familiar ring for those who know Bayreuth. There is always the inherent risk in the memorialization and insitutionalization of an aesthetic legacy of a historic figure that rigidity and a tendency to monopolistic control will predominate. Posthumous enthusiasm quickly deteriorates into warring camps of claimants, almost hagiographical devotion to preserving and sorting out biographical details, and intolerance towards so-called "deviant," unsanctioned interpretations. Schoenberg's own penchant for domineering habits and fiercely held opinions and loyalties easily become routines in the insitutional shrines created to preserve his music and ideas

15. Rainer Maria Rilke, *Sämtliche Werke*, vol. 2: *Gedichte 1906–26* (Leipzig, 1957), p. 111.

16. Karol Szymanowski, "W sprawie 'muzyki wspólczesnej,'" in Szymanowski, *Z Pism*, vol. 6 (Krakow, 1958), pp. 107–18. The text in question, from pp. 114–18, is contained in the appendix to this essay.

17. Alban Berg,"Why is Schoenberg's Music so Difficult to Understand" quoted in Willi Reich, *Alban Berg* (New York, 1974), p. 204

18. See Tadeusz A. Zieliński, *Szymanowski. Liryka i ekstaza* (Krakow, 1997), pp. 227–43.

19. Despite Szymanowski's extensive praise and doubtless admiration, he did not follow suit in his own work precisely because he could not quite abandon this communicative nexus. He could not sacrifice "psychologism" in music on behalf of music's absolute nature. Szymanowski's argument is quite similar to what Adorno would write in 1948, particularly on Schoenberg's departure from conventions of expressivity in music. See Adorno, *Philosophy of Modern Music*, trans. Anne G. Mitchell and Wesley Blomster (New York, 1973), pp. 37–60.

20. In Arnold Zweig, *Novellen*, vol. 1 (Frankfurt/Main, 1987), pp. 301–7. See also Wilhelm von Sternburg, *'Um Deutschland geht es uns.' Arnold Zweig. Die Biographie* (Berlin, 1998), p. 68.

21. See Job Ijzerman, "Schönberg's Pursuit of Musical Truth: Truth as a Central Category in Expressionism," in *Schönberg & Kandinsky*, pp. 183–98, and Leon Botstein, "Music and the Critique of Culture. Arnold Schoenberg, Heinrich Schenker and the Emergence of Modernism in Fin-de-Siècle Vienna," in *Constructive Dissonance: Arnold Schoenberg and the Transformation of Twentieth Century Culture*, ed. Juliane Brand and Christopher Hailey (Berkley and Los Angeles, 1997), p. 19.

22. Furthermore, Op. 7 and Op. 9 were both performed in Leipzig in 1912, by the Flonzaley Quartet and the Gewandhaus under Nikisch.

23. For this group of works see Walter Frisch, *The Early Works of Arnold Schoenberg* (Berkeley and Los Angeles, 1993), pp. 181–247, esp. pp. 186–87, and Christian Martin Schmidt, "Schönbergs 'very definite-but private" Programm zum Streichquartett op. 7," in *Bericht über den 2. Kongreß*, pp. 233-34.

24. See Alexander L. Ringer, *Arnold Schoenberg. The Composer as Jew* (Oxford, 1990), and his essay, "Assimilation and the Emancipation of Historical Dissonance," in *Constructive Dissonance*, 23–24; and Leon Botstein, "Arnold Schoenberg: Language, Modernism and Jewish Identity," in *Austrians and Jews in the Twentieth Century*, ed. Robert S. Wistrich (New York, 1992), pp. 162–83.

25. See Hans-Christoph Hoffmann, Walter Krause and Werner Kitlitschka, *Das Wiener Opernhaus* (Wiesbaden, 1972); also *Das K.K. Hofoperntheater in Wien* (Vienna, 1894), plates 50–52.

26. Consider for example the neoclassicism of the new Musikverein in Vienna designed by Theophil von Hansen and completed in 1870, the year of an extensive and influential Beethoven centenary festival held in the new hall.

27. The best English-language introduction to Karl Kraus remains Edward Timms, *Karl Kraus: Apocalyptic Satirist* (New Haven, 1986), see esp. pp. 30–62.

28. See Manfred Wagner, *Alfred Roller in seiner Zeit* (Salzburg, 1996), pp. 71–112 and pp. 177–85. The attitudes and function of the Viennese critics and the public at the fin de siècle cannot be inferred from the vitriolic attitudes of either Kraus or Schoenberg. It is curious, for example, that Bruno Walter praises the staunchly conservative anti-Schoenberg critic Robert Hirschfeld (who also had his reservations about Mahler) in a letter to Hans Pfitzner in 1903 as a "wonderful and smart" man. In Bruno Walter, *Briefe 1894–1962* (Frankfurt/Main, 1969), p. 64.

29. See H. H. Stuckenschmidt, *Schönberg. Leben-Umwelt-Wirkung* (Munich, 1989), p. 50.

30. In *Im Heim—Die Welt* (Vienna, 1909); on Schoenberg and Lehár see Otto Schneidereit, *Franz Lehár. Eine Biographie in Zitaten* (Innsbruck, 1984), pp. 204-6.

31. See the essays collected in *Josef Frank, Architect and Designer. An Alternative Vision of the Modern Home*, exhibition catalog, ed. Nina Stritzler-Levine (New Haven, 1996), and Haus Nr. 12 (Josef Frank) and Nos. 49–52 (Adolf Loos) in *Werkbundsiedlung. Internationale Austellung Wien 1932*, ed. Josef Frank (Vienna, 1932). Frank's critique of architectural modernism parallels Eisler's doubts in the 1920s about Schoenberg.

32. *Wiener Almanach. Jahrbuch für Literatur, Kunst und öffentliches Leben* xxi, ed. Jacques Jaeger (Vienna and Leipzig, 1912), pp. 204ff.

33. These are the phrases used about Strauss in 1932 by Richard Eichenauer in *Musik und Rasse*; quoted in Tim Ashley, *Richard Strauss* (London, 1999), p. 164

34. This radical break was precisely what Schoenberg sought to achieve. He made this point explicitly in his own discussion of Op. 9. See Claus-Steffen Mahnkopf, *Gestalt und Stil. Arnold Schönbergs Erste Kammersymphonie und ihr Umfeld* (Kassel, 1994), pp. 186ff.

35. Leon Botstein, "Egon Schiele and Arnold Schoenberg: The Cultural Politics of Aesthetic Innovation in Vienna 1890–1918," in *Egon Schiele. Art, Sexuality and Viennese Modernism*, ed. Patrick Werkner (Palo Alto, 1994), pp. 101–18.

36. See Eduard Hanslick, *On the Musically Beautiful*, trans. and ed. Geoffrey Payzant (Indianapolis, 1986), pp. 6–7 and 36–40; also pp. 82–83. These sections are selected to highlight the idea that although the content of music is autonomous, and the source of its beauty likewise, music remains a human and natural phenomenon in history, making its adaptation to individualized forms of appropriation, even "false" ones, understandable. See also Thrasybulos Georgiades, *Musik und Sprache* (Berlin, 1954), pp. 138–42. I differ therefore with key points in the reading of Hanslick and the mid-nineteenth century debate articulated by Lydia Goehr in *The Quest for Voice* (Berkeley and Los Angeles, 1998), pp. 63–65 and 91–98.

37. See Konrad Boehmer, "Expressionism and Rationality" in *Schönberg & Kandinsky*, pp. 169–81. For Fontane and reader expectations, as well as parallels with the visual arts, see Theodor Fontane, *Der Stechlin* (Berlin, 1993) and *Fontane und die bildende Kunst*, eds. Claude Keisch, Peter-Klaus Schuster and Moritz Wullen (Berlin, 1998). On Stifter see *Der Nachsommer* (Munich, 1987) and Marina van Zuylen, *Difficulty as an Aesthetic Principle. Realism and Unreadability in Stifter, Melville and Flaubert* (Tübingen, 1994), pp. 1–46.

38. See Franz Hadamowsky and Heinz Otte, *Die Wiener Operette* (Vienna, 1947), pp. 399–402.

39. As Siegfried Krakauer's 1937 book on Offenbach and Karl Kraus's fanatical enthusiasm indicated, Schoenberg's generation of modernists understood and admired the mix of parody, social critique, dramatic rigor, and refinement that characterized the great operettas of Offenbach and Johann Strauss; what was disturbing was the routinization and trivialization of the form as well as the loss of the critical edge that marked the operetta in the twentieth century. The attraction on the part of Schoenberg and Kraus to operetta of the nineteenth century (and the comic theatre and farce of an earlier epoch, that of Nestroy) is connected to the modernist impulse to fashion, in a new, rigorous and honest language inherently as devastatingly critical of mid- and late-nineteenth century mores as operetta had been. See Georg Knepler, *Karl Kraus liest Offenbach* (Vienna, 1984), and Karl Kraus, "Offenbach-Renaissance" in *Die Fackel* (April 1927), pp. 757–58; Siegfried Krakauer, *Jacques Offenbach und das Paris seiner Zeit* (Frankfurt, 1980).

40. See Otto Breicha, *Gerstl und Schönberg. Eine Beziehung* (Salzburg, 1993), p. 7.

41. Arnold Schoenberg, "How One Becomes Lonely" (1937), in *Style and Idea*, ed. Leonard Stein (New York, 1975), pp. 30–52.

42. In the comparison between twelve-tone composition and Zionism it must be pointed out that Herzl's debt to nineteenth-century concepts of nationalism and statehood was powerful. What was radical was the notion of a modern Jewish political entity.

43. See Leon Botstein, "Music and Its Public," (Ph.D. diss., Harvard University, 1985), vol. 4, pp. 1202ff.

44. "Die Moderne in der Tonkunst," *Die Zeit* (8 February 1907).

45. The notion of a specifically Jewish and sophistically complex music written by Jews seeking to partake in European culture—gratuitously ugly, but justifiable on technical grounds—was rendered concrete in a parody of "Ostjuden" in Strauss's 1905 *Salome* in the music for the five Jews (Rehearsal Nos. 188–207). This example was used by anti-Semitic critics from the 1920s and 1930s. See Sander L. Gilman, "Salome, Syphilis, Sarah Bernhardt, and the Modern Jewess," in *The Jew in the Text. Modernity and the Construction of Identity*, ed. Linda Nochlin and Tamar Garb (London, 1995), pp. 101–2. Examples of this criticism in its Nazi form can be found in Ernst Bücken, *Die Musik der Nationen* (Leipzig, 1937), p. 451; and his *Wörterbuch der Musik* (Leipzig, 1940), pp. 389–90.

46. *Die Zeit* (8 February 1907).

47. Consider, for example Arthur Schnitzler's exemplary novel from 1908 *Der Weg ins Freie*.

48. See Oscar Bie, "Die Neue Musik," *Berliner Börsen-Courier* (22 March 1920). Steininger Sammlung, Geheimes Staatsarchiv, Preussischer Kulturbesitz, Berlin.

49. See Leopold Schmidt, "Die österreichische Musikwoche in Berlin," *Neue Freie Presse*, and "Aus den Konzerten," *Berliner Tagblatt* (1 April 1925). Steininger Sammlung, Berlin.

50. See Hans Kleemann, "Futuristische Musik" (3 October 1919), Steininger Sammlung, Berlin.

51. See Adolf Weissmann, "Von Wagner bis Schönberg," from Arnold Schönberg Center, Vienna.

52. See Adolf Weissmann, "Die Ausdruckskunst Arnold Schönbergs," in Weissmann, *Die Musik in der Weltkrise* (Stuttgart and Berlin, 1922), p. 183.

53. See Paul Bekker, "An Arnold Schönberg," in Bekker, *Briefe an zeitgenössische Musiker* (Berlin, 1932), pp. 57–67, and Bekker, "Zwischen Vergangenheit und Zukunft." Steininger Sammlung, Eugen Püschel, writing about the twelve-tone system, concurred with Szymanowski's assessment. Music was no longer "psychologically grounded," and century old habits were set aside. The intellectual is construed as the absence of emotional connection with the audience, which in turn becomes a metaphor for the nation. See Eugen Püschel, "Vom Impressionismus zur abstrakten Musik," in Steininger Nachlass, Geheimes Staatsarchiv, Preussischer Kulturbesitz, Berlin.

54. As Felix Galimir recounted, when Schoenberg received back from Rudolf Kolisch the manuscript of Op. 37, the Fourth Quartet, Kolisch had written out the tone rows; Schoenberg was outraged. That was not the sort of response he wanted. After all, what did such analysis have to do with music! Video interview with Felix Galimir, Fall 1998, courtesy of Robert Martin.

55. See Leon Botstein, "Brahms and his Audience. The Later Viennese Years 1875–1897," in *The Cambridge Companion to Brahms*, ed. Michael Musgrave (forthcoming, Cambridge, 1999).

56. Josef Rufer, *Das Werk Arnold Schoenbergs* (Kassel, 1959), p. 139.

57. See Alban Berg, "Prospekt des Vereins für musikalische Privataufführungen," in *Schönbergs Verein für Musikalische Privataufführungen*, ed. Heinz-Klaus Metzger and Rainer Riehn, Musik-Konzepte 36 (Munich, 1984): 4–7.

58. Eberhard Preussner, *Die bürgerliche Musikkultur* (Hamburg, 1935), pp. 200–10.

59. See Jost Hermand, "'Der Biblische Weg.' Zur Radikalität von Schönbergs zionistischer Wende," in *3. Kongreß der Internationalen Schönberg-Gesellschaft*, pp. 195–206, and particularly p. 206, in which Hermand speaks of the "unpolitical dodecaphonic music" Schoenberg wrote in the 1930s, of which there is, in my view, none. See also a later extension of this argument in Hermand's "Ein Überlebender aus Deutschland. Zur Radikalität von Arnold Schönbergs zionistischer Wende," *Judentum und deutsche Kultur* (Köln, 1996), pp. 160–85,

which contains comparable characterizations of Schoenberg's chamber and orchestral work from the 1930s (p. 179).

60. See Schoenberg's 1951 letter to the director of the Israel Academy of Music in *Arnold Schönberg. Ausgewählte Briefe*, ed. Erwin Stein (Mainz, n.d.), pp. 297f.

61. See Karol Szymanowski, "Zagadnienie 'ludowści' w stosunku do muzyki wspólczesnej (Na marginesie artikulu Béli Bartóka 'U źródel muzyki ludowej')" from 1925 (On the Question of Folk Music in Relation to Contemporary Music [Marginalia on Bela Bartók's article on the sources of folk music]), in Szymanowski, *Z Pism*, pp. 77–85.

62. Consider Schoenberg student Erich Itor Kahn's post-war "Thoughts about the Twelve Tone Technique" which makes the same point and links Schoenberg's mode of composition with the historical moment and the intense search for an "adequate" expressive and "spiritual" vision, in Juan Allende-Blin, *Erich Itor Kahn*, Musik-Konzepte 85 (Munich, 1994): 105.

63. Janáček was able to utilize the Czech language, his own idiosyncratic harmonic theories (put forward in 1913, two years after Schoenberg's *Harmonielehre*) and fashion a modernism that openly embraced the psychological, once again relying on pre-modern elements but ultimately contemporary notions of national identity. Compare for example *Katá Kabanová* from 1921 with Schoenberg's music from the same period. Both may be divergent resolutions of the same historical process.

64. See Bela Bartók, "Harvard Lectures" (1943), in *Essays,* ed. Benjamin Suchoff (Lincoln, Nebraska, 1992), pp. 354–92.

Schoenberg as Theorist:
Three Forms of Presentation

The crucial fact about Schoenberg the theorist is contained in his own statement, "I am still more of a composer than a theorist."[1] He is always conscious of the limitations of theory, including his own, and despite his constant efforts, all Schoenberg's theoretical works after *Harmonielehre* remain torsos.[2] Generations of students and disciples have taken up Schoenberg's ideas and tried with varying degrees of success to make them whole.[3] But the incompleteness of Schoenberg's theoretical works is inevitable, mirroring his own philosophical and compositional conviction that any theory of art is inherently preliminary. For him it is not possible to understand an artistic accomplishment rationally and completely through any defined system or finite set of laws.[4] He wrote: "Theory is guided by an ideal case—however sensitively it might track down the facts—but it [cannot] aim to arrive at one. . . .In the realm of thought, everything is merely a preliminary stage, even if it is right, if only it comes from an accomplishment" (*MI* 88–89, 92–93).[5]

For Schoenberg the "accomplishment," the musical composition, is ultimately the expression of a "musical idea"—lying beyond time and space essentially metaphysical in nature (*ZKIF* 4–5).[6] Schoenberg accepts that he can never capture in words the true essence of the "musical idea."[7] His theoretical remarks constitute instead the intuitions of a composer who is constantly drawing consequences from musical material that he is studying, whether in his own compositions or those of someone else. Thus Schoenberg's aspiration as a theorist is to throw light—necessarily incomplete—on the meaning of *presentation*, the ways in which musical ideas are portrayed in various contexts.

In his writings, Schoenberg has only one direct description of presentation (*Darstellung*): "*Darstellung* signifies the presentation of an object to a spectator in such a way that he perceives its composite parts as if in functional motion."[8] The two crucial terms here are "component parts" and "functional motion," which define Schoenberg's well-known epistemological belief in the artwork as organism.[9] For Schoenberg the presentation of the organic form is always based on his twofold notion of motive (*Motiv*). On the one hand, a motive is the ultimate source of formal unity:

> Everyone with a knowledge of music is aware that each piece has certain parts, the smallest, which always recur: the so-called motives. . . . [E]very form no matter where or how it appears may be traced back to these motives. (*SI* 279)

On the other hand, a motive can also be "something that gives rise to motion . . . that change in a state of rest, which turns it into its opposite" (*ZKIF* 26–7). Such motives "allow new ideas to arise" (*ZKIF* 38–39), thus creating the dynamic of a tonal form.

Schoenberg mentions several techniques of motivic presentation: "development" (*Entwicklung*) or "developing variation" (*entwickelnde Variation*), "stringing together" (*Aneinander-Reihung*) or "juxtaposition" (*Juxtaposition*), and "unfolding" or "envelopment" (*Abwicklung*) (*MI* 379–80). "Development" or "developing variation" is the method of long-term motivic association typical of classical forms such as the sonata. [10] Here, "something new always has to come into being" through the manipulation of a basic motive or several motive-forms that act as a gestalt (*MI* 365). "Stringing together" or "juxtaposition" denote slow motivic presentation with little or no variation. Schoenberg associates this form of presentation with folksongs, popular songs, and classical melodies emulating vernacular idioms. Schoenberg sees "unfolding" or "envelopment" as strictly a form of contrapuntal presentation typical of invention or fugue. Here the "kaleidoscopic" shifting of an "initial formulation" or "contrapuntal combination" accounts for new material. The variations of the contrapuntal combination "differ greatly from one another in the total sound but differ very little from one another in thematic [or motivic] content, because the same voices, after all, make up the harmonies. . . . Clearly, a certain working-out of 'independent' voices, with or without *leitmotivic* or motivic or thematic 'work,' is not in accord with this compositional method" (*MI* 110–11). This essay will consider Schoenberg's three forms of presentation and the specific forms of motivic working out associated with them.

Development and Homophonic Music

Motivic working out is predicated on Schoenberg's organic view of tonality:

> To symbolize the construction of a musical form, perhaps one ought to think of a living body that is whole and centrally controlled. . . . One [can] presume by way of comparison, that one such whole body could be the tonality of a piece of music. (*MI* 120–21)

Thus for Schoenberg tonality is not a system but "a formal possibility that emerges from the nature of the tonal material, a possibility of attaining a certain completion or closure by means of a certain uniformity."[11] Schoenberg conceived of tonality itself as analogous to a centrally controlled organism, a *body* called monotonality (*Monotonalität*).

The natural basis of monotonality is the *Grundton*, the fundamental of the overtone series. In the artistic realm the *Grundton* is understood to be the tonic, and the overtones, the regions of the tonic. Schoenberg himself explains:

> The primitive ear hears the *Grundton* as irreducible, but physics recognizes it to be complex. In the meantime, however, musicians discovered that it is capable of continuation, i. e. that movement is latent within it. That problems are concealed in it, problems that clash with one another, that the *Grundton* lives and seeks to propagate itself. (*TH* 313)

Monotonality is described in its most developed form in *Structural Functions of Harmony*:

> According to this principle, every digression from the tonic is considered to be still within the tonality, whether directly or indirectly, closely or remotely related. In other words, there is only one tonality in a piece, and every segment considered as another tonality is only a region, a harmonic contrast within that tonality.[12]

Thus the body called monotonality is formed by a centrally controlled tonic and the regions which present all possible key areas in relation to that tonic.

Schoenberg pictures this body in the major and minor charts of the regions: see the minor chart of the regions in figure 1 (*SFH* 20, 30). Schoenberg's chart is constructed with the circle of fifths running vertically, while relationships of parallel and relative major and minor are presented horizontally. Together these relationships picture all possible regions, the functional potential of all tonal pieces. Thus, the chart itself must be viewed as a teleological organic model in which each key is functionally related to each other and ultimately to the tonic. The chart is not a model based on the logic of cause and effect but a *Darstellungs-system* (system of presentation): a presentation of the organism of tonality, in which all parts relate to a whole.

Figure 1: The minor chart of the regions

np	NP	subt	subT	v	D	♯m	♯M		
subtsm	subtSM	m	M	t	T	♯sm	♯SM		
		sm	SM	sd	SD	dor	S/T	♯subt	♯subT

KEY
T means tonic
D means dominant
SD means subdominant
t means minor tonic
sd means subdominant minor
v means five minor
sm means submediant minor
mm means mediant minor
SM means submediant minor
Np means Neapolitan
dor means Dorian
S/T means supertonic
subt means subtonic minor
subT means subtonic major

CLASSIFICATIONS
Direct and close: **T, M, v, sd**
Indirect but close: **D, SM**
Indirect: **sm, m, SD**
Indrect and remote: **♯M,**
   ♯m, ♯SM, ♯sm, subt,
   subT, NP, np
Distant: **subtsm, subtSM, S/T,**
   dor, ♯subt, ♯subT

N.B. All symbols in capitals refer to major keys, those in small letters refer to minor keys.

Schoenberg viewed the functions of tonality as consisting of a field of forces: those moving away from the tonic, *centrifugal* forces, and those moving toward it, *centripetal*. For example, a centrifugal move toward the subdominant could be counteracted by a centripetal one toward the dominant and tonic. Schoenberg understood such forces as creating a network of functional classifications that describe distances between keys. "Direct and Close" regions are those which share six or seven pitches with the tonic collection (see figure 1). The next groupings, "Indirect but Close" and "Indirect," have tonics related by major/minor interchange to those of a previous grouping. The "Indirect and Remote" and "Distant" regions are related to previous groupings either through functions of the subdominant minor region, through fifth relations, or substitution (*SFH* 68–69).

In a tonal piece, functional relationships can be defined by scale degrees expressed on three levels: as single pitches, harmonies, or regions. Such events can express three different structuring principles: "binding" or adhering to the key, "driving apart" or "leaving the key," or "neutral, static, fluctuating" (*ZKIF* 44–45). These relations may be exploited in the expression of a tonality so long as the relation to the tonic is ultimately clarified. The single pitch, harmony, or key most crucial for the work is presented at the beginning through a *Grundgestalt* or basic motive (*MI* 134–35). The organic presentation of the consequences of these structures causes the work to become an articulated whole whose parts, like the organs and limbs of a living organism, exercise their specific hierarchy of functions.

Schoenberg left us only one, highly general definition for Grundgestalt, which is found in the "Gedanke" manuscript of 1934–36:

> Grundgestalten are such gestalten as (possibly) occur repeatedly within a whole piece and to which derived gestalten can be traced back. (Formerly, this was called the motive; but that is a very superficial designation, for gestalten and Grundgestalten are usually composed of several motive-forms; but the motive is *at any one time the smallest* part.) (*MI* 168–69)

Schoenberg's student Josef Rufer interpreted such general statements as describing the first phrase of a piece, establishing a characteristic sound and usually asserting the tonic.[13] In this study I have adopted Rufer's interpretation.

In his extant writings Schoenberg gave several different definitions for motive (*Motiv*). In 1917, 1934, and 1943, he defined a motive as "a unit which contains one or more features of interval and rhythm [whose] presence is manifested in constant use throughout a piece."[14] The variation of motive by either pitch or rhythm accounts for its "development" or "developing variation." In *Harmonielehre* (1911), however, when commenting on Brahms's Third Symphony, he distinguished between a motive and a basic motive (*Hauptmotiv*) (*TH* 164). I take the basic motive to be the first interval of a work whose later multiple reinterpretations in light of monotonality generates the composition's tonal form.

In later studies such as the "Gedanke" manuscript of 1934, Schoenberg described what I call the first chromatic version of the basic motive as the "tonal problem," which is stated either in the Grundgestalt itself or in a subsequent reinterpretation. Schoenberg considers as the "tonal problem" that which makes a tonic "capable of continuation" through its inherent centrifugal motion. For an organicist, such a motion to outlying regions literally creates a problem because it contradicts the functions characteristic of the tonal center. This outward motion must be turned back toward the tonal center by a corresponding centripetal force, solving the problem and thus shaping the form of the piece. In Schoenberg's words, each composition

> raises a question, puts up a problem, which in the course of the piece has to be answered, resolved, carried through. It has to be carried through many contradictory situation [sic]; it has to be developed by drawing consequences from what it postulates . . . and all this might lead to a conclusion, a *pronunciamento*.[15]

For Schoenberg the motivic transformations of the Grundgestalt and the "tonal problem" thus produce the functioning parts of a piece, its tonal form. The statement of a theme introduces the relationships of the Grundgestalt and sets up the "tonal problem." This "problem" demands expansion and continuation in regions away from the tonic, eventually including the most tonally distant reinterpretation of the opening material, the climax of the centrifugal force. But in an organically tonal piece this leads to a retransition as the centripetal force begins to overcome the centrifugal one. The final section or coda eliminates all centrifugal tendencies of the "tonal problem," reinterpreting both the material of the Grundgestalt and the "tonal problem" in the tonic. Thus in a truly organic work the opening already presents the tonal form of the whole.

In his teaching Schoenberg did not work out all transformations of the basic motive, Grundgestalt, and "tonal problem"—indeed, he left no "complete" analysis in all his writings. Instead, through succinct analytic observations he guided students to pursue their own observations, to develop their own analytic craft. Schoenberg's comments on Brahms's String Quartet, Op. 51, no. 1, point the analyst toward the extraordinary single F♯ in m. 20, a pitch evoking the "distant" key of B minor within the tonic, C minor.[16] Schoenberg explains:

[In the C-Minor String Quartet] the figure of the second violin, gradually prepared in bars 15 and 17, takes a turn in bar 19 toward a scale step which looks almost as if the F♯ wanted to become an (artificial)[17] dominant of B; it is supported by the similarly long preparatory progression of the bass and is strengthened through the repetition in bar 20, so that the exposed F♯ of the viola and cello could hardly be comprehended differently.—This far-reaching digression is the result of the one that began in bars 9 and 10: its consequence. Having gone so far, one cannot go back with an easy gesture. One must go further and employ powerful means.

Brahms, especially beginning with his second period (approximately around Op. 40), usually attempts in the first form of his theme to introduce a characteristic turn toward the outer regions of his key. This serves several purposes, testifies to great wisdom, and is in accordance with the highly developed stage of harmony at this time: I.) Primarily, it provides the theme with a very distinct characteristic. II.) The return to the tonic has a strong effect. III.) It provides him with the possibility of unfolding this turn in the elaboration [i. e., development] and of creating new twists out of this idea. IV.) Then in the recapitulation he usually introduces a new turn, developed from the underlying basic change.—In summary, it can be said that this turn engenders a common *basis for the varying* of the theme, one, moreover, that *points the way toward the continuation*. (*MI* 320–23)

With regard to Schoenberg's remark about the F♯ in m. 20, we notice that the first phrase of the theme, a series of motives outlining the tonic triad and a descending diminished seventh—a Grundgestalt—ends on an F♯ that finds no clear immediate resolution,[18] thus creating a point of "unrest," a "tonal problem" (see example 1a). In contrast, the F♯ in the main theme that introduces the coda of the movement resolves to G in the dominant triad, thus creating a point of integration, of tonal "balance," of "rest" (see example 1b). Moreover, the coda does not contain a single further F♯. Instead F♮ takes the place of F♯ in the diminution of the theme in the cello, part of the shift to C major in mm. 245–51 (example 1c). Tonal balance has been restored.

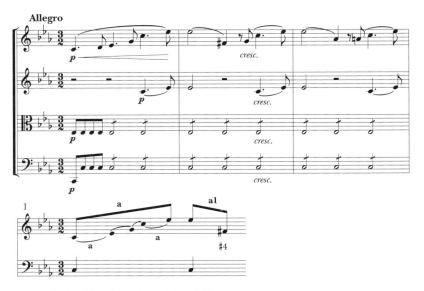

Example 1a: The "tonal problem," ♯4

Example 1b: The resolution at the coda

Example 1c: The introduction of F♮

The F♯ in m. 1 functions as ♯4 in the tonic. The use of ♯4 relations remains crucial to formal articulations of the work. For example, the region of the first half of the second theme group is E♭ minor, the "indirect" region of the minor mediant (compare figure 1). The tonic triad of this region is introduced by the cello E♭–G♭ (mm. 29–30), the enharmonic equivalent of E♭–F♯ in the Grundgestalt. While the E♭–F♯ descent in the Grundgestalt generated maximum "unrest," its enharmonic form E♭–G♭ points out a temporary stability in the minor mediant that extends until m. 44. At this point the first violin line persistently reiterates the ♯4 of E♭ minor, A♮, for no less than eight measures (see example 2). The same ♯4 relation is reiterated between the tonic E♭ of this second group, (mm. 32–83), and the "indirect and remote" region of A minor that begins the development section (mm. 84–92). The tonal problem of the Grundgestalt, the tritone relation of C–F♯, has now become a tritone relation, E♭–A, between regions.

Example 2: ♯4 in the second group

   In the opening, the tonal problem F♯ continues to G and A♭, the 5 and
♭6 scale degrees, and these scale degrees are featured in a familiar nexus
of relationships. Thus, the A♮ reiterated across mm. 46–53 resolves to a
striking B♭ 4/2 chord that could function as ♭VI in the region of D minor.
This is prevented by the bass-note A♭ (the ♭5 of D minor, the enharmonic
equivalent of ♯4). The B♭ dominant seventh instead functions as V in E♭
major: ♭6 of D minor has been reinterpreted as 5 of E♭ (see example 3a).
The notion of pitches functioning as both ♭6 and 5 in different regions
has a precedent in mm. 20–21—the events that so interested
Schoenberg. Here F♯ functions as 5 of the "distant" region of B minor. At
first the G in the subsequent measure seems to be ♭6 in B minor, only to
become the 5 in the tonic (see example 3b). The same functional move
appears directly at the retransition to the tonic at mm. 132–33: the V of
the D♭ minor region (spelled enharmonically as C♯ minor) becomes the
♭VI of C minor: see example 3c.

Example 3a: The ♭6/5 shift, in the second theme group

Example 3b: The ♭6/5 shift, in the first theme group

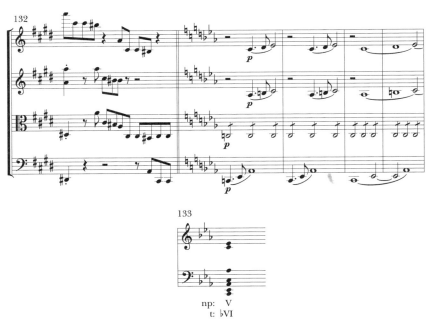

Example 3c: The ♭6/5 shift, in the retransition

The network of tonal functions derived from the motives of the Grundgestalt thus emphasize the tonal problem at many crucial formal junctures of the work. Their tonal force produces the inherent "unrest" that shapes the movement's organic presentation, finding "rest" only in the coda.

Presentation in Popular Forms

Despite Schoenberg's unfailing devotion to European art music, he frequently analyzes Johann Strauss's *On the Beautiful Blue Danube*—a piece also admired by Johannes Brahms (*MI* 182–83, 184–85, 302; *SI*, 103, 399–400). The relation of classical and popular music is a major theme throughout Schoenberg's writings.[19] "Higher and lower forms" and "primitivism and art music" are two topics Schoenberg lists for inclusion in his main treatise on the "musical idea." The incomplete draft also contains verbal comment on "popular music" and detailed analyses of Strauss's *Laguna Waltzes*, *Roses from the South*, and *On the Beautiful Blue Danube*; Johann Strauss Sr.'s *Radetzky March*; and Franz Lehár's "Love Unspoken" from *The Merry Widow* (*MI* 302–5). Schoenberg's interest in popular forms is not only a theoretical concern but also a life-long compositional preoccupation. As a young man, he composed his early cycle of theater songs, the *Brettl-Lieder*, and worked for Ernst von Wolzogen's cabaret group in Berlin.[20] Later he arranged Johann Strauss's waltzes for concerts at the Society for Private Musical Performances. Like Karl Kraus, Schoenberg admires "people who can write in a popular and generally comprehensible way, [who were] born with an inventive talent, turn of mind, and mode of presentation that are popular. The best examples are Johann Strauss and Nestroy" (*SI* 268).[21] Schoenberg acknowledges that he was not among those "few composers, like Offenbach, Johann Strauss, and Gershwin, whose feelings actually coincide with those of the 'average man in the street,' dwell[ing] intensely within the sphere of human sentiment" (*SI* 124).

Why then did this creator of some of the densest, most complex European art music take such an interest in popular works? Schoenberg responds:

> [I] do not see why, when other people are entertained, I, too, should not sometimes be entertained; I know indeed that I really ought at every single moment to behave like my own

monument; but it would be hypocritical of me to conceal the fact that I occasionally step down from my pedestal and enjoy light music. . . . [But] light music could not entertain me unless something interested me about its substance and its working out. (*SI* 178)

Unsurprisingly Schoenberg's theoretical approach to the "working-out" of popular music is strictly from his own notion of the "presentation of the musical idea."

In his main theoretical text on "idea," Schoenberg specifies aspects of popular "presentation" that engaged his compositional sense:

The popular effect of popular music is based on its broad understandability. Nevertheless, real connoisseurs (who exist in this area, too) distinguish the original from the unoriginal, the good from the bad. [B]road understandability [here] is mainly achieved through an extremely slow *tempo of presentation*. This means: 1) the Grundgestalten themselves usually contain only a very few motivic forms; 2) are very often repeated in nearly unvaried form; and 3) if after several (2–5 or more) such repetitions a more developed variation appears, it often changes so much that it could be hard to comprehend, were not the entire section repeated again and again, or, if it is varied more in pitch, the rhythm remains (almost) unchanged. (*MI* 300–01)

Schoenberg concretized his ideas of extremely slow presentation—literal repetition of motives, and juxtaposition of virtually unrelated motive-forms—in the analyses of popular works mentioned above. The layout of these analyses physically manifests their presentation. In these analytic examples, such as figure 2 ("Love Unspoken" from *The Merry Widow*), motives and gestalten remain "set *next to* each other . . . like columns of items that are to be added together and indeed are added up at the end" (*MI* 158–59). Wavy lines alone outline the actual progress of the score. The columns emphasize that when one of the motives or gestalten ends, another begins; there is no varied interconnection by the fitting together of endings (*MI* 158–59). The many literal or virtually literal repetitions of motives determine the "slow" presentation.

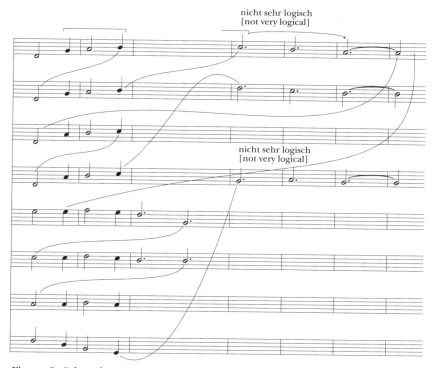

Figure 2: Schoenberg's analysis of "Love Unspoken" from *The Merry Widow*

In Schoenberg's analysis of "Love Unspoken" (figure 2) he demon-strates that there is no intermediate structure shared between aspects of the two gestalten of the theme. While the main half-note/quarter-note motive is either repeated literally or replaced by three dotted-half notes, the pitches of the first four gestalten in the first column are distinct in contour and intervallic shape from the second. The final four gestalten in the first column are succeeded by a gestalt in the second that shares *no* rhythmic and melodic characteristic with its immediate antecedent: G–A–G is preceded by D–B–G–E. For this reason Schoenberg terms the first rhythmic gestalt followed by the second as "not very logical"—that is, not varied and joined through connectives in the organic sense of "developing variation." Thus although the literal repetition of gestalten as well as the sequential phrase structure give the work a "continuous action," gestalten at the most local level are merely juxtaposed, never subtly fused together into a more complex whole.

This lack of continuous local development between parts gives the work "a certain unproblematic or relaxed quality, *a certain rest between the constituent parts* of the components which just barely allows continuation without demanding it" (*MI* 379). As Schoenberg explains:

> Structurally, there never remains in popular tunes an unsolved problem, the consequences of which will show up only later. The segments do not need much of a connective; they can be added by juxtaposition, because of the absence of variation in them. There is nothing that asks for expansion. The small form holds the contents firmly, constituting thus a small expansion but an independent structure. (*SI* 164)

Schoenberg likens this "problem-less" presentation of the musical *Gedanke* to a literary form:

> [The] popular art of presenting thoughts belongs wholly to [those], who can only relate an orderly succession of things just as they happen, who have no grasp of the whole, who can therefore neither anticipate nor go back nor connect one sentence with another except by means of the copula 'and' . . .'And then I said . . . and then he said and then we laughed . . . and . . . and so on.' The narrative goes on only because the story that is being told goes on, because a continuous action drives the story-teller on. The climax is then only dynamic. (*SI* 256)

In this way, "and" functions not as a organic connective intertwining one action with another and the whole, but as a mechanical divider of a "continuous action." In a musical presentation formed by "stringing together" or "juxtaposition," the perception of "wholeness" depends on the memory of the addition of segments that are themselves wholes. Schoenberg sees such a presentation as geared to an undisciplined, "uneducated" mind whose ability for comprehension depends on replication, not variation. Nonetheless, he still maintains that such a presentation is valid for certain musical ideas.

Schoenberg's concept of a popular form extends to passages which are not literally "strung together" but are merely "melodic" in nature. Such passages depend on the principles of the "concentration of all events in a single voice, extensive unification of all figuration, and frequent repetition of slightly varied phrases" (*MI* 180–81). Thus Schoenberg defines a melodic passage or melody as having "extremely slow and sparing development" of motives and gestalten (*MI* 180–81), as opposed to popular works like "Love Unspoken," which has virtually no development at all.

"Melodic" presentation is illustrated by Schoenberg's analytic remarks on Papageno's first aria from Mozart's *Magic Flute* (see example 4). Schoenberg focuses on the continuity of rhythmic motives and gestalten which lie within basic rhythmic groupings: see, for example, the positioning of the sixteenth-eighth-note gestalt, A–G–F♯ (m. 15). The use of such rhythmic connectives makes the passage a "melodic" rather than a purely popular form. With the category of "melodic" presentation, certain repertories traditionally labeled "classical" become "popular," not only Mozart, but some of Schubert and Verdi (*SI* 128, 395; *MI* 180–95).

Only once does Schoenberg analytically discuss the relation of his own music to "melodic" forms, comparing retrograded motives and contours in Verdi's "La donna è mobile" with the second theme of the First Chamber Symphony. Schoenberg concludes:

> If you consider the analysis of this Verdi theme you will per-haps agree, that possibly I could have written it—although with other notes. But if you compare it with [the] theme of my Chamber-Symphony, you will see, that the relation between myself and Verdi is not as strange [as] it seems!

Schoenberg's comments appear in a late, undated (c. 1936?) manu-script (see figure 3) catalogued by the composer himself among his most prized theoretical works.[22]

Example 4: Schoenberg's analysis of Papageno's aria from *The Magic Flute*

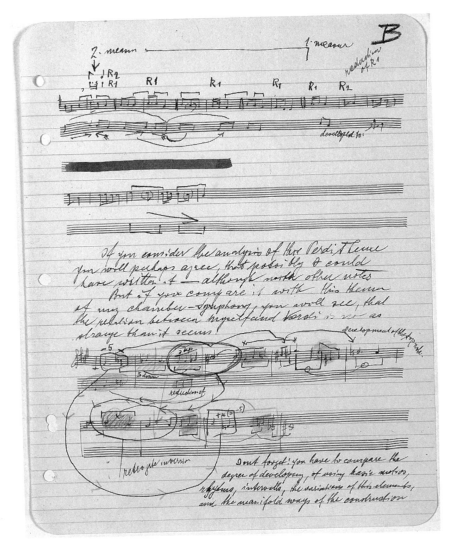

Figure 3: Schoenberg's analysis of "La donna è mobile" and the First
Chamber Symphony, Op. 9. Arnold Schönberg Center, Vienna.

Presenting Contrapuntal Combinations

A pencil sketch from 1921 portrays Schoenberg's basic notion of contrapuntal form (see figure 4). The torso of the little figure playing the Ibach piano is shaped like an unfolded coil or roll, an image mirroring Schoenberg's description of presentation in the contrapuntal work:

Figure 4: Schoenberg's sketch depicting contrapuntal presentation

> In a contrapuntal piece the idea is compressed in the form of a theme whose constituent elements, sounding together, form a kind of "point of departure.". . . This "point of departure," this theme, contains all the possibilities for future redeployment of the elementary material. . . . In the course of the piece, the new shapes formed by rearrangements (varied forms of the new theme, new ways for its elements to sound) are unfolded, *rather as a film is unrolled*. And the way the pictures follow each other (like the "cutting" in a film) produces the "form." (*SI* 290–91; italics mine)

Contrapuntal combination is Schoenberg's term for the theme or "point of departure" whose varied repetition generates the contrapuntal work. This varied repetition of the contrapuntal combination constitutes the third possibility of presentation, contrapuntal presentation. Unfortunately, Schoenberg wrote little on this topic.[23] Those few remarks that do exist make several crucial technical points. First of all, in the contrapuntal piece "there is a basic combination which is the source of all combinations" (*SI* 397). This combination constitutes at least two lines in invertible counterpoint such as the subject and countersubject of a fugue. The combination always contains a motivic content that remains basically the same throughout the work: "[Combinations] differ greatly from one another in the total sound . . . but differ very little from one another in thematic [or motivic] content, because the same voices, after all, make up [the harmonies]" (*MI* 110–11). Variation is achieved by a "disassembling and reassembling" of the basic combination:

> [A] basic configuration . . . taken asunder and reassembled in a different order contains everything which will later produce a different sound than that of the original formulation. Thus, a canon of two or more voices can be written in one single line, yet furnishes various sounds. If multiple counterpoints are applied, a combination of three voices, invertible in the octave, tenth, and twelfth, offers so many combinations that even longer pieces can be derived from it. (*SI* 397)

Because no complete analysis of a contrapuntal piece survives in Schoenberg's manuscripts, we are forced to rely on students' notes and recollections of his procedures. Examples 5–8 are an adaptation and expansion of a classroom analysis of Bach's Invention in C Major (BWV 772) by Schoenberg's student, Patricia Carpenter.[24] Example 5a shows the contrapuntal combination on which the invention is based, labeling as motive *a* the rising fourth that begins the work. The contrapuntal combination of the Invention can be seen as a working out of the tonal "unrest" or ambiguity of motive *a* which can be construed in three possible keys: C major, F major, and A minor (see example 5b). Bach presents these possibilities in a three-part form delineated by clear cadences: first, and virtually inevitable, in the dominant (m. 7) but then in A minor (m. 15) and at the end of the piece in the tonic (m. 22). The last phrase moves back to the tonic through F major (mm. 18–20). The ambiguity of the C/F relation in motive *a* is ultimately brought to "rest" at the end of the work when the combination is realized in F major, then in C.

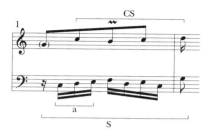

Example 5a: The contrapuntal combination

Tonalities:
C major: 1 2 3 4
F major: 5 6 7 8
A minor: 3 4 5 6

Example 5b: Motive *a*

A rhythmically displaced variant of the combinations enters in m. 3 after the statement of the main combination on the dominant (see example 6a). In this variant the inverted subject is in the upper voice, and the lower line features a rhythmic displacement of the countersubject, leading into an augmentation of a scalar displacement of motive *a* —a perfect illustration of what Schoenberg calls a "'kaleidoscopic" shifting of "an initial formulation" (*MI* 110–11). This variant becomes the model for a series of sequences ending in a liquidation of the combination (mm. 7–8) and an eventual cadence in the dominant (m. 7).

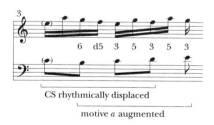

Example 6a: Variant combination at m. 3

Schoenberg describes the process of liquidation as follows:

> Development implies not only growth, augmentation, exten-
> sion and expansion, but also reduction, condensation, and
> intensification. The purpose of liquidation is to counteract the
> tendency toward unlimited extension. *Liquidation* consists in
> gradually eliminating characteristic features, until only
> uncharacteristic ones remain, which no longer demand a con-
> tinuation. Often only residues remain, which have little in
> common with the basic motive. . . . This is accomplished . . .
> by gradually depriving the motive-forms of their characteris-
> tic features and dissolving them into uncharacteristic forms.[25]

In contrapuntal music liquidation consists of disassembling a combination, leaving only a basic skeleton of its initial motives. The disassembling of the variant combination (m. 3) begins in m. 4 with the extension
of the rising eighth-note scale leading to C (mm. 4–5). The rising fourth
line associated with the combination has thus been dissolved into a simple scale (example 6b). The C moves to a D in the upper line, a voice-
crossing leading to a combination remarkable for the registral
displacement of the first pitch of the countersubject. This registral displacement not only continues the rising scale from the lower part, but
it is then itself followed by an E in the same register, which continues the
rising scale up to D in m. 6. Here the dissolution is complete, and it is
succeeded by the dominant cadence in m. 7, slightly undermined by the
sixteenth rest on the downbeat in the lower line, which allows the subject to begin immediately in the dominant.

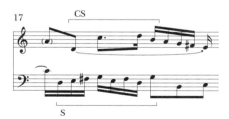

Example 6b: Liquidation of the variant combination

The first two measures of the second section correspond to mm.
1–2, but the basic combination appears in invertible counterpoint at the
fifteenth (m. 7) and the twelfth (m. 8). Measure 9, however, does not
correspond to m. 3. Instead Bach introduces sequential statements of

the inverted subject followed by a new variant combination (see example 7a). Its upper line is derived from the variant in m. 3; its lower introduces a "double neighbor" formula in eighth notes. This formula is related by augmented retrograde to the sequential figures of the inverted subject in mm. 3–4 (example 7b). The new combination is followed by a recapitulation of mm. 3–7 transposed and inverted at the fifteenth (mm. 11–13), altered material being found in the upper line from m. 13, beat 3, and in the lower line only at m. 14, beat 3. This new material in the upper line produces a registral climax featuring a diminution and transposition of the "double neighbor" figure introduced in the new combination, A–G♯–B–A, thus confirming the tonality of A minor at the ensuing cadence (m. 15).

Example 7a: The new combination at mm. 9–10

Example 7b: The derivation of the combination

The final section of the work opens with the inversion of the subject in the same register as it appeared in m. 3. The fourth, A–G–F–E, which in m. 3 was clearly referable to C major, is now equally clearly heard in A minor. The sequence that follows prolongs this fourth on a broader structural level, leading into a restatement of the subject in the tonic. [26] But now the rising fourth C–D–E–F, motive *a*, is clearly heard in F major, its one harmonic possibility not so far presented in the Invention (m. 19). The combination producing F major, however, derives not from the opening combination but corresponds exactly to the variant combination in m. 3 inverted in contour (example 8). Most remarkably, this contour inversion also gives Bach the vertical intervals characteristic of normal registral invertible counterpoint at the fifteenth. This nexus of relations is perhaps the consummate expression of organic unity in the work.

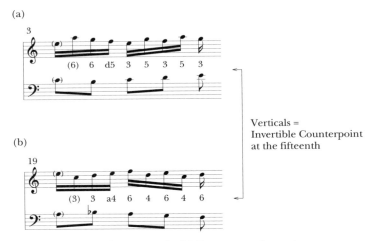

Verticals =
Invertible Counterpoint
at the fifteenth

Example 8: (a) The variant at m. 3; (b) Its contour inversion

For Schoenberg, however, presentation through contrapuntal combination finds its highest expression not in the invention but in the fugue: he terms the combinations in *The Art of Fugue* a "miracle" (*SI* 396). At the same time, however, Schoenberg distinguishes certain fugues which have no such working out of a contrapuntal combination, thus limiting the applicability of his own theories:

> I have speculated much about the fact that Bach writes, on the one hand, so many fugues which deal with the most complex contrapuntal combinations of canons of all forms and of multiple counterpoint of countersubjects, and, on the other hand, composes a great number in which nothing of this kind can be observed, and which seem to correspond to the most superficial concept of several entrances of themes 'fleeing from one another.' Such examples are, among others, in volume 1, numbers 1, 3, 6, 9, 10, and 17 (*Das wohltemperierte Klavier*).
>
> It is difficult to believe that there should not be present here the same high art which we observed in those pieces

where it is quite obvious. I rather believe there is a hidden mystery which has not yet been discovered. I have frequently tried to discover such a principle therein, but in vain. Nevertheless, I always feel that something is going on that catches my attention in a peculiar way. What is it? (*SI* 396)

In singling out fugues which do not conform to his theory of contrapuntal combination, Schoenberg says that their presentation is illustrative of the traditional derivation of "fugue" from the Latin *fuga*, "to flee." In contrast, he understands fugues using contrapuntal combination in terms of the word, *Fuge*, as derived from a German etymology—that is, from *fügen*, to bind together or to structure:

I believe that the word [fugue] derives from the complex of German words: *Fuge, fügen, Gefüge, Gefügtes.* A structure [Gefüge] is something that is a composite. . . Composition. thus: fugue=composition![27]

This notion of "fugue" as composition itself first appears in 1924, immediately after the publication of the first twelve-tone work.[28] Subsequently Schoenberg makes reference to connections between methods of contrapuntal combination and twelve-tone composition. In an early "Gedanke" manuscript he even directly claims:

I will show that counterpoint is based on the laws of contrapuntal composition which correctly presented, reveal the Bach family's secrets of the art of the fugue and appropriately expanded, will pave the way theoretically for composition with twelve tones.[29]

Tonal counterpoint and twelve-tone music continues to be a topic in later theoretical writings. For example, in a manuscript about *Modern Psalms*, Op. 50c, he comments that the hexachordal forms of the row

produce a greater variety than double counterpoint of all sorts. Of course you have to invent your theme as ordinarily; but you have more possibilities of producing strongly related configurations, which in sound are essentially different.[30]

Finally, a manuscript dating from the last decade of his life analyzes as a twelve-tone work Bach's Fugue 24 from Book I of the *Well-Tempered Clavier* (see figure 5).[31] Such references to tonal counterpoint and twelve-tone composition, however, remain sporadic comments or musical examples that receive no extensive verbal explanation. Was he working out his theories of contrapuntal combination through his twelve-tone compositions? Perhaps that was enough for Schoenberg, who knew himself to be "more a composer than a theorist."

Figure 5: Schoenberg's twelve-tone analysis of Fugue 24 from Book I of the *Well-Tempered Clavier.* Arnold Schönberg Center, Vienna.

NOTES

1. Arnold Schoenberg, *Style and Idea*, ed. Leonard Stein (New York, 1975), pp. 91–92 (henceforth *SI*; further references will be given in the text).

2. For a list of Schoenberg's theoretical works, see Arnold Schoenberg, *Zusammenhang, Kontrapunkt, Instrumentation, Formenlehre: Coherence, Counterpoint, Instrumentation, Instruction in Form*, ed. Severine Neff, trans. Charlotte M. Cross and Severine Neff (Lincoln and London, 1994), xxxiv–xli (henceforth *ZKIF*; further references will be given in the text). See also Alexander Goehr, "The Theoretical Writings of Arnold Schoenberg," *Perspectives of New Music* 13/2 (1975): 3–16.

3. Theodor Adorno "On the Problem of Musical Analysis," *Music Analysis* 1 (1982): 169–87; Alban Berg, "Why is Schoenberg's Music So Hard to Understand?" in *Schoenberg, Webern, Berg: The String Quartets* (Hamburg, 1971), pp. 20–30; Patricia Carpenter, "*Grundgestalt* as Tonal Function," *Music Theory Spectrum* 5 (1983): 15–38; Alexander Goehr, "Schoenberg and Karl Kraus: The Idea Behind the Music," *Music Analysis* 4 (1985): 59–71; Philip Herschovitch, "On Bach's F-Minor Invention," in *O Muziki* (About Music) (Moscow, 1991), pp.190–213 (English trans. Mikhail Krishtal, unpublished); Erwin Ratz, *Einführung in die musikalische Formenlehre* (Vienna, 1951); Rudolph Réti, *The Thematic Process in Music* (1951; repr. Westport, Conn., 1978); Josef Rufer, *Composition with Twelve Notes Related Only to One Another*, trans. Humphrey Searle (London, 1954); Erwin Stein, *Orpheus in New Guises* (London, 1953); Edward Steuermann, *The Not Quite Innocent Bystander: Writings of Edward Steuermann*, ed. Clara Steuermann, David Porter, and Gunther Schuller (Lincoln and London, 1989); Anton Webern, *The Path to the New Music*, ed. Willi Reich, trans. Leo Black (Bryn Mawr, Penna., 1963); Adolph Weiss, "The *Lyceum* of Arnold Schoenberg," *Modern Music* 9/3 (1932): 99–107.

4. For discussions of the nature and theory of the artwork, see Arnold Schoenberg, *The Musical Idea and the Logic, Technique, and Art of Its Presentation*, ed. and trans. Patricia Carpenter and Severine Neff (New York, 1995), pp. 7–10, 92–93, 114–15 (henceforth *MI*; further references will be given in the text).

5. For a further discussion of Schoenberg's concept of theory, see *ZKIF* liii–lvii.

6. For a discussion of "musical idea," see *MI* 15–21, 102–13; R. Wayne Shoaf, "Schoenberg on Inspiration," *Newsletter of the Arnold Schoenberg Institute* I/1(1987): 3; Patricia Carpenter, "Musical Form and Musical Idea: Reflections on a Theme of Schoenberg, Hanslick, and Kant," in *Music and Civilization: Essays in Honor of Paul Henry Lang*, ed. Edmond Strainchamps and Maria Rika Maniates, with Christopher Hatch (New York, 1984), pp. 394–427; Charlotte M. Cross, "Three Levels of 'Idea' in Schoenberg's Thought and Work," *Current Musicology* 30 (1980): 24–36.

7. He acknowledges that such an activity "is probably not the task of a musician who, at least as a musician, could at most contribute symptomatic experiences"; see *MI* 376–77.

8. Letter of 1931 cited in Bryan Simms, Review of Arnold Schoenberg, *Theory of Harmony*, trans. Roy E. Carter, *Music Theory Spectrum* 4 (1982): 160.

9. For a detailed discussions of Schoenberg's organicism, see Severine Neff, "Goethe and Schoenberg: Organicism and Analysis," in *Music Theory and the Exploration of the Past*, ed. Christopher Hatch and David W. Bernstein (Chicago, 1993), pp. 409–33; Patricia Carpenter and Severine Neff, "Schoenberg's Philosophy of Composition: Thoughts on the 'Musical Idea and Its Presentation'," in *Constructive Dissonance: Arnold Schoenberg and the Transformations of Twentieth-Century Culture*, ed. Juliane Brand and Christopher Hailey (Berkeley and Los Angeles, 1997), pp.146–59.

10. Schoenberg uses both terms to describe this motivic procedure. See also Walter Frisch, *Brahms and the Principle of Developing Variation* (Berkeley and Los Angeles, 1984), Chapter 1.

11. Arnold Schoenberg, *Theory of Harmony*, trans. Roy E. Carter (Berkeley and Los Angeles, 1978), p. 27 (henceforth *TH*; further references will be given in the text).

12. Arnold Schoenberg, *Structural Functions of Harmony*, 2nd ed., ed. Leonard Stein (New York, 1969), p. 19. (henceforth *SFH*; further references will be given in the text).

13. Rufer, *Composition*, p. 32.

14. Arnold Schoenberg, *Models for Beginners in Composition* (New York, 1943), p. 15.

15. Arnold Schoenberg, "My Subject: Beauty and Logic in Music." See Jean and Jesper Christensen, *From Arnold Schoenberg's Literary Legacy: A Catalogue of Neglected Items* (Warren, Mich., 1988), p. 99.

16. Compare Frisch, *Brahms and the Principle*, pp. 113–16. See also Songtaik Ahn-Kwon, "Brahms's C-Minor String Quartet, Op. 51, no.1: Schoenberg's Analytic Methods," *The Journal of the Institute for Western Music Research* [Seoul National University] 3 (1998): 105–20.

17. Schoenberg's term for secondary dominant.

18. It is true that one can consider the F♯ to be resolved by the G immediately following after the eighth-note rest. But the eighth rest connects G into an upbeat to the next gestalt, and an upbeat can function only weakly, if at all, as the resolution of a strong and prominent dissonance like the F♯.

19. See *SI* 124, 134–35, 138–39, 148, 164, 176–77, 178, 256, 268, 311, 336, 395, 415. Schoenberg's composition of the *Brettl-Lieder* and his arrangements of Strauss's *Roses from the South* further attest to his interest. See Josef Rufer, *The Works of Arnold Schoenberg*, trans. Dika Newlin (New York, 1962), p. 125.

20. These were named for the famous collection *Deutsche Chansons* of Otto Julius Bierbaum. For a discussion of Wolzogen's cabaret, see Harold B. Segel, *Turn-of-the-Century Cabaret* (New York, 1987), chapter 3.

21. See Edward Timms, *Karl Kraus, Apocalyptic Satirist* (New Haven, 1986), pp. 6, 225–26.

22. Arnold Schoenberg, "Rigoletto and the *Kammersymphonie*: An Analysis"; see no. 175b, in Rufer, *Works*, p. 161. The manuscript is catalogued with Schoenberg's "Gedanke" manuscripts, *Zusammenhang, Kontrapunkt, Instrumentation, Formenlehre*, and his incomplete counterpoint texts. See *ZKIF*, Appendix 3, p.122.

23. For a discussion of contrapuntal combination in Schoenberg's works, see P. Murray Dineen, "The Contrapuntal Combination: Schoenberg's Old Hat," in *Music Theory and the Exploration of the Past*, ed. Hatch and Bernstein, pp. 435–71.
Schoenberg never published extensively on "contrapuntal combination." The only extended work on counterpoint is *Preliminary Exercises in Counterpoint*, whose title emphasizes the preliminary nature of the species exercises it discusses compared to the study of contrapuntal combination and fugue. Projected works on these topics were never realized: see Arnold Schoenberg, *Preliminary Exercises in Counterpoint*, ed. Leonard Stein (London, 1962), Appendix B. For a list of Schoenberg's writings on counterpoint, see *ZKIF*, Appendix 3, pp. 121–22.

24. The analysis is dated October 12, 1986. The illustrations in this article are my own. Compare Erwin Ratz's approach: Ratz, *Einführung*, pp. 45–57.

25. Arnold Schoenberg, *Fundamentals of Musical Composition*, ed. Gerald Strang and Leonard Stein (New York, 1967), pp. 58, 152.

26. The fourth is A (m. 13, beat 1) and the half-note succession G–F–E in the upper line (mm. 15–18).

27. Arnold Schoenberg, "Fuga-Flucht," Mödling, 1/10/24; manuscript no. 78a in Schoenberg's catalogue, no. 39, in Rufer, *Works*, p.166.

28. Twelve-tone exercises do appear in the counterpoint section of *ZKIF* (1917) but receive no verbal comment; see *ZKIF* 70–77.

29. Arnold Schoenberg, "Der musikalische Gedanke, seine Darstellung und Durch-führung" ("The Musical Idea: its Presentation and Development"), 3; no. 3a: b in Rufer, *Works*, p.137 (translation by Charlotte M. Cross).

30. Rufer, *Works*, Plate 25, p.112. See also the essay "Linear Counterpoint: Linear Polyphony" (*SI* 296), in which he distinguishes between the vertical forms of combinations of rows and tonal combination.

31. From the annotated collection of Bach's works in Schoenberg's library, Arnold Schönberg Center, Vienna. See Kathryn P. Glennan, Jerry L. McBride, and R. Wayne Shoaf, *Arnold Schoenberg Institute Archives Preliminary Catalogue* (Los Angeles, 1986), vol. 1, pp. 19–20; ID-CASG84-C8, call no. SCO B21. "1" = B♮ in Schoenberg's row count. For additional comments on this fugue as a twelve-tone work, see Arnold Schoenberg, "Bach und die Zwölf Töne" ("Bach and the Twelve Tones"), 7/23/1932; manuscript no. 214 in Schoenberg's catalogue, no. 84 in Rufer, *Works*, p.167; see also *SI* 393.

Schoenberg and His Public in 1930:

The Six Pieces for Male Chorus, Op. 35

JOSEPH H. AUNER

Schoenberg begins his 1930 essay "My Public" with a sentence that would seem to sum up the well-established image of the isolated, embattled composer in self-imposed exile from the world: "Called upon to say something about my public, I have to confess: I do not have one." In the space of a few pages Schoenberg retraces the familiar stations of his troubled relationship with the public. He cites the hissing and disturbances that greeted performances of his works, the hostility and incomprehension of critics and musicians, and the short-lived popularity and subsequent rejection of his music by the younger generation after World War I. To counterbalance such opposition he mentions only the occasional friendly comments by strangers over the years and the support of his small circle of friends, "as true as few."[1]

Schoenberg's words resonate today with the accounts of his music and historical position by such figures as Leibowitz, Adorno, Babbitt, and Boulez. In his claims of isolation we see foreshadowed the central themes of Schoenberg reception: the "difficult path," music into which "no social function falls—indeed, which even severs the last communication with the listener," the complexities of twelve-tone composition accessible only to an elect, and "Schoenberg the unloved."[2] That such formulations stem from those essentially sympathetic to Schoenberg only underscores the degree of consensus on this issue; it goes without saying that generations of less sympathetic critics have come to very similar conclusions.

It was undoubtedly to reflect Schoenberg's image as the icon of a modernism marked by its autonomy and hostility to mass culture that "My Public" was chosen to be included in *The Weimar Republic Sourcebook*, an assemblage of documents pertaining to all aspects of

German culture, politics, and society in the interwar period.[3] The essay is reprinted in a section concerning *Zeitoper* and *Gebrauchsmusik* to show Schoenberg's distance from contemporary efforts by Weill, Hindemith, and others to promote a new social function for art. The accompanying editorial commentary contrasts Schoenberg's "tone of resignation . . . about his audience" with the critical and popular success of such works as Weill's *Three-Penny Opera*. Other selections in the book present a similar view, such as that by Hanns Gutman on Gebrauchsmusik, published in *Melos* in 1929, which describes Schoenberg as "removing himself as a creative individualist so far from the common disposition that the lack of resonance in his work becomes comprehensible."[4]

To present the founder of the Society for Private Musical Performances in such a light is by no means unjustified. On the contrary, there is plentiful evidence from Schoenberg's works and his writings of his commitment to the principle of *l'art pour l'art* and his suspicion of any sort of what he called "Publikumsmusik."[5] In an unpublished commentary on "Gemeinschaftskunst" (communal art) from February 1928, he wrote:

> I have surely said it often enough already: I do not believe that the artist creates for others. If others want to establish a relationship between themselves and the artwork that is their concern, and the artist cannot be expected to deny this to them. Although he should! . . . Art for the people: one can also see it in this. Art is from the outset naturally not for the people.

As in other writings from this period, he relegates the notion of a socially committed art to the realm of shifting fashion, " . . . what is one supposed to think of Gemeinschaftskunst? (But I don't want to say what that is, for in ten years in any case no one will know anymore, and so why should I introduce the term into music history)."[6]

It is to be expected, therefore, that when Schoenberg is viewed in the Weimar context, he can appear to have little to do with the defining "Weimarish" notions, as characterized by Richard Taruskin: "great artist as good citizen, high art reduced to social transaction, music making as activity not speculation, classicism as antiaestheticism . . ."[7] When Schoenberg is discussed it is primarily as a foil to those more in tune with the times. Stephen Hinton, for example, in his study of Hindemith and the idea of Gebrauchsmusik, writes that "Schoenberg was well aware that his music and views had nothing in common with recent developments." Discounting connections between the neoclassical features of Schoenberg's twelve-tone works and *Neue Sachlichkeit*, Hinton concludes: "In the minds of most his contemporaries and in the composer's own mind Schoenberg's music embodied the very antipode of Neue Sachlichkeit and Gebrauchsmusik."[8] Hinton and others have consequently interpreted *Moses und Aron*, composed in 1930–32, as Schoenberg's personal aesthetic testament on Weimar culture, with Schoenberg as Moses dedicated to the pure idea, standing alone and misunderstood, in contrast to the numerous Arons of the time who cheapened and falsified the idea in pursuit of broader understanding.[9]

So pervasive are these accounts of Schoenberg's enforced withdrawal from the public sphere and so abundant is the evidence of his rejection of the defining trends of Weimar musical life that it is easy to overlook aspects of his works and activities from these years that suggest a more complex and ambivalent relationship with contemporary developments and to the broader public. Striking evidence of this blind spot is that the concluding sentences of the "My Public" essay were omitted when it was reprinted in the *Weimar Republic Sourcebook*. Yet the silent omission significantly obscures the actual intent of the essay. Just as the opening sentence apparently presents the verdict of his solitude as a settled matter, the deleted final line calls such claims into question: "But whether I am really so unacceptable to the public as the expert judges always assert, and whether it is really so scared of my music—that often seems to me highly doubtful."[10] Rather than resigning himself to a breach with the public, he attempts in the essay both an analysis of the factors that led to his problematic position and a challenge to how the idea of the public should be understood.

My purpose here is to reexamine Schoenberg's relationship to the public and his attitude toward the social function of art during the period around 1930. When Schoenberg's words, such as the "My Public" essay, are read in context and weighed against his compositional output and other activities at this time, there is evidence of a deeper engagement with the new mass audience and the problems posed by Gebrauchsmusik and Gemeinschaftskunst than many contemporaneous and present-day representations might suggest. I have chosen to focus this inquiry on the year 1930 not only because it coincides with the publication of the "My Public" essay, but also because it was a time when Schoenberg was particularly involved with the problems of speaking to a broader public. The Six Pieces for Male Chorus, Op. 35, are arguably the most intriguing and problematic works in the context of Schoenberg's attitudes on the social function of art.

Sunday, January 31, 1932, 3:00 p.m.
in the Singakademie in Berlin
Sunday, January 31, 1932, 8:00 p.m.
in the Gesellschaftshaus Grünau

CONTEMPORARY CHORAL MUSIC

PROGRAM

Arnold Schönberg (b. 1874): Three Arrangements for Mixed Chorus:
"Schein uns, du liebe Sonne" (after Antonius Scandellus, 1517–80),
"Herzlieblich Lieb, durch Scheiden" (15th-cent. melody), "Es gingen
zwei Gespielen gut" (melody before 1540)
Lendvai Quartet and members of the Youth Choir. Director: Walter
Hänel

Arnold Schönberg: Six Pieces for Male Chorus, Op. 35
13er-Quartet. Director: Franz Schmitt, Frankfurt am Main

Inge Eschbach (b. 1918): "Lied der Arbeit"
13er-Quartet, Lendvai Quartet, Youth Choir. Director: Walter Hänel

Hugo Hermann (b. 1896): "Chorburlesken im Zoo," Op. 73
13er-Quartet. Director: Franz Schmitt, Frankfurt am Main

Armin Knab (b. 1881): Five Unison Choral Songs
13er-Quartet, Lendvai Quartet, Youth Choir. Director: Walter Hänel

Hanns Eisler (b. 1898): Three Male Choruses
13er-Quartet and Lendvai Quartet. Director: Franz Schmitt

Ernst-Lothar v. Knorr (b. 1896): "Soziale Unordnung"
13er-Quartet, Lendvai Quartet, Youth Choir. Director: Ernst-Lothar v.
Knorr

Josef Vorsmann (b. 1903): "Wir bauen eine neue Welt"
13er-Quartet, Lendvai Quartet, Youth Choir. Director: Walter Hänel

Performers:
13er-Quartet of the Arbeitergesangverein *Vorwärts*, Hanau (Members of
the DAS), Director: Franz Schmitt, Frankfurt a.M.; Lendvai Quartet,
Leipzig; and Youth Choir of the Berlin People's Choir (Members of the
DAS), Director: Walter Hänel. Piano: Ludwig Belitzer

Figure 1: Text for program of the January 1932 Berlin Concert, Contemporary
Choral Music

Closely coinciding with the "My Public" essay, the six pieces were written in two periods of composition, March–April 1929, and February–March 1930, and were published by Bote & Bock in Berlin in the summer of 1930.[11]

In light of the usual representations of Schoenberg's position in Weimar musical life, it comes as something of a shock to read in the few studies of these pieces that two movements, No. 4, "Glück," and No. 6, "Verbundenheit," were commissioned and first published by the *Deutsche Arbeiter-Sängerbund* of Berlin in 1929 and 1930, respectively. Following earlier performances of individual movements by various worker's choruses beginning in 1929, the complete set was premiered, widely performed, and eventually broadcast by the 13er-Quartett of the Arbeitergesangverein Vorwärts from Hanau in the 1931–32 season. After extensive rehearsals, this group of thirteen amateur singers performed the works from memory before large and enthusiastic audiences.[12] Alfred Einstein in the *Berliner Tageblatt* reviewed a Berlin Singakademie performance by the group included in a concert of worker's music from January 1932 (figure 1).[13] Schoenberg's Op. 35, and a set of his choral arrangements appeared alongside works by Hanns Eisler, many lesser-known composers associated with the worker's chorus movement, and what Einstein describes as "a primitive song of work" composed by the thirteen-year-old Inge Eschbach that was presented as evidence of the "creative-power awakened by musical training." Einstein writes of the audience that it was made up of "people who were not able to go to Furtwängler, Walter, or to the Opera, but for whom music is nevertheless a necessity." While he wonders at the inclusion of Schoenberg's music with the other works in which "all the efforts of the new community-social musical endeavors run together," he concludes: "here is a germ-cell for a truly fruitful development; these two hours are a hundred times more important for what is known as musical life than two hundred soloist concerts."[14]

Without denying the fundamental ideological distinctions between Schoenberg's response to the problem of the social function of art and that of his contemporaries such as Eisler, Weill, and Hindemith, the presence of these pieces written for a workers' chorus in a concert of workers' music suggests that in actual practice there were significant points of contact as well. It is precisely this aspect of the Six Pieces for Male Chorus that Alban Berg identified in a letter to Schoenberg from February 1931:

> . . . behind the absolute, eternal values of this opus there
> seems to be something timely as well: just as in the magnifi-

cent texts (especially in II, III, and V and VI) you reflect upon today's communal ideas [Gemeinschaftsideen] in such a way that they also become those of tomorrow and of all times. . . . It also appears that you (you who have always shown the younger generation the way) for once wished to show something after the fact, thereby demonstrating that the simple forms generally associated with the low "communal music" can also lay claim to the highest standards of artistry and skill and that their level need not be so debased as to make them suited to be sung only by children or on the street.[15]

Through an examination of the last two movements of Op. 35, "Landsknechte" and "Verbundenheit," I will explore ways in which Schoenberg sought to facilitate accessibility and comprehensibility and to find a common ground between his own compositional concerns and the practical demands of performance and the audience. Schoenberg's interest in bridging the "great divide" between himself and the broader public is evident in his texts, which deal directly with the relationship of the individual to the group, and in the mediation between the tonal and twelve-tone realms in the musical settings. Rather than representing a withdrawal from the public sphere, the textual and musical structure of the Op. 35 choruses show Schoenberg attempting to stake out a new terrain that would preserve an individualistic idea of art while responding to its changing social situation.

Schoenberg and the Public Sphere

Schoenberg's claims of isolation in "My Public" need to be understood less as a statement of fact than as an aesthetic declaration and even a provocation by a prominent figure who was in many ways at the height of his public status. This is particularly evident in the broad dissemination of the "My Public" essay shortly after it was written. Indeed it is ironic that Schoenberg's "message in a bottle" was published in several places including the *Blätter der Staatsoper der Republik*, and as far afield as the *Eisenacher Zeitung* (August 16, 1930). The most significant publication of "My Public" in the present context was its appearance in the April 1930 edition of the Berlin journal of art and society *Der Querschnitt* (figure 2).[16] With *Der Querschnitt*, Schoenberg could have scarcely found a platform with a higher profile or one more connected to the defining trends of the time. Together with the *Weltbühne* and the *Neue Rundschau*, *Der Querschnitt* was one of the lead-

Joseph H. Auner

ing periodicals of Weimar Germany, with an estimated readership throughout Europe of 125,000 at its high point in 1931.[17] The overriding aim of the journal to be as up-to-date as possible is reflected in this special music issue timed to coincide with the New Music Berlin festival, an outgrowth of the Donaueschingen festivals, that took place on June 18–21, 1930.

DER QUERSCHNITT

X. Jahrgang   Berlin. Ende April 1930   Heft 4

INHALT

Marginalien:

H. v. Wedderkop: Berliner Theaterbilanz / Paul Schiller: Röntgenaufnahmen aus dem Konzertsaal / Anton: Lieber Richard Romanowsky / Norbert Schiller: Das Bombardon in Loge 12 / Hannen Swaffer: Der Roman der Sophie Tucker / Richard Strauß in Anekdoten / Heinrich Hemmer: Mjusik, wie sie die Engländer hören / Hans Leip: Die Elefanten und die Musik / Hans Reimann: Am sausenden Webstuhl der Musik / Bücher und Schallplatten usw.

Mit vielen Abbildungen im Text und auf Tafeln

*

Umschlagbild nach einer Zeichnung von Carl Hofer

Figure 2: Text for title page of *Der Querschnitt* 10/4 (April, 1930)

The publication of this essay in *Der Querschnitt* can serve as a particularly appropriate symbol of the complexity of Schoenberg's position in Weimar cultural life. At first glance his contribution can appear very much out of place in the journal. Indeed, as a leading exponent of the Neue Sachlichkeit, *Der Querschnitt* was closely connected to many trends apparently antithetical to Schoenberg and his music. This context may shed light on the ironic and defensive tone of the "My Public" essay, along with its complaints about the corrupting influence of those guiding the public taste. But at the same time, his inclusion demonstrates that even those who were unsympathetic to his music had to acknowledge his prominence.

Schoenberg had since 1926 served as Busoni's successor at the Prussian Academy of the Arts in Berlin, one of the most important teaching positions in Europe. With the great success of Berg's *Wozzeck*, and with such talented younger students in his master class as Hannenheim, Zillig, and Skallkottas, whose works were performed by the Berlin Symphony Orchestra on May 20, 1930, his teaching found considerable confirmation.[18] During this period Schoenberg was extremely active as a composer and his works were widely performed. Among the major performances in 1930 were *Von heute auf morgen*, premiered in Frankfurt in early February and shortly after broadcast in Berlin; *Erwartung* and *Die glückliche Hand* in June at the Kroll Opera in Berlin; and the *Begleitungsmusik zu einer Lichtspielszene* at a symphony concert of the Kroll Opera in November. In April alone, when "My Public" appeared, *Pierrot lunaire* was performed in Cologne, *Gurrelieder* in Mannheim, and *Die glückliche Hand* in Philadelphia. Significantly, this partial list of performances includes works dating from Schoenberg's earliest to his most recent periods.

Merely to establish that such performances took place does not, of course, constitute a measure of their success or of their public resonance. On the contrary, it is undeniable that many works were met with incomprehension and even hostility. But a survey of concert reviews from the years around 1930 demonstrates that Schoenberg enjoyed a number of successes as well, and a still greater number of concerts that if not warmly received were at least met with interest. The critic of the *Hanauer Anzeiger*, for example, described the premiere of the Six Pieces for Male Chorus in October 1931 as an event of "highest musical significance." As confirmation of the "magnificent structural beauties" of the choral pieces he wrote of the "reverent silence with which the six pieces . . . were then received, the applause after these choral works, each of which reaches dizzying heights of compositional structure and musically vivid creation . . ."[19]

Present day and contemporaneous perceptions of Schoenberg's Berlin years are strongly colored by the concert scandals that occurred, perhaps most prominent among them the tumultuous reception in December 1928 of the premiere of the Variations for Orchestra by the Berlin Philharmonic under Furtwängler. Yet to interpret such scandals as indications of the public verdict on Schoenberg is to neglect the cultural politics, which as is well known were conducted with extreme vehemence in Berlin. It is precisely to this aspect of the reception of his music that Schoenberg draws our attention in "My Public." He attributes the most violent reactions not to the general public, which he says is usually "either friendly or indifferent . . . and rather inclined to enjoy something they have devoted time and money to," but to the "small but active 'expert' minority" that intimidated or provoked members of the audience. The example he provides is that of a conservatory director who created "the loudest disturbances" during a performance of *Pierrot* in Italy. But he surely must have had in mind journalists who intentionally provoked scandals through their writings or their own actions.[20] Such a context must be kept in mind when reading Schoenberg's analysis in "My Public" of "a concert where there was hissing":

> In the front third of the hall, roughly, there was little applause and little hissing; most people sat unconcerned, many stood looking around in amazement or amusement toward the parts of the hall farther back, where things were livelier. There the applauders were in the majority—there were fewer unconcerned, and a few hissers. But the most noise, both applause and hisses, always came from the standing space at the back and from the galleries. It was there that the people instructed or influenced by the expert judges went into battle against those who were impressed. [21]

Through his position at the Prussian Academy, Schoenberg was viewed as a representative of the cultural policies of the Republic, and was linked by its harshest opponents with the still more controversial figure of Leo Kestenberg, who was in charge in musical matters. Although many undoubtedly opposed Schoenberg's music on aesthetic grounds, the political nature of many attacks and scandals should not be underestimated. One example of what Schoenberg meant in his essay by "those who get between him and the public" is an article by Paul Zschorlich that appeared in the right-wing *Deutsche Zeitung* (June 11, 1930) about the Kroll Opera performances of

Erwartung and *Die glückliche Hand*. While he begins by claiming that Schoenberg's reputation was exclusively the result of his numerous concert scandals, his main point is to bewail the lack of a scandal in the performances:

> Schoenberg's "creations" represent a negation of all German musical culture, as the extermination of all taste, feelings, traditions, and all aesthetic principles. To perform Schoenberg means the same as to open a cocaine bar for the people. Cocaine is poison. Schoenberg's music is cocaine. In justifiable self-defense the German concert public has defended itself for years against this poison, most recently in December . . . with Furtwängler. But now it has gone to sleep. In the Kroll Opera there was no scandal, only boredom.

He writes that while it is bad enough that such music would be offered to the public, what is still worse is the sheeplike patience with which it is accepted. "One is tired, in music as in politics. One lets these things go on. It is a shame." Zschorlich's conclusion demonstrates the self-perpetuating nature of these attacks. With this concert, he writes, "we have reached a low point that is a scandal in itself, regardless of whether one broke out or not."[22]

Just as such polemics have led to an overemphasis on the degree of public hostility to Schoenberg's works, his distance from contemporary developments has been similarly overstated.[23] Yet taking the April 1930 issue of *Querschnitt* as a guide, we can see that there were significant points of contact between Schoenberg's activities and the dominant trends of Weimar music. Although a much more detailed discussion would be necessary to explore Schoenberg's ambivalent relationship to these developments, his works and writings show that he was deeply concerned with current debates about the future of opera, the relationship to popular styles, and the impact of the mass audience created by film and radio. Indeed from his position at the Prussian Academy of the Arts, Schoenberg could hardly have avoided dealing with these issues, since the goals of encouraging composers to reach out to the masses, and of making music of every sort accessible to the broad public through concerts and active participation in music making were central to the cultural policy of the Minister of Education and the Arts, Carl Heinrich Becker, and more directly of Leo Kestenberg, who was responsible for bringing Schoenberg to Berlin.[24] One example of the pressure he felt is an aphorism from April 1929 called "Telegraphic Delivery," which simultaneously comments on the limited frequency range of radio broadcasts as well as the implications of the contemporary cultural policy:

> The Prussian Minister of Education, (and on his behalf Mr. Kestenberg) have telegraphically ordered Gemeinschaftsmusik, and expect now not only that it will come, but that it will be telegraphically delivered. But lo and behold: now it comes through the radio! The upper half of all music for the lower ten thousand times ten thousand.[25]

In "My Public" Schoenberg deals only with earlier conceptions of a public defined through direct personal contact. At the most immediate level this consists of the personal circle of acquaintances that supported his music—his friends "as true as few." The largest level he explicitly discusses is the concert audience. But as "Telegraphic Delivery" makes clear, Schoenberg was well aware that the nature of the public for art had been profoundly changed by the new technologies. This can be best illustrated by his involvement with radio. In a reply to a questionnaire about the influence of radio Schoenberg identified it as a foe, singling out the damage done by its poor tone quality and the "boundless surfeit" of music it provided that could so harden the listener that music would be reduced to background noise. Yet he ends the essay on a more optimistic note, comparing the radio to publishing, which had resulted in the "virtual extinction of illiteracy." He suggests that the easy availability of music similarly had the potential of making music available to "every human being," with the possibility that they might be "moved, touched, taken hold of, gripped, by music."[26]

Far from turning his back on the new medium, Schoenberg used the radio for important broadcasts of his works, such as *Von heute auf morgen*, for lectures such as those on the Variations for Orchestra and the Four Orchestral Songs aimed at helping listeners understand his music, and for more general propaganda for modern music. It is noteworthy that Schoenberg's Op. 35 choral pieces were broadcast on several occasions. Indeed a *Deutsche Arbeiter-Sängerzeitung* review of the radio premiere of "Glück" reports that it was his enthusiasm after hearing the broadcast that inspired Schoenberg to write the additional movements.[27]

Of special significance in this context, Schoenberg saw in the radio the possibility of bypassing those "musical experts" who stood between him and the general public. In the spring of 1930 he wrote several letters to the Intendant of the Berlin radio, Hans Flesch, about how a program could be arranged to allow the composer, a critic, and members of the public to meet on a level playing field to discuss modern music.

> For the sake of variety one might also consider: One critic only, another specialist, a member of the public, and the author.
>
> Further one could occasionally also interpolate, for variety, singly, the views of members of the public, well-sifted, interestingly arranged, if necessary with comments by author or critic.

His confidence that the public, if given such a chance, would have interesting things to say is evident in his remark: "I have for years had the idea of getting someone to start a periodical in which the public could express opinions in the manner described above."[28]

Schoenberg's paradoxical notion of using a mass medium like the radio to reach a larger number of interested individuals is in fact characteristic of his whole approach to the idea of the "public" during this period. In this letter to Flesch, the "My Public" essay, and, as we shall see, in the texts of the Six Pieces for Male Chorus, he challenges the image of the public as a faceless mass, seeking instead to subdivide it into its component individuals. This is already evident in his categorization of the concert hall audience into the three factions cited above, but even more so in the dissection of those hissing.

> And yet I never had the impression that the number of people hissing was particularly great. It never sounded full, like a chord of solid applause entering with precision, but more like an ad hoc group of ill-assorted soloists, the extent of whose ensemble was limited to the fact that their noises told one the direction they were approaching from.[29]

This potential of the new media to transcend a mass public to reach a group of interested individuals is reflected in the overall shape of the "My Public" essay. Starting from a disavowal of a "public," and moving through the analysis of the concert audience and the factors influencing reception, Schoenberg concludes with those chance personal encounters with his commanding officer in the army, a taxi driver, and an elevator operator who complimented him on his music they knew from concerts, or in the case of a "hired man," from singing in the chorus of *Gurrelieder*.

If there is no doubt that Schoenberg took advantage of the mass media for the purposes of propaganda and for the dissemination of his music, it is also clear that he confronted the more fundamental problem of writing music that would be accessible to the broader public created by these technologies. Schoenberg's compositional activities during the Weimar years are most often represented by the canonical twelve-tone works like the Third String Quartet, Op. 30, the Variations for Orchestra, and *Moses und Aron*. Without denying the importance of these works, it must be stressed that they by no means dominated his contemporary reception. Paralleling these pieces are many compositions that are more difficult to reconcile with his image of isolation and elitism, including the arrangements and recompositions of Bach, Monn, and Handel; compositions like the Suite, Op. 29, the Zeitoper *Von heute auf morgen*, the *Accompaniment to a Film Scene*, Op. 34; and a large number of choral works. Each of these pieces is deeply engaged with contemporary debates about the fashion for popular music, the return to tonality, and the desire to reflect contemporary life. While it cannot be said that he had an unerring sense of how to achieve popular success, it is just as misleading to suggest that he avoided it. Schoenberg was in fact so convinced of the prospects for the success of *Von heute auf morgen* that he undertook considerable financial risk to publish it himself, rejecting a substantial offer from Bote & Bock.[30]

Choral Music and the Social Function of Art

Most significant in the context of his engagement with the communal artistic ideals of the Weimar republic are the choral compositions from this period. These include, along with the Six Pieces for Male Chorus, two sets of folk song arrangements written in 1928–29 and published the following year. While the preceding choral works, the Three Satires and the Four Pieces for Mixed Chorus, Op. 27, have received some scholarly attention because of the historical interest of their texts and twelve-tone structural features, the folk song arrangements and the Six Pieces for Male Chorus have been largely overlooked. Such neglect can be attributed to a range of reasons, including their genre, the use of tonality, or in the case of Op. 35, their hybrid tonal/twelve-tone structure, and their awkward ideological position for those to whom Schoenberg's isolation is an article of faith either to be praised or censured. But it is important to stress that both the choral arrangements and the Six Pieces for Male Chorus had a significantly higher profile at the time. Indeed it is striking that the last movement of Op. 35, "Verbundenheit," was the only work discussed in detail in the 1934 volume published on the occasion of Schoenberg's sixtieth birthday, while the text was printed at the beginning of the book as a sort of epigraph. The essay by Schoenberg's pupil Josef Polnauer remains the most insightful study of Op. 35—a sign of the extent of the work's subsequent eclipse.[31]

Such choral compositions occupied the centerpiece of Kestenberg's program for involving the masses in music as a means for building community and for raising the level of musical education. Significantly, choral music for amateurs and children was one of the main themes of the Neue Musik Berlin festival in 1930.[32] Schoenberg's folk song arrangements from this period, consisting of three pieces for mixed choir and four for voice and piano, were written as part of the *Volksliederbuch für die Jugend*, published by Peters, and resulting from a state commission. Reflecting Kestenberg's ideal of enlisting modern composers in service of the broader public, those asked to contribute such arrangements included Hindemith and Křenek.[33] One need not think that only altruism could have motivated such compositional concerns; by 1929 there were thousands of choral organizations throughout Germany involving more than three-quarters of a million participants. The *Deutsche Arbeiter-Sängerzeitung* alone had a monthly circulation of over 80,000. While the performance level of the group from Hanau that premiered Schoenberg's Op. 35 may not have been typical, many ensembles performed the most challenging choral repertoire.[34]

In writing his choral works, Schoenberg could draw on his own early experience with workers' choruses in turn-of-the-century Vienna. Shortly after leaving his job as a bank clerk in 1895, and probably through the influence of his life-long friend David Josef Bach, Schoenberg began conducting and composing for several suburban workers' choirs.[35] It is not exactly clear how long he was involved in these activities, but it is likely that they continued up to the time of his first move to Berlin in 1901. While Schoenberg's early experience with workers' choirs is given little attention today, it was prominently mentioned in a complimentary *Deutsche Arbeiter-Sängerzeitung* review of the premiere of "Glück," Op. 35, no. 4, in a broadcast by the Erwin Lendvai Quartet.

> Maestro Arnold Schoenberg was active in his youth as the director of five Viennese workers' choral organizations. That he still has a lively interest in our movement is proven by his

giving us an original composition for our collection of male choruses, for which he specifically wrote the work just premiered.[36]

To claim Schoenberg as a friend of music for the proletariat, of course, strikes us today as very peculiar. Despite evidence of an early interest in Marxism, it is clear that by 1930 Schoenberg's politics had moved far away from these socialist sympathies. Yet we need to recognize that the political faultlines that can seem so clear today were considerably more obscure in the 1920s and 1930s.[37] On the one hand, many of the documents that shape our current understanding were not published at the time, such as "National Music" (1931). During his Berlin years, on the contrary, Schoenberg often cultivated an "apolitical" public face. In the short essay, "Does the World Lack a Peace-Hymn?" published with a group of responses to the question in the *8-Uhr Abendblatt der Berliner National-Zeitung* (May 26, 1928), he wrote:

> I have nothing to do with politics—in whose utterances, at even their most nonsensical, human, artistic or any other similar feelings still have no influence. . . . [B]y what chord would one diagnose the Marxist confession in a piece of music, and by what colour the Fascist one in a picture? [38]

His public statements with political implications were most often put forward in relatively circumspect terms. The 1931 radio lecture on the Variations for Orchestra, Op. 31, for example, begins by defending the rights of the minority against the majority: "Far be it from me to question the rights of the majority. But one thing is certain: somewhere there is a limit to the *power* of the majority; it occurs, in fact, wherever the essential step is one that cannot be taken by all and sundry."[39] On the other hand, regardless of Schoenberg's personal politics, his harshest critics came from the right wing and centrist parties, while figures on the left, such as Hermann Scherchen, championed Schoenberg, Busoni, and other composers of the new music.[40] Thus we should not be surprised to see him praised in the pages of the *Deutsche Arbeiter-Sängerzeitung* as a sympathetic friend of the workers' chorus movement, or to see his works featured in the twenty-fifth anniversary concert of the "Arbeiter-Sinfonie-Konzerte" in Vienna, founded by D. J. Bach, and conducted by Anton Webern.[41]
The point is not that these representations of Schoenberg as composer for the proletariat are more accurate than his familiar picture as

the lonely elitist.[42] But the image of an uncompromising Schoenberg making no concessions to the performer or the listener is just as mistaken. In an unpublished reply from 1927 to an article in the *Neues Wiener Tagblatt* concerning the future of opera, Schoenberg wrote:

> So it is self-evident that art which treats deeper ideas cannot address itself to the many. "Art for everyone": anyone regarding that as possible is unaware how "everyone" is constituted and how art is constituted. So here, in the end, art and success will yet again have to part company.

While such statements are used to show Schoenberg's elitism, the corollary claim with which this passage begins is often overlooked: "To be understood by many, ideas need expressing in a particular way."[43]

The larger point—and the issue that occupies the bulk of his theoretical writings, in particular the recently published *Gedanke* manuscripts—is that there is an intimate relationship between the nature of the musical idea, the means of presentation, and the intended audience. In some handwritten remarks from 1929 published as "Glosses on the Theories of Others," Schoenberg responded to recent writings by Hindemith, Křenek, and Hanns Guttman on Gebrauchsmusik and the *Lehrstück*:

> I have, above all, repeatedly pointed out the *purpose of all forms*: a layout which guarantees comprehensibility. I have then shown what are the conditions that go with comprehensibility; how it is a question of the kind of listener one is writing for (and in doing so, defined the difference between light and serious music, something else which troubles him); and how there is always a manifest relationship between an *idea's difficulty* and the way it is presented [44]

That Schoenberg did in fact take into consideration the conditions of performance and the intended listeners and performers is evident in his tonal and relatively conventional folk song arrangements from the *Volksliederbuch für die Jugend*. Many aspects of the Six Pieces for Male Chorus similarly suggest that Schoenberg kept the fact that he was writing for a workers' chorus very much in mind during the composition of these pieces. This is apparent in his use of tonality, his treatment of the twelve-tone system, and other compositional features designed to ensure more immediate accessibility and comprehensibility. His concern for the practicalities of performance is also indicated by a note in the *Deutsche Arbeiter-Sängerbund* publication of "Verbundenheit," not carried over to the Bote & Bock publication, that if needed the chorus could be accompanied by cello and contrabass, or piano.

Yet while the folk song arrangements fit comfortably within the model of a socially committed, nonautonomous artwork, the Six Pieces for Male Chorus clearly move well beyond what is typical of the music for workers' choruses. The challenges this work poses should not be underestimated; in his discussion of the pieces shortly after they appeared, Willi Reich compared Schoenberg's difficulty to that of Kant, Einstein, and Bach.[45] It is precisely the complex and even contradictory way that these pieces simultaneously participate in and challenge their genre that is most typical of Schoenberg's relationship to the compositional and aesthetic trends of the Weimar Republic. Just as *Von heute auf morgen* or the *Accompaniment to a Film Scene* are both exemplars and critiques of Zeitoper and film music respectively, the Six Pieces for Male Chorus show how seriously Schoenberg sought to come to terms with as well as to transform the sphere of music for workers' choruses.

Schoenberg attempted to articulate this position in his annotations to Hindemith's essay "Demands made to the amateur" ["Forderungen an den Laien"] from the inaugural issue of *Musik and Gesellschaft* (April 1930).[46] Figure 3a is a facscimile of Hindemith's text, with Schoenberg's marginal notations. Figure 3b is a translation. Schoenberg added a long marginal note covering most of the blank parts of the page, the conclusion of which is translated in figure 3c. As Hinton points out in his discussion of this article, Hindemith issued a challenge both to the amateur and the composer to live up to their mutual responsibilities.[47] After criticizing the "arrogance" of laypeople who value too highly their amateur status, Hindemith characterized the excesses of composers in terms that Schoenberg clearly took personally.

Instead of meeting the public on its own terms, as Schoenberg felt that Hindemith and Weill were proposing, the Six Pieces for Male Chorus reflect his commitment to the idea of using art to push performers and audiences forward. This is the position that underlies Schoenberg's ironic aphorism from March 1929: "It is never too soon to start writing Gemeinschaftsmusik, and even more so Gebrauchsmusik (an awful word). I figure that one would certainly have to begin fifty to one hundred years in advance."[48]

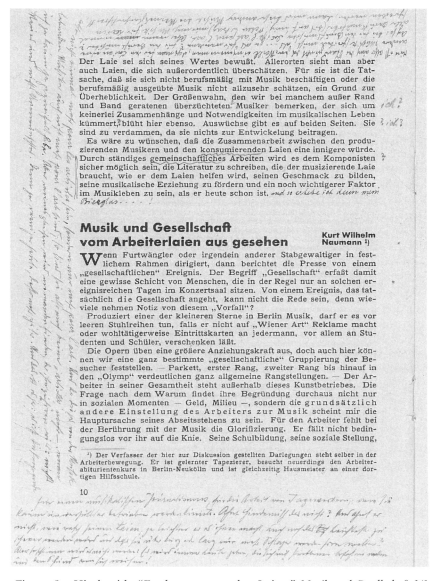

Figure 3a: Hindemith, "Forderungen an den Laien," *Musik und Gesellschaft* 1/1 (April 1930): 13, with annotations by Schoenberg. Arnold Schönberg Center, Vienna.

The megalomania, that we notice in many overbred[?] musicians [me?] who run amok and in no way concern[?] themselves with the relationships [?me?] and necessities of musical life, also thrives here as well. There are excesses on both sides. They are to be condemned since they contribute nothing to the development.

It is to be hoped that the cooperation between the producing musician and the *consuming* laymen would become more profound. Through constant *communal* work it will certainly be possible for the composer to write [?] literature that the music-making layman needs, as he helps the layman to educate his taste, promote his musical upbringing, and to be a still more important factor in musical life than he is today. [and so I raise my beerglass. . . . !]

Figure 3b: Hindemith, excerpt from "Forderungen an den Laien" (My translation; Schoenberg's handwritten interjections are in brackets.)

This also takes up Herr Weill's standpoint, that one must write a different music for laymen than . . . yes, for whom then? For the professional musician? Ah, that written for the professional musician is *l'art pour l'art*. But now if all professional musicians (except for me, Webern, and Berg,) will only write more music for laymen, then what other music people like me write is not *pour les artistes* any longer, but is only *pour l'art*. And since these musicians who make their living off music are also no longer *pour l'art* then they are also therefore no longer "artistes"—something which I have hardly doubted anyway. But people like me will find no one who will listen to them: nothing new and nothing undesirable. For the less today, the more later. And that is indeed the point: it is propaganda for a musical journalism, for the product of a day's work, as it would become a scarcely disguised business. Doesn't Hindemith suspect this? And doesn't he suspect how quickly his laymen, as he makes it easier for them, will find the easiest things still too difficult and that sooner or later they will only want to hear more hit tunes? But it won't get so bad: there will always be people who will want to concern themselves with valuables and reject the rubbish!

Figure 3c: Schoenberg's marginal annotations to Hindemith, "Forderungen an den Laien." Arnold Schönberg Center, Vienna.

Bridging the "Great Divide":
"Landsknechte" and "Verbundenheit"

The seriousness of his purpose in the Six Pieces is reflected in the texts that depart from the more limited concerns of the Three Satires to deal with the largest moral and social problems. Even where he does approach satire, especially in the first movement, "Hemmung," which lampoons artists who babble on without thinking too deeply, he presents the issue in his most deeply felt terms: "Wie schwer ist es, einen Gedanken zu sagen." The religious themes that had already emerged in the Op. 27 choruses, and that would become more dominant in *Moses und Aron,* also appear here, particularly in the second movement, "The Law." Several poems take a largely critical stand on issues of human nature and the relationship of the individual to society, thus reflecting other Schoenberg writings on the masses and the majority.[49] As in *Moses und Aron* and *Der biblische Weg,* the masses are portrayed as unthinking mobs driven, easily provoked into a violence that serves as their sole unifying force. This pessimistic view is put in particularly vivid terms in the fifth movement, "Landsknechte," which depicts humanity as beasts of the field, living for the moment, constantly battling one another, until they are slaughtered—mercenaries for a cause they never investigate (see Appendix on pp. 118–19 for texts and translations).[50] Seen from the perspective of Schoenberg as Moses, such texts can justifiably be taken as his rejection of the masses, but if we keep in mind that these pieces were written for and performed by workers' choruses, the element of social criticism acquires a different impetus. With the title "mercenaries," Schoenberg evokes not only those slaughtered on the battlefield, but those who sent them to die.

Such an interpretation is supported by the undoubtedly problematic, but ultimately much more sympathetic, representation of the relationship of the individual to the social sphere in "Verbundenheit." The text recounts the hardships of life from birth to the grave in short phrases alternating in a responsorial form. On first glance the text could appear to be a bitter sarcastic denunciation of a world lacking any sort of *Verbundenheit.*[51] This reading is supported by the very uncharacteristic appearances in the first half of the piece, lines 1–5, of such clichés as "Sei gesegnet," "Ruhe sanft," and "Gute Besserung" as scarcely adequate responses to the accounts of the various tribulations of injury, fire, drowning, and death. But in the second half, lines 6–10, the impersonal third person structure "man hilft," "man gräbt" is replaced by a direct form of address, "du läßt," "du hebst," while the responses become simple factual statements about the circumstances of social action instead of empty clichés. The final line is an exhortation to a social Verbundenheit in which the individual acts in the common good.

Significantly, the text focuses on the suffering of the world. In this it recalls one of the defining statements of Schoenberg's expressionist period from 1909: "Art is the cry of distress uttered by those who experience at firsthand the fate of mankind. Who are not reconciled to it, but come to grips with it. Who do not apathetically wait upon the motor called 'hidden forces,' but hurl themselves in among the moving wheels, to understand how it all works."[52] The difference is that now the individual not only reports the experience, but is called on to take action in response to this fate.

Thus the point of the piece, in my view, is the way that these verbal, and as we shall see, musical clichés, can be reanimated to become newly meaningful. Berg suggests a similar reaction in a letter to Schoenberg from December 13, 1932, after hearing a performance of "Verbundenheit" by the Freie Typographia chorus, one of the oldest and most important workers' ensembles:

> I *must* see you again sometime: when I heard your chorus "Verbundenheit" the day before yesterday (for the first time): I was truly heartsick with longing for you. To be sure, *this* is the kind of music that even one *not* so bound to you as *I* would be filled with deep melancholy at the sound of those mysterious triads. I say mysterious because the *tone* of the music defies any attempt to define it *analytically*. "Bless you." . . .[53]

Many aspects of the musical structure of the set reflect a desire to define a common ground with the listener. In all the movements Schoenberg seems to have been particularly concerned with settings that, as Malcolm MacDonald has written, "give passionate expression to subjects which could remain forbiddingly abstract."[54] Rhythm and texture play an important role in all six movements in clearly expressing the texts and articulating the structure. In "Verbundenheit" the responsorial textual structure is reflected in the alternation of single melodic lines followed by a homorhythmic choral answer.[55] One form this takes is the use of vivid and quite literal text painting throughout. In "Landsknechte" Schoenberg's evokes the world of Mahler's *Wunderhorn* settings by dividing the chorus into eight parts with various subgroups presenting a continuous accompaniment of onomatopoeic percussive sounds in characteristic march rhythms. The resulting energetic depiction of the text makes this arguably one of Schoenberg's most immediately accessible and effective twelve-tone works. Rufer wrote to Schoenberg after hearing the 1932 performance, "Das ist ja direkt ein 'Schlager.'" ("Now, that's a direct 'hit.' ")[56]

Perhaps the most significant feature of the Six Pieces for Male Chorus in terms of the idea of creating a common ground with a broader public is the interaction of twelve-tone and tonal elements. Indeed, "Landsknechte" can be viewed as an attempt to create a twelve-tone composition that preserves many tonal features, while "Verbundenheit" is a tonal work that appropriates many aspects of the twelve-tone system. The hybrid nature of Op. 35 has led to its status as a unified work being called into question. Jan Maegaard, for example, comments that the work "consists of two separate groups of pieces, numbers 4 and 6 which are not dodecaphonic, and the dodecaphonic pieces, numbers 1, 2, 3, and 5."[57] From the perspective of Schoenberg's mature twelve-tone style as it has been defined by Ethan Haimo, the piece is atypical not only in the mixture of tonal and twelve-tone movements, but because the twelve-tone movements are not based on a single row.[58] Yet rather than viewing the mixture of twelve-tone and tonal movements as a shortcoming, it is precisely this apparent heterogeneity that is the point of the piece. And while individual movements can be and were performed separately, Schoenberg indicates his own view of the six pieces as a cycle with his note in the score that the movements should be presented in the order given.

The earliest stages of the commission provide evidence for how closely the tonal versus twelve-tone issue is bound up with the entire conception of the set. When he was first approached by Alfred Guttmann, in a letter of September 5, 1928, to write one or two pieces for the *Deutsche Arbeiter-Sängerbund,* Schoenberg initially reacted angrily because of the small amount of money offered and because he felt that the topic was not raised with the appropriate respect.[59] But by early 1929 Schoenberg had agreed to write a piece, "Glück," that became the fourth movement, completed on March 15, 1929. The final version of this piece, however, differs considerably from his first draft, as Schoenberg noted in letter to Guttmann from March 17, 1929:

> The first, which was already three-quarters complete (a four-voice canon, tonal), did not please me so I wrote a new one that is closely in keeping to my true style, but which is not therefore as unmanageable as it might first appear. For the individual voices are not that difficult, but are very singable. . . .[60]

The original fourteen-measure draft, transcribed in the *Sämtliche Werke*, is a four-voice double canon at the fifth based on rich consonant harmonies, and thus not so different in style from the recently completed folk song settings. Schoenberg did not mention, however, that this was in turn preceded by a two-measure sketch that shows the beginning of a canon using a similar rhythmic figure to the theme in the tonal draft, but based on a combinatorial twelve-tone row and with the canon at the tritone.[61] The final version of the movement, as published in the *Deutsche Arbeiter-Sängerzeitung* and as it appears in Op. 35, is a hybrid, characterized by Richard Specht as "a paradoxical combination of opposing styles, utilizing an ambiguous sort of double tonality on the one hand, and the procedures of atonal serialism on the other." Specht demonstrates how the piece, which replaces the canonic structure of the early drafts with a homophonic texture contrasting single melodic voices with chordal accompaniments, uses various serial transformations of an eight-note row together with harmonies suggesting tonal chords and pitch centricity on A♭ and F.[62]

The progression in Schoenberg's thinking about the movement from his initial notion of a twelve-tone piece, to a tonal work, to an attempt to bridge the two styles—a solution with important ramifications for all the movements of the completed opus— reflects how profoundly he sought to balance a concern for the nature of the commission with a commitment to preserving the essentials of his "true style." Each of the twelve-tone movements explores different solutions to this problem. Schoenberg's approach in "Landsknechte" was to severely reduce the amount of pitch material. His row table for the work shows that the row is designed so that all of the dyads in the prime form are held invariant, though obviously reordered, in the combinatorial pair I^5. (See example 1. I will refer to the dyads by the following labels: "a" [F♯–C], "b" [A–F], "c" [F–E], "d" [E–G♯], "e" [B–D♯], "f" [G–C♯], "g" [D–E♭].) These two row forms are the basis for over sixty of the work's ninety-seven measures; the other row forms used such as P^5 and I^{10} also feature many of the same dyads. Thus underlying the complex and shifting rhythms and textures of the movement, there is a constant return of the same pairs of pitch classes. As shown in example 2, these row relationships do not remain abstract, but are explicitly emphasized on the surface of the music. Compare, for example, the prominence of the shared dyads in the two passages shown in examples 2a and 2b, which are based on different forms of the row, I^5 and P^5 respectively. The resulting extreme reduction in the pitch material of the piece is a major factor in the relative ease of comprehensibility and would also facilitate the process of teaching the work to a chorus. As shown in example 2c, Schoenberg also exploits the row structure for one of the more arcane examples of text painting. At the words "One is paralyzed"

Example 1a: Schoenberg's row table for "Landsknechte." Arnold Schönberg Center, Vienna.

Example 1b: Trichords in the "Landsknechte" row

Example 1c: "Voice leading" between the "Landsknechte" dyads

(Man ist gelähmt), the otherwise fairly clear row statements crystallize into the component dyads, making both forward motion and precise identification of the rows problematic.

That the row structure of the work also permits Schoenberg to make analogies to tonal composition is significant in this regard. As indicated in example 1b, the row includes several diminished (036), augmented (048), and major/minor triads (037), along with the (014) trichord. Similarly, four of the six dyads of the row noted above are major thirds

Example 2a: "Landsknechte," mm. 24–26

Example 2b: "Landsknechte," mm. 48–50

(example 1c). Unlike Berg's practice, however, Schoenberg does not take advantage of the potential for emphasizing the tonal triads explicitly on the surface or for writing harmonic progressions. Rather he develops more subtle allusions to tonal practice while preserving a unified sound world defined more by the augmented and diminished triads. One example of this is the quasi-tonal voice leading created by a succession of the row's component dyads, shown in example 1c. Such stepwise motion between voices moving in thirds or sixths is characteristic of the entire piece. In formal terms as well Schoenberg makes analogies to tonal structure by establishing the combinatorial pair of row forms P⁰/I⁵ at the opening, moving to other transpositions during transitional and contrasting passages, and returning to the original pair at the conclusion of the piece. This technique is common to most of Schoenberg's twelve-tone works, but in "Landsknechte" it is particularly apparent owing to the frequent use of ostinato figures and pedal tones that establish areas with a clearly defined pitch focus.

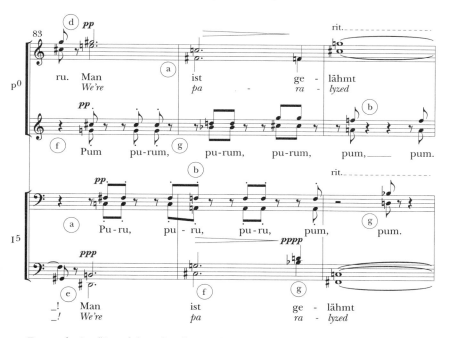

Example 2c: "Landsknechte," mm. 83–85

The analogies to tonal practice in "Landsknechte," also present in the other twelve-tone movements, become explicit in the last movement, "Verbundenheit." The role of tonality in Schoenberg's works from this period is of course a crucial issue in the context of his relationship to the public. With his reputation as the father of atonality, and his role in what he described as the "battle" of tonality and dissonance, the matter of "tonal or atonal" was obviously a central concern.[63] In the essay "Schoenberg's quasi-tonal style around 1930" Maegaard points out that while Schoenberg had been involved with tonal composition with the Bach arrangements of several years before, "Verbundenheit" from 1929 marks the first newly composed tonal piece for over two decades. From this point on Schoenberg was often involved with tonal composition, including the folk song arrangements, the Cello and String Quartet Concertos, along with several fragmentary tonal works such as a piece for violin and piano from 1930 and a piano concerto from 1933, both in D major. Maegaard links this return to tonality with Schoenberg's reaction to the cultural-political situation that made atonal and twelve-tone composition appear increasingly less viable.[64] While it can be argued that works such as the String Quartet Concerto and the Cello Concerto from 1933 need to be interpreted in the context of the Nazis' seizure of power, the significance of tonality and tonal composition for Schoenberg in these years can not be reduced to any single interpretation. Schoenberg's situation in 1930 was very different from what it was in 1933. Indeed an important sign of this is the mixture of tonal and twelve-tone movements in the Six Pieces for Male Chorus, which from an ideological perspective at least, was likely to please no one.

Why Schoenberg chose to use tonality for "Verbundenheit," as well as for the fourth movement "Glück," thus presents a complex problem. If the piece is interpreted as a satire, the cadential progressions that resolve deceptively could be viewed as the evocation of familiar formula, comparable to the textual clichés, and the pseudo-religious responsorial form. Thus tonality would serve as a further sign of the empty solace offered by society. But the overall effect of the piece does not at all support this interpretation; neither do Berg's comments about the "deep melancholy at the sound of those mysterious triads," nor Polnauer's probing analytical remarks about Schoenberg's form-building function of tonality in the work. Rather, the use of tonality in the context of this set of pieces, as well as the particular form it takes in this movement, can be explained in terms of Schoenberg reaffirming a bond between his music and the tonal tradition, while at the same time using familiar means to educate performers and listeners about the essentials of his compositional language. As with the textual clichés that are made newly meaningful, "Verbundenheit" demonstrates how the familiar materials of tonal music can be rethought and renewed through contact with his serial techniques.

The most important means by which Schoenberg carries this out is in the relationship between the two halves of the piece, mm. 1–18 and mm. 19–36, corresponding to the two five-line stanzas of the text (the opening of each section is given in example 3). As Polnauer describes, the second half of the piece is a strict inversion of the first half, with the voices exchanged so that the original leading voice is transferred from Bass 1 to become the top melodic line in Tenor 1. The inversion is strict except for small changes in the last four measures to better prepare the final cadence. This is not merely a display of compositional skill, but serves to bring out the important change of character between the two halves of the text. As a result of the inversion the harmonies and voice leading of the first part are all transformed. Thus all major triads become minor triads, and vice versa; more noticeably, the many dominant sevenths are transformed into half-diminished sevenths.

Just as the second stanza of the text dispenses with the clichés and shifts from the third person to a direct form of address, the formulaic and familiar musical elements in the first half are reworked into something more ambiguous and individual. Schoenberg exploited precisely such intervallic relationships in his twelve-tone works such as the Piano Piece, Op. 33a (1929), the opening chords of which feature a similar transformation of a dominant seventh to a half-diminished seventh. Complementing the structural function of the melodic and harmonic inversion, many other features of "Verbundenheit" suggest analogies to twelve-tone composition. For example, in addition to allowing a final cadence on D minor in reference to the F-major opening, the level of transposition chosen for the inversion creates many pitch-class invariances between the two parts. Because the second half begins on F♯, many of the same pitch classes and triads are emphasized in the two halves, while a network of relationships is created between the cadential points.

Example 3a: "Verbundenheit," mm. 1–9

invariant p.c. collections
invariant p.c. subsets

Example 3b: "Verbundenheit," mm. 19–28

Example 3a continued

Example 3b continued

After 1930

By arguing that Schoenberg's Six Pieces for Male Chorus represent his own attempt to come to terms with the problems raised by Gebrauchsmusik, Neue Sachlichkeit, and Gemeinschaftskunst, I by no means intend to minimize the distinctions between Schoenberg and his contemporaries that loomed so large at the time and in historical retrospect. If Schoenberg did compose Gebrauchsmusik, it was a utopian Gebrauchsmusik with as much attention to ideals of the future as to present-day circumstances. But, as I hope to have shown, our sense of where the differences lie needs to be reconsidered with a better understanding of the complexity of the historical record and with close attention to how recent musical developments have colored our perception of the past. If there is no doubt that Schoenberg did identify with Moses, there is also considerable evidence that he had more of an affinity with Aron than is usually granted. Moreover, it is just this tension and ambivalence in his relationship to the public that made the metaphor of Moses and Aron so meaningful for him during the Weimar years. Similarly, many compositions following his move to America, not to mention his tireless teaching, writing, and lecturing on music, show that Schoenberg did not give up the search for points of contact between himself and a broader audience. Works such as the Suite for String Orchestra, Theme and Variations for Wind Band, and *Kol Nidre* show an obvious concern for their function and conditions of performance.[65]

Yet Alfred Einstein's hopeful characterization of the 1932 Berlin workers' chorus concert as a "germ-cell for a truly fruitful development" can only strike us today as poignant or naive in light of the collapse of the Republic scarcely more than a year later. Not long after the Berlin performances of the choral pieces, Schoenberg left Germany never to return. One of the first acts of the Prussian Academy of the Arts under Nazi control in May 1933 was to ban the workers' choral organizations. Already in 1930 the worldwide economic crisis had brought to an end the period of prosperity in Germany. The rapid increase in unemployment and the ensuing social unrest resulted in a period of sustained governmental crisis following the March 1930 elections that led over the next months to the demise of parliamentary politics.[66] One sign of the changing situation was a polarization within the Deutsche Arbeiter-Sängerbund between those who like Alfred Guttmann advocated "elevating" the repertoire, and those who called for making the groups more explicitly political by placing revolutionary songs at the center of the repertoire.[67]

It is also clear that the "bond" Schoenberg attempts to define in "Verbundenheit" or "My Public"—a bond based on aesthetic experience among like-minded individuals that transcended the traditional ties of nation, religion, race, class, and party—proved illusory in the Weimar years. Schoenberg's "apolitical" stance opens him to the same charge leveled at many Weimar intellectuals, that by holding himself aloof to a significant degree from the present-day circumstances of many members of the public and from political action he deprived the Republic of an advocate in difficult times. Taruskin and others have commented on the easy metamorphosis of the notion of Gemeinschaft into a Volksgemeinschaft; clearly, such a reconfigured community had no place for Schoenberg. He wrote to Berg in September 1932 of being forced to confront the question of "regarding myself as belonging here or there, and whether it is forced upon me."

> Of course I know perfectly well where I belong. I've had it hammered into me so loudly and so long that only by being deaf to begin with could I have failed to understand it. And it's a long time now since it wrung any regrets from me. Today I'm proud to call myself a Jew; but I know the difficulties of really being one.[68]

But in early 1930 the end was not yet clear and despite the growing financial crisis, many of the possibilities of the earlier more hopeful years of the Republic remained. It is just this contradictory quality that I believe defines both the "My Public" essay and the Six Pieces for Male Chorus. Both works acknowledge the existence of destructive, irrational social forces, but there is an underlying optimism as well. To allow our perspective to be totally determined by subsequent events risks obscuring the real achievements of these years and limiting the potential for our present day musical life.[69] We should be cautious of accepting too readily the apparent verdict of history about such forgotten works as the Six Pieces for Male Chorus, particularly when thinking about such historical moments when the notions of history and tradition were so hotly contested. Increased awareness of the range of his compositional activities and the contexts for his writings suggest that we need to rethink the image of Schoenberg as a solitary prophet, as an artist without a public.

APPENDIX
Texts and translations for "Landsknechte" and "Verbundenheit"

LANDSKNECHTE
(Arnold Schoenberg)

MERCENARIES
(translation by Joseph Auner)

Einmal muß man sterben,
aber wer denkt daran?
Und wie ist das: Sterben?
Ach was!

We all have to die once,
but who thinks about it?
And how is it: to die?
So what!

Leben weiß man in jedem
  Augenblick.
Ebensolang: aber es geht weiter.

We know how to live in each moment.
Just for that very moment, but things
  go on.

Tapp, tapp, hopp, hopp!
Auf die Weide!
Oh, heute regnets; wenig Gras –
  kein gutes –.
Herrlich: hier bin ich allein!
Der beste Platz! Kein andrer findet
  her.
Eine fette Weide für alle.
Vertragt euch: es ist genug für jeden!

Tapp, tapp, hopp, hopp!
To the pasture!
Oh, it's raining today; little grass—
  none good—
Marvellous: I am alone here!
The best spot! No one else will find it.
A luxuriant pasture for us all.
Make peace: There's enough for
  everyone!

Weg! Die Weiber sind mein!
Lauf, oder ich spieß dich auf!
Stirb! So, hier bin ich Herr!
Für die Jungen ist gesorgt.
Ach was, Junge!
Man lebt jetzt eben!

Go away! the women are mine.
Run, or I'll run you through.
Die! Now I'm the master here!
The young are provided for.
The young—So what!
Live for the moment!

Oho, es riecht nach Blut?
Nach unserm Blut und Fleisch.
Also dorthin gehts?
Werden wir jetzt schon geschlachtet?
Man sollte fliehen:
Man ist gelähmt!
Was könnte es nützen?
Landsknechtsschicksal!

Oh, there's a smell of blood?
Of our flesh and blood.
So, that's the way it goes?
Will we be slaughtered already?
One ought to flee:
One is paralyzed!
What's the use of that?
Mercenaries' fate!

Joseph H. Auner

VERBUNDENHEIT
(Arnold Schoenberg)

Man hilft zur Welt dir kommen,

man gräbt ein Grab für dich,

man flickt die Wunden dir im Spital,

löscht dein Haus, zieht dich aus dem Wasser

du hast selbst doch auch mit andern Mitleid!

Du läßt den Greis nicht liegen,

du hebst die Last des Schwachen,

du hemmst im Laufe das scheue Pferd,

wehrst dem Dieb, schützt des Nachbarn Leben

leugne doch, daß du auch dazu gehörst!

– – – – – – –
Sei gesegnet!
– – – – – – –
Ruhe sanft!
– – – – – – –
Gute Bessrung!

Fürchte nichts,

Hilfe naht, du bist micht allein!

– – – – – – –
fällst einst selbst so,
– – – – – – –
ohne Lohn,
– – – – – – –
schonst dich selbst nicht,

ohne Zögern bringst du Hilfe:
– – – – – – –
bleibst nicht allein.

BOND
(translation by Joseph Auner)

You are helped into this world, – – – – – – – – – – – – – – – – – Be blessed!
a grave is dug for you, – – – – – – – – – – – – – – – – – – – Rest in peace!
your wounds are patched up in the hospital, – – – – – – – – – Get well soon!
the fire in your house is put out, you're pulled from the water
– – – – – – – – – – Don't be afraid!
after all, you yourself have compassion for others!
– – – – – – Help is near, you are not alone!

You don't leave the old man behind – – – – – you yourself will fall someday,
you lift the burden from the weak – – – – – – – – – – – – – – without reward,
you slow the flight of the skittish horse – – – – – – – – – not sparing yourself,
you fight off the thief, protect your neighbor's life
– – – – – you bring help without hesitation:
try denying that you too are part of all this! – – – – – – you won't stay alone.

NOTES

Earlier versions of the essay were presented at the Boston meeting of the American Musicological Society (1998), and in colloquia at the Humboldt University in Berlin, Yale University, and the State University of New York at Stony Brook. I wish to thank in particular Klaus Kropfinger, Hermann Danuser, Albrecht Riethmüller, James Hepokoski, and Robert Morgan for their suggestions on earlier drafts. Special thanks to Ulrich Krämer and the Arnold Schönberg Gesamtausgabe in Berlin for providing access to documentary materials and to R. Wayne Shoaf at the Arnold Schoenberg Institute for all his help over the years. Research on this topic was conducted with the support of the Alexander von Humboldt-Stiftung.

1. Arnold Schoenberg, "My Public," in *Style and Idea*, ed. Leonard Stein (New York, 1975), pp. 96–99.

2. René Leibowitz, *Schoenberg and His School: The Contemporary Stage of the Language of Music*, trans. Dika Newlin (New York, 1949; reprint: New York, 1979), pp. 287–88; Theodor Adorno, "On the Social Situation of Music" (1932), *Telos* 35 (1978): 134; Milton Babbitt, "Who Cares if You Listen?" *High Fidelity* 8 (1958): 38–40, 126–27; Pierre Boulez, "Schoenberg the Unloved?" in *Orientations*, ed. Jean-Jacques Nattiez, trans. Martin Cooper (Cambridge, Mass., 1986), pp. 325–29. And see more recently Susan McClary, "Terminal Prestige: The Case of Avant-Garde Music Composition," *Cultural Critique* 12 (1989): 60–61.

3. *The Weimar Republic Sourcebook*, ed. Anton Kaes, Martin Jay, and Edward Dimendberg (Berkeley and Los Angeles, 1994), pp. 584–86. See also Andreas Huyssen, *After the Great Divide: Modernism, Mass Culture, and Postmodernism* (Bloomington, 1986), pp. 53–54.

4. *Weimar Republic Sourcebook*, pp. 569 and 581.

5. Schoenberg, "Neue und veraltete Musik, oder Stil und Gedanke" (1930–33), *Stil und Gedanke: Aufsätze zur Musik*, ed. Ivan Vojtěch (Frankfurt, 1976), p. 471.

6. Schoenberg, "Gemeinschaftskunst" (February 28, 1928). Arnold Schönberg Center, Vienna. My translation.

7. Richard Taruskin, "Back to Whom? Neoclassicism as Ideology," *19th-Century Music* 16 (1993): 296. He places Schoenberg with the "latter-day Romantics of the transcendental strain," for whom such ideas posed the greatest threat.

8. Stephen Hinton, *The Idea of Gebrauchsmusik: A Study of Musical Aesthetics in the Weimar Republic (1919-1933) with Particular Reference to the Works of Paul Hindemith* (New York and London, 1989), pp. 102–03.

9. Alexander Ringer extends the metaphor of Moses to make still broader claims about what he calls "Schoenberg's splendid isolation." He writes of Schoenberg "aligning himself with the visionary prophets of old who lived and acted bereft of peace but in the certainty of an ideal future." Ringer too concludes that Schoenberg "shunned Aron, the practical man of experience, fact, and compromise. Instead he chose Moses, unbending in the proclamation and defense of revealed truth yet human enough to err and pay for his error with burial in an unknown grave." Alexander Ringer, *Arnold Schoenberg: The Composer as Jew* (New York and Oxford, 1990), pp. 21 and 23.

10. Compare the conclusion of Schoenberg, "My Public," *Style and Idea*, p. 99, to the version in the *Weimar Republic Sourcebook*, p. 586. It is possible that the final four sentences of the essay were accidentally left out; the missing passage corresponds precisely to what appears on p. 99.

11. "Glück" appeared in *Männer-Chöre ohne Begleitung* (Berlin, 1929), pp. 687–90. "Verbundenheit" was published in July 1930 as publication No. 1382 of the Deutsche Arbeiter-Sängerbund. The most detailed documentation of the genesis of the pieces is

given in the critical commentary in Schoenberg, *Sämtliche Werke*, Chorwerke. Series B, vol. 18/2, ed. Tadeusz Okuljar and Dorothee Schubel (Mainz and Vienna, 1996), pp. XXIX–LI. See also Robert John Specht, "Relationships Between Text and Music in the Choral Works of Arnold Schoenberg" (Ph.D. dissertation, Case Western Reserve University, 1976); Anthony Payne, "First Performances," *Tempo* 71 (1964): 24–25; and Willi Reich, "Schoenberg's New Männerchor," *Modern Music* 9 (1932): 62–66. As I was completing this article I learned of another study by Robert Falck, "Schoenberg in Shirtsleeves: The Male Choruses, Op. 35," which will appear in *Religious and Political Ideas in Schoenberg's Works*, ed. Charlotte Cross (New York, forthcoming.)

12. Joan Evans, "New Light on the First Performances of Arnold Schoenberg's Opera 34 and 35," *Journal of the Arnold Schoenberg Institute* 11 (1988): 163–73. Additional information is provided in Schoenberg, *Sämtliche Werke*. On November 2, 1929, the Erwin Lendvai-Quartett, directed by Walter Hänel, performed "Glück" on the Berliner Rundfunk in a broadcast, "Modern Workers' Poetry and Music." The complete set was premiered by the 13er-Quartett of the AGV Vorwärts, on October 24, 1931. Hans Rosbaud offered a complete performance on the Frankfurt Radio on November 29, 1931.

13. The program is reproduced in Inge Lammel, *Arbeitermusikkultur in Deutschland 1844–1945: Bilder und Dokumente* (Leipzig, 1984), item 192.

14. Alfred Einstein, "Chormusik der Gegenwart," *Berliner Tageblatt* 53 (February 1, 1932), reprinted in Schoenberg, *Sämtliche Werke*, p. XLVIII (my translation). There was a substantial recording industry associated with the worker's choruses. At least one 78 rpm record was released with performances by the 13er-Quartett on the Gloria Carl Lindstöm G.O. label (10265 B. 536), containing "Wir bauen eine Neue Welt" by Vorsmann and the "Lied der Arbeit" by Eschbach. A copy of the recording is contained in the Arbeiterliedarchiv of the Akademie der Künste, Berlin.

15. *The Berg-Schoenberg Correspondence, Selected Letters*, ed. and trans. Juliane Brand, Christopher Hailey, and Donald Harris (New York, 1988), pp. 412–13.

16. Schoenberg's article appeared in the vol. 10, no. 4 (1930), issue of *Der Querschnitt*, which was published at the end of April 1930. The manuscript is dated March 17, 1930.

17. *Der Querschnitt* was concerned above all with the visual arts, but also with society, sports—boxing in particular—business, travel, and, without taking any definite position, politics. See *Berlin im "Querschnitt*," ed. Rolf-Peter Baacke (Landshut, 1990), pp. 254–60.

18. In preparation for the event Schoenberg had distributed 1,500 invitations (Archives of the Akademie der Künste, Berlin). In April 1930 he published an enthusiastic tribute to Alban Berg in *Die Theaterwelt*, Düsseldorf, where *Wozzeck* was being performed. See Schoenberg, "Alban Berg (2)," in *Style and Idea*, p. 475.

19. Evans, "New Light," p. 169.

20. A particularly telling instance of this behavior is described in an article about the 1920 Music Festival in Weimar, in which Paul Bekker challenges the account of a scandal around a performance of Schoenberg's Five Orchestral Pieces, Op. 16, written by Paul Zschorlich in the *Deutsche Zeitung*. Bekker writes that in contrast to the other works, the orchestral pieces were not a success, but he adds, "in no way was it a 'scandal beyond compare' as the *Deutsche Zeitung* falsely reported. It is only correct that the representative of this paper that reported the scandal attempted himself to provoke a scandal through continual disturbances and anti-Semitic outbursts without achieving the desired effect. This is an example of how artistic politics are 'made' by that side. First one creates a scandal and then reports that the public had done it." Paul Bekker, "Zwischen Vergangenheit und Zukunft—Zum Tonkünstlerfest in Weimar," *Frankfurter Zeitung* (June 22, 1920).

21. Schoenberg, "My Public," in *Style and Idea*, p. 98. This typology of the audience reinforces Schoenberg's affinity with those of the middle rank, positioned between the bemused patrons in the best seats and the chaotic masses of the gallery. It is striking to compare Schoenberg's description to Adorno's "Natural History of the Theater," written in 1931–33. Adorno writes of the gallery as the one place in the theater open to change—in contrast to the bourgeois orchestra seats and the aristocratic boxes populated only by ghosts. See Adorno, *Quasi una Fantasia: Essays on Modern Music*, trans. Rodney Livingstone (London, 1992), pp. 65–80.

22. Paul Zschorlich, "Schönberg-Heuchelei bei Kroll: 'Erwartung' und 'Die glückliche Hand,'" *Deutsche Zeitung* (June 11, 1930). My translation.

23. This is not to deny, as noted above, that he himself and his followers repeatedly stressed his isolation from the concerns of the younger generation. Yet along with the significant aesthetic differences, cultural politics played an important role in the way these distinctions were defined. See Scott Messing, *Neoclassicism in Music: From the Genesis of the Concept Through the Schoenberg/Stravinsky Polemic* (Ann Arbor and London, 1988); Susan C. Cook, *Opera for a New Republic: The Zeitopern of Křenek, Weill, and Hindemith* (Ann Arbor and London, 1988); and Joseph Auner, "The Second Viennese School as a Historical Concept," in *Schoenberg, Berg, Webern: A Companion to the Second Viennese School*, ed. Bryan Simms (Westport, Conn., 1999) pp. 1–36.

24. Tamara Levitz, *Teaching New Classicality: Ferruccio Busoni's Master Class in Composition* (Frankfurt, 1996), pp. 80–82.

25. Schoenberg, "Telegraphic Delivery" (April 9, 1929). Arnold Schönberg Center, Vienna. My translation.

26. Schoenberg, "The Radio: Reply to a Questionnaire" (1930), in *Style and Idea*, pp. 147–48.

27. "Arnold Schoenberg was so enthusiastic about the performance of this uncommonly difficult chorus, which owing to illness he was only able to hear on the radio, that he has entrusted the premiere of a further five male choruses on his own texts, now in preparation, to this tirelessly-advancing eight-man proletarian singing group." "Arnold Schönberg-Uraufführung," *Deutsche Arbeiter-Sängerzeitung* 30/11 (1929): 234. Reprinted in Schoenberg, *Sämtliche Werke*, pp. XLV–XLVI. (My translation.) The review was written by "W.H." (presumably Walter Hänel) and Rudolf Brauner.

28. Arnold Schoenberg, *Letters*, ed. Erwin Stein, trans. Eithne Wilkins and Ernst Kaiser (New York, 1965), pp. 141–42.

29. Schoenberg, "My Public," in *Style and Idea*, p. 98.

30. Stephen Davison, "Of its time, or out of step? Schoenberg's Zeitoper, *Von heute auf morgen*," *Journal of the Arnold Schoenberg Institute* 14 (1991): 271–98.

31. Josef Polnauer, "Schönbergs 'Verbundenheit,'" in *Schönberg zum 60. Geburtstag* (Vienna, 1934), pp. 44–49.

32. See Pamela M. Potter, *Most German of the Arts: Musicology and Society from the Weimar Republic to the End of Hitler's Reich* (New Haven, 1998), pp. 4–9. The role of choral music in the cultural policy of the Republic was extensively discussed at the First Choral Music Congress in Essen in 1929, which included statements by Kestenberg and Carl Heinrich Becker. See *Organisationsfragen des Chorgesangwesens: Vorträge des I. Kongress für Chorgesangwesen in Essen* (Leipzig, 1929). Hinton cites an article by Karl Laux that appeared in the *Zeitschrift für Musik* in 1929 concerning the Baden-Baden Festival, which included the premiere of the Brecht-Hindemith *Lehrstück*: "'Just as the audience's sociological mix has changed—the working masses rising upward, wishing to participate in cultural activities–so the internal structure has also changed. People no longer sit in subscription seats. They sit together in rows wishing to form a community. Moreover, this community is no longer content with just listening. They want to make music themselves. Inner involvement is thus guaranteed. *Activity of the community replaces passivity of the individual.*'" Hinton, "*Lehrstück*: An Aesthetics of Performance,"

in *Music and Performance during the Weimar Republic*, ed. Bryan Gilliam (Cambridge, 1994), p. 67.

33. See Specht, "The Choral Works of Arnold Schoenberg," pp. 401–12. Most other contributions were by those with close connections to the youth music movement, such as Fritz Jöde, Hans Mersmann, and Georg Schünemann. Schoenberg commented on Hindemith's settings in "Linear Counterpoint," in *Style and Idea*, p. 294.

34. See Lammel, *Arbeitermusikkultur in Deutschland 1844–1945*, pp. 141–56.

35. See Specht, "Schoenberg Among the Workers: Choral Conducting in Pre-1900 Vienna," *Journal of the Arnold Schoenberg Institute* 10 (1987): 28–37; and Albrecht Dümling, "Im Zeichen der Erkenntnis der sozialen Verhältnisse: Der junge Schönberg und der Arbeitersängerbewegung," *Zeitschrift für Musiktheorie* 6 (1975): 11–12.

36. "Arnold Schönberg-Uraufführung," reprinted in Schoenberg, *Sämtliche Werke*, pp. XLV–XLVI.

37. In the review/essay "Back to Whom? Neoclassicism as Ideology," Taruskin's "Bach of the Right and . . . Bach of the Left" framework, for example, links Schoenberg to "Stravinsky's snooty art" rather than to the "socially motivated *Gemeinschaftsmusik* of his fellow Germans, toward which his attitude would always remain ironical." Taruskin, "Back to Whom? Neoclassicism as Ideology," p. 298.

38. Schoenberg, "Does the World Lack a Peace-Hymn?" in *Style and Idea*, p. 500.

39. Schoenberg, "*Variations for Orchestra*, Opus 31: Frankfurt Radio Talk" (March 22, 1931) as reprinted in, *Arnold Schoenberg Self Portrait*, ed. Nuria Schoenberg Nono (Pacific Palisades, 1988), p. 41.

40. Levitz, *Teaching New Classicality*, pp. 62–74. As with all art work there is no necessary link between the creator's ideology and the reception of the work. Hinton, for example, shows that even a work such as the Brecht-Weill school opera, *Der Jasager*, could be significantly misconstrued by critics, "Some on the right, for example, even greeted what they saw as endorsement of their conservative Christian principles, while others on the left interpreted the piece as lending support to authoritarian and reactionary tendencies, despite the authors' clear intentions to the contrary." Hinton, "*Lehrstück*: An Aesthetics of Performance," p. 69.

41. The jubilee concert featured Schoenberg's arrangement of Bach's Prelude and Fugue in E♭ ("St. Anne") and of Three German Folk Songs (see Josef Rufer, *The Works of Arnold Schoenberg*, trans. Dika Newlin [New York, 1962], p. 92). Webern served as director of the Singverein between 1923 and 1934. See Christopher Hailey, "Webern's letters to David Joseph Bach," *Mitteilungen der Paul Sacher Stiftung* 9 (1996): 35–40.

42. Indeed, Stuckenschmidt reports that Schoenberg rejected a request from his former student Paul Pisk to "add his signature to a proclamation for the Workers' Symphony Concerts," though he did send personal "greetings to Dr. D. J. Bach on the occasion of the jubilee of these concerts." Hans Heinz Stuckenschmidt, *Schoenberg: His Life, World and Work*, trans. H. Searle (New York, 1978), p. 329.

43. Schoenberg, "The Future of Opera," in *Style and Idea*, p. 336.

44. Schoenberg, "Glosses on the Theories of Others," in *Style and Idea*, p. 316.

45. Reich, "Schönberg's New Männerchor," p. 62.

46. This issue of *Musik und Gesellschaft* 1/1 (April 1930) included articles by Fritz Jöde, Heinrich Besseler, Hindemith, and others. See Hinton, *The Idea of Gebrauchsmusik*, p. 6ff.

47. Hinton, *The Idea of Gebrauchsmusik*, p. 201.

48. Schoenberg, "Gemeinschaftsmusik: mehr aber noch; Gebrauchsmusik. . . ." (March 15, 1929). Arnold Schoenberg Center, Vienna. My translation. It should be pointed out that this position in fact shares important elements with the views of those whom Schoenberg criticizes. Hinton quotes Weill making a similar point in 1930 about a "dialectical aesthetic" that would bring about "the sublation of '*Kunst*musik' and '*Gebrauch*smusik'": "Precisely in an art which is meant for use, the concept of quality

must again be emphasised, because otherwise the danger will repeatedly emerge of confusing it with the *Gebrauchskunst* that has always been around as an 'everyday commodity.'" Hinton, *The Idea of Gebrauchsmusik*, p. 212; see also pp. 84–86.

49. There are striking parallels between the concerns of Schoenberg's texts and Freud's discussion of the relationship to the individual and the community in *Civilization and Its Discontents*, first published in 1930.

50. On the wide-spread fascination with mass spectacle during these years, see Detlev Peukert, *The Weimar Republic: The Crisis of Classical Modernity*, trans. Richard Deveson (New York, 1989), p. 161.

51. Reich, for examples, says that all the texts but the fifth, "Landsknechte," "express some philosophical aphorism of a pessimistic nature." Reich, "Schönberg's New Männerchor," p. 63.

52. Quoted in Willi Reich, *Schoenberg: A Critical Biography*, trans. Leo Black (New York, 1971), p. 57.

53. *Berg-Schoenberg Correspondence*, p. 438.

54. Malcolm MacDonald, "Schoenberg's Opus 35," *Tempo* 71 (1964): 105–07.

55. Such a texture is common to the repertoire, as can be seen by a comparison of "Verbundenheit" with Copland's "Into the Streets May First," written in 1934 and published in the *Workers Song Book 2* (1935), as well as to contemporary works by Eisler and Blitzstein. See Carol J. Oja, "Marc Blitzstein's *The Cradle Will Rock* and Mass-Song Style of the 1930s," *Musical Quarterly* 73 (1989): 445–75.

56. Schoenberg, *Sämtliche Werke*, p. XXXIV.

57. Jan Maegaard, *Studien zur Entwicklung des dodekaphonen Satzes bei Arnold Schönberg* (Copenhagen, 1972), vol. 1, p. 134.

58. Ethan Haimo, *Schoenberg's Serial Odyssey: The Evolution of his Twelve-Tone Method, 1914–1928* (Oxford, 1990), pp. 7–41. Yet underlying this surface dissimilarity, the four twelve-tone rows do have important connections with each other as well as with the pitch structure of the tonal movements. Significantly, these are pitch class rather than intervallic relationships based on many recurring dyads as well as larger segments that appear reordered in other rows. For example, the first five pitch classes of the row of "Hemmung," no. 1, return as the last five pcs of the row of "Ausdrucksweise," no. 3. Schoenberg's approach to twelve-tone composition in Op. 35 suggests interesting parallels to Berg's compositional techniques with the references to tonality and the mixture of twelve-tone and non-twelve-tone movements.

59. Schoenberg's letter is dated September 22, 1928. Guttmann's reply in a letter of September 28 expressed considerable shock in return about the level of Schoenberg's hostility, noting that in years of correspondence with prominent composers only Hans Pfitzner had written such a sharp response. Schoenberg, *Sämtliche Werke*, p. XXIX.

60. Schoenberg, *Sämtliche Werke*, p. XXX. My translation.

61. Since the sketch breaks off two notes before the leading voice has completed the row, the piece is not definitively twelve-tone. But the use of the combinatorial (012345) hexachord at the tritone transposition in the opening voices makes this likely. Schoenberg, *Sämtliche Werke*, p. 253.

62. Specht, "The Choral Works of Arnold Schoenberg," pp. 299–306.

63. See my "Schoenberg's Handel Concerto and the Ruins of Tradition," *Journal of the American Musicological Society* 49 (1996): 282–87.

64. Maegaard, "Schönbergs quasi-tonaler Stil um 1930," *Bericht über den 1. Kongreß der Internationalen Schönberg-Gesellschaft*, ed. Rudolf Stephan (Vienna, 1978), pp. 132–33.

65. Hinton also points out the importance of commissions for Schoenberg's American works and the possible connection to the development of his musical language and the use of tonality, but he concludes "this did not mean a change in his overall musical aesthetic, which was still part of his nineteenth-century heritage." Hinton, *The Idea of Gebrauchsmusik*, p. 115.

66. See Peukert, *The Weimar Republic*, pp. 248–72.

67. See Guttmann's letter to Schoenberg from September 5, 1928, in Schoenberg, *Sämtliche Werke*, p. XXIX. Among the leaders of the new "Kampfgemeinschaft der Arbeitersänger" were Schoenberg's pupils Hanns Eisler and Karl Rankl. Lammel, *Arbeitermusikkultur in Deutschland 1844–1945*, p. 156.

68. Schoenberg, *Letters*, p. 167.

69. Hinton describes the historian's task as restoring "to past events the openness in which they occurred; otherwise the very essence of the historical fact (as opposed to the scientific fact) — freedom — would be extinguished." Hinton, *The Idea of Gebrauchsmusik*, p. 81. And see Taruskin's critique of this point in "Back to Whom? Neoclassicism as Ideology," pp. 301–02.

Schoenberg and Bach

RUDOLF STEPHAN

TRANSLATED BY WALTER FRISCH

The topic Schoenberg and Bach deserves a comprehensive treatment, especially because of its importance for understanding the origin and the language of the new music. Bach was the great stimulus for the new musical thought, and at the same time he furnished it with what we may call—borrowing the terminology of Arnold Gehlen—the "musical framework" (Aussenhalt).[1] After the tradition of classical forms and compositional methods gradually began to wane, Bach provided the model for this kind of musical framework, especially to the classicists, who sought to draw directly on the great works of the past. Bach also stimulated further progress in musical thought among the composers who not only did not want to give up the traditional aspiration of music as art, but wanted to develop it further, to enhance it, yet who at the same time were obliged by the changed circumstances to seek out the necessary consequences. This applies above all to Schoenberg himself.[2]

There are two critical moments in Schoenberg's involvement with Bach. The first comes around 1910, the second in the 1920s. In his later years Schoenberg oriented his teaching methods in counterpoint toward Bach (and toward the Italian contrapuntal tradition, which had been the leading one in Austria since the seventeenth century). The clearest evidence of this orientation is his late textbook *Preliminary Exercises in Counterpoint*. In the foreword he gives the following justification of why the book contains contrapuntal exercises in major and minor, but not in the church modes:

> And . . . there is no greater perfection in music than in Bach! Not Beethoven or Haydn, not even Mozart who was closest to it, ever attained such perfection. But it seems that this perfec-

tion does not result in a style which a student can imitate. This perfection is one of idea, of basic conception, not one of elaboration. The latter is only the natural consequence of the profundity of the idea, and this cannot be imitated, nor can it be taught.[3]

As early as *Harmonielehre* Schoenberg reveals an extraordinary, and in many respects uncustomary, estimation of Bach. *Harmonielehre* appeared in 1911, before the epoch-making books by August Halm that were the earliest to assign Bach the top position that he has assumed unchallenged ever since, even for the musical public.[4] Bach is the composer cited most often in *Harmonielehre*; he appears even more frequently than Beethoven or any modern composer, including Wagner, whom one would expect to see cited the most in any harmony book of the post-Wagnerian era.

By this time Schoenberg had already been intensively involved with Bach, even as a performing musician. A concert program included in the Vienna Schoenberg exhibit of 1974 showed that Schoenberg had rehearsed and performed Bach motets in 1907— something that was anything but self-evident at that time in Catholic Vienna, since there was no tradition for performing those kinds of pieces.[5] Schoenberg may have felt himself drawn to the works as a religiously active Protestant. In any case, this might explain the deep affinity to the motets evident in *Harmonielehre*. (The excerpts in this treatise, drawn mainly from the motet "Komm, Jesu, komm" [BWV 229], figure as models in the discussion of the problem of "nonharmonic tones.")

In *Harmonielehre* Schoenberg formulated for the first time the insight that was to be crucial for all later music: that tonality is merely an artificial means, albeit an extraordinarily versatile and powerful one. What had heretofore been understood as something given by nature—conservative theorists like Heinrich Schenker still held firmly to the antiquated viewpoint—was now recognized as a means to an end: the creation of musical coherence and articulation, and thus the construction of form. This realization, made possible by Schoenberg's own compositional experience of the years 1908–09—during which he wrote the Second String Quartet, Op. 10; the George-Lieder, Op. 15; the Three Piano Pieces, Op. 11; the Five Pieces for Orchestra, Op. 16; and the monodrama *Erwartung*, Op. 17—implied that the emancipation of the dissonance had been fully accomplished. Thereafter it was no longer necessary to justify nonharmonic tones as dissonances.

About Bach he wrote:

> Bach's solution is wonderful. . . .True, it would hardly be pos-
> sible without the passing tones and changing tones, which
> therefore are not ornamental here, but structural; they are
> not incidentals, not non-harmonic, they are rather necessities,
> they are chords.[6]

And Schoenberg's thesis that "there are no non-harmonic tones, for harmony means tones sounding together" (*Theory of Harmony*, p. 318) must
be recognized as the expression of a new way of musical thinking that no
longer acknowledges a qualitative difference between consonance and
dissonance (which does not, however, mean that there is no longer any
distinction to be made). The quotations from Bach's motets (*Theory of
Harmony*, pp. 324, 327) play a role in the discussion of whether the "dis-
cords" that arise can be interpreted as free-standing chords. For
Schoenberg this was no longer an issue since, even presupposing a foundation of harmony in the natural properties of the overtone series, he
could explain dissonances as more distant overtones: "Dissonances are
the more remote consonances of the overtone series" (*Theory of Harmony*,
p. 329). There was no longer a reason for Schoenberg to deny the status
of a chord to any sonority that might appear.

We can surmise that this realization came to Schoenberg through
not only his own creative work, but the works of Bach that he cited.
In these pieces, the continuous motion and the lack of strongly differentiated accent patterns give rise to a relationship between the different sonorites within a particular context that is distinct from the
music of the classical composers, especially Beethoven. Is it not thus
amazing that Schoenberg immediately sought to affirm the musical
framework displayed by Bach's compositional technique, above all
since the challenge was to create the greatest possible diversity of
musical characters?

This was in fact the case in 1912, one year after the appearance of
Harmonielehre. For the cycle of melodramas *Pierrot lunaire* is precisely a
succession of distinct character pieces. Besides contrapuntal numbers,
we find character pieces in the nineteenth-century style; dances; and a
movement, "Madonna" (no. 6), that links up directly with Bach.
"Madonna" (see example 1) corresponds to the type of setting that in
this case is characterized principally by three elements: the lack of a bass
(that is, a figured bass), "walking" lower parts, and sigh motives. For
Schoenberg, the avoidance of the figured bass finds its analogy in the
avoidance of the piano, and the walking lower voice is evident in the

Example 1: "Madonna," no. 6 of *Pierrot lunaire,* mm. 1–7

cello pizzicato. The sigh motives are everywhere apparent: above all in the flute part at the end of m. 1, which is marked as the *Hauptstimme*; at the beginning of m. 3; in the middle of mm. 4 and 5; and especially in mm. 12–14. Schoenberg constructs the melodies from phrases of different lengths, which as a consequence of the procedures of developing variation exhibit structural coherence to the highest possible degree. This aspect needs as little discussion as does the new structure of the chords, all of which presuppose the emancipation of the dissonance. Clearly, only the first half of "Madonna" is indebted to this kind of texture, which is most clearly audible in a movement like "Gute Nacht, o Wesen," from the motet *Jesu, meine Freude* (BWV 227), and which can also be found to some extent, though in modified form, in the duet for the Men in Armor in the Act II finale of *Die Zauberflöte*.

This kind of setting by Bach serves as "musical framework," very much like the character pieces and dances alluded to by Schoenberg himself in the movement titles or performance indications (Barcarole, Waltz) of *Pierrot*—Schoenberg once even referred to them as "baroque dance forms"—and like the contrapuntal procedures of "Parodie" and "Mondfleck" already mentioned. (In the Passacaglia, however, which Schoenberg mentions in this context, things are somewhat different.) Schoenberg himself is entirely correct when he observes a connection with the older musical types (dance forms), which he used a decade later in the Five Piano Pieces, Op. 23; the Serenade, Op. 24; and the Piano Suite, Op. 25—all of which since their publication have been readily understood as classicist.

It would certainly be possible to link the first of the Five Piano Pieces, Op. 23, with "Madonna" from *Pierrot* as attempts to compose a three-voice setting whose individual parts are independent of one another in both articulation and phrase length. And above all, imitation should be avoided: imitation, which for Schoenberg was nothing less than the contrapuntal corollary to sequence. Counterpoint played a decisive role in the makeup of the new musical language, which made possible composition with twelve notes related only to one another. Reinhold Brinkmann has alluded to this fact in an essay;[7] and the drafts and sketches he edited for the Piano Pieces, Op. 23, and the Piano Suite, Op. 25, provide enough evidence to give a good impression of the situation.[8] Only with the publication of the sketches for the Serenade, as well as of fragments and drafts that cannot be interpreted as having been destined for any particular work, will this development be comprehensively demonstrated. This work was begun by Jan Maegaard in his extensive *Studien zur Entwicklung des dodekaphonen Satzes bei Arnold Schönberg* (Copenhagen, 1972).[9]

Here I would like to discuss two documents from the early 1920s: first, Schoenberg's well-known orchestration of Bach's organ chorale, "Schmucke dich, o liebe Seele" (BWV 654). If in "Madonna" the type of setting adopted by Schoenberg serves as framework, then in this organ chorale the traditional setting loses its unifying force because each musical detail is filled with expression. Schoenberg once wrote: "The principal goal of all musical reproduction must be: to realize in sound what the composer has written such that each note will be truly audible, and to assure that everything, whether it sounds simultaneously or separately, stands in a relationship to everything else such that at no point will one voice hide another, but, on the contrary, that each voice will stand out against the others."[10]

In order to make such a performance possible, Schoenberg occasionally orchestrated pieces or works by other composers. For once he wanted to hear everything. What did Schoenberg really seek to clarify? First, motivic events, which his ear picks up from within the counterpoint, and which he perceives as constituting musical meaning. The principal voice—the upper voice before the entry of the actual melody—is divided into individual motives, and these motives are assigned to different instruments (see example 2). It is in fact characteristic of the melody to conceal innumerable motives such that they do not so much follow one another as overlap, such that individual notes can belong to different motives. Thus a single note can be at the same time the last note of one motive and the upbeat to the next. The secondary voice, the middle one of the three-voiced texture, is in this case not divided up into such motives. The two upper voices are thus arranged in different ways, in order to make possible a diversified

Example 2: Bach, chorale prelude, "Schmücke dich," mm. 1–6, with indications of Schoenberg's orchestration

realization in sound. The motivic articulation of the principal voice, which in Schoenberg's autograph is moreover supplied with the brackets that later become customary for the *Hauptstimme*—they are missing in the printed edition—entails a continuous change in tone color and even turns the melody into a tone-color melody (Klangfarbenmelodie). Thus its higher status becomes visible. At the same time it was possible for Schoenberg to color the octave registers differently: the principal voice is doubled at the octave, while the secondary one is not, except in the first measure. Thus the two voices are also distinguished from one another in this respect .

The beginning of the piece, whose special quality we have just discussed, is presented in a homogeneous tone color, because here both upper voices are parallel, thus making differentiation seem inappropriate. Differentiation begins only in the second measure, when both voices take on independent motion. The differing instrumentation corresponds to the altered compositional circumstances.

The degree to which each note is charged with meaning is shown by many individual features: first, added signs like crescendo markings, swells (on individual and sometimes short notes), slurs, articulation signs, etc. And even passages that seem to be merely figurative are differentiated by performance markings and separated into motives. A particularly impressive example is offered by mm. 17–18 (example 3). The succession of tones, which comments upon the first chorale phrase now concluding—played "dolce" by the high solo cello—is performed by four each of solo violins, solo violas, and solo cellos, whose articulation is shown in example 3.

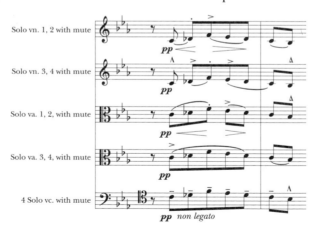

Example 3: Schoenberg's orchestration of Bach, "Schmucke dich," mm. 17–18

The result of this articulation is that each individual note becomes accented in one or several instrumental parts. The first note is accented by the third and fourth violas; the second, by the third and fourth violins; the third, by the first and second violins; the fourth, by the third and fourth violins and first and second violas. These accents appear each time at the beginning of a group of notes that are phrased together. The signs • and ^ show still further differentiation: the dot indicates a slight shortening, possibly with separation; the carat tells a performer to avoid deemphasizing a note that is in itself unstressed. If we observe the notes that are not marked and consider that they too must be accented or remain unaccented according to their different positions within the measure, the result is an extraordinarily rich gradation.

What is intended here is less a gradation of dynamics than a coherence of articulation with respect to the motivic coherence of the individual phrases, as indicated by these signs. Each note thus attains its own weight, its own distinctive meaning. The differentiation, which is a manifestation of the desire for infinitely enhanced expressivity and musical animation, had to be completely realized in the mind before it could be adequately represented. Motivic richness to guarantee wealth of expression and motivic subdivision and thereby enrichment to create animation: these were the factors that stimulated Schoenberg's orchestration of the organ chorale. His orchestration is not only an analytical but also a constructive document of a new kind of musical thought. It unites constructivity with expressivity, both of which appear greatly intensified, and it thereby legitimates one through the other.

There are many other documents that show Schoenberg's tendency to uncover motivic connections even where according to traditional views they are not at all present. Here I will discuss one that fits particularly well in this context.

In the first volume of his periodical *Der Tonwille* Heinrich Schenker presented an analysis of the E♭-minor Prelude from Book I of the *Well-Tempered Clavier*. In addition to showing the establishment of the *Urlinie* in the first four measures (b♭,' [c♭,"]–a♭,'–g♭,'–[g♭,"]), Schenker describes the motivic development of the upper voice. Although he does not make clear what really delimits a motive, the beginning of his analysis is relevant here:

The first note of the Urlinie, in m. 1, gives life to an arpeggiation which nevertheless lays claim to individual motivic significance. . .

In m. 4 the line comes to a pause on g♭'. If the repetition of the motive had departed from this same note in the Urlinie, the motive, since it always descends, would have had to sink into a deeper register, in which, because of the extreme proximity of both outer voices, scarcely any diminution would be manageable. Moreover, letting the upper octaves lie fallow would create a purely sonorous disadvantage. With a simple but ingenious device:

the Urlinie is shifted upward into the register of the octave above c". Each time the same danger and problem recur, they are handled in the same fashion. Hence this device, too, seems to have risen to the level of an independent motive, which in its own right contributes to increase the illusion that we are dealing here with a completely independent world, in which the freest unfolding of motives becomes the one and only law.

We again encounter the device we have just described as early as m. 8, where it helps to raise the Urlinie, which meanwhile had fallen, up to the level of c♭². This time, however, the master prepares us for this register a measure earlier (m. 7), where he inverts the note b♭² above the e♭² that initiates the motive. Notwithstanding its particular function, however, this b♭ retains the character of a filler tone. . . . We are justified in perceiving a law here: indeed, the law, as it were, of an obligatory treatment of register as well as voices.[11]

Schoenberg provides a commentary on this page to the extent that he underlines the words *give* (*gibt*), *life* (*Leben*), and *nevertheless* (*gleichwohl*), and also puts *life* in quotation marks. It is evident what he wants to say with these markings: one note alone cannot give life, and an arpeggiation can surely not sustain a claim to be life, which can be created only through motivic work, not "nevertheless."

After the second musical example (Schenker's figure 3) Schoenberg underlines the first two syllables of the word for "raised up" (emporgesteigert) and observes as follows in the margin: "lowered" (herabgemindert). At the very beginning of the next paragraph he highlights the word *device* (Griff) by encircling it; he does the same with the "inverts" (stülpt). Schoenberg's next annotations refer to two places in Schenker: first to the phenomenon illustrated in Schenker's figure 3, second to the "law of a voice-leading of register." About the figure Schoenberg writes: "the transformation of the rhythm is much more important here. From ♩. ♪♪♪♩ comes ♩♩|♩ (see the tenor in m. 6, the bass in m. 9, also mm. 8–10, 11, 13, 14, 16, etc.). A new form has arisen from the first." And Schoenberg illustrates all this as in the following example:

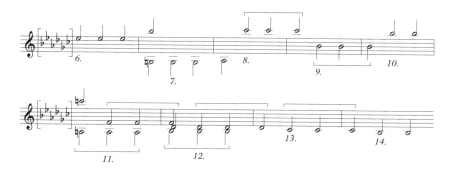

A further comment by Schoenberg on Schenker's analysis is significant in the present context. He writes on the following page, "I see the following":

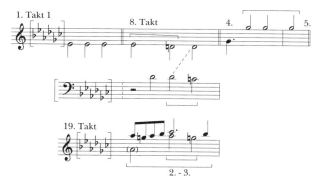

And at the passage where Schenker describes the art of diminution in m. 12ff., Schoenberg makes notations as follows:

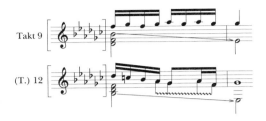

These musical examples are significant insofar as they make readily apparent what Schoenberg brings in from his own perspective. His proposed reading of m. 19, which is motivically derived, is that of the Forkel-Hoffmeister edition[12] (apparently taken over by Kroll in the Peters Edition, which we know Schoenberg owned), and is thus hardly authentic. What is most interesting about these remarks is the insight they allow into Schoenberg's musical thought. For him, no musical coherence is imaginable without a motivic relationship. Schoenberg even gives motivic significance to the chords in the accompaniment; through the motivic life which they make possible, they obtain a musical meaning beyond that of mere accompaniment. The motives that impart life are often the simplest possible intervals, seconds. According to traditional motivic theory these are not motives at all, only motivic elements. What is significant is the step from the concrete motive, or the smallest element recognizable as a motive, to a more abstract motivic element: the intervallic relationship, which lies behind the motive and which itself takes on a thematic significance like that of the abstract rhythmic shape.

Should we be surprised that Schoenberg welcomed, as a confirmation of so many of his own ideas (despite more than a few differences), the investigations of Wilhelm Werker, which appeared in the following year under the title *Studien über die Symmetrie im Bau der Fugen und die motivische Zusammengehörigkeit der Präludien und Fugen des "Wohltemperierten Klaviers" von Johann Sebastian Bach* (Studies of the symmetry in the construction of fugues and of the motivic coherence of the preludes and fugues of the "Well-Tempered Clavier" of Johann Sebastian Bach) (Leipzig, 1922). Werker's main idea, that behind musical themes there are motivic entities that give meaning, must have seemed a most welcome confirmation to Schoenberg at the time that he was developing his method of composition with twelve tones. And even Werker's reference to numerous correspondences and the most cryptic relationships were welcome to Schoenberg, who always had something similar in mind.

The remarks that Schoenberg scribbled in the margins of Schenker's analysis and that we have examined above are, like most of his comments, not to be understood as sketches for essays or larger studies. Rather, they served exclusively the composer's process of self-awareness. They are also the result of complete spontaneity and thus offer an unmediated glimpse into Schoenberg's ideas and ways of thinking. Such jottings often served primarily as vehicles for emotional release. In the heat of emotion Schoenberg often wrote down things that upon more tranquil consideration he not only could not have maintained, but would not have maintained. There is in fact much evidence to suggest that an idea that had been phrased in a radical form in spontaneous jottings would be formulated more carefully in a text destined for publication. Sometimes upon closer examination Schoenberg even rejected an idea written down spontaneously (perhaps in great agitation). In his essay on Bach of March 1950, which was certainly intended for publication and is one of his last critical writings—it remained unfortunately incomplete—Schoenberg no longer expressed himself spontaneously, but thought everything through carefully.[13] Two ideas from this essay, which is characterized by a certain skepticism, are relevant for our investigation.

Schoenberg begins by recalling his earlier claim that Bach was the first twelve-tone composer. He says that this was obviously a joke. But was it a joke, or was it an exaggeration or one of those paradoxes for which Schoenberg was known as a young man? As the "only" basis for the claim Schoenberg offers the twelve-note subject of the B-Minor Fugue from Book I of the *Well-Tempered Clavier*, and he says, at the end of the section, after the discussion of other fugue themes: "In Fugue 24 the chromatically altered tones are neither substitutes nor parts of scales. They possess distinctly an independence resembling the unrelated tones of the chromatic scale in a basic set of a twelve-tone composition. The only essential difference between their nature and modern chromaticism is that they do not yet take advantage of their multiple meaning as a means of changing direction in a modulatory fashion."[14] This excerpt becomes completely understandable only to the reader who thinks of it in connection with Schoenberg's earlier statements. The twelve-tone nature of the theme is in itself not necessary for the perception of what is meant here as the twelve-tone concept. The idea of "twelve-toneness" means in this context simply a tonal space that keeps all twelve notes equally available and that, as Schoenberg formulated it in a manuscript from 1932, makes it possible for a work like the *Well-Tempered Clavier* to "take account of all twelve tones."[15]

Thus Bach realized twelve-toneness not through twelve-tone rows, but through conceptualizing with, or rather in, twelve tones. Schoenberg also says this in the manuscript already cited (which is also written in a style of aphoristic overstatement): "Bach is (paradoxically speaking) the first twelve-tone composer. . . . Bach extended to all twelve notes the technique of bringing seven notes into such opposing positions that, through the motion of the voices each simultaneity is perceived as a consonance."

The essay of 1950 almost retracts this thesis, though not in its entirety. Schoenberg modifies it only on the basis of another idea that likewise is not exemplified in the later essay, but which he had advocated since the early 1920s: the idea that the fugue theme is the source of all possible subsequent musical events. The fugue subject should, in Schoenberg's view, contain within itself all the "possibilities of coherence that are only later uncovered, unfolded, or unleashed (taken apart, disclosed, represented by the musical development."[16] Or: "In the purest form, which perhaps may be only a theoretical construction, nothing would appear in a fugue that could not be derived at least indirectly from the subject."[17] From this point of view a theme would of course be ideal when it represented the entire tonal spectrum, even if only in *nuce*. From this point of view the twelve-tone fugue subject in fact appears as a unique piece of evidence—though not the only one—for Schoenberg's thesis.

It appears, then, that at the time that he wrote his Bach essay, in the Bach year 1950, Schoenberg had attained a somewhat more distanced relationship to the contrapuntal arts. Now he wished to fathom the secrets of all the fugues that renounce the use of many contrapuntal procedures. The idea that a subject could completely predetermine the course of a fugue had apparently lost some of its relevance.

In the second section of his Bach essay Schoenberg had again retreated somewhat from an earlier point of view (without completely abandoning the basic thesis). Here he holds the view that in Potsdam Bach became the "victim" of a joke. The royal theme, which Schoenberg here attributes to Carl Philipp Emanuel Bach, is intentionally constructed so as to resist all contrapuntal techniques. Schoenberg thus sees the theme as the result of a cleverly contrived conspiracy. Earlier on, Schoenberg took it for something different: "The fugue subject is undoubtedly a completely unusable piece of trash. . . . Not a single stretto is possible with this theme. . . .The theme is bad from all musical points of view. Senseless, unimaginative and schematic, superficial, garrulous, uncharacteristic, internally incoherent and above all uncontrapuntal!! A companion piece to the Diabelli waltz. Bach has to attempt the most remote devices in order to do anything with it, specifically *with it*!!! . . ." The theme that is so highly valued in the Bach literature, which Bach himself called "excellent" (trefflich),[18] poses the greatest difficulties for contrapuntal treatment, although as Erich Schenk has shown, it is actually comprised of two conventional melodic models that are suited for contrapuntal development.[19] In Potsdam Bach improvised only a three-voice fugue on this theme; for the six-voice one he chose his own theme. Even the worked-out version of the three-voice fugue shows, as Philipp Spitta long ago pointed out, "an intentionally light, preludial character" and thus might have recalled the improvisation that had been so well received by the king. What Schoenberg said applies completely to the six-voice fugue: the object of contrapuntal technique is not the (royal) theme, but what Bach himself brought to it.

NOTES

This article originally appeared as "Zum Thema 'Schönberg und Bach,'" in *Bach Jahrbuch 1978* (Berlin, 1979), pp. 232–44.

1. See Arnold Gehlen, *Urmensch und Sprachkultur: Philosophische Ergebnisse und Aussagen*, 3rd ed. (Frankfurt, 1975).
2. The importance of Max Reger in this connection has yet to be clarified. In general the opinion prevails today that his relation to Bach was more or less secondary, but the question really demands another look. Schoenberg, at any rate, found in studying Reger's Violin Concerto what he "had not counted on finding: a familiarity with tonal relationships reminiscent of Bach" (Ms. of July 1923, in Arnold Schönberg Center, Vienna; Rufer D 21 [Josef Rufer, *The Works of Arnold Schoenberg*, trans. Dika Newlin, New York, 1962]; Christensen Mus 46b [Jean and Jesper Christensen, *From Arnold Schoenberg's Literary Legacy: A Catalog of Neglected Items*, Detroit, 1988]). Unless otherwise noted, all manuscript sources cited in this article are now housed at the Arnold Schönberg Center, Vienna. Further references to the inventories of Rufer and Christensen will be given in short form.
3. Arnold Schoenberg, *Preliminary Exercises in Counterpoint*, ed. Leonard Stein (London, 1963), p. 223.
4. See especially *Von zwei Kulturen der Musik* (Munich, 1913).
5. *Arnold Schönberg: Gedenkausstellung 1974*, ed. Ernst Hilmar (Vienna, 1974), p. 199.
6. Arnold Schoenberg, *Theory of Harmony*, trans. Roy E. Carter (Berkeley and Los Angeles, 1978), p. 303. Further references to this work will be given in the text.
7. Reinhold Brinkmann, "Zur Entstehung der Zwölftontechnik," in *Bericht über den Internationalen Musikwissenschaftlichen Kongreß Bonn 1970*, ed. Carl Dahlhaus et al. (Kassel, 1970), pp. 284–88.
8. Arnold Schönberg, *Sämtliche Werke*, Series B, vol. 4 (Mainz and Vienna, 1975).

9. See also, more recently, Martina Sichardt, *Die Entstehung der Zwölftonmethode Arnold Schönbergs* (Mainz, 1990).

10. Rufer D 100; Christensen Mus 299.

11. Heinrich Schenker, *Der Tonwille*, vol. 1 (Vienna and Leipzig, 1921), p. 39.

12. Johann Sebastian Bach, *Clavierwerke*, Kritische Ausgabe. . .von Dr. H. Bischoff, vol. 5 (Leipzig, 1883), p. 40, n. 19.

13. Arnold Schoenberg, "Bach," in *Style and Idea*, ed. Leonard Stein (New York, 1975), pp. 393–97.

14. Schoenberg, "Bach," pp. 393–94.

15. Rufer D 84; Christensen Mus 214

16. Draft of June 11, 1923; Rufer D 18; Christensen Mus 40.

17. August 8, 1936; Rufer D 124 (with obliterated names); Christensen 374.

18. *The New Bach Reader*, ed. Hans T. David and Arthur Mendel, rev. Christoph Wolff (New York, 1998), p. 226.

19. Erich Schenk, *Barock bei Beethoven* (Bonn, 1937), p. 177ff.

The Compressed Symphony:

On the Historical Content of

Schoenberg's Op. 9

REINHOLD BRINKMANN

TRANSLATED BY IRENE ZEDLACHER

Schoenberg considered the First Chamber Symphony, Op. 9, one of
his most important compositions. He wrote to Alexander Siloti in
1914: "It is my ewe lamb, one of my very best works, and yet up to
now (owing to bad performances!!) it has hardly been understood by
anyone."[1] However, the work's difficult reception history is not
explained by poor performances alone but rather is caused by the
innermost constitution of the work itself. And it is this constitution
that legitimizes the work's historical and aesthetic importance. The
historical place of the work—a place it fills consciously—determines
the difficulty of the encounter precisely because of the work's uncompromising embrace of the notion of difficulty itself, as defined
by comprehensibility. The aural impression—and we have to start
with this experience—does not confirm the "clarity and transparency"
achieved with "solo instruments of opposite tone color" correctly (but
only theoretically) claimed by an encyclopedia article.[2] Rather, the
piece seems unwieldy and complex. This is because the individual
lines are emphasized by a distinctly delimiting instrumentation. For
example, in the multi-voiced polyphony of the large development section no line is ever allowed to become secondary, and every line
presses to the foreground. And because every line can be heard at
every moment, the enormous effort behind this unruly complexity is
on display. The aesthetic experience, the immense irritation that the
process of active concentration arouses in the listener, obviously is still

(even today) occasioned by the above-mentioned process of compression. I will proceed in this article by beginning to describe that element of compression as it occurs in discrete elements of the composition, that is, in (1) harmony, (2) themes, (3) polyphony, (4) instrumentation, (5) form, and (6) tone. I will then attempt to define the historical consciousness articulated in the specific compositional style of the Chamber Symphony and in that context I shall return to the philological issues to be considered beforehand.

The Chamber Symphony, Op. 9, that we know today and that is treated here is in many ways—but in no way marginally—not the work of 1906. The facts important to my line of argument present themselves roughly as follows.[3] The first printed score from 1912 departs in some essential aspects from the printed score that is commercially available today. The divergences concern the realm of dynamics and agogics, but primarily affect the instrumental complexity. Moreover, the first edition explicitly states the possibility of doubling the individual voices. Before 1918 Schoenberg began to enter numerous corrections in his personal copy of the first print; these involve primarily extensive cutting of the multiple voices in sections of the main sonata movement. This corrected version was obviously the basis for rehearsals and performances that took place before the creation of the Society for Private Musical Performances of 1918–19, and later at the Society itself.[4] In connection with those concerts, Schoenberg made further extensive changes in the dynamic-agogic realm in the individual voices. All corrections were then included in the 1924 edition of the revised score in the Philharmonia series.

What is of interest here, though, is the structure of the work as shown in the first printed version, and the tendency toward revision. Some examples:

• In m. 10 the main theme of the cello is doubled in the English horn with the whole tone series G♯–A♯–C on the first three quarter notes and the triplets D–F♯–D on the last quarter note, while flute and clarinet complete the whole tone series—the basis of the theme—to augmented triads on top with the line E–F♯–G♯–A♯ or B–D–E–F♯. In his copy of the score Schoenberg cut all instrumental and sonic additions in the three instruments.

• Similarly, in the first version of mm. 11–13, the secondary voices of the bass clarinet and the bass are continued by bassoon and contrabassoon beyond the E-major entry in m. 11. This instrumental doubling is also cut in Schoenberg's personal copy.

- Parallel cuts appear in m. 12, where oboe and English horn originally had executed a figure following the cello theme (analogous to m. 13). An even more intrusive cut appears in m. 15, where oboe, English horn, clarinet, bassoon, contrabassoon, and second horn had further split up and enriched the amalgam of voices.

- Extensive reductions also affect—to name but a few more instances—mm. 26–29 where flute and oboe in the original version had doubled other voices throughout; neither did the two clarinets alternate. A similar reduction occurs in mm. 35 (end)–38 in oboe, English horn and contrabassoon. Particularly extensive cuts were made in mm. 62–67, where in the first printed version all the wind instruments had participated in the musical events almost constantly and without rests. The reduction, in contrast, resulted in a lighter sounding ensemble. (A cut in the first violins made in Schoenberg's personal copy is withdrawn from the later printing.)

The tendency expressed by the individual revisions is clear: all changes are directed toward increased transparency and stress on the particular color of a voice in the instrumentation. The overall result is an emphasis on the solo character of the instrumentation. But at the same time, polyphonic relationships emerge more distinctly, especially where originally an additional instrument had traced the central motif of the main voice but deviated slightly because of a difference in rhythm or articulation and thus had been given its own weight as if it were an independent line. In some places, as in m. 10, a harmonic complexity is withdrawn. Whatever Schoenberg's remark on a four-hand piano reduction for Op. 9, related by Rufer, may have referred to and whatever its date might be, it fits the tendency of the revisions: "That is all much too overloaded!!! There should always be just half as many parts!"[5]

When I now turn to the final score from the perspective mentioned above, the facts of the work's genesis should stay in our minds.

1. Harmony

Decades later Webern would recount in his lectures, intended for a general audience, the exhilarating impression made by the Chamber Symphony at the time of its creation:

In 1906 Schoenberg came back from a stay in the country, bringing the Chamber Symphony. It made a colossal impression. I'd been his pupil for three years, and immediately felt "You must write something like that, too!" Under the influence of the work I wrote a sonata movement the very next day. In that movement I reached the farthest limits of tonality.[6]

According to this statement, for Webern the central progressive element of the work was its treatment of harmony. In another context, I have pointed out how Schoenberg himself had discussed the work's harmonic construction, particularly the use of fourths.[7] He wrote in *Harmonielehre*:

> Then, not until long afterwards, in my Kammersymphonie, did I take up the fourth chords again, without recalling the previous case [Op. 5], and without having got to know in the meantime the music of Debussy or Dukas. Here the fourths, springing from an entirely different expressive urge (stormy jubilation), shape themselves into a definite horn theme, spread themselves out architectonically over the whole piece, and place their stamp on everything that happens. Thus it turns out that they do not appear here merely as melody or as a purely impressionistic chord effect; their character permeates the total harmonic structure, and they are chords like all others.[8]

And in a later program note he states: "The harmonic idea of the piece is exhibited at once: the fourth-tone row in melodic and harmonic relation to the whole-tone scale."[9] Hermann Erpf's well-known theoretical insight is much more comprehensive:

> In the Chamber Symphony Schoenberg makes not incidental, but thematically structural, use of interval relations between whole-tone, minor-seventh and fourth chords and between major-third and whole-tone chords; of the extension of fourth chords that have only a few notes into twelve-tone chords; and of the possibilities of combining functional chords with symmetrical ones.[10]

It is important how this was achieved. The status of Op. 9 in the history of harmony as a reference point between tonality and atonality has been discussed before.[11] So as not to repeat myself I will only recount the results of that analysis. First, the individual steps of an extended cadence are loaded, systematically and within the smallest space, with all the means to explode tonality that were available at this time to Schoenberg's creative mind. Second is the unifying force of the cadences themselves preserved with emphatic constancy. Such compression without any reduction in complexity consciously brings the already precarious development of harmonic tonality to a critical point. Important for Schoenberg's musical thought finally is the interdependence of vertical and horizontal lines, as can be seen in the side-by-side use of fourth chords and successive thematic fourths at the beginning of the symphony. Schoenberg himself explained this:

> The climax of my first period is definitely reached in the Kammersymphonie, Op. 9. Here is established a very intimate reciprocation between melody and harmony, in that both connect remote relations of the tonality into a perfect unity, draw logical consequences from the problems they attempt to solve, and simultaneously make great progress in the direction of the emancipation of the dissonance.[12]

In the above-mentioned lectures, Webern identified this new cohesive integration of the musical materials using the vertical and horizontal dimensions as the central idea of the Schoenberg School. This idea was—as is well-known—crucial in the formulation of twelve-tone music, for which Schoenberg envisioned a "musical space" where all dimensions became equal. In terms of compositional technique, the Chamber Symphony has to be regarded as the first decisive step toward this goal. In the passage quoted above Schoenberg identified the logical result of the horizontal/vertical congruence of Op. 9 as harmonic progress. But equally important is what happens with the contours of the themes. And with that I arrive at my second analytical perspective.

2. Themes

In his early Schoenberg biography Egon Wellesz correctly observed: "Here Schönberg had already found a way to a concise form of theme construction, the like of which he had not quite fully achieved in the string quartet [Op. 7]."[13] The First String Quartet, the backdrop for this observation, was Schoenberg's first work without a literary basis. However, the composition's musical proclivity is toward a latent musico-dramatic character, particularly in the expressive gestures of the rich and spacious themes and thematic complexes and in its sometimes associative (but sometimes also very strict) thematic connections. The themes of Op. 9, on the other hand, are all stark, brief, concise, and each possessed of a clearly defined character. Wellesz recognized that fact. Two further aspects seem more important, however. The first is the result of the interdependence of vertical and horizontal line discussed above: the themes of the Chamber Symphony tend to act as the substratum of a theory. The horn motive at the beginning is nothing but the open and direct unfolding of a series of fourths; the main theme that follows is a representation of the whole-tone scale enriched by figuration. This quality lends the themes their impact. The second aspect is the function of the meticulously constructed themes in the multi-voiced texture of the piece, its polyphony. With this, my third analytical perspective, we have arrived at a nerve center of the piece.

3. Polyphony

"The main difficulty in the chamber symphony is the great amount of polyphony," wrote Schoenberg in 1922.[14] Consider first the closing section of the exposition, which is introduced by the combination of a transition theme and a secondary theme with a new theme, all in triple counterpoint, to which, when the constellation is repeated for the second time, a fourth voice is added in the horn, a voice that itself contains elements from the main thematic group. Then consider the three three-voice canonic structures of the third section of the development, which consists of three strettos using the transition theme (initially entering first four and then two quarter notes apart, whereby in the second configuration a fourth voice, derived from the main theme, is added, with the result that the second and third configurations relate to each other as fourfold counterpoint). "An enormous number [Unzahl] of imitative entrances" (as Alban Berg formulated it in his analysis of Op. 9[15]) of the other themes is added. (Berg's thematic analysis is a reference point for this part of my discussion.) Three aspects of this intensified polyphony seem significant:

1. The dissolution of functional harmony and particularly the use of equidistant sounds demand a legitimization of the chord structures different from that which "harmonic" analysis could provide.

"If harmony of the voices can no longer be understood in tonal terms, it has at least to be motivated by counterpoint."[16] This refers to the relationship of polyphony to the evolution of harmony discussed in section 1.

2. The four-voice polyphony allows—at least implicitly—the entire thematic material, all the exposed musical characters, to be present in compressed form in the smallest space. Thus the wealth of meaning of the whole is actually present virtually in every one of its elements. In this context it should be pointed out that in the recapitulation/finale not only are themes of the exposition repeated, but elements of the "slow movement" are included as well—a tendency analogous to the one discussed. We should also mention Schoenberg's famous preface to Webern's Bagatelles for String Quartet (Vienna, 1924), which understands the piece's brevity as an example of compressed and extremely concentrated length: one gesture is said to stand in for the entire novel. The permeation of polyphony in the structure of the Chamber Symphony —the transformation of succession into simultaneity—is born of the same spirit. This is the relationship between polyphony and thematic design discussed in section 2.

3. The density of the polyphony and the rigorousness of the thematic contours are direct correlates of the mode of instrumentation. This brings me to my fourth analytical perspective.

4. Instrumentation

There is, first, the soloistic character of the instrumentation. Egon Wellesz again touched on one of the decisive points:

> The evolutionary tendency to replace the massive effect of the large orchestra with the thinner, more piercing sound of solo instrumentation, in order to make the thematic and motivic fabric more readily recognizable can be detected in the orchestration of Mahler's songs as well as in Schoenberg's Chamber Symphony. . . . However, the true breakthrough of a distinctive chamber symphony style came only with works which had abandoned symphonic methods altogether, that is, in connection with a tendency that pushed toward innovation in the creation of form.[17]

Three points can be made about this topic:

1. The individual thematic penetration by each voice corresponds to its soloistic formulation; the clarification of each voice in the polyphonic instrumental texture corresponds to the elaboration of contrasts in color. This is, as Wellesz rightly stated, a decisive moment in the history of composition:

> His labours at the *Chamber-Symphony* gave Schoenberg a decisive impulse in search of a new style of orchestratation. All that he has orchestrated since the *Chamber-Symphony* bears the stamp of being written for solo-players; that is to say, every instrument in the orchestra attains to importance and is treated in accordance with its nature. The problems to be faced in a composition for ten wind instruments and five strings had the effect of maturating this new principle in orchestration, and quite early in these works they led to a most highly individual colouring.[18]

Certainly, the idea of soloistic orchestration was already the basis for the first version of the Chamber Symphony. However, the genesis of the different versions of the score, as discussed above, reveals that it crystallized in its final form only after Schoenberg worked on or maybe had already composed the pieces cited by Wellesz. The "authentic" instrumental version of the First Chamber Symphony thus moves closer to the context of the Four Orchestral Songs, Op. 22 (composed between 1913 and 1916), which are each scored differently and have a much greater soloistic fragmentation of instrumental color, as in the division of the string choir (violins, cellos) into as many as six parts in the first song.[19]

2. A significant dimension of the Chamber Symphony is the actual hearing experience referred to previously: the brittle, astringent, even intractable character of the sound. It is one of the symphony's most oppositional elements and is based, in terms of instrumentation (as measured against the traditional concept of a beautiful orchestral sound), in the disproportionate balance between sections—i.e., the predominance of wind instruments over strings, but not in that alone. Theodor W. Adorno mentioned other factors: "The *First Chamber Symphony*—with its preponderance of the woodwinds, the excessive demands made upon the string soloists, and the

compressed linear figures—sounds as if Schoenberg had never advanced beyond the lush and radiant Wagnerian orchestra."[20]

The compressed sound, which characterizes the work almost throughout, does indeed rest on its intricate polyphony and the extreme thematic contrasts. Rarely (only at the beginning of both the second subject of the exposition and the slow movement) does a voice have enough space to fulfill itself melodically; there are always equally significant counter- or at least thematically secondary voices demanding definition and differentiation. Metaphorically speaking: the price of individualization is the necessity of self-assertion, therefore relentless competition. And all of it is related simultaneously to the increasingly sharper harmonic edge of the movement. The work's specific sound character arises from the interdependence of all these factors, which are predetermined by the particular character of the orchestration.

3. The background for this sound strategy is Schoenberg's anticlassicism. At first glance the idea of balance, the interdependence of all dimensions, appears to be classical in origin. But in Schoenberg's case we are not dealing with a principle of economy that demands that complexity in one plane has to be balanced with simplicity in another. Just the opposite: everything has to be developed to the same degree.[21] That is, if harmony consciously is advanced to a critical point, it had to be accomplished by an analogous thematic concentration, which in turn is connected to the work's enormous polyphonic structure. And all of this corresponds again to the specific style of instrumentation. That which is put forward collectively has to be understood as requiring unity to be grasped at every moment of the composition. As to the unity of the whole, everything relates to a form whose signature is expansive wealth on the one hand, and concentration on the other. With this I come to my fifth and next-to-last analytical perspective.

5. Form

The Chamber Symphony draws consequences from the nineteenth-century problem of symphonic form as understood by Schoenberg's notion of tradition, and declares this problem to be solved. In parenthesis: on this level—and in contrast to other aspects of the composition—the Chamber Symphony is an endpoint. If we were to establish the historical place of Op. 9 with regard to ideas of innovation based on the relation of the individual levels of the work to each other, the work could be positioned as follows. The problem of form in the nineteenth-century sense of the search for overall unity in a multimovement work is solved. The problem of tonality is brought to a crisis point. It will be solved in immediately succeeding works (Opp. 10, 14, and 15). The individualization of sound color is clarified; it will become crucial at a later stage. The problem of the emancipation of structure (which I shall not discuss here) appears, as in Op. 7, only in extraterritorial moments, even though the wealth of counterpoint within moments of compression indicates possible solutions. The First Chamber Symphony thus is a focal point for differing levels of innovation.

The problem of symphonic form in the nineteenth century is well known and does not need a more thorough discussion here. However, the issue can be articulated superficially as the problem of unity in a multimovement work. The different approaches to a solution are well known. Roughly, we can distinguish two models. First, the classicist approach that seeks to establish unity through the musical material alone, primarily through motivic-thematic connections and the character of closure. Form here becomes the problem of the finale, which achieves its status through summarization of the material. This pattern applies, since Beethoven, both to sonata-form first movements (the recapitulation as endpoint) and to the symphony as a whole (the Fifth Symphony, with its linkage of scherzo to last movement; the Ninth Symphony, with its collective recapitulation of themes and the vocal culmination in the finale). Bruckner's finales are probably the most explicit example of a combination of both tendencies (as in the finale of the Fifth Symphony, in which all previous movements are cited in ways that make the main theme the result of them all, and where we find linking of themes on the one hand, and hymnic, almost eschatological final culmination on the other). The second model is that of the New German School: resolution through a unifying third dimension, the program. The symphony becomes a symphonic poem, as in Liszt and Strauss. A possible result of both models is the merger, or the contamination, of the multi-movement work into a one-movement work. That is the point at which Schoenberg the composer of instrumental music enters the picture.

As is well-known, Schoenberg's first two instrumental works, Opp. 4 and 5, are one-movement works following the New German School model of program music. Op. 5—at times also Op. 4 (as Pfannkuch, following Berg's analytical approach, has made plain[22])—simultaneously shows debt to the first model as well. This trend continues in the

First String Quartet, Op. 7, and in the Chamber Symphony, Op. 9, in an increasingly concentrated manner.[23] Two formal schemata can elucidate this point (see figure 1).

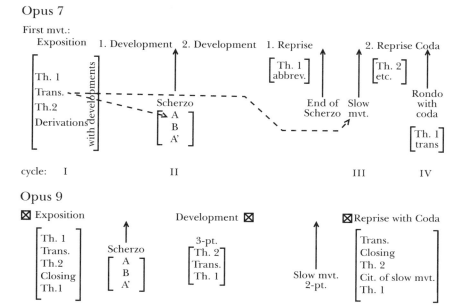

Figure 1: Form overviews of First String Quartet, Op. 7, and Chamber Symphony, Op. 9

A comparison of the two schematic outlines reveals the distinct and transparent formal configuration of the Chamber Symphony in comparison with the String Quartet. The pronounced thematic individuality corresponds to the individuality of the formal sections. In the quartet, however, the sections of the sonata form—as well as the thematic characters—are interlaced in manifold ways. The development, where everything seems related to everything, corresponds to the extremely complex individual organization of an already complicated form in general. The step from the quartet toward the symphony discloses a process of more pronounced outlining and integration. (Also notable is the conscious change in the thematic groupings in the development and, above all, in the recapitulation in relationship to the exposition.)

Schoenberg himself later thought about the path he took in his compositional odyssey. In 1938 he wrote about the First String Quartet: "It is composed in one very long movement, without the conventional interruptions after each movement. Influenced by Beethoven's C# minor Quartet, by Liszt's Piano Sonata, Bruckner and Gustav Mahler's symphonies, we young composers believed this to be the artistic way to compose."[24] From the distance of later years, in 1950 he reflected once more: "In accommodation to the faith of the time, this large form was to include all the four characteristics of the sonata type in one single, uninterrupted movement."[25] The term "faith of the time" is not accidental. Hidden in it is the idea that music history was a history of compositional problems that needed to be solved.

The essay "About Music Criticism" from 1909 contains sentences that indirectly reveal a consciousness of the Chamber Symphony's historic status in the evolution of musical form:

> Our music critics are in very truth unfit to be even canon-fodder in the battles of art. They wailed about dissonances while the problem of the one-movement symphony swept by; they wailed about dissonances while new possibilities of melodic development were showing themselves; they even wailed about dissonances when none was there.[26]

According to Schoenberg's own words, the evolution from Op. 7 to Op. 9 was directed toward the liquidation of the traditional "problem of form" through an extreme working out of the issues by adherence to the principle of economy and concentration:

> It was one of the first symptoms [of the trend toward a new music] that the period of greatly expanded forms—which had been initiated by Beethoven's C# minor quartet—was passing, and that a new period aimed for shorter forms, in size and content and also in expression.[27]

But this emphasis on concentration and integration was—in a positive way—a polemical one. It was directed, *expressis verbis*, against the monumental form of the contemporary symphony. Schoenberg writes:

> The length of the earlier compositions was one of the features that linked me with the style of my predecessors, Bruckner and Mahler, whose symphonies often exceed an hour, and

Strauss, whose symphonic poems last a half hour. I had become tired—not as a listener but as a composer—of writing music of such length. . .

Students of my works will recognize how in my career the tendency to condense has gradually changed my entire style of composition.[28]

In this sense Opp. 7 and 9 fit together. The formal development of Schoenberg's music from this phase is motivated by the critique of the large symphony, or less superficially: his music is meant as an alternative to the worldview of Bruckner and Mahler, to the epic and expansive nature of the symphony of late Romanticism. The nerve center of this counterproject is the reappropriation of subjectivity.

A preliminary summary: the burden placed on this compressed symphony consists not only in taking up the central issues of musical evolution of the nineteenth century and bringing them to a conclusion. The symphony reaches the limits of new music "with exultant jubilation." Furthermore, this does not occur in a work of monumental epic scope but within the dimensions of a piece hardly twenty minutes long, a piece that retains the complexity of the grand scale despite its diminished size, which virtually attempts to concentrate epic succession into simultaneity all in one single moment. If anything in music can be called expressionist it is the Chamber Symphony, Op. 9, by Arnold Schoenberg.

With this I arrive at the sixth and last point on my list of analytical perspectives.

6. Tone

In his *Harmonielehre*, Schoenberg described the horn theme at the beginning in expressive language. In the first edition (1911) he calls it "stürmisch und aufwärtsstrebend." In the revised edition (1922) he characterizes it as "stürmischer Jubel." That is accurate, but only to a point. This (almost Straussian) moment of energy (the marking "schwungvoll" in fact appears quite frequently in the piece) is only one side of the coin. The other side (explicitly so and particularly at the beginning, where the horn theme merges into the sharply tautened melody of the strings) is the insistence and compression of sound, the forced nature of this music as already alluded to in the discussion of the orchestration. (This quality is evident particularly in the hectic melodic gestures of the scherzo and development sections.)

The combination of expression and reflexivity seems to be responsible for this effect. "Stürmischer Jubel"—the horn theme certainly expresses that. At the same time it is also, with its construction in fourths and the relation of those notes to the harmonic idea of the whole and to the historical situation of music in general, a piece of pure theory. Schoenberg's reflexivity aims at two things. First, at the historical continuum, at the identification of his own place in a historical process that was considered logical and from which one had to draw consequences. ("While the problem of the one-movement symphony swept by," critics complained about dissonances; Schoenberg's reproach is that historical awareness was lacking.) Second, reflexivity becomes part of each aspect of the aesthetic structure. No single note remains that is not essential to the process of integration; that is, every note becomes individualized. Both points can be understood in a historical context.

The dichotomy of chamber music and symphony (behind it stands the dichotomy of the private and public sphere) is part of the special character of nineteenth-century self-analysis. Two examples suffice, one from 1865, the other from 1882:

> Equally explicit differences can be noticed in concert and in chamber music. The former presents its content through many different genres, with large masses of sound and dynamic effect, with various shadings of color, etc. Chamber music has no means of such diversity available and therefore has to strive to replace what is lacking in tonal variety, or in volume, etc., by offering the most artful creations . . . Orchestral music paints with fullness and scale using rich colors; chamber music creates a delicate ink drawing or a lithograph. . . .
>
> Chamber music had to compensate through quality for the quantity of effect which church music, and theater music as well, could create through external action on the one hand, and the fixed meaning of the word on the other. It had itself to become a language whose fine dialectic quality could offer the connoisseur a surrogate for the captivating al fresco traits and the wealth of tone color not only of those two style genres, but of the concert style as well as developed since Haydn and particularly since Beethoven.... It is obvious that . . . through such renunciation of help from any exterior stage effect and dramatic action, music suddenly was thrown back ¬onto itself and interest was focused on the sound itself. After

music's emancipation from the word the expressive quality of music had to be increased continually to finally allow pure instrumental music to stand on its own feet. [29]

It does not matter here if such evaluations are ideologically colored, that is, if they cannot be contradicted by the works themselves or by performance practice, as Carl Dahlhaus pointed out in his essay "Brahms and the Idea of Chamber Music."[30] What is important is that such contrasts (as well as their social background) confirmed Schoenberg's own experience, the encounters in turn-of-the-century Vienna that would determine his later musical ideas. Schoenberg's reaction to the historical situation was to attempt to invalidate these established contrasts in his own work. All his early work—as he himself conceded—is part of that context. From our point of view, it meant the reconciliation of chamber and symphonic music. The way it was done in Schoenberg's work is significant.

Schoenberg's answer was individualization. Technically it meant the annulment of the general compulsory conventions of tonal harmony, and the assignment of sonic structure to specific individual solutions arrived at through the "mental power of the great composer." Individualization of the voices was achieved through concise thematic material and solo instrumentation. A tendential freedom to create individualistically without "appropriations of external conventions" (in Adorno's words) resulted historically in the transformation of symphonic music into chamber music. Hans Werner Henze characterized this as follows:

> The significance of chamber music is that in dealing with the intimate it can attain to the ineffable. Chamber music conceives itself as a world of sound that has external boundaries but no internal ones. It is music to reflect upon and develop with one's own thoughts, to a far greater extent than that heard in large concert halls and opera houses, which must aim at more direct effects than music that is in fact addressed only to the players, and demands much practice and patient rehearsal.[31]

The historical place of the Chamber Symphony becomes apparent through its rejection of an epic worldview and by its withdrawal into the subject. The artistic subject of this symphony no longer sees itself capable of experiencing reality as unity and encompassing and transcending it with one grand design. Only through extreme immersion into the self, through grounding artistic production in the isolated subject alone, does the artistic subject attempt to preserve its identity. This has to be understood as the general artistic problem characterizing the decades around the turn of the century. The problematic situation of artistic consciousness in turn can be taken as representative of the historical condition of bourgeois subjectivity in general.

However, before I pursue my topic in that direction with some sketchy concluding remarks, I have to return to Schoenberg's inner biography via the philological facts regarding the Chamber Symphony recounted in the first part of this essay. The revisions show that Schoenberg's Op. 9 was the first decisive step on the route toward "concentration" described above. More specifically, it mirrored the pre-conditions of historical change. The definitive "concentrated" version of the work however reminds us at the same time of a new beginning that appeared only in other, later works. One might say that Op. 9—to say it in formulaic ways—simultaneously produces and presupposes atonality. This means, on a more general level of intellectual history, that Schoenberg's artistic response to the crisis of the subject, evident at the time the Chamber Symphony was created in 1906, came to its conscious fruition only in the phase of free atonality. Historiography and philology do not stand so far apart from one another.

A collection of essays by the Viennese writer Hermann Bahr published in 1891 contains the following sentences:

> Sensations, nothing but sensations, unconnected momentary images of fleeting events on the nerves—this characterizes the last phase into which truth has driven literature. It will not reach its extreme form for a while. . . . And only when this inner naturalism finally will have copied and written out all that anxiety, just as the picturesque exhausts external reality, only then will this phase be done with again. But the principle of truth in literature will be done with as well, empty and done with, because it will have played its last trump cards and exhausted its last possibilities, just as in painting, which also began initially with celebratory courage to conquer reality, only to retreat beaten and despondent soon after the recognition of the illusion of vision. It lost in the end the sense of form in mere specks of color. So too literature lost the self in the multitude of sensations. For self and form never can be established and we have no guarantee of their existence other than this peculiar longing which will not be stilled. . . .[32]

No matter how one wants to judge Bahr as a representative phenomenon,[33] he knew how to assimilate everything new briskly, and he was therefore equipped with a specific sensor for the turn of an era—as well as for its dangers. Bahr's writings thus seem particularly articulate witnesses for the change experienced in Vienna's artistic scene around 1900, and in the German-speaking world as a whole. The topics he wrote about in his essays of the 1890s—European subjectivism and aestheticism—are important for our context, Schoenberg's turn "to the internal." The critical literary commentary on the above-quoted passage rightly stresses Bahr's "unusual anticipatory quality."[34] Only about a decade later will the connection between the "loss of form" and the "loss of the self," for which the critical relation between interior and exterior, self and reality forms a background, become central to artistic thought. Hofmannsthal's oft-quoted Chandos Letter from 1902 portrays the disintegration of the experience of reality, the "estrangement" of "things." He reflects them in the artistic realm as loss of language:

> For me everything disintegrated into parts, those parts again into parts; no longer would anything let itself be encompassed by one idea. Single words floated round me; they congealed into eyes which stared at me and into which I was forced to stare back—whirlpools which gave me vertigo and, reeling incessantly, led into the void.[35]

Loss of identity as the result of an alienated reality, which withdraws or seems to withdraw from the subject, is essential also for the compositional strategy in Musil's novel *Die Verwirrungen des Zöglings Törleß* (1906). The Maeterlinck quote at the beginning brings that immediately into focus:

> In some strange way we devalue things as soon as we give utterance to them. We believe to have dived to the utmost depths of the abyss, and yet when we return to the surface the drop of water clinging to our pale fingertips no longer resembles the sea from which it came. We believe we have discovered a treasure trove of marvelous riches, yet when we emerge again into daylight we see that all we have brought back are fake stones and chips of glass. But the treasure goes on glimmering in the dark, unchanged.[36]

Gert Mattenklott has shown how in Musil's early novel internalization is the result of the experience of a "hiatus between language and thing, between experience and object, between perception and reality. . . , which only can be bridged through longing,"[37] a seemingly a priori opposition that cannot be resolved by the historical subject. He has shown how and why the "subjective factor" moves into the center of attention; how a theory of alienation of object and self places an interior "reality," taken as essential, against the exterior one. Ultimately this interior reality is positioned as the only authority. Schoenberg's famous aphorism from 1909, which defines art as a "cry of desperation from those who experience in their own being the fate of humankind,"[38] essentially does the same. It is true, the aphorism (a confession) puts into words the necessity to "confront" reality, but it unequivocally invokes the primacy of the "internal." The artist has "to close his eyes to perceive what the senses do not convey, to see inside what only seems to happen outside. And inside . . . is the movement of the world. . . ."[39]

Schoenberg's grounding of artistic production in subjectivity without a doubt was part of the historical context outlined here through passages quoted from the work of Bahr, Hofmannsthal, and Musil. His aphorism concludes this in most extreme terms, and it is also represented by his evolution from *Gurrelieder* to the symphonic works, to chamber music and the preeminence of poetry at the threshold to atonality, with the Chamber Symphony as a decisive station on the way. And this trajectory would have to be extended beyond the first decade of the new century to Ernst Bloch's *Geist der Utopie* from 1918 (second edition, 1923), a philosophic draft that "was created in the last days of expressionism and reflected the creation of its ornament."[40] It is introduced programmatically with the "incipit vita nova":

> The *internal* path, also called encounter with the self, leads so deeply towards the preparation of the inner word, without which any glance to the outside has to remain invalid; and no outside magnet, no outside power can attract the inner word to come to the fore or can help it to break free from the errors of the world.[41]

Without being able to discuss, within this historical development, the diverse stylistic trends (neo-Romanticism, Impressionism, Jugendstil, Expressionism . . .) with their subjectivity and their very specific variance in the individual arts, we can nevertheless assume a unity or continuity in the artistic experience of the world and the self from the end of the nineteenth century into the third decade of the twentieth century. In such historical dimensions the turn of the Schoenberg circle toward atonality around 1908–10, generally represented in musicology as an epoch-making event, is relativized. A really decisive historical caesura comes only after World War I (in Austria after the end of the Habsburg monarchy) in the 1920s.[42] (This is not the place to show that in a musical-compositional context.) Carl Einstein's novel *Bebuquin* (written between 1906 and 1909) deals with the crisis in the form of the self of the "highly consolidated intellect" by combining inner bewilderment and shock with critical distance, but still in the form of a poetic presentation. More than twenty years later, the draft of the pamphlet "Die Fabrikation der Fiktionen" (The fabrication of fictions) by the same author, subtitled tellingly and not without reason "Eine Verteidigung der Wirklichkeit" (A defense of reality), vehemently criticized intellectual individualism.[43] Einstein's turn (in his later terminology) from "private mythical conception" to a "collectively usable reality" paradigmatically explains a change beginning in the 1920s. It also marks the end of an era.

Schoenberg's artistic stance as I have tried to determine it from the particulars of the First Chamber Symphony has to be seen in the context of this history of ideas. In the sociopolitical context it has become fashionable to describe the turn of the subject onto itself as an escapist phenomenon, and then to pass judgment. But such turn to the "interior" is in fact typical for the nineteenth-century German intelligentsia and is implied in Goethe's concept of renunciation, in Wagner's shift after the 1848 revolution, as in Schoenberg's founding of atonality out of the self-discovery of the I. To address the historical relevance of such processes of internalization appropriately I prefer to speak of concentration rather than flight. And I believe that Hans Werner Henze's statement quoted above relates directly to my topic and is valid by analogy beyond the realm of music: "It is music to reflect upon and develop with one's own thoughts."

NOTES

This article appeared originally as "Die gepreßte Sinfonie: Zum geschichtlichen Gehalt von Schönbergs Opus 9," in *Gustav Mahler: Sinfonie und Wirklichkeit*, ed. Otto Kolleritsch (Graz, 1977), pp. 133–56.

1. Arnold Schoenberg, *Letters*, ed. Erwin Stein, trans. Eithne Wilkins and Ernst Kaiser (London, 1964), p. 52.
2. Wilfried Brennecke, "Symphonie," *Die Musik in Geschichte und Gegenwart*, vol. 12 (Kassel, 1965), p. 1857.
3. For information on problems of source material and reworkings, see the critical report prepared by Christian M. Schmidt in Arnold Schoenberg, *Sämtliche Werke*, Series B, vol. 11.
4. See the report by Erwin Ratz, "Die zehn öffentlichen Proben zur Kammersymphonie im Juni 1918 und der 'Verein für musikalische Privataufführungen,' in *Arnold Schönberg: Gedenkausstellug 1974*, ed. Ernst Hilmar, pp. 68–70.
5. "Das ist alles viel zu überladen!!! Immer nur halb so viel Stimmen!" Cited in Josef Rufer, *The Works of Arnold Schoenberg*, trans. Dika Newlin (New York, 1962), p. 29.
6. Anton Webern, *The Path to the New Music* (London, 1975), p. 48.
7. Reinhold Brinkmann, *Arnold Schönberg: Drei Klavierstücke, op. 11*, Beihefte zum Archiv für Musikwissenschaft, vol. 7 (Wiesbaden, 1969), pp. 5–8.
8. Schoenberg, *Theory of Harmony*, trans. Roy E. Carter (Berkeley and Los Angeles, 1978), pp. 403–04.
9. Schoenberg, liner notes to Columbia M2S 709, p. 32.
10. Hermann Erpf, *Studien zur Harmonie- und Klangtechnik der neueren Musik* (Leipzig, 1927), pp. 75ff.
11. See Reinhold Brinkmann, "Max Reger und die neue Musik," *Max Reger, 1873 bis 1973. Ein Symposium* (Wiesbaden, 1974), pp. 90ff.
12. Arnold Schoenberg, *Style and Idea*, ed. Leonard Stein (New York, 1975), p. 84.
13. Egon Wellesz, *Arnold Schönberg: The Formative Years* (London, 1921), p. 106.
14. Schoenberg, *Letters*, pp. 76–77.
15. Alban Berg, *Arnold Schoenberg: Chamber Symphony, op. 9*, trans. Mark de Voto, *Journal of the Arnold Schoenberg Institute* 16 (1993): 255.
16. Carl Dahlhaus, "Brahms und die Idee der Kammermusik," *Neue Zeitschrift für Musik* 134 (1973): 560. Schoenberg's words at the end of *Harmonielehre* and the formulation "justification through melody alone" in the third edition of 1922 (p. 466) articulate the logical conclusion from a connection that had already been realized in composition. The study cited in footnote 7 quotes related remarks by Busoni.
17. Egon Wellesz, *Die neue Instrumentation*, vol. 2 (Berlin, 1929), p. 151.
18. Wellesz, *Arnold Schönberg*, p. 106.
19. See Reinhold Brinkmann, "Schönbergs Lieder," in *Arnold Schönberg*, [Publication of the Archive of the] Academy of Arts Berlin, Berliner Festwochen 1974 (Berlin, 1974), p. 49.
20. Theodor Adorno, *Philosophy of Modern Music*, trans. Anne Mitchell and Wesley Blomster (New York, 1980), p. 122.
21. Brinkmann, *Schönberg: Drei Klavierstücke*, pp. 11ff.
22. Wilhelm Pfannkuch, "Zur Thematik und Form in Schönbergs Streichsextett," *Festschrift Friedrich Blume*, ed. Anna Amalie Abert and Wilhelm Pfannkuch (Kassel, 1963), pp. 258–71.

23. See also Adorno's remark in the essay, "Zur Vorgeschichte der Reihenkomposition" (1959) from *Klangfiguren*, in *Gesammelte Schriften*, vol. 16, ed. Rolf Tiedemann (Frankfurt, 1978), pp. 72–76.

24. Album notes for private recordings made by the Kolisch Quartet in 1938; reprinted in Fred Steiner, "A History of the First Complete Recordings of the Schoenberg String Quartet," *Journal of the Arnold Schoenberg Institute* 2 (1978): 132.

25. Schoenberg, "Notes on the Four String Quartets," in *Schoenberg, Berg, Webern: The String Quartets*, ed. Ursula von Rauchhaupt (Hamburg, 1971), p. 35.

26. Schoenberg, *Style and Idea*, p. 194.

27. Quoted in *Schoenberg, Berg, Webern*, p. 160.

28. Liner notes to Columbia M2S 709, p. 32.

29. Quoted in Erich Reimer, "Kammermusik," *Handwörterbuch der musikalischen Terminologie*, vol. 3 (Stuttgart, n.d.), pp. 11–12 (Dommer, 1865; Tottmann, in Ersch and Gruber, 1882).

30. Dahlhaus, "Brahms und die Idee der Kammermusik."

31. Hans Werner Henze, *Music and Politics: Collected Writings, 1953–81*, trans. Peter Labanyi (London, 1982), p. 130.

32. Quoted in Erich Ruprecht and Dieter Bänsch, *Literarische Manifeste der Jahrhundertwende, 1890–1910* (Stuttgart, 1970), p. 169.

33. See the critical evaluation of William Johnston, *The Austrian Mind: An Intellectual and Social History, 1848–1938* (Berkeley and Los Angeles, 1972), pp. 119–20.

34. Ruprecht and Bänsch, *Literarische Manifeste*, p. 169.

35. Hugo von Hofmannsthal, *Selected Prose*, trans. Mary Hottinger, Tania Stern, and James Stern (New York, 1952), pp. 134–35.

36. Robert Musil, *Die Verwirrung des Zöglings Törleß* (Reinbek, 1957), p. 6.

37. Gert Mattenklott, "Der 'subjektive Faktor' in Musils 'Törleß'," *Neue Hefte für Philosophie* 4 (1973): 61.

38. Schoenberg, "Aphorismen," *Die Musik* 9/21 (1909/10): 159.

39. Ernst Bloch, *Erbschaft dieser Zeit* (Frankfurt, 1962), p. 262.

40. Bloch, *Geist der Utopie*, rev. ed. (Frankfurt, 1964), p. 13. For a discussion of the connections between this philosophy and Schoenberg's aesthetic views around 1910, see Brinkmann, "Schönberg und das expressionistische Ausdrucksprinzip," *Bericht über den Internationalen Schönberg-Kongreß Wien 1974*, ed. Rudolf Stephan (Vienna, 1978), pp. 13–19.

41. See also Schoenberg's letter to Kandinsky dated July 20, 1922: "I expect you know we've had our trials here too: famine! It really was pretty awful. But perhaps—for we Viennese seem to be a patient lot—perhaps the worst was after all the overturning of everything one has believed in. That was probably the most grievous thing of all. When one's been used, where one's work was concerned, to clearing away all obstacles often by means of one immense intellectual effort and in those 8 years found oneself constantly faced with new obstacles against which all thinking, all power of invention, all energy, all ideas, proved helpless, for a man for whom ideas have been everything it means nothing less than the total collapse of things, unless he has come to find support, in ever increasing measure, in belief in something higher, beyond" (Schoenberg, *Letters*, pp. 70–71). Rudolf Stephan rightly stressed this passage in "Schönberg und der Klassizismus," in Stephan, *Vom musicalischen Denken: Gesammelte Vorträge*, ed. Rainer Damm and Andreas Traub (Mainz, 1985), pp. 146–54.

42 Hans-Ulrich Wehler, *The German Empire: 1871–1918*, trans. Kim Traynor (Leamington Spa, 1985), p. 245.

43 For Einstein's *Bebuquin*, see the edition in the *Gesammelte Werke*, ed. E. Nef (Wiesbaden, 1962); "Die Fabrikation der Fiktion" is available in the edition prepared by S. Penkert (Reinbek, 1973).

Schoenberg the Reactionary

J. PETER BURKHOLDER

I, in my reactionary way, stick to writing [my music] on orders from The Most High.
—Arnold Schoenberg, "Italian National Music" (*Style and Idea*)

Born in 1874 in Vienna, the very center of the classical tradition, Arnold Schoenberg was acutely aware of his historical position at the end of a long line of composers from Bach through Brahms, Mahler, and Strauss. He began his career writing in a late Romantic style deeply influenced by Brahms and Wagner.[1] By the time of his death in Los Angeles in 1951, his Romantic, tonal music had been eclipsed by the two radically new idioms that he had pioneered and that made him famous: atonality and twelve-tone music. What is paradoxical about his career and his music is that these apparently revolutionary changes of idiom sprang directly from his concern for the continuation of the German tradition. Indeed his twelve-tone music is simultaneously progressive and reactionary: progressive because it extends and codifies techniques present in his earlier music to create something truly new; reactionary because it resurrects through new musical techniques the structural functions of tonality and recapitulates the major forms of the common-practice period.

This paradox reflects Schoenberg's Januslike view of the tradition of German art music, in which the new and the classic were the same. For Schoenberg, the earlier composers Bach, Mozart, Beethoven, Wagner, and Brahms, seemed to be concerned with one objective above all: saying something new.

> In higher art, only that is worth being presented which has never before been presented. There is no great work of art

which does not convey a new message to humanity; there is no great artist who fails in this respect. This is the code of honour of all the great in art, and consequently in all great works of the great we will find that newness which never perishes, whether it be of Josquin des Prés, of Bach or Haydn, or of any other great master.[2]

In pursuing this objective, the great composers of the past developed new procedures and styles that were needed to express their ideas. In Schoenberg's view, "A truly new idea—at least as musical history reveals—is hardly imaginable without significant changes in musical technique."[3] Yet this was achieved, not through revolution, but by extending past procedures: "no new technique in the arts is created that has not had its roots in the past."[4]

Schoenberg aspired to match or exceed the achievement of the best German composers, so he did what he believed they had done: seek to say something new, while preserving and extending what was of highest value in the music of his predecessors. By emulating their music while seeking to move beyond it, Schoenberg sought for his music the same immortal status as the classics he chose as his models. As he wrote in 1931:

> My teachers were primarily Bach and Mozart, and secondarily Beethoven, Brahms, and Wagner. . . .
>
> I also learned much from Schubert and Mahler, Strauss and Reger too. I shut myself off from no one, and so I could say of myself:
>
> My originality comes from this: I immediately imitated everything I saw that was good, even when I had not first seen it in someone else's work.
>
> And I may say: often enough I saw it first in myself. For if I saw something I did not leave it at that; I acquired it, in order to possess it; I worked on it and extended it, and it led me to something new.
>
> I am convinced that eventually people will recognize how immediately this "something new" is linked to the loftiest models that have been granted us. I venture to credit myself with having written truly new music which, being based on tradition, is destined to become tradition.[5]

The view of himself expressed here paralleled Schoenberg's view of Brahms in his article "Brahms the Progressive." He argued that

Brahms combined Mozart's irregular phrasing, Bach's chromatic counterpoint, Beethoven's approach to form, and other procedures from earlier composers into a unique, progressive idiom of his own.[6] By arguing for the progressivism of Brahms, widely regarded as a conservative composer, through parallels with his own work, he was also arguing for his own traditionalism, despite his enduring reputation as a radical.[7]

There are two major concerns here: to continue the tradition and to say something new. These concerns were shared widely by the modernist composers of Schoenberg's generation, all of whom confronted the enduring presence of the classical masters and sought ways to contribute to the repertoire while establishing a distinctive and individual style.[8] What is so remarkable about Schoenberg is how precisely his music reflects this intertwining of new and old. Within each piece, he created a world in which exact repetition is avoided, while each new idea is derived from what has come before, a process he termed "developing variation."[9] As he wrote in an unfinished essay, "I say something only once. . . . With me, variation almost completely takes the place of repetition (there is hardly a single exception to this)."[10] Over the course of his career, the same process applies; he sought not to repeat himself, nor to repeat what previous composers had done, but at the same time to develop each new work from the ideas that he and earlier composers had used before.[11] In a sense, his entire output represents a process of developing variation based on ideas he had gleaned from the classical masters, while avoiding repetition both within and between pieces—a strategy that Schoenberg did not name, but that might be termed "the principle of nonrepetition."[12] The combination of nonrepetition and developing variation, both within pieces and from each work to the next, led to "truly new music" that was nevertheless "based on tradition," and for Schoenberg these were the essential requirements of any music that might claim to be "destined to become tradition."

Developing Variation and Nonrepetition

The interplay of developing variation and nonrepetition can be seen in the opening of Schoenberg's early song "Erwartung" (Expectation), Op. 2, no. 1 (1899), shown in example 1.[13] The first vocal phrase leaps up a fifth from E♭ to B♭, then circles around the upper note using its two chromatic neighbors, C♭ and A, before closing on B♭. This interplay of the perfect fifth with neighbor-tone motion is reflected in the harmony. At the beginning and end of the phrase is an E♭-major triad, scored in a way that emphasizes the same E♭–B♭ fifth as the melody, with an open fifth at the bottom and an octave and fifth between the outer notes. Between these two E♭ triads is a chord created from chromatic neighbor-tones to the triad, with the C♭ and A of the melody joined by G♭ and D, chromatic lower neighbors to G and E♭, respectively, all over E♭ sustained as a pedal point. The melodic idea of a rising fifth, chromatic motion to C♭, and A, and back is developed in the realm of harmony into the motion between a triad and a chord comprising these and two other chromatic neighbor tones.

Example 1: "Erwartung" (Expectation), Op. 2, no. 1, mm. 1–5

The rest of the passage is created by developing variation, with each seemingly new element derived from one or more elements that have preceded it. The melodic filigree that fills out m. 1 in the piano is based on the neighbor-tone idea, now a whole step from E♭ to F and back, and on arpeggiation of the E♭ major triad. This filigree in turn is varied over the next several measures. The second vocal phrase (m.

2) varies the first, over the same accompaniment. Here the voice states as melodic intervals the dissonant E♭–A and C♭–A from the second chord, strengthening the connection between melody and harmony by using the same intervals. The rising major triad in the voice in mm. 3–4 derives from the opening major chord and the arpeggiated figures in the piano, and the half step and tritone (E–F–B) that close the vocal melody echo the similar intervals in the second chord (D–E♭ and E♭–A) and in the second vocal phrase (E♭–A–B♭).

In m. 3, the second chord reappears, but its resolution is now varied. The tones of the chord again move chromatically, but in new directions; whereas before C♭ went down and A up to converge on B♭, here they reverse direction to arrive at an E♭–A♭–E♭–G♭–C chord in the second half of the measure. In other words, the motion to this chord varies the motion from the first to the second chord, and in so doing arrives at a new destination. Example 2 shows the chord sequence of mm. 0–5 as a series of seven five-note chords, omitting the repetitions of the first and last pairs of chords and some octave doublings. A tie or slur indicates that a note is sustained from the previous chord, sometimes with a change of register; a diagonal straight line indicates motion up or down by half step, and a double line motion by whole step. Each chord is derived from the previous one through a process analogous to the motion from the first to the second chord: one to three notes stay the same; one or two move up a half step; and the rest move down a half step (in one case a whole step). The exception is the motion from chord 4 to chord 5 (in m. 4), with two of the three sustained "voices" (the C and G) dropping an octave or two and the others rising a half or whole step. But even this is only a more distant variation on the process of moving from chord to chord that was initiated at the beginning of the piece. The result is an extraordinary sequence in which each new chord is a surprise, yet follows logically from what has preceded it. Moreover, each chord is novel, a type of sonority that has not been heard previously in this piece.[14] Schoenberg's interest in creating something new by varying the old is marvelously represented here in miniature, with both developing variation and the principle of nonrepetition clearly in play.

Example 2: The chords in "Erwartung," mm. 0–5

The Shape of Schoenberg's Career

Schoenberg's extension of the past to say something new can be seen throughout his career. Indeed, his entire development can be viewed as a series of variations on what he and others have done. We can trace two main paths. The first is a fairly linear progression (noting Jan Swafford's caveat that "in its logical trajectory an artist's development resembles more the butterfly than the arrow").[15] From his tonal works through the atonal period, Schoenberg consistently developed two main ideas that became codified in his twelve-tone music: the integration of melody and harmony into a unified space through the use in both of collections of notes that were identical or related through the simple transformations of transposition, inversion, and reordering; and the use of all twelve notes of the chromatic scale to create a sense of harmonic completion coordinated with the music's form, phrasing, and meter.[16]

The second main path is not linear, but is characterized by departure and return, or progress and reaction. In pursuing the first path, Schoenberg was led out of tonality into a new world in which, as he put it, dissonance was "emancipated" from the requirement in earlier music that it resolve to consonance.[17] The principle of nonrepetition led quickly to a point in which the relation of his music to the previous tradition was largely one of negation, in which tonality, thematic and motivic repetition, and use of traditional forms were all avoided. From this point of furthest remove, his subsequent career shows an attempt to return to the initial condition, using traditional forms, emphasizing motives and themes, and finding new ways to mimic tonality and tonal structures. He found the key to this in his development of the twelve-tone method.[18]

The song just discussed provides a good starting point for tracing both paths. For the sake of clarity, I will subdivide the first path into two themes and treat them separately: the integration of melody and harmony, and the circulation of the twelve chromatic notes.

Extensions

In his *Harmonielehre,* Schoenberg strongly criticized the traditional notion of "non-harmonic tones," the passing tones, neighbor tones, appoggiaturas, and other melodic notes that lie outside the prevailing harmony and are dissonant with it: "non-harmonic tones do form chords (*Zusammenklänge*), hence are not non-harmonic; the musical phenomena they help to create are harmonies, as is everything that sounds simultaneously."[19] This manner of thinking rejects the traditional view that some notes are part of the harmony and others are dissonant with it, and instead implies a close integration between melody and harmony.

We have already seen this exemplified in the song "Erwartung" from 1899. For much of the next decade, this integration coexisted with functional tonality in Schoenberg's music. Yet the desire not to repeat himself pushed him to find novel and unconventional progressions and to avoid standard cadential formulas. Since tonality is based on convention, the avoidance of conventional cadences attenuated the sense of a tonal center. In composing the Second String Quartet, Op. 10, in 1907–08, and his Op. 15 songs on texts from Stefan George's *The Book of the Hanging Gardens* in 1908–09, Schoenberg came to feel that resolution to a tonic was no longer necessary.[20] In this atmosphere, harmony no longer had to serve traditional functions and could be organized instead through developing variation, especially by using collections of notes derived from melodic motives.

The passage in example 3 from "Das schöne Beet," no. 10 of *The Book of the Hanging Gardens,* will illustrate. The first three notes of the melody, G♯–A–D, are also contained in the opening harmony. This same set of notes, often transposed, inverted, or reordered, occurs numerous times melodically and harmonically throughout the song, sometimes overlapping. Its appearances in mm. 11–19 are shown in boxes in the example. The melodic statements include an exact repetition (mm. 13–14, piano), a transposed and rhythmically altered repetition (mm. 15–16, voice), and several more or less distant variants (mm. 12–14, voice and bass, mm. 15–16, bass, and m. 19, bass); most of the harmonic statements are simple transpositions of the opening A–D–G♯ chord, while others involve inversion or changes in registration.[21] Thus much of the melodic material and many of the accompanying chords derive from the initial motive through developing variation. Schoenberg came to call this "working with tones of the motif."[22] By this he meant that the notes of a melodic motive could be used to generate everything from other motives to chords and accompanimental figures.

Example 3: "Das schöne Beet," Op. 15, no. 10, mm. 11–19

Example 3 continued

This unification of melody and harmony through the use in both of the same sets of notes is typical of Schoenberg's atonal music, and becomes codified in his twelve-tone music. Example 4 shows the beginning of the Minuet movement of the Suite for Piano, Op. 25, the first completely twelve-tone work. Here there are three main pitch motives, each of four notes:

1   E–F–G–D♭, first presented in the bass in mm. 1–2
2   G♭–E♭–A♭–D, in the treble in m. 1
3   B–C–A–B♭, in the treble in m. 2

Each of these is varied in the following music, often transposed, inverted, or reordered, sometimes part of the melody, sometimes played or arpeggiated as a chord, and frequently varied in rhythm. This is shown in the example, where the collections derived from these three motives are enclosed in boxes and labeled by number each time they occur. The use of these collections is here more systematic than it was in "Das schöne Beet" or "Erwartung"; each note of the piece is part of a statement of one of these sets, and the harmony is entirely integrated with the melody.

The use of collections in both melody and harmony that are related to one another through transposition, inversion, or reordering thus shows a fairly linear progress in Schoenberg's career, present already in his tonal music, suffusing the atonal music, and rigorously organized in the twelve-tone music to account for every note. As astonishing as the move from tonality to atonality and then to twelve-tone procedures may have been at the time, both new manners of composition continue to depend on the traditional concepts of variation and development, and both extend the traditional idea of a harmonic accompaniment that relates closely to and supports the melody above it.

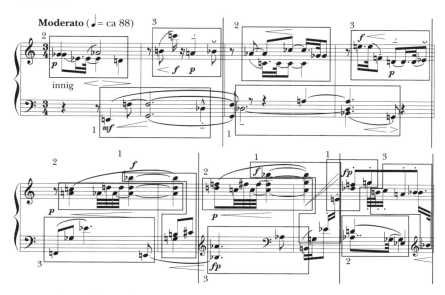

Example 4: Minuet, from Suite for Piano, Op. 25, mm. 1–7

Schoenberg's extension of this idea from "Erwartung" through his twelve-tone music exemplifies the view stated in his writings that "possessing" and "extending" "everything that was good" from the past led him to "something new," a "truly new idea" that required "significant changes in musical technique."[23] What in *Harmonielehre* was an observation that all melodic pitches are part of the harmony, "as is everything that sounds simultaneously," became in the twelve-tone music a concept of complete equivalence between melody and harmony:

> THE TWO-OR-MORE DIMENSIONAL SPACE IN WHICH MUSICAL IDEAS ARE PRESENTED IS A UNIT. . . . The elements of a musical idea are partly incorporated in the horizontal plane as successive sounds, and partly in the vertical plane as simultaneous sounds. The mutual relation of tones regulates the succession of intervals as well as their association into harmonies. . .

> *The unity of musical space demands an absolute and unitary percep-tion.* In this space, as in Swedenborg's heaven (described in Balzac's *Seraphita*), there is no absolute down, no right or left, forward or backward. Every musical configuration, every movement of tones has to be comprehended primarily as a mutual relation of sounds, of oscillatory vibrations, appearing at different places and times.[24]

Within such a space, not only is tonality unnecessary, but it simply cannot function. Tonal progressions require a sense of succession, a syntax; they move forward to the cadence, and to move backward is to create a special effect. Similarly, tonal resolution requires a kind of gravity, as the melodic line descends to its final note and the harmonic progression typically descends through the circle of fifths; the reverse would be just as likely in a musical space without an "absolute down," and that would make the sense of tonal closure impossible. This truly new idea about music, though derived from Schoenberg's observations of the relatedness of melody and harmony in tonal music, required a truly new music, foreshadowed in the atonal period and codified in twelve-tone procedures.

Example 4 also shows another trait of Schoenberg's music, the use of all twelve notes of the chromatic scale to create a sense of harmonic completion coordinated with the music's form, phrasing, or meter. Schoenberg noticed a tendency in the music of the late nineteenth and early twentieth centuries for chord successions to involve the presentation of new notes. This is related to the principle of non-repetition. In discussing chords of five and six notes in his *Harmonielehre,* Schoenberg comments on an example from Alban Berg's Op. 2, no. 4 (still a tonal work):

> It seems that the progression of such chords can be justified by the chromatic scale. The chord progression seems to be regulated by the tendency to include in the second chord tones that were missing in the first, generally those a half step higher or lower.[25]

But one can only go so far in this before all twelve notes of the chro-matic scale have been heard. When this happens, a kind of local limit on nonrepetition has been reached, demarking a harmonic unit; the forward motion initiated by introducing new notes has been com-pleted, all possible notes explored, creating a temporary point of rest before a new motion is begun. This has been called "the saturation of chromatic space" or "chromatic completion."[26]

In the Minuet from Schoenberg's Piano Suite, all twelve notes appear at least once by the end of m. 2. All twelve appear again in mm. 3–4; again in m. 5 and the first beat of m. 6; again in the remainder of m. 6 and the first beat of m. 7; and again in the remainder of m. 7 (the E is shared between these two statements). These are marked off by lines in example 4. This creates a kind of harmonic rhythm: the first unit of two measures is balanced by another, to create a four-bar phrase; this is followed by an acceleration of harmonic rhythm, as the next three statements of all twelve chromatic notes are completed in four beats, three beats, and two beats respectively. The following measures settle into a steady pace of completing one statement each measure, twice the pace at the beginning. There is a clear coordination between chromatic completion and phrasing and meter, as if the statement of all twelve notes has taken over the rhythmic, metric, and phrasing functions of harmony.[27]

Like the use of sets, this is very systematic here, but present in less systematic ways in the earlier music. In "Das schöne Beet," the statement of all twelve chromatic notes at least once happens slowly at the beginning and end of the song but accelerates in the middle, creating a kind of harmonic rhythm akin to that in the Minuet. In example 3, vertical lines show the groupings suggested by chromatic completion, and the twelfth note to appear in each unit is circled. The order in which notes appear, and which notes repeat, changes from group to group, but the acceleration in pace is very clear, from four measures (mm. 11–14) to one and a half (mm. 15–16), one and a quarter (mm. 16–18), and a single measure (m. 19). This is followed by a relaxation of pace to two-measure groupings (mm. 20–27) and five measures at the end. These groupings begin and end either with the vocal phrases or with the barlines, once again showing a coordination with phrasing and meter.[28] In "Erwartung" the statement of all twelve chromatic notes happens more slowly and is associated with sections rather than meter or phrasing, but there is a similar sense of chromatic completion signalling the end of a harmonic unit, with acceleration in the middle of the song. The first section, shown in example 1, includes only eleven notes; the twelfth, D♭, appears near the end of the varied repetition in mm. 6–10. The middle section goes through all twelve quite quickly (once in mm. 11–14 and again in mm. 14–17), then begins again to withhold notes; this continues through the reprise of the opening section, so that only as the voice cadences and the coda begins in m. 30 do we finally hear the twelfth note (once again, C♯, not heard since m. 15). Like the variation of melodic and harmonic collections discussed earlier, this takes place within a framework that is still tonal. The process of chromatic completion complements and is coordinated with the major events of the piece as determined by traditional harmonic and formal parameters. This is not new with Schoenberg; the same coordination can be found in Wolf, Mahler, and other nineteenth-century composers, and it has been traced as far back as the eighteenth century.[29]

Over the course of Schoenberg's career, this process becomes more systematic. As tonality is attenuated, the twelve chromatic notes can circulate more often, and in the atonal music from 1908 on, the process of chromatic completion takes over some of the traditional functions of harmony, such as its role in shaping phrase rhythm. The application of the principle of nonrepetition at a very local level leads to the circulation of all twelve notes with little or no repetition and ultimately to twelve-tone music, which depends upon chromatic completion for its harmonic rhythm and effective meter.[30] What is interesting here is how far chromatic completion has developed from its role in "Erwartung" and other late-nineteenth-century tonal music as a complement to other harmonic forces, to an element that takes a leading role ("something new"), and yet how closely linked to tradition are the notions of phrasing, harmonic rhythm, and meter. Schoenberg has found a new way to do familiar things, in the process creating "truly new music" that is "based on tradition."

Reaction

We have seen both for the integration of melody and harmony through the use of sets and for the idea of chromatic completion that there is a fairly linear progress in Schoenberg's music culminating in the systematic use of these ideas in his twelve-tone music. But the twelve-tone music was not only the culmination of a progressive development of these procedures. It also represented a reaction, a retreat.

From his early works through 1908, Schoenberg wrote music that was tonal; that presented, developed, and recapitulated themes and motives; and that clearly related to traditional forms and genres, however they might vary or reinterpret them. Following the principle that he should not repeat himself, his tonal music tended increasingly to vary rather than repeat large sections. His first atonal works continued to present, develop, and reprise motives and themes, but featured even less large-scale repetition. Without the need to articulate the tonal structure through repetition, as in tonal music, the trend toward nonrepetition led quickly to an extreme in the opera *Erwartung*, Op. 17 (1909), which is not only atonal, but athematic, amotivic, and without reference to traditional forms. There is in every aspect of the music a negation of repetition, an unremitting pursuit of the new.

One can go only so far in avoiding repetition; ironically, after *Erwartung*, Schoenberg could not write another such work without repeating himself.[31] Instead, he turned backward—not in his use of sets and chromatic completion, which continued to develop, but in increasing repetition and evocation of traditional forms and of the functions of tonality. Among the twenty-one songs of *Pierrot lunaire*, Op. 21 (1912), for example, are two waltzes, a barcarolle, a canonic passacaglia, and an aria over a walking bass, reminiscent of Bach. There is repetition at all levels, from motives and chords to varied returns of themes, sections, and one entire song. Perhaps most telling is a return to the idea of a pitch level from which the music departs and to which it returns, analogous to the tonic in tonal music. The first song exemplifies this, as the opening figure repeats several times, is developed at various pitch levels, and returns at the end to its original pitch level.

When Schoenberg developed the twelve-tone method, he saw it not only as a way to systematize the procedures of chromatic completion and "working with tones of the motif," but also as "a new procedure in musical construction which seemed fitted to replace those structural differentiations provided formerly by tonal harmonies."[32] After focusing on vocal works in his atonal period, he turned to traditional instrumental forms in his twelve-tone works, writing the Piano Suite in emulation of the Bach keyboard suites, a waltz for piano, sonata and other classic forms in a wind quintet and two string quartets, a set of orchestral variations in the Brahms mold, and concertos for violin and for piano reminiscent in form and virtuosity of the great Romantic concertos. In these pieces, melodic and rhythmic motives that are repeated, developed, and transformed are everywhere, repetition of large sections returns, and long-breathed themes are used in ways that parallel the concert music of the eighteenth and nineteenth centuries. In genre, form, gesture, and motivic development, these works are deeply historicist. Most fundamentally, and perhaps most surprisingly, they also recreate through analogy the structural functions of tonality.

The principles of twelve-tone music are briefly stated.[33] A twelve-tone row is an ordering of the twelve notes of the chromatic scale. Schoenberg typically used a single row in composing a piece, but found ingenious ways to permute or divide the row while in principle maintaining the ordering. The row may be transposed to begin on another pitch, inverted, retrograded, or some combination of these, without losing its identity, because the order of intervals within the row is preserved. It may be stated melodically or divided into segments to be used melodically or harmonically. Each statement of the row in any of its permutations completes a circulation of all twelve notes, so that twelve-tone music naturally produces chromatic completion in a relatively rapid harmonic rhythm, as we saw in example 4, the opening of the Minuet from the Piano Suite. In the Minuet, Schoenberg almost exclusively divides the twelve notes of his row into three groups of four, producing the three pitch motives identified in example 4. Every permutation of the row includes a similar permutation of each of these motives; that is, a transposition will transpose each of them the same distance, and an inverted row will invert all of them. So Schoenberg's twelve-tone music combines his practice of chromatic completion with the constant variation of melodic motives and the sets derived from them. This is by no means true of all twelve-tone music, but it is consistently true of Schoenberg's.

This will produce considerable motivic unity and a very close integration between melody and harmony, while the circulation of the twelve chromatic notes regulates meter and phrasing in ways analogous to the alternation and cadencing of chords in tonal music. But Schoenberg had already glimpsed in atonal works such as *Pierrot lunaire* the possibility of recreating some of the other functions of tonal harmony in a post-tonal language, and he sought to do so in the twelve-tone music as well. In the Waltz, no. 5 of the Five Piano Pieces, Op. 23, he uses only one form of the row, without any transpositions or inversions (there is one retrograde presentation), analogous to the idea of staying in the same key throughout. The Piano Suite, Op. 25, accomplishes this in a more complex way. Here Schoenberg uses only two transpositions each of the original or prime form (P-0, the untransposed prime form, and P-6, its transposition up six half steps), the inverted form (I-0 and I-6), and their retrogrades, shown in figure 1. The row is so designed that each of these begins on either E or B♭ and ends on the other, and all the prime and inverted forms have G and D♭ as the second pair of notes (enclosed in a box in the figure), giving a consistency of sound. That Schoenberg was thinking in terms of a tonal field analogous to a key is clear from a sketch in which he labeled P-0 "T" (for "tonic") and P-6 "D" (for "dominant"); here the tritone relationship substitutes for the normal interval of a fifth between tonic and dominant in tonal music.[34]

```
PRIMES ⇒                                              ⇐ RETROGRADES
P-0 ⇒   E  F  |G  D♭|G♭ E♭ A♭ D  B  C  A  B♭   ⇐ R-0
P-6 ⇒   B♭ C♭ |D♭ G |C  A  D  A♭ F  G♭ E♭ E    ⇐ R-6
INVERSIONS ⇒                                          ⇐ RETROGRADE INVERSIONS
I-0 ⇒   E  E♭ |D♭ G |D  F  C  F♯ A  A♭ C♭ B♭   ⇐ RI-0
I-6 ⇒   B♭ A  |G  D♭|A♭ C♭ G♭ C  E♭ D  F  E    ⇐ RI-6
```

Figure 1: Row forms used in Suite for Piano, Op. 25

In his later twelve-tone works, Schoenberg developed an even more sophisticated analogy to tonal procedures, one that permitted him to use all twelve possible transpositions of each form of the row and to suggest the idea of a home key, modulation to other keys, and return to the home key at the end, as in sonata and other forms. As he put it,

> the inversion a fifth below of the first six tones, the antecedent, should not produce a repetition of one of these six tones, but should bring forth the hitherto unused six tones of the chromatic scale.[35]

When this occurs, the first six notes of the inversion combined with the first six notes of the prime form complete a statement of all twelve notes of the chromatic scale. Since the essential harmonic unit of twelve-tone music is a complete statement of all twelve notes, the inversion a fifth below "fits together" harmonically with the prime form and thus can be combined in counterpoint with it. Of course, not all twelve-tone rows work this way; some cannot combine like this with any inversion, some combine with more than one, and some combine with an inversion other than the one that begins a perfect fifth below the prime form. These are features that the composer must design in. Having done so, Schoenberg now has a prime form, inverted form, and their retrogrades—one of each type of row form—which can be used in combination. Taken together, they define a kind of tonal field, and Schoenberg used this as an analogue to a key in tonal music.[36] In this light, his insistence that the inversion be at a fifth below is sug-

Example 5: Fourth String Quartet, Op. 37, first movement, mm. 1–22

Example 5 continued

gestive, recalling the interval of a fifth between the tonic and the dominant in tonal music.

The Fourth String Quartet

The first movement of the Fourth String Quartet, Op. 37 (1936), offers an example. Figure 2 shows the prime form that begins on D (P-0) and the inversion that begins a fifth below or a fourth above on G (I-5, for the inversion that begins five half steps above the first note of P-0), along with their retrogrades. The first six notes of P-0 and I-5 together state all twelve notes, as do the last six notes of each. As a corollary, the last six notes of P-0 are the same as the first six of I-5 (and vice versa), only in a different order. These row forms are always used in conjunction and never used in direct combination with other transpositions of the row. Within the tonal field these forms create,

Figure 2: Row forms used in Fourth String Quartet, Op. 37

they may alternate or appear together, somewhat like dominant and tonic chords defining a key in traditional tonal music.

At the opening, shown in example 5, P-0 appears melodically in the first violin. This is the first theme of the sonata form. It is accompanied by three-note segments of P-0 played as chords in imitation of a chordal accompaniment in a quartet by Mozart or Beethoven. Each three-note segment of the row in the melody, labeled by letters from *a* to *d*, is accompanied by the other three such segments, as shown in the example, so that approximately each measure there is a statement of all twelve notes of the row. In mm. 6–9, the second violin presents I-5 as a contrasting melody. This is again accompanied by three-note chords from the row, the last one excluding the row's twelfth note since it is already sounding in the second violin, and Schoenberg's method excludes such doublings. In mm. 10–15, the first violin returns with R-0 more or less in the rhythm of the first theme, accompanied with chords as at the beginning, and a tag in mm. 15–16 closes off the first period with a retrograde of the previous three chords.

Further development of these ideas occurs in the ensuing measures, continuing to stay within the tonal field established by P-0, I-5, and their retrogrades through the middle of m. 31. This transposition is the "tonic," the tonal field in which the piece begins and ends. As shown in figure 3, it is also the tonal field that takes up the largest pro-

TONAL FIELD	FIRST PITCH OF PRIME FORM	NO. OF MEASURES FIELD IS PRESENT	NO. OF TIMES FIELD OCCURS	THEMATIC ASSOCIATIONS
P-0 + I-5	D	60.5	3	Theme I in exposition, coda
P-6 + I-11	A♭	44.5	3	Theme I in recapitulation
P-2 + I-7	E	39	3	Theme III in development
P-1 + I-6	E♭	28.5	3	Theme I in coda
P-3 + I-8	F	19.5	2	
P-7 + I-0	A	18.5	1	Theme II in exposition
P-4 + I-9	F♯	17.5	3	Themes II & III in recapitulation and Theme II in coda
P-8 + I-1	B♭	15.5	3	
P-5 + I-10	G	12	2	
P-10 + I-3	C	10	1	Theme I at development
P-11 + I-4	C♯	10	3	
P-9 + I-2	B	9	1	Theme III in recapitulation

Figure 3: Frequency of row transpositions in Fourth String Quartet, first movement

portion of musical time in the movement, occurring three separate times and covering over 60 of the movement's 284 measures.

Figure 4 shows the form of the movement and the placement of the different transpositions of the tonal field, designated by the opening note of the prime form in each tonal field and the measures in which each transposition appears (using *a* and *b* to indicate the first and second half of a measure). The movement is in sonata form, with two contrasting themes in the exposition, a development section that introduces a new theme, a recapitulation that brings back all three themes in the order they first appeared, a "second development section," and a coda that functions almost as a second recapitulation, bringing back short statements of both principal themes. Many of these features recall the *Eroica* Symphony and other works of Beethoven's middle period.

ROW TRANSPOSITION	MEASURE NUMBERS	THEMATIC ANALYSIS
		EXPOSITION
		First theme group and transition
D	1–31a	Theme I, subtheme i at m. 27
G	31b–41	transition, subtheme i at 40–41
E	42–50a	subtheme ii
B♭	50b–54	
F♯	55–60a	subtheme ii
A	60b–65	bridge: sul ponticello and harmonics
		Second theme group and close
A	66–78	Theme II
F	79–94a	close: sul ponticello and harmonics
		DEVELOPMENT
C	94b–104a	Theme I in inversion
A♭	104b–110	sul ponticello and harmonics
E	111–140a	Theme III (new theme) at 116
C♯	140b–145b	
B♭	145b–153a	
E♭	153b–164	
		RECAPITULATION
		First theme group
A♭	165–184	Theme I in counterpoint with subtheme ii
C♯	185–187a	
		Second theme group
F♯	187b–194	Themes II and III in counterpoint
E♭	195–202	subtheme i at 198
B	203–211	continued development; Theme III at 207
G	212–213a	
E	213b–214a	
C♯	214b–216	
F	217–220	
A♭	221–238	fragmentation preparing return
		CODA ("second recapitulation")
D	239–257	Theme I
F♯	258–262a	Theme II
B♭	262b–264	
E♭	265–273	Theme I
D	274–284	fragments of Theme I, cadential chords

Figure 4: Row and thematic analysis of Fourth String Quartet, first movement

The "tonic" transposition provides the frame. It appears at the beginning, at the end, and at the beginning of the coda, always associated with the first theme. At the beginning of the recapitulation in m. 165, the first theme appears in a different transposition, half an octave away, on A♭ (P-6 and I-11). This is the second most prominent transposition in the work. One reason it is an appropriate row for the recapitulation is that the first theme strongly stresses the descending half steps D–C♯ and A♭–G in the original row (see example 5, mm. 1-4) through duration and accent; when the theme is transposed up a tritone the same half steps, A♭–G and D–C♯, are emphasized.[37] Because of this repetition, the reprise of the main theme a tritone higher will be satisfying in many respects, but not completely satisfying. This allows Schoenberg to set up a "second recapitulation" in the coda after what amounts to a "false recapitulation"—the right theme in the wrong key. The coda is preceded by this same transposition on A♭, for a lengthy period of disintegration, as themes and even the sense of the continuity of the row fall away in the repetition of single intervals, producing a sense of harmonic stasis. Following this virtual breakdown, the recurrence at the beginning of the coda of the opening theme in its original transposition—a row transposition that has not been heard from m. 31 to m. 239—is strong and perceptible. Despite the 200 intervening measures of "twelve tones which are related only with one another" (in Schoenberg's phrase),[38] we hear this moment as the return of the tonic. It helps that the row, and thus the theme, begin with the notes D–C♯–A, like the tonic, leading tone, and dominant in a tonal melody, for the use of such a familiar formula makes it easy to hear and remember. Thus the transposition on A♭, having served as a substitute tonic at the beginning of the recapitulation, serves as a kind of dominant preparation before the return of the tonic.

The third most prominent transposition of the tonal field is the prime form on E (P-2), with the inversion on A (I-7). The latter relates to the original transposition in an interesting way, as shown in figure 5; the first, second, and third groups of four notes in the inversion on A use the same notes as the first, third, and second groups respectively of the prime form on D. Considering this relationship, which is perhaps analogous to the common tone between tonic and subdominant chords, and taking into account the duration of this transposition at the center of the development section (only one measure shorter than the duration of the opening transposition, which is the longest of any), it might be fair to think of this transposition as an analogue to the subdominant in a tonal framework.

The other row transpositions that carry major thematic material, as indicated in figures 3 and 4, are also important. Three of them occur only once, at the point they bear thematic material, and they are the only three unique transpositions in the piece: A for the second theme and its preparation in the exposition; C for the inverted first theme at the opening of the development; and B for the "recapitulation" of Theme III. The first of these is relatively extensive, the sixth most prominent row transposition, but the latter two are among the rarest and have a rather special function. All three were apparently saved precisely to carry thematic material. The fact that the transposition on A carries the second theme and happens to be a fifth above D, the "key" of the first theme, suggests of course that Schoenberg is deliberately evoking the traditional relationship between the first and second themes of tonal sonata forms, in which the second theme is usually in the key of the dominant. The second theme returns transposed to F♯ in both the recapitulation and coda. The prime form in this transposition (P-4) has an interesting relationship to the inverted form from the opening tonal field (I-5); as shown in figure 6, the first five notes of one are the same as the second five notes of the other, reordered. Perhaps this suggested the transposition on F♯ as a substitute for the tonic at these reappearances of the second theme. The first theme appears briefly in the transposition on E♭ just before the final return of the tonic transposition on D, perhaps reflecting in this drop of a half step the half-step motive that opens the theme itself. Elsewhere, this transposition immediately precedes the recapitulation of the first theme and again of Theme III. The prime form in this transposition (P-1) shares the same three-note groupings as the inverted form in the opening transposition (I-5), but in a different order, as shown in figure 7, which may explain why this is the fourth most common transposition. The other four transpositions, on F, B♭, G, and C♯, do not carry important thematic material, and seem primarily to serve as bridges, modulatory fields, and preparation for other rows.

This analysis is complex and is arguable in its details. Is this the best way to describe the form? What is the exact role of each row, and why is each tonal field used where it is? These are debatable issues. But the very fact that we can debate them is a sign of how well Schoenberg met his goal of emulating the classical master composers. Analytical questions such as the role of a recapitulation in the "wrong key," the recapitulation of two themes at once, the introduction of a new theme in the development, what modulation means and when it begins, the return to the tonic only after thematic material has already been recalled—these are issues precisely like those posed by the classic quartets of Haydn, Mozart, and Beethoven. In other words, the analogy is perfect. Schoenberg has created with his twelve-tone tools a plastic, living, newly grown form that shows the same organic relationship of form and material as in the music of those for whom the sonata principle was still a method or idea rather than a mold or pattern. Schoenberg's sonata does not follow a rigid pattern, but approaches the form in exactly the same way as his classical teachers and creates a unique expression of the sonata idea.

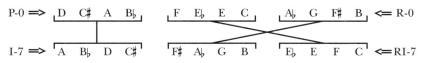

Figure 5: Relation of P-0 and I-7

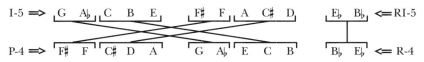

Figure 6: Relation of I-5 and P-4

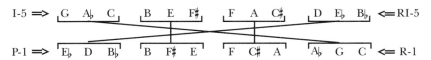

Figure 7: Relation of I-5 and P-1

To do this, he had to use transpositions of his row complexes as his analogue to tonal motion. Row usage—such as division into different units, or the distinction between prime and inversional forms—would not work, because there are not enough possibilities and because the contrasts and similarities are not clear enough. Having established through combinations of related rows the idea of a tonal field, the notion that this tonal field might be transposed, and that transposition might be a source of the musical structure, was of course obvious, and it had ample precedent in such atonal works as *Pierrot lunaire*. Yet Schoenberg chose to transpose his tonal fields in ways exactly analogous to older tonal procedures. All twelve possible transpositions are used; surely that was intentional. Yet some are used much more prominently than others. In a system of composing in which the twelve notes are related only to one another, why should one transposition be more important than others by a factor of six times? Why should not the order of these transpositions be determined by a twelve-tone row? Only the urge to create an analogue to tonal form fully explains Schoenberg's choices.

The interrelationships between rows through groupings of three, four, or five notes, as shown in figures 5, 6, and 7, help to explain why particular transpositions were chosen to be featured prominently, and it can be argued that these relationships are intrinsic to twelve-tone music.[39] But what these relationships create is a gradation of relatedness between row forms that corresponds by analogy to the relatedness between keys in major-minor tonality. Showing the intrinsic set relationships between these rows shows how good Schoenberg's analogue to tonality is, since the relationships among keys are likewise intrinsic to the tonal system. That is, it would be a poor analogue indeed if the only thing that made the music coherent were its resemblances to tonal motion; to be a true analogue, it must *both* be internally coherent, as tonal music is, *and* create relationships analogous to those in tonal music. Meanwhile, the surface of the music is marked everywhere with gestures that recall tonality, from the "chordal accompaniment" of the opening measures to the familiar tonal patterns (D–C♯–A and G–F♯–B) that open and close the row, from the coordination of themes with important transpositions to the fragmentation that precedes significant thematic statements and the audible return of the opening tonal field at the end. In other words, Schoenberg *chose* to use his twelve-tone method to create analogues to the tonal forms of the eighteenth and nineteenth centuries, and he made his analogue both as obvious and as deep and rich as possible.

The Progressive and the Reactionary

Progress itself was not satisfactory for Schoenberg. Rather, his development of twelve-tone procedures had a reactionary program at its base. His aim was to resurrect the ideals of abstract musical form he had learned from his primary teachers, Bach and Mozart. He said as much, as early as 1926:

> From the very beginning, this was clear in my mind: tonality's aids to articulation having dropped out, one must find some substitute, so that longer forms can once more be constructed.[40]

Having been driven forward by his commitment to developing variation and the principle of nonrepetition to a style based on "working with tones of the motif" and the circulation of the twelve chromatic notes, he found that by regularizing these procedures in the twelve-tone method he could go backward and reclaim what he had lost. Historical time became like the musical space he imagined, in which "there is no absolute down, no right or left, forward or backward"—in which claiming the "truly new ideas" he had developed by extending what he had learned from past masters did not preclude a more direct borrowing of their accustomed genres, forms, and gestures. His path took him to a place where the progressive and the reactionary, the new and the old, were so intertwined that they became one.

Just as Schoenberg argued that Brahms was a progressive composer, contributing to the forward progress of music by extending the techniques of the past, so I have argued that Schoenberg was a reactionary composer, seeking to restore the ideals of the past. Part of Brahms's project, of course, was to demonstrate the continuing viability of the traditional classical forms of symphony, variations, sonata, and chamber music and to put the new virtuosity and expanded harmonic resources of the late nineteenth century to work in their behalf. Ultimately Schoenberg's project was similar, although the new tools were ones he had made himself. To Schoenberg, it was the spirit of creation, not the piece itself, that was of utmost importance, for it was from that spirit that the works of the past masters arose. This attitude underlies both his centrality in the modernist tradition and his enduring unpopularity; while his audiences loved the classical masters of the past as much as he did, they were unable to love his own music, because what he sought to continue was a tradition of the spirit of composition, including technical innovation, an ideal of structural complexity, and classical approaches to form, rather than the more familiar tradition of musical style and convention.

NOTES

My thanks to Dana Gorzelany for research assistance, to Walter Frisch for his careful editing, and to Robert P. Morgan and Joseph N. Straus for their comments on a much earlier version of this essay, written in 1982.

1. On the depth of these influences, especially that of Brahms, and on the tonal music as a whole, see Walter Frisch, *The Early Works of Arnold Schoenberg 1893–1908* (Berkeley and Los Angeles, 1993).

2. "New Music, Outmoded Music, Style and Idea" (1946), in Arnold Schoenberg, *Style and Idea,* ed. Leonard Stein (New York, 1975), pp. 114–15 (henceforth *SI*). See also his comment in "Folkloristic Symphonies" (1947), *SI* 165: "A composer—a real creator—composes only if he has something to say which has not yet been said and which he feels must be said."

3. "Problems of Harmony" (1934), *SI* 269. See also "New Music, Outmoded Music, Style and Idea," *SI* 121.

4. "A Self-Analysis" (1948), *SI* 76. He explicitly denied that his own work was revolutionary; see "How One Becomes Lonely" (1937), *SI* 50, and "My Evolution" (1949), *SI* 86.

5. "National Music (2)" (February 24, 1931), *SI* 172–74.

6. "Brahms the Progressive," *SI* 398–441. This essay was first presented as a lecture in 1933, the centenary of Brahms's birth, and revised in 1947, the fiftieth anniversary of Brahms's death.

7. See for example the discussion of this essay in Joseph N. Straus, *Remaking the Past: Musical Modernism and the Influence of the Tonal Tradition* (Cambridge, Mass., 1990), pp. 27–34. Through his analyses, Schoenberg "establishes a link between his music and Brahms's" and "thus justifies his own music by showing that its structural principles are not revolutionary but are hallowed by tradition"; by analyzing the music as if Brahms were "a proto-typical Schoenberg," he tries to cast himself as "the culmination of all that has come before" (p. 31).

8. See J. Peter Burkholder, "Museum Pieces: The Historicist Mainstream in Music of the Last Hundred Years," *Journal of Musicology* 2 (1983): 115–34; and id., "Brahms and Twentieth-Century Classical Music," *19th-Century Music* 8 (1984): 75–83.

9. See Schoenberg's comments in *Fundamentals of Musical Composition*, ed. Gerald Strang and Leonard Stein (New York, 1967 [written 1937–48]) and throughout *SI*, including "Twelve-Tone Composition" (1923), *SI* 207–08; "National Music (1)" (1931), *SI* 171; "Linear Counterpoint" (1931), *SI* 290; "New Music, Outmoded Music, Style and Idea" (1946), *SI* 115–18; "Criteria for the Evaluation of Music" (1946), *SI* 129–30; "A Self-Analysis" (1948), *SI* 78; "Composition with Twelve Tones (2)" (ca. 1948), *SI* 248; "My Evolution" (1948), *SI* 80; "On Revient Toujours" (1948), *SI* 109; and "Bach" (1950), *SI* 397. The fullest exploration of the concept is in Walter Frisch, *Brahms and the Principle of Developing Variation* (Berkeley and Los Angeles, 1984), who summarizes

Schoenberg's writings on the subject on pp. 1–18. David Epstein, *Beyond Orpheus: Studies in Musical Structure* (Cambridge, Mass., 1979; repr. Oxford, 1987), pp. 207–10, provides another useful summary. Carl Dahlhaus, "What Is 'Developing Variation'?" in *Schoenberg and the New Music*, trans. Derrick Puffett and Alfred Clayton (Cambridge, 1987), pp. 128–33, argues that developing variation is more broadly an idea, not just a technique.

10. "New Music: My Music" (before 1930), *SI* 102.

11. I have suggested parallels between Schoenberg's music and his career before, in "Musical Time and Continuity as a Reflection of the Historical Situation of Modern Composers," *Journal of Musicology* 9 (1991): 412–29.

12. Elliott Antokoletz, *Twentieth-Century Music* (Englewood Cliffs, N.J., 1992), p. 38, uses this phrase in regard to Webern's avoidance of pitch repetition in his atonal works. I use it here in a much broader sense.

13. This song is analyzed by Frisch, *The Early Works of Arnold Schoenberg*, pp. 92–98, building on an analysis by Edward T. Cone, "Sound and Syntax: An Introduction to Schoenberg's Harmony," *Perspectives of New Music* 13/1 (1974): 28–29.

14. These are in turn (1) a major triad, (2) the dissonant chord, (3) a dominant seventh chord, (4) a minor triad, (5) a minor-major ninth chord, (6) a new dissonant sonority equivalent to four notes of the second chord (D–E♭–G♭–C♭) transposed down a fifth, and (7) a major-minor ninth chord. Even the inversions are unusual; only the first and last chords are in root position, and chords 3–5 are in second, first, and fourth inversion respectively.

15. Jan Swafford, *Charles Ives: A Life with Music* (New York, 1996), p. 101. See Schoenberg's comment in "My Technique and Style" (c. 1950), *SI* 110: "My technique and style have not been developed by a conscious procedure. Reviewing this development today, it seems to me that I have moved in many roundabout ways, sometimes advancing slowly, sometimes speedily, sometimes even falling back several steps."

16. Cf. Ethan Haimo, *Schoenberg's Serial Odyssey: The Evolution of His Twelve-Tone Method, 1914–1928* (Oxford, 1990), p. 69.

17. See Schoenberg's discussion of "the emancipation of the dissonance" in "Opinion or Insight?" (1926), *SI* 258–61, and "Composition with Twelve Tones (1)" (1941), *SI* 216–17.

18. Interestingly, this path represents a further parallel between his career and his music, for his works often vary and extend the initial ideas until a point of furthest remove is reached, then work their way back to the opening material for a varied reprise, recognizable but thoroughly refashioned and suffused with all that has come before.

19. Arnold Schoenberg, *Theory of Harmony*, trans. Roy E. Carter (Berkeley and Los Angeles, 1978), p. 309. This is a translation of the 3rd edition of *Harmonielehre*, from 1922.

20. See his comments in "How One Becomes Lonely," *SI* 49–50, and "My Evolution," *SI* 86. See also Ethan Haimo, "Schoenberg and the Origins of Atonality," in *Constructive Dissonance: Arnold Schoenberg and the Transformations of Twentieth-Century Culture*, ed. Juliane Brand and Christopher Hailey (Berkeley and Los Angeles, 1997), pp. 71–86, for a suggestion that atonality arose as a natural extension of Schoenberg's theories concerning chord formation and progression in tonal music as articulated in his 1911 *Harmonielehre*.

21. Music theorists use the term "pitch-class set" for these groups of notes that can be projected either harmonically or melodically, and consider collections that can

be transformed into each other through transposition, inversion, or reordering to be instances of the same basic set, in this case 016 or set 3–5. Set theory was standardized by Allen Forte, *The Structure of Atonal Music* (New Haven, 1973). The most accessible introduction to it is Joseph N. Straus, *Introduction to Post-Tonal Theory* (Englewood Cliffs, N.J., 1990). Example 3 presents only a very partial analysis, showing the role of a single set (and only its most obvious statements). See Ethan Haimo, "Atonality, Analysis, and the Intentional Fallacy," *Music Theory Spectrum* 18 (1996): 191–99, for an intelligent critique of set theory as applied to Schoenberg's atonal music; Haimo relies instead on developing variation. But both approaches highlight the interrelationship of melodic motives and harmonies, which is my point here.

22. "Composition with Twelve Tones (2)," *SI* 248.

23. See the passages quoted above from "National Music (2)," *SI* 174, and "Problems of Harmony," *SI* 269.

24. "Composition with Twelve Tones (2)," *SI* 220 and 223. Emphasis original. This idea is foreshadowed in an early short essay on "Twelve-Tone Composition" (1923), *SI* 207: "Whatever sounds together (harmonies, chords, the result of part-writing) plays its part in expression and in presentation of the musical idea in just the same way as does all that sounds successively (motive, shape, phrase, sentence, melody, etc.)." On the aesthetic background to this and other concepts in Schoenberg's thought, including the influence of Emanuel Swedenborg, see John Covach, "The Sources of Schoenberg's 'Aesthetic Theology,'" *19th-Century Music* 19 (1996): 252–62.

25. Schoenberg, *Theory of Harmony*, p. 420.

26. The former is used by Charles Rosen, *Arnold Schoenberg* (New York, 1975), pp. 57–62 (quoting p. 58), and the latter by Ethan Haimo, *Schoenberg's Serial Odyssey*, defined on pp. 12 and 183, and used *passim*.

27. See Martha Hyde, "A Theory of Twelve-Tone Meter," *Music Theory Spectrum* 6 (1984): 14–51, and Haimo, *Schoenberg's Serial Odyssey*, pp. 35–37.

28. Of course, I have not always drawn the line immediately after the twelfth note, but have looked for the closest appropriate place to suggest the end of a group. Still, the coordination is striking, with a phrase ending or a barline on the next beat in half of the cases, and within half a measure in the others. Chromatic completion is also evident in the song's piano prelude (mm. 1–10); the first grouping ends with the low D♯ in m. 7, the lowest note in the piece, and the second begins there and ends with the D that accompanies the vocal entrance in m. 11.

29. James K. Baker shows this for Mozart in "Chromaticism in Classical Music," in *Music Theory and the Exploration of the Past*, ed. Christopher Hatch and David W. Bernstein (Chicago, 1993), pp. 233–307; Henry Burnett and Shaugn O'Donnell for classic-era composers back to C. P. E. Bach, in "Linear Ordering of the Chromatic Aggregate in Classical Symphonic Music," *Music Theory Spectrum* 18 (1996): 22–50.

30. This is an important aspect of the development Haimo traces in *Schoenberg's Serial Odyssey*.

31. He began his next work, *Die glückliche Hand*, Op. 18 (1910–13), in the same vein, but changed during composition from avoiding repetition to reintroducing motivic and thematic development, canons, and repetition as an element of form. See Joseph Auner, "Schoenberg's Compositional and Aesthetic Transformations, 1910–1913: The Genesis of *Die glückliche Hand*" (Ph.D. dissertation, University of Chicago, 1991), and idem, "In Schoenberg's Workshop: Aggregates and Referential Collections in *Die glückliche Hand*," *Music Theory Spectrum* 18 (1996): 77–105.

32. "Composition with Twelve Tones (1)," *SI* 218. See also "Composition with Twelve Tones (2)," *SI* 245: "The method of composing with twelve tones purports reinstatement of the effects formerly furnished by the structural functions of the harmony."

33. The classic statement of these principles is in "Composition with Twelve Tones (1)," in *SI*.

34. Haimo, *Schoenberg's Serial Odyssey*, p. 101. Interestingly, Schoenberg considered I-0 to be the "dominant inversion," leaving I-6 as the inversion of the "tonic." P-0 and I-6 both have G and D♭ as the third and fourth notes of the row respectively, and both pair E with F and B♭ with A, as shown in figure 1; perhaps these commonalities explain why Schoenberg considered I-6 the "tonic" inversion.

35. "Composition with Twelve Tones (1)," *SI* 225. The pioneering work on this and most other aspects of Schoenberg's twelve-tone music was done by Milton Babbitt, who coined the term "combinatoriality" for this kind of relationship between two rows. See the discussions of combinatoriality in Haimo, *Schoenberg's Serial Odyssey*, pp. 8–15; Straus, *Introduction to Post-Tonal Theory*, pp. 152–58; and Babbitt's articles "Some Aspects of Twelve-Tone Composition," *The Score and I.M.A. Magazine* 12 (1955): 53–61, and "Set Structure as a Compositional Determinant," *Journal of Music Theory* 5/2 (1961): 72–94.

36. Straus, *Introduction to Post-Tonal Theory*, pp. 158–61, discusses this under the term "twelve-tone area" and notes that "For Schoenberg in particular, these twelve-tone areas are something like the keys in a tonal piece. Large-scale motion in his music often involves movement from area to area" (p. 158). The concept of twelve-tone areas is developed in three articles by David Lewin, "*Moses und Aron*: Some General Remarks, and Analytic Notes for Act I, Scene 1," *Perspectives of New Music* 6/1 (1967): 1–17; "A Study of Hexachord Levels in Schoenberg's Violin Fantasy," *Perspectives of New Music* 6/1 (1967): 18–32; and "Inversional Balance as an Organizing Force in Schoenberg's Music and Thought," *Perspectives of New Music* 6/2 (1968): 1–21. Haimo, *Schoenberg's Serial Odyssey*, pp. 28–30, discusses this concept as "hexachordal levels."

37. There are other relationships between the original row and its transposition up a tritone as well; see Haimo, *Schoenberg's Serial Odyssey*, pp. 27–28, and William E. Lake, "Structural Functions of Segmental Interval-Class 1 Dyads in Schoenberg's Fourth Quartet, First Movement," *In Theory Only* 8/2 (1984): 21–29. Lake introduces a general principle on the relatedness of non-combinatorial rows in this movement, based on the number of identical half-steps the row shares with P-0. See Ethan Haimo and Paul Johnson, "Isomorphic Partitioning and Schoenberg's Fourth String Quartet," *Journal of Music Theory* 28 (1984): 47–72, for a consideration of relatedness of rows through shared segments.

38. "Composition with Twelve Tones (1)," *SI* 218.

39. This has been argued for the Wind Quintet, Op. 26, by Andrew Mead, "'Tonal Forms' in Arnold Schoenberg's Twelve-Tone Music," *Music Theory Spectrum* 9 (1987): 67–92. Mead argues that "each feature, even the transposition in the recapitulation [of the second theme up a fourth, as in a tonal work], reflects relations within the piece's row class working in an overriding compositional strategy for the whole movement." Yet Schoenberg designed his row precisely so that this would be possible.

40. "Opinion or Insight?," *SI* 263.

PART II
ARNOLD SCHÖNBERG

•

Arnold Schönberg

(1912)

TRANSLATED BY BARBARA Z. SCHOENBERG
INTRODUCED BY WALTER FRISCH

Editor's Introduction

Schoenberg, whose following among pupils and members of his circle approached the cultlike, was honored on several occasions with books or special issues of periodicals devoted to him, his activities, and his music. These volumes were essentially in the tradition of the German *Festschrift*, or celebratory collections of essays presented to important scholar-teachers on milestone birthdays—with the important difference that in these cases all the contributions centered on Schoenberg. The Schoenberg *Festschriften* are among the most important sources of information now available about the composer.[1]

Unique among them is *Arnold Schönberg*, which appeared in February 1912, when the composer was not yet thirty-eight years old. This ninety-page volume, the first about Schoenberg published in any language, was issued by Piper Verlag, the progressive publisher in Munich, which in the previous year had published a monograph on Mahler by Paul Stefan—one of the first studies on that composer— and would in May 1912 issue the landmark *Blue Rider Almanac*, edited by Wassily Kandinsky and Franz Marc.[2]

The volume *Arnold Schönberg* presciently celebrates the four areas of activity for which Schoenberg is recognized at the end of the twentieth century: composition, music theory, teaching, and painting. It also gives us an invaluable glimpse of Schoenberg—as seen, of course, by true believers—at an early and critical stage of his career, when he had just completed the first group of atonal works and was about to embark on their capstone, *Pierrot lunaire;* when *Harmonielehre* was still barely off the press and beginning to be absorbed; when Schoenberg was active and gaining some attention as a painter. *Arnold Schönberg* also captures something of the interdisciplinary fervor and the intense spirit of discovery that was shared by many who came in contact with Schoenberg during this period.

The book was handsomely produced with five tipped-in black-and-white illustrations—a photograph of Schoenberg and four of his paintings (discussed by Kandinsky in his essay). We have reproduced these with the present translation, which also includes the entire text in English for the first time.

The contributors to this volume were mostly Schoenberg's pupils past and present, including the two who were to become the most famous, Berg (who studied with Schoenberg 1904–11) and Webern (studied 1904–08), whose account of Schoenberg's musical development here is the earliest such assessment to have appeared in print. Other students represented, most of them much less familiar to us today, include Karl Horwitz (1884–1925), who studied with Schoenberg 1904–08; Heinrich Jalowetz (1882–1946; studied 1904–08); Paul Königer (1882–1943; studied 1911–12); Karl Linke (1884–1938; studied 1909–12); Erwin Stein (1885–1958; studied 1906–10); and Egon Wellesz (1885–1974; studied 1904–05), who would in 1921 publish the first monograph on Schoenberg.

From outside music, the contributors to the volume included the painter Kandinsky, the writer-turned-artist Albert Paris von Gütersloh, and the philosopher Robert Neumann. Kandinsky had initiated a now-famous correspondence with Schoenberg in January 1911 and had included some of Schoenberg's paintings in the first Blue Rider exhibition in Munich in December of the same year. Schoenberg would in turn contribute an essay and a facsimile of a musical composition to Kandinsky's and Marc's *Blue Rider Almanac*. Gütersloh (1887–1973) had written one of the first German expressionist novels, *Die tanzende Törin* (The dancing fool) in 1910. After he turned to the visual arts, he became a stage designer working under Max Reinhardt. Robert Neumann (1864–?) perhaps counts among the first modern theorists of microtonality. In a lengthy footnote in *Harmonielehre* Schoenberg discussed Neumann's idea of a fifty-three-part division of the octave that would assure pure intonation of intervals without giving up the practicality of temperament.[3]

Schoenberg was deeply moved by *Arnold Schönberg*, but was also made somewhat uncomfortable by it. After the volume was presented to him by Webern, Schoenberg reported his feelings and reactions at some length in a diary entry of March 11, 1912:

> I feel I am being talked about in really much too effusive a way. I am too young for this kind of praise, have accomplished too little, and too little that is perfect. My present accomplishments I can still only regard as a hope for the future, as a promise that I may keep; but not as anything more. And I have to say, were I not spoiling the joy of my students by doing so, I might possibly have rejected the book. On the other hand, however, I was so overwhelmed by the great love which shows in all this, that I really had been happy, insofar as something like this can provide happiness. And I was proud as well: I find everything, almost everything, written so well and with such beautiful words, that I really should have a high opinion of a group of human beings like these. Above all, of course, Webern! He is a wonderful human being. How moved he was when he handed the book to me. Solemn and yet so unpretentious. Almost like a school boy; but like one who only prepared something so as not to be overwhelmed. . . . Then Berg, and Linke and Jalowetz. Yes, even Horwitz. And: Kandinsky. A magnificent essay![4]

Although the prose style of most of the contributors is relatively uncomplicated and straightforward, and thus lends itself readily to translation, the introduction by Karl Linke and especially the essay "Schoenberg the Painter" by Paris von Gütersloh present special challenges. Gütersloh's contribution is really a full-blown example of expressionist prose—dense, abstract, and obscure even in German. We have attempted to render it in an English that is as idiomatic as possible, yet also captures the style of the original.

(Notes appear on p. 261.)

ARNOLD SCHOENBERG, FROM AN AMATEUR'S SNAPSHOT

ARNOLD SCHÖNBERG

MIT BEITRÄGEN VON ALBAN BERG
PARIS VON GÜTERSLOH · K. HORWITZ
HEINRICH JALOWETZ · W. KANDINSKY
PAUL KÖNIGER · KARL LINKE
ROBERT NEUMANN · ERWIN STEIN
ANT. V. WEBERN · EGON WELLESZ

R. PIPER & CO · MÜNCHEN 1912

Facsimile of original title page

TO ARNOLD SCHOENBERG
IN HIGHEST ESTEEM

Contents

BIOGRAPHICAL

Arnold Schoenberg was born in Vienna on September 13, 1874. He lived there until 1901. In December of that year he moved to Berlin where he served as conductor for Wolzogen's Buntes Theater for a short period of time, after which he served as a teacher of composition at the Stern Conservatory. In 1903 he returned to Vienna where he quickly gained a reputation as a highly regarded teacher of numerous students. In 1910 he was "permitted" to hold courses in composition at the imperial-royal Academy of Music and Representational Arts in Vienna as an adjunct instructor. In the fall of 1911 he moved back to Berlin once again.

THE WORKS

Opp. 1, 2 and 3, Songs (composed 1898–1900); Op. 4, String Sextet, *Verklärte Nacht* (1899); these works are published by Verlag Dreililien, Berlin; *Gurrelieder*, text by J. P. Jacobsen, for soloists, chorus and orchestra (1900), to be released forthwith by Universal-Edition, Vienna; Op. 5, *Pelleas and Melisande*, symphonic poem for orchestra (1902), Universal-Edition; Op. 6, Eight Songs (ca. 1905), Dreililien; Op. 7, First String Quartet in D Minor (1905), Dreililien; Op. 8, Six Orchestral Songs (1904), U-E; Op. 9, Chamber Symphony (1906), Two Ballads for voice and piano (1907), *Friede auf Erden*, for mixed chorus a capella (1908), manuscripts; Op.10, Second String Quartet in F♯ Minor (1907–08), U-E; Fifteen Songs with texts by Stefan George (1908), manuscript; Op. 11, Three Piano Pieces (1908), U-E; Five Pieces for Orchestra (1909), to be published by Edition Peters; Monodrama *Erwartung* (1909), *Glückliche Hand*, Drama with Music (1910), and Six Piano Pieces (1911), acquired by U-E. In addition: *Harmonielehre* (1910), U-E.

AS INTRODUCTION

Artists who have arrived at a full understanding of themselves always say exactly what they are and not what others want to hear. Each wants to listen only to himself, or to only as much about another person as he can comprehend with his own self. If the boundary line of comprehensibility has been overstepped, then the very dissonances that originate between the artist and his audience will allegedly be found in his works as well. The artist could be considerate and attempt to control his feelings. But being considerate is a compromise that will one day seek revenge. There can be no rapprochement from without, and the sensitive listener will never be deceived. He will sense when the artist goes out of his way to extend his hand to someone.

Schoenberg does not reach out his hand. But those who have understood him through feeling are suddenly so close to him that they no longer need a helping hand. They are the chosen who hear his word even if he has not spoken it, who already perceive the willpower with which the thought strives to express itself. They, within whom everything stands at the ready to pour forth, would have to express the word themselves, were it not duly expressed by the master. Those who do not have this feeling can make every effort and will nevertheless achieve nothing. It is like a secret that only those attuned to one another can understand without needing to speak about it. There is a kind of silent expressiveness between Schoenberg and his friends, and when he finally does speak, he does so only to those who would be close to him even without the word. His art does not lend itself to being lectured about like subject matter. And his works often gaze at us with such large and fixed eyes that we grow afraid and step back as if trying to create a protective layer of air between them and us. This stepping back has a secret meaning that involves not only fear. It is an unconscious reaction to the close-up view we have of the work. A new work always stands so near the eye that its perspective appears distorted in time. We thus want to distance ourselves from it, because we hope thereby to perceive its correct proportions. This distancing ought to occur in time and backward. We, however, childlike and groping, take the actual step spatially, in order to overcome time. It is just as impossible for us to go back in time as it is to push the work ahead in time. There is no alternative but to wait, until time distances itself from us.

Those attuned to one another, who share Schoenberg's blood, can understand the work without having to wait. For them the distortion in perspective does not exist, because for them it is not a close-up image. They see it in its larger perspective the way others can only perceive through temporal distance. The organs have developed ahead of the time and at the start are already adjusted to see objects simply and upright, even though they may be produced doubled and reversed.

There is something that those who have the will could do if they wish to approach Schoenberg: be open and devoted. Throw away everything to which they are accustomed and about which they are so proud: fundamentals, eloquence, conviction, infallibility, arm movements, nervousness. Be completely still and turn off the distracting lights in the house. To listen deeply within and not prevent themselves from feeling anything. Then suddenly there will be light, unexpectedly and from somewhere. Windows will open to let the light in. It will be bright in every corner. But they will have to be able to wait, and that is even more difficult than comprehending. Because waiting might take a long time, and it is possible that it may never cease. Comprehension is the matter of a moment. Only those who have unconditional trust in the veracity of the artist will be able to wait. Those who have no faith will see only the distortion produced by the close-up image, and will mistake for the effect precisely that which in reality hinders the effect. They will blame the work because it does not reveal itself to them, and will want to hear nothing about distance. Their judgments will have the same distortion in perspective as the close-up image that evinced them, and such judgments will seem just as incomprehensible to a later time, when the distance will have been sufficient, as the fact that these works are considered incomprehensible today. Because the apparent distortion of the work will have been corrected with time, whereas the distortions in judgment will have remained because they are not art.

Nonetheless, there are several who believe in Schoenberg the composer. Here paths are still visible that he has traversed and that remain open to everyone. Much more about that must be said in this book. But at best people just shake their heads about Schoenberg the painter. There is a weeping countenance with a clear forehead and veiled face. No child, woman, or man weeps that way; no living being can experience that kind of sorrow. For they will remain in the world and will be diverted from their pain by a thousand things. But within the artist sorrow comes alive in such a way that reality could never reproduce as completely. Inner sorrow is the clearest and most vitally intensified form of external sorrow. In longing for redemption it forms an image. Colors stubbornly take positions that they no longer leave, despite the objections of reason, which doubts their validity, their possibility, and their reality. Everything occurs as a result of strong drives, against which the creative person is defenseless. He has only a feeling: Something is happening to me. My hand is being led.

Once he strokes the head of a child. Suddenly he desists and stares at his hand, which is arched and cramped. An arched, cramped hand is something terrible. It remains in the retina and then slips beyond consciousness where it lies in waiting until the sentinel of the brain is asleep. Then, adjusting itself, it follows the pressure upward into the medium of a thinner atmosphere. All of this follows laws which hover above the physical realm like specters over people. This kind of projection into reality is scorned by the irritated eye and newly awakened reason, which see no hand, no face. There is absolutely no resemblance to what a human hand or face looks like in reality. Light on sensitive glass plates takes care of that with painstaking clarity. The human organism is even more complicated than the photographic camera. The painted canvas contains only those elements of the head and face that are still present within, a face that exists only externally, the mask and a hand which serve only as instruments and leave no traces. But a countenance in which momentary anger flares up, or love, and a hand raised in an unintended gesture: all the chaste reflexes that mean nothing in real life and are overlooked—often intentionally—collapse within the artist in order to become pure and born anew.

Such are Schoenberg's paintings of an inner visage brought to the surface. How it grows and matures internally, heeding no objection of the mind, expressing nothing but itself, and, with the surest instinct, how it places objects next to one another in a fashion the synthesizing mind could never accomplish: all of this removes itself completely from outside observation and control. Perhaps we could have some notion of it in a dream.

Like-minded spirits received the strongest impressions. Those who were not attuned became receptive suddenly, in a clairvoyant hour. Some were left behind. The doubt in their minds asked: What is this trying to represent? But reason should not ask questions, and the eye might be closed and still ought to be able to see. The pictures are nothing physical that can be understood and examined like a body; they are metaphysical, something that we possess but cannot see or grasp. This is no art the eye can perceive, nor can words describe these pictures. For then they would no longer be pictures. They have come by way of a long and strange path and they are searching for peace. One ought not to disturb them by using words. They are delicate and have blossomed in a dark sanctuary. That is why they are so incomprehensible.

These were images fixed in space. But some extend even farther along into time and have their own distinct life. Thus does drama arise. The forms bundle together, grow into one another and separate themselves into new ones. They remain like that, without peace, until they find themselves repeatedly in accordance with the same inner principles, laws that are completely incomprehensible seen from the vantage point of the outside world, laws governed by shadows and ghosts. Once they subside, the time has come to expose them to the outside world. That would be the profoundest pantomime. But the forms have voices which can be heard. It is not the mouth that speaks, because it says only what the head knows. The excitations do not follow a path toward consciousness, or they would no longer exist. Their essence lies in the unconscious. Here the blood, the eye, and the brain speak in sounds which are not our language. The blood has not learned our language, nor the brain the language of the blood. Each speaks its own kind; the blood speaks ecstatically, the brain perceives out loud. The eye places the soul on the outside and the things of this world disappear. The world is the inner person turned outward. The knowledge of the brain beams into this world and is the only light that shines. But it has not yet reached into all the depths. It is the drama of an astounding subjectivity.

However, there still are some excitations where the word, the light, and the gestures grow silent and are no longer able to find the expression they are seeking. But now Schoenberg has the strongest and most elemental thing that he can give: music. The place where everything else stops is where music begins. To the outer ear, inaudible noises of our trembling interior emerge and consolidate along their path toward sound. Everything that lives like a dream beneath consciousness can be heard and becomes conscious in a favorable hour. This is already music. It has an enormous, flowing energy and is not constructed according to any of the laws that we know. It has its own rhythm, just as blood pulsates in rhythm, and just as all life within us is rhythm. It has a key, much like the sea or a storm has. It has harmonies, but we cannot grasp them, nor analyze them, and we cannot find its themes. There is always an edifice present, but we are unable to reconstruct it in ourselves. All the handiwork of technique has foundered. Everything is the same and at one with content. No longer can we find any difference between idea and technique, because what dissolved entirely into and out of itself has matured. There can be no adaptation; to divide something that has never been divided would be to misunderstand this music.

This is what seems so new and shocking to us in Schoenberg's music: this amazingly secure maneuverability through the chaos of new sounds, and the total charting of depths into which no paths had ever led before, and from which we receive no messages; to have recognized as music that which some may have listened to timidly, but which they never had experienced because the time was not yet ripe for it. Everything that was called music or tradition had to topple. This wall had been so alive once, but it died at the precise moment that it became tradition. The idols of a dead era had to be crushed by someone who felt our era so completely within himself that he could express it and could offer his heart for it. Progress proceeds intermittently, and what remains between the old and the new is revised at the hands of imitators, who, by their industry and their perseverance, build the bridge which the conqueror, because of the white-hot energy of his will, did not need.

The person who, even in a lucid moment, remains in the dark about what it is he actually has before him, who has no keen sense of hearing enabling him to hear beyond his horizons: such a one has to wait patiently until he has time along the long path over the bridge to develop his inner person toward the new music. For this new music demands not only a culture of the ear, but also a culture of the whole person.

This is not a dream. Schoenberg is no longer alone. There are people who had only one feeling when they heard this music for the first time: This is what we have thirsted for, this is us exactly, with the ghostly, restless things within us and above us—a release from a torpid sentimentality. This handful of people understood each other so well, without having spoken a word to one another. A stronger language had brought them together.

Schoenberg's music does not serve the ear in the way that has been customary up to now. Because it is the *ear* that should serve. It has at most the function that a pen has for writing: it is a medium. But it assumes the rights of a king and wants to rule. Only the inner person who has produced music can hear it. But the inner person cannot serve, because he is free of the outside world. He follows no rules, knows no aesthetics. He knows only compulsion, the inexorable compulsion of expressing that which oppresses him, without the least consideration for what it will become. Beauty becomes so unspeakably small and a minuscule occurrence in this compulsion, which has so much power and wealth it cannot drape itself with glitter. The glitter would only be for the ear. The triad and tonality have been lost with the fulfillment of a new kind of urgency of expression. An attempt was once made to prove that the desire for tonality lay in the way our ear was constructed, but the attempt proved unsuccessful. Had it succeeded, however, what would have been proven would have been the ear itself, which is merely a servant of the greater force. The source, the most important thing in our being, has been suppressed in favor of the ear and an acquired method of feeling. The rubble of centuries has to be cleared away before we can become ourselves, pure and free of dross.

Thus pure and free of everything that has been heard are the latest works of Schoenberg, which will be addressed in greater detail later. They are works that will resist those who try to grasp them. Most probably it is we who resist and read our own prejudices into the work. Because our fears have been fulfilled here. Our unconscious spasms have been given expression; our premonitions, which we may not have believed, have become credible; and our fear of ghosts, which we deride during broad daylight, has come alive in these works and overcomes us while we hear this music, while we view the paintings and witness the performance of the drama *Die glückliche Hand*.

It is impossible for our emotions to separate clearly Schoenberg's music, painting, and poetry. A compelling spirit speaks everywhere, someone who is so at one with himself in everything, and who takes hold of his own development with ironfisted, unfailing certainty. Nothing will be able to prevent him from striding further along his path, even were he to wish it otherwise himself. No one can get beyond his own self, because beyond it there is nothing else.

KARL LINKE

SCHOENBERG'S MUSIC

"The artist does nothing that others deem beautiful, but rather only what to him is a necessity."
—Arnold Schoenberg, *Harmonielehre*[5]

Arnold Schoenberg is an autodidact. For a short time he received instruction in composition from Alexander von Zemlinsky, but not so much by way of lessons as by friendly discussions.

Nevertheless his works demonstrate the phenomenally high level of his ability and, in a marvelous way, his *Harmonielehre* proclaims to the world the incredible wealth of his knowledge.

The virtuosity of his ability has even been acknowledged by his opponents. They have spoken about his works as if they were theoretical speculations. They have called him a theoretician. The unprecedented art of his counterpoint has even been the subject of reproach.

But theory does not bring you any closer to his works. There is only one thing that is necessary: your heart must remain open. Schoenberg's work should be listened to without inhibition or prejudice of any kind. Put theory and philosophy aside. In Schoenberg's work there is purely music, music as in the case of Beethoven and Mahler. The experiences of his heart become tones. Schoenberg's relationship to art is rooted exclusively in the necessity for expression. His emotion is that of scorching flames; it creates completely new standards of expression, thus it needs entirely new means of expression. Content and form are inseparable.

The first-large scale work that Schoenberg gave the world is the String Sextet Op. 4, *Verklärte Nacht*. The poem by Richard Dehmel precedes the score. Schoenberg is one of the few who turned to chamber music at a time when Wagner's music dramas served almost exclusively as a model for German composers, and almost everyone sought to express himself in the form of opera and larger orchestral works. However, he trod this ground not by following the classical path of Johannes Brahms, but rather by way of Richard Wagner.

The sextet is in one movement, the form of the movement freely improvised. The excessive wealth of themes and their variations immediately reveal Schoenberg's great art. In the brevity of its themes, the unrestricted way they succeed one another, and the free structure that results, the Sextet anticipates Schoenberg's works today. Its new tonal and harmonic effects surpass anything written at the time. It is a miracle of sound and without prototype in chamber music. I will cite from it a theme that already contains the seed of all the features so characteristic of Schoenberg's tonality.

Nonharmonic tones, chromatic progressions clearly point in the direction of ever-progressing, and ultimately complete separation from tonality, as in Schoenberg's recent works. In addition, there is the freely suspended rhythm for which the barline is of absolutely no consequence. The Sextet was played for the first time in Vienna by the Arnold Rosé Quartet. Since then it has been given repeated performances in cities around Germany and Austria.

Similarly revolutionary are the songs that precede the Sextet, Opp. 1, 2, and 3, with poems by Levetzow, Dehmel, Schlaf, Keller, Jacobsen, Lingg, and from the *Knaben Wunderhorn*. Schoenberg's songs are far removed from declamatory and pictorial intention. They are songs in the style of Schubert, Schumann, or Mahler, and are thoroughly imbued with Schoenberg's astonishingly expressive melodic style.

Closely following the Sextet are the *Gurrelieder* after poems by J. P. Jacobsen. The work breaks up into three completely self-contained parts and is for large orchestra, soloists, three four-part men's choruses, and, at the conclusion of the work, a mixed chorus. In addition, preceding the final chorus there is an episode of melodrama with a speaker.

Gurrelieder is scored for the following forces: 8 flutes (piccolos), 5 oboes (English horns), 7 clarinets, 5 bassoons (contrabassoon), 10 horns (Wagner tubas), and, in addition, 6 kettle drums, several timpani, 4 harps, celesta, and as large a string section as possible.

Schoenberg wrote this work in 1900 and to date it has not been given a complete performance. The first part alone was performed in Vienna in 1909 (!) with piano (!!). It is the foremost duty of those who are in a position to do so, to see to it that this work be given a worthy performance. It makes great demands, but similar tasks have been accomplished before; why not in this instance?

The individual songs of each section are self-contained compositions, but are connected by way of symphonic interludes which lead into one another.

I will cite a theme from the *Gurrelieder* in order to pursue further the path of Schoenberg's melodic style:

Especially noticeable are the wide intervals so prevalent in Schoenberg's music.

The four songs of Waldemar's men in the third section, sung by three male choruses, are remarkably elaborate and use entirely novel sound effects. The poem following the last of these, which concludes the work, is entitled "The Summer Wind's Wild Hunt." It was shaped by Schoenberg as follows: After a longer orchestral interlude, a speaker accompanied by the orchestra recites the poem in a slow, singing intonation until the words *See the sun!*; from this point on the mixed chorus takes over from the speaker with eight insertions of "See!" The effect of this choral entry is indescribable. The chorus which then follows and concludes the work is one of overwhelming beauty. As harmonic support a wonderfully expressive male chorus together with first and second soprano, alto and half of the first tenors, execute a double canon. The two simultaneously entering themes are the following:

In the first quarter of the second measure the second alto and the first tenor enter. Who could possibly shut himself off from the beauty of this music!

This part is performed by a small group of individual voices. It is followed by an entirely canonic, imitative passage of extreme rapture for all the choral forces.

The instrumentation of *Gurrelieder* creates the most colossal effect. One need only imagine the sensitivity to sound as expressed in Schoenberg's Sextet carried over into the enormous apparatus of this orchestra to get an idea of the grandeur and richness of this instrumentation.

Gurrelieder are followed by the symphonic poem *Pelleas and Melisande*, based on the drama of Maurice Maeterlinck (composed in Berlin in 1902). The instrumentation: 4 flutes (piccolos), 4 oboes (English horn), 4 bassoons (contrabassoon), 8 horns, 4 trumpets, 5 trombones, contrabass-tuba, timpani, 2 harps, 32 violins, 12 each of violas and cellos, 8 contra-basses.

This instrumental work by Schoenberg is also in one movement. It lasts almost one hour. Its structure is quite free. It has a gigantic number of themes. They are for the most part short and improvisational—with the exception of a scherzo-like theme and a long, spun-out Adagio—and are most artfully manipulated.

The richness of these modulations and variations is boundless. Each theme shows itself in a thousand shapes. The range of interpretation in Schoenberg's art is immeasurable. The instrumentation of this work is of a wonderful pathos and full of heretofore unknown colors.

I will cite two themes from *Pelleas*, in order to show how new they are with regard to harmony and melody, and how very much the tonal element of this music has slipped into the background.

In *Pelleas*, Schoenberg is one of the first to utilize the whole-tone scale and the chords that are based on it. I cite a section where these are represented in a series of major thirds.

Now I relate a fact that shows how Schoenberg accomplishes his harmonic conquests following nothing other than his immediate inspiration: in only one instance in *Pelleas*, in the following two measures, do we find one of the fourth chords (indicated by * in the example) that Schoenberg uses much later in the Chamber Symphony, Op. 9, where they were recently given conscious shape for the first time.

Pelleas was performed for the first time in Vienna in January 1905, with Schoenberg conducting, at a concert of the Society of Creative Composers. The work was given its second and up-to-now last performance in October 1910, in Berlin, under Oskar Fried. Schoenberg himself will conduct it in Prague in February 1912.

After *Pelleas* follow instrumental works in which Schoenberg, turning from the freely improvisational character of his earlier works, has created a new form harkening back to the classical quartet and symphony. These are: the First String Quartet in D Minor, Op. 7; the Chamber Symphony in E Major, Op. 9; and the Second String Quartet in F♯ Minor, Op. 10. The latter leads directly into the style of Schoenberg's present creations.

Between *Pelleas* and the First Quartet are the Six Orchestral Songs, Op. 8. They are set to poems by Hart, others from the *Knaben Wunderhorn,* and the sonnets of Petrarch. Their strict, thematic structure forms a transition to the works that follow.

In the First String Quartet, Schoenberg fuses the individual movement types of a classical quartet into a single large movement whose central section assumes the role of a large development. The development is the internal bond of this fusion. Preceding this section is the part that seems like the main movement of a sonata, with a long fugato between the main theme and secondary theme and the scherzo (with trio); following it comes the reprise of the main theme, followed by the Adagio, the repetition of the secondary theme, and at the end a rondo finale, the themes of which are modifications of the preceding sections. Basically the form of this quartet is that of one large movement of a sonata. The scherzo and the large development are inserted between the first development and the restatement of the secondary theme, and the reprise is extended by the Adagio, which comes between the main theme and the secondary theme. One could consider the rondo finale in this case to be a broadly expanded coda.

Like his awareness of form, the artistry of Schoenberg's themes is also greatly intensified in Op. 7. It is amazing how he builds an accompaniment figure out of the smallest part of a motive, how he introduces the themes, how he conceives of the connections between the individual main sections. And it is all done thematically! There is, so to say, no note in this work that doesn't become thematic. This is unprecedented. Most likely this is still a connection to Johannes Brahms.

Through the art of thematic development Schoenberg's quartet becomes a work of outstanding polyphony.

I introduce a theme from the Adagio as an example of Schoenberg's melodic style in this work:

The sonic effect of this quartet is completely new. This has an internal reason first of all: the new melodic and harmonic style of the themes. But then it also has an external reason—the utilization of new sonic possibilities developed in the string section of the modern orchestra: mutes, playing on the bridge, *col legno*, harmonics, etc. There is no question of external instrumental effects here. These new means of sound are born as a result of the expressiveness of this music. To this must be added the most wonderful utilization of the sounds of the strings and their different ranges.

This quartet had its premiere in Vienna by the Rosé Quartet. It was also played by them at the Thirty-Third Composer's Festival in Dresden, after the resident Petri Quartet had rejected it as "unperformable."

Then follows the Chamber Symphony in E Major, Op. 9. Schoenberg chose the title because of the completely solistic quality and treatment of the instruments, which give it the character of a work of chamber music. At its first and only (!) performance in Vienna by the Rosé Quartet and the Wind Instruments' Association [Bläservereinigung] of the Vienna Court Opera Orchestra, it was also performed without a conductor.

The instrumentation is as follows: 1 flute (alternating with piccolo), 1 oboe (alternating with English horn), one D (also E♭) clarinet, 1 A (also B♭) clarinet, 1 bass clarinet (A and B♭), 1 bassoon, 1 contrabassoon, 2 horns, one first and one second violin, 1 viola, 1 violoncello, one contrabass. Schoenberg adds: "Should it be necessary, the strings can also be increased in multiples: (6,6,4,4,3)."

The form of this work is also a fusion of the classical movement types whose sequence is similar to that of the First String Quartet. But the relationships are completely different here. The Chamber Symphony is in essence shorter. It is of a lighter and thoroughly lively character. In comparison to the First Quartet, the thematic artistry is intensified, since Schoenberg now works in the same manner with fifteen instruments. Harmonically and melodically the work introduces something quite new: the fourth harmonies and the melodic phrases stemming from the series of fourths. The beginning of the work shows both:

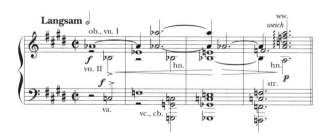

In addition, the whole-tone scale and the harmonies that develop from it achieve enormous significance.

Still greater artistry is found in Schoenberg's treatment of tonality. It is clearly present whenever strived for, but now only in paraphrases and oppositions.

I use as an example the secondary theme of the first main part; while unfolding, it seems not to belong to any key and yet gives the distinct impression of being in A major.

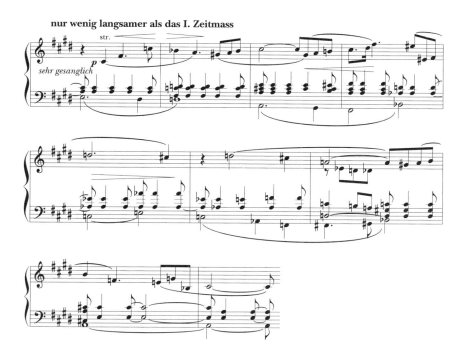

The theme of the slow part offers something similar:

But these examples show very clearly how Schoenberg's music forces itself away from tonality, which is completely undermined by the whole-tone scale, fourth chords and this type of melody.

The Eight Songs, Op. 6, also partake of all these principles. They were composed at approximately the same time as the First Quartet. Often Schoenberg's songs are studies for the revolutionary ideas of the larger works. The songs Op. 6 confront the problem of piano style. The poems are by Hart, Dehmel, Remer, Conradi, Keller, Mackay, Aram, and Nietzsche.

Between the Chamber Symphony and the Second String Quartet is a piece for eight-part mixed chorus a cappella [*Friede auf Erden*, Op. 13], a work of the most artful polyphony, most wonderful tonal effect, and sublimest expression. The first performance of this chorus was in December 1911 in Vienna under the direction of Franz Schreker (Philharmonic Chorus). Also written at this time were the Two Ballads for Voice and Piano [Op. 12].

Now to the Second String Quartet (F♯ Minor), with voice in the third and fourth movements.

First movement, moderate; second movement, very fast; third movement, "Litanei"; fourth movement, "Entrückung." The poems for the movements with voice are from *Der siebente Ring* by Stefan George.

As previously mentioned, in spite of its four movements this quartet has a formal relationship to Opp. 7 and 9: Here there is also a large, developmental section after the Scherzo, "Litanei." It is a variation movement, the theme of which is a combination of motives from the first and second movements.

The "model" of the large development in the Chamber Symphony is similarly constructed. The vocal part introduces new motives, which are developed together in the variations. The last movement, "Entrückung," has no connection to any recognizable instrumental form. It follows the poem freely. With its fragmentary quality and rich alternation of motives, the long instrumental introduction already prepares the way for Schoenberg's later works.

This quartet brings something new to Schoenberg's creative output: brevity. This quality first showed itself in the conciseness of the Chamber Symphony and is clearly evident in the F♯ Minor Quartet with the division into four shorter movements. It is but a small step from the harmony of this work to the complete abandonment of key. However, the last movement, although belonging mainly in F♯ major, has no signature. Through alteration the fourth chords change into never-before-heard harmonies that are free from any tonal relationship. A theme from the fourth movement is as follows:

ARNOLD SCHÖNBERG

Langsame Halbe

Ich lö - se mich in tö - nen, krei-

sehr ausdrucksvoll

send,____ we - bend un - grün-dig-en danks und

un - be nam - ten lo - bes dem gross - en a - tem wun - schlos____

____ mich er ge - bend.

(Ton!)

espr.

(Ton!)

A comparison of this melody with the musical example from the Sextet reveals what sort of development Schoenberg's melodic style has now taken. The inner ear feels the deeper relationship of these melodies. Chromaticism, notes that are dissonant with the accompanying harmony, broad and previously unusual intervals (eg. the major seventh)—these are the exclusive components of this melody.

This quartet was also given its premiere by Arnold Rosé, in December 1908.

All this leads directly to the style of the next work, to the fifteen songs from *The Book of the Hanging Gardens* by Stefan George.

In January 1910, when the Society for Art and Culture [Verein für Kunst und Kultur] in Vienna sponsored the first performances of Part I of *Gurrelieder*, with piano accompaniment, the George-Lieder, and the Piano Pieces Op. 11, Schoenberg wrote the following preface in the program:

"I composed the *Gurrelieder* early in 1900, the George songs and piano pieces in 1908. The time between perhaps justifies their great difference in style. Since the combination of such heterogeneous works within the confines of a single concert is a striking expression of one particular person's will, it, too, perhaps needs a word of justification.

"With the George songs I have for the first time succeeded in approaching an ideal of expression and form which has been in my mind for years. Until now, I lacked the strength and confidence to make it a reality. But now that I have set out along this path once and for all, I am conscious of having broken through every restriction of a bygone aesthetic; and though the goal towards which I am striving appears to me a certain one, I am, nonetheless, already feeling the resistance I shall have to overcome; I feel how hotly even the least of temperaments will rise in revolt, and suspect that even those who have so far believed in me will not want to acknowledge the necessary nature of this development.

"So it seemed a good thing to point out, by performing the *Gurrelieder*—which eight years ago were friendless, but today have friends enough—that I am being forced in this direction not because my invention or technique is inadequate, nor because I am uninformed about all the other things the prevailing aesthetics demand, but that I am obeying an inner compulsion, which is stronger than any upbringing: that I am obeying the formative process which, being the natural one to me, is stronger than my artistic education."[6]

The George-Lieder have to be performed in their totality and in immediate succession. Their relationship is not thematic; yet an inner architectonic design can clearly be felt. Schoenberg has created a wholly congruent, highly expressive melodic style, ideally suited to vocal recitation. He also achieves a marvelous wealth of tonal effects for the piano.

The George-Lieder were created in part before the Second Quartet. They fulfilled what had specifically been prepared for harmonically by the works immediately preceding them: key has completely disappeared. But an absolutely compelling necessity keeps watch over this harmonic style.

Schoenberg writes about this in his *Harmonielehre*:

"In composing I make decisions only according to feeling, according to the feeling for form. This tells me what I must write; everything else is excluded. Every chord I put down corresponds to a necessity, to a necessity of my urge to expression; perhaps, however, also to the necessity of an inexorable but unconscious logic in the harmonic structure. I am firmly convinced that logic is present here, too, at least as much so as in the previously cultivated fields of harmony. And as proof of this I can cite the fact that corrections of the inspiration, the idea (Einfall), out of external formal considerations, to which the alert consciousness is only too often disposed, have generally spoiled the idea. This proves to me that the idea was obligatory, that it had necessity, that the harmonies present in it are components of the idea, in which one may change nothing."[7]

The Three Piano Pieces, Op. 11, follow the songs based on George.

Each of these pieces is short. The first and second have a slight relationship formally to the three-part *lied* form. The short motives which immediately detach from one another are repeated again and then are spun out further. But even this fetter is removed in the third piece. Schoenberg abandons motivic working. No motive is developed further; at the most, a short succession of notes is immediately repeated. Once established, the theme expresses everything it has to say. Again something new has to follow. I demonstrate a section from the first piece, which gives an idea of the individuality of these themes, the combination of motives that are completely oppositional, the richness of this piano writing, and, moreover, the use of a heretofore utterly neglected sound effect from the piano, its harmonic tones.

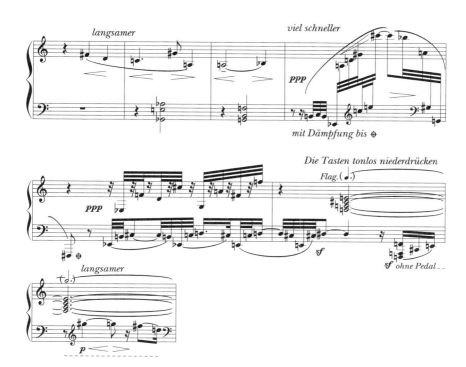

After the Piano Pieces Schoenberg composed Five Pieces for Orchestra.

The themes of these pieces are succinct but undergo elaboration. Only in the monodrama *Erwartung* did Schoenberg achieve the abandonment of all thematic work for the first time. There is no trace of any kind of traditional form in the Orchestra Pieces. The form is entirely free. One could perhaps speak of a kind of musical prose here. What Schoenberg said with reference to his harmonic style in the passage quoted above from *Harmonielehre* pertains as well to these forms. Here too an adherence to theoretical principles holds sway. The convincing power of this music vouches for it.

Here is a theme from the second piece:

How infinitely delicate is the expression of this theme, how marvelous the linking of the voices. This section also provides a glimpse into the instrumental miracle of this score. How remarkably the first chord is scored. More about this in conjunction with the orchestration of the monodrama.

The third piece offers a completely original sound effect.

The initial measures are as follows:

Schoenberg remarks: "The chord changes have to occur so gently that no accentuation of the entering instruments is noticeable; the changes should be perceptible only through the different coloration."

Due to the variation in color of the chords, which extends throughout the entire piece, a characteristically shimmering sound results, comparable, as Schoenberg says, to the ever-changing impressions of color in a moderately agitated sea surface.

Immediately following the orchestral pieces, Schoenberg wrote his first work for the stage, *Erwartung*, a monodrama by Elsa Pappenheim. A woman is the sole party responsible for an event presented in a series of short transformations connected by brief musical interludes. Late in the evening by the edge of a forest, a woman awaits her lover, searches for him in the forest throughout the night, and at last finds him killed next to the highway as morning dawns.

The work lasts approximately one-half hour. What brevity here, even in a theater work!

The score of this monodrama is an unprecedented event. All traditional formal principles have been severed; there is always something new, presented with the most rapidly shifting expression.

This is also true of the orchestration: a continuous succession of sounds never heard before. There is no measure in the score that doesn't demonstrate a completely new sound pattern. The treatment of the instruments is entirely soloistic. The registers of the instruments are fully utilized with a marvelous sense of timbre. Schoenberg scores chords in a completely new way.

An example:

Observe closely the singular compositional technique: the muted trumpet given the highest note, then the solo cello, below that the oboe (!), the muted trombone with the fourth, and the muted horn with the fifth note. In the second measure the contrabass adds a sixth note. Finally, interwoven into the whole is the sound of the vocal part. Each color derives from an entirely different timbral family. There is absolutely no blended sound here; each color resounds solistically, unbroken. But since each is selected so that no note overpowers the next in dynamics, a sonic unity results nevertheless.

The harmonic and melodic style of this work is of an unimagined richness. In it Schoenberg constructs eleven—and occasionally even twelve-part chords. Here is an example of an eleven-part chord:

What was said before concerning the instrumentation pertains here as well. I cite the following example in order to illustrate the melodic style of this work and the manner in which Schoenberg combines themes:

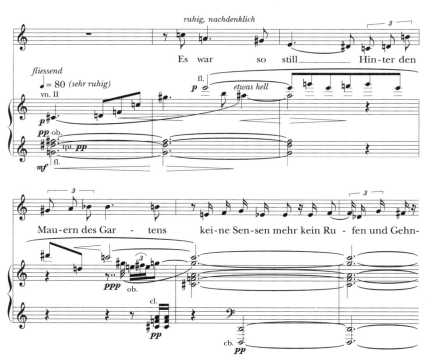

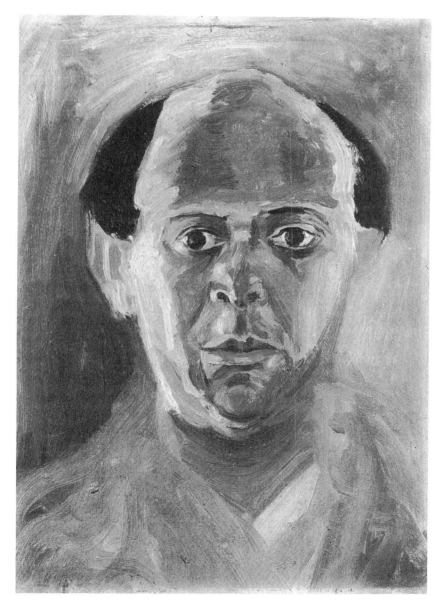

SELF-PORTRAIT

PAINTING

The melody of the second violin is taken over by that of the flute; the vocal line catches hold of both. In the fifth measure an orchestral chord closes off these melodic phrases; the vocal part, approaching a speaking tone in its expression, continues the sixteenth note movement begun by the entrance of the oboe in the fourth measure. Thus this music flows by, tightly bound forms along with disintegrating ones, breaking up recitative forms, giving expression to the most hidden and faintest stirrings of emotion.

Now follow six new piano pieces [Op. 19] and the second stage-work, *Glückliche Hand*, drama with music.

The new piano pieces are very short, unbelievably delicate and expressive structures. Say what you will about it, it all is mere lip-service in light of this music. The music of *Glückliche Hand* is still incomplete. The poem of this work is by Schoenberg himself. It appeared in volume 17 (2nd year) of the Viennese musical journal *Der Merker*, devoted to Schoenberg.[8]

What I have attempted to show is the relentless necessity with which everything in Schoenberg's creative work is accomplished.

Those who devote themselves lovingly to this work must recognize this. Only those blinded by envy and ill-will could speak of "sensationalism mania" and the like. Since such assertions impede the influence of Schoenberg's work, they must be eradicated. But as for the work itself, no harm can come to it: it is beyond the realm of time.

ANTON VON WEBERN

THE *HARMONIELEHRE*

The important teacher is always effective through his example. Even if he does not demonstrate the skill to be learned, but only explains it, he influences by the example of his whole essence. A good textbook presupposes a certain suggestive personality who stands tangibly before his pupils in every sentence. Therefore Arnold Schoenberg had an absolute calling to write *the* musical textbook. For he possesses that true multifacetedness based on *one* homogenous spirit that permeates his whole essence. All his utterances become avowals and reveal a deeper unity that of itself serves as a model. That phenomenon is so extensive, that one could learn more composition from hearing him speak about the most remote things than from thick-bodied theoretical books. And, on the other hand, this textbook of harmony instruction has meaning not only for the musician but also anyone who considers artistic problems to be life's problems. For the creator of this book possesses a brilliant creative power combined with the insatiable craving for knowledge characteristic of the true philosopher, to whom it is granted to see problems everywhere. For him there is nothing that is extrinsic, even the most insignificant things are given a perspective, because at no point does he ever lose sight of the life of art and ultimately of life itself. It is precisely for this reason that the pupil acquires a disproportionately greater respect for artistic material than precepts or inhibitions could ever instill; because he learns to be conscious of the relationship between the most insignificant detail and the deepest essence of artistic things, and by way of that is trained to achieve the highest goal of education, honesty.

From this it is self-evident that strictest objectivity is the earmark of Schoenberg's style. There are no decorative words of secondary importance here, there are only primary words. You have the feeling that were you to omit just one sentence, the balance of this book so laden with deep thoughts would be upset. Style is produced as the direct result of point of view, verbal richness from the virtually tremendous profusion of ideas. And for all his severity he is so personal that were you acquainted with Schoenberg you would think that while reading you heard his voice. You can never grow tired of this work whose verbal purity seems miraculous in journalistic times, and you repeatedly find passages which will remain unforgettable because of the immortal way they are expressed.

What differentiates this book on harmony in its purely musical content from all contemporary textbooks is the circumstance that it was written by someone who understands music from his innermost being and not merely at second hand like the "theoreticians." Only someone whose knowledge stems directly from his experience could succeed in transforming the false presupposition from which music education has proceeded up to now and give it a natural basis. It shows, namely, that so-called music theory can never really be that which it claims to be: a system of explanations able to establish eternal rules and aesthetic principles, but rather at best a system of representation, which distinctly orders artistic phenomena. Schoenberg has the courage to designate and comprehend the instruction of composition as what it can only be, an "instruction of handicraft." That premise is never abandoned in this work: the pupil is never given just rules, but instead receives directions for the appropriate use of artistic tools that are put into his hand in a careful, pedagogically systematic and reflective manner. The pupil is not about to be permitted to write down everything; quite the contrary, he is bound to follow formulae that are stricter by far than those of the ordinary theory teachers. But the pupil knows he must avoid certain things because he is not mature enough to use them yet, and not, as it were, because they are bad or not beautiful. Of course Schoenberg also gives explanations for his instructions, and even to a far greater degree than is usually the case. The essential difference is that he does not give aesthetic but instead gives physical and psychological proof, and does not search for rules in order to find inflexible artistic norms, for searching becomes an end in itself. Because he continually finds relationships, the subject comes to life as never before. The entire process of harmony no longer appears to be the result of dead formulae; rather a psychology of harmony is created. Therefore precisely the talented person, who barely understood before what that boring system had to do with music, now will find what is uniquely important for him.

The physical basis to which Schoenberg attempts to trace back all phenomena is for him as well as for science the theory of overtones. And even in this he succeeds in exhibiting entirely new relationships. Schoenberg points out, first of all, that not only the basic major triad, but also the major scale is given in the overtone series. He thus explains the origin of the most primitive musical tools, scale and triad, as an imitation of a model found in nature: the tone as a result of its overtones, in its horizontal as well as vertical manifestation. This principle of imitating a model is communicated throughout the entire book as the psychological foundation for the development of musical technique. In accordance with the theory of the triad, Schoenberg also casts aside the second false premise of "music theory": the *distinction* between consonance and dissonance, which we might be inclined to call the grand delusion of harmonic theory. He proves unequivocally that there is no essential difference, but rather a gradual one, between consonance and dissonance. That means that there are only nearer and more distant composite sounds, all of which exist in nature and are therefore of equal value for the artist, and their applicability depends solely upon the training of the ear. The proof is so convincing that the result seems immediately obvious, as obvious as brilliant discoveries which never presume anything but the ability to see with our own eyes what we had picked up by way of the senses from our ancestors. Just like the prejudice against dissonance, the generally accepted view of forbidden parallels is also dismissed. Schoenberg demonstrates that this prohibition like many others, can have only historical meaning, that originally "octaves and fifths were not in themselves *bad*, but on the contrary, were in themselves *good*; that they had merely come to be considered outdated, primitive, relatively artless; that there was no physical nor aesthetic reason, however, why they should not on occasion still be used."9 Thus Schoenberg points out the emptiness of all those formulae to which theory holds fast, because it would be able to find no standpoint in the eternal flow of artistic development. That is how the breach in the old system of harmonic instruction, pointed out in the chapter on nonharmonic tones, comes to light. For the chords resulting from those notes that are nonharmonic, as Schoenberg points out in a brilliant polemic, are harmonies like any other. They are not random, because in masterworks nothing can be viewed as random; their legitimacy just hasn't been acknowledged as yet. The difference between random chord structures and those acknowledged as independent is only a historical one, because the dominant seventh chord was only possible, originally, as a passing sonority. "There are, then, no nonharmonic tones, no tones foreign to harmony, but merely tones foreign to the harmonic system."10 There is no reason, therefore, why every chord arising originally from voice-leading cannot be used independently. This means: any chord is possible. Ultimately the staunchest prejudice, the belief in the necessity of tonal boundaries for a piece of music, must give way. Schoenberg doesn't consider harmony "to be a natural law nor a constraint exerted by the substance of music, but rather an artistic device that makes it possible for us to lend musical thoughts the aura of completeness."11 And he shows that even those contemporary compositions that still officially acknowledge tonality carry within themselves the seeds of its death; that their harmonic design no longer consistently expresses the relationship to key, that all that is needed, therefore, for the total disintegration of tonality is a small step. For the artist, as Schoenberg explains—and this is the most valuable consequence of this work—there are absolutely no aesthetic prerequisites: "Beauty exists only from that moment on when the unproductive begin to miss it. Before that it does not exist, for the artist does not need it. To him integrity is enough. To him it is enough to have expressed himself. To have said what had to be said; according to the laws of *his* nature."[12] Thus this textbook turns *unintentionally* into one of the most brilliant vindications of modern music, because Schoenberg's interest lies primarily in showing the pupil that art need not concern itself with rules, that the latter have only a limited validity with regard to a certain style and are of value to us only pedagogically. This is stressed repeatedly, of course, and in a very forceful manner. He says so himself: "After I have shown the pupil to what extent these rules are absolutely not mandatory, I place a check on his desire to unleash his disdain for them, by developing his sense of form so profoundly according to the old rules, that he will be able to tell in time just how far he may go, and what state a composition must be in, in order for rules to be disregarded."

The way Schoenberg develops a pupil's feeling for form is fundamentally different from the way it is usually done today, in that, in the first place, he specifies precisely the function of the theory of harmony. He differentiates much more sharply than is customary between the subject areas of harmony and counterpoint, and puts major emphasis on the exercise in working with harmonics, that is, on fundamentals, on purely harmonic structure. This is again self-evident, but demonstrates precisely why it is not customary with present-day teachers. As in other instances, Schoenberg harkens back to the method used by older theoreticians, because they are closer to fulfilling his need for objectivity. Therefore he provides the pupil no figured basses but instead, from the first day on, has him compose little pieces with the simplest means given him. The pupil himself has to sketch the voice that determines harmonic structure, the bass, thereby paving the way in advance for the development of his specifically harmonic sense of form. Just as Schoenberg proceeds from no other hypotheses but those that are revealed within himself, he presupposes nothing on the part of the pupil. He hands him the tools that will be used gradually, in sequence, and with increasing difficulty, so that the pupil is hardly conscious of them. Nothing is regarded as a matter of course, because nothing is trifling, nothing is too insignificant for the person for whom the material of his art is sacred. On account of the unusual thoroughness with which everything is treated here, the precepts that the pupil never has to accept blindly take on far greater importance for him. He knows why he has to keep very precisely to all the old rules, whose limited validity he is reminded of time and again. He knows that he should try first to strive for one goal: to bring clearly to expression the simplest possible style. If the means accessible to the pupil are somewhat richer, then the standard fundamental steps are given an exhaustive investigation. At this point, which has to be the true center of harmony instruction, Schoenberg once again takes up and develops independently an idea alluded to by older theoreticians and long forgotten today— one, of course, obligatory for the pupil—that of giving considerable value to the fundamental steps as they result from the harmonic structure of classical works. The division of the fundamental steps that results serves as groundwork for the entire remainder of the instruction. It can only be touched upon cursorily here that in the chapters on inversions, origins of the minor mode, and the treatment of dissonances, entirely new psychological perspectives are opened up, and the pupil learns to handle these in an unusually conscientious manner. The extraordinary objectivity and rigor with which Schoenberg leads the pupil from step to step features prominently in the chapters that treat cadence and modulation. The pupil is not shown the usual practicable maneuvers by which he can modulate anywhere without hesitation, rather he is obliged to apply a modulation methodically. Thus a very rigorous system is developed, based upon the simplest tonal relationships, whereby the pupil learns to work out modulations in which every chord has meaning and which demonstrate a well-thought-out construction. Step by step broader relationships are made accessible, without losing sight of the goal-oriented design. As an enriching element, the chords designated by Schoenberg as secondary dominants are inserted into the system, then the altered ones harkening back to the accidentals of the church modes, and finally the "vagrant" chords. The diminished seventh chord, formerly handed the pupil so that he could skip from key to key without a second thought, obtains its clear position in the tonal system by being classified as a ninth chord with its root omitted, and is treated exactly like tonal chords in the narrower sense. The kindred relationships that the modulation had opened up are then used for the enrichment of the cadence. These now shift into the foreground, systematically providing greater possibilities for their expansion, so that the ultimate result is a plastic image of the infinite wealth of relationships within the scope of tonality. Eventually all known harmonic means are included in the system, even the ninth chords usually treated as stepchildren and finally even the whole-tone chords and the fourth chords whose derivation and systematic treatment are offered here for the first time.

These are only a few of the most obvious characteristics of the book. To cite each special feature would be impossible, because *everything* is special. There would be no page we could skip over; in the end we would rather copy down the book from A to Z. For this textbook has the richness and the expressive power of a work of art, and who could possibly conceptualize such a thing for a person unacquainted with it? If only our era, which likes to lie dormant during great events, could be made aware of *this* work. Especially the young, the really young musicians, for whom this book will be an artistic gospel. And the nonspecialists, who already place some trust in the name Schoenberg but who shrink away in fear from the title *Harmonielehre*, because they do not understand that this work is a confession that speaks to everyone. Ultimately also those who are perhaps looking for a theory of harmony, but who shy away from the name Schoenberg because they believe all those who shape public opinion negatively, who, knowing that several of Schoenberg's pupils have written dissonances, have drawn the faulty conclusion that their teacher had forced them to do so. It is quite obvious that those who expressly wanted to study with Schoenberg didn't become his pupils by chance, but rather because, even before they began to study with him, they had felt an affinity to those forbidden sounds within themselves. There are people who would opt more easily for a slanderous statement than for such a simple reflection. But this book will prove in black and white to all those who do not wish to understand that Schoenberg is the best teacher because he is the sternest. Only there is an essential difference between his severity and that of the accredited theoreticians: the latter fear "that which abideth not by their rules"; Schoenberg shuns all artistic dishonesty and wants to bring the pupil to the point of understanding that everything he does must stem from an inner necessity.

HEINRICH JALOWETZ

SELF-PORTRAIT

THE PAINTINGS

The paintings of Schoenberg fall into two categories: those that are drawn perfectly true to nature, such as people or landscapes, and those that are intuitively conceived heads, which he calls "Visions."

Schoenberg himself refers to the first group as necessary finger exercises, does not value them especially, and is reluctant to exhibit them.

The second group he paints, just as infrequently as the first, in order to bring to expression those stirrings of his soul that cannot find any musical form.

These two kinds are outwardly quite different. Inwardly they stem from one and the same soul, which is made to vibrate sometimes by external nature and at other times by nature within.

This division is naturally a generalization, and is strongly colored schematically.

In a wider reality, one can hardly separate outer and inner experiences so bluntly. Both kinds of experiences have, so to speak, many long roots, fibers, and branches, which penetrate each other, intertwine, and in the end form a complex that is and remains significant for the artistic soul.

This complex is, so to speak, the digestive organ of the soul, its transforming, creative force. It is the originator of the transforming inner activity, which manifests itself in a transformed external form. By means of the qualities of this complex, unique in each case, the art-forming apparatus of the individual artist produces works that bear his imprint, so to speak, and reveal the "handwriting" of the artist. Of course, these popular designations are completely superficial, since they stress only the external, the formal, and neglect the internal almost entirely. That means that here, as so often, the external is given altogether too much respect.

With the artist, the external is not only defined by the internal, but it is also created by the internal, as in any other creation, even that of the cosmos.

Seen from this vantage point, the artworks of Schoenberg permit us to recognize his emotional complex beneath the imprint of his form.

First of all, we see *immediately* that Schoenberg paints not in order to paint something "beautiful" or "charming," but that he paints without even thinking about the picture itself. Renouncing the objective result, he seeks to affix only his subjective feelings, and for that purpose uses only the means that seem to him indispensable at that moment. Not every professional artist can lay claim to this mode of creativity! Or stated differently, infinitely few professional artists possess this fortunate power, and at times this heroism, this energy of renunciation, whereby all kinds of artistic diamonds and pearls, when they fall of themselves into their hands, are quietly left aside unnoticed, or are even discarded. Schoenberg proceeds directly toward his goal, or, led by his goal, directly toward the necessary resolution.

*   *
*

The purpose of a picture is to give an outward expression to an inner impression through the medium of painting. That may sound like a well-known definition! If we can follow it to its logical conclusion, that a picture actually has no other purpose, then I should like to ask: How many pictures are perfectly clear examples of works unsullied by what is unnecessary? Or, how many pictures actually remain pictures when measured by this very harsh and inflexible test, and not mere "objets d'art" that deceitfully simulate the necessity of their existence?

*   *
*

A picture is an external expression of an inner impression in painted form.

He who accepts this definition after painstaking and exact examination, thereby receives a correct—and it should be stressed— an *inalterable* standard for every picture, be it recently created, still wet upon the easel, or whether it be discovered as a mural, unearthed from a bygone city deeply buried in time.

Many a viewpoint concerning matters of art must change if this definition be accepted. In passing, I would like to take one of these views, and, in the light of the above definition, forcibly remove it from the blindness of the usual prejudices. Not only the art critics and the public, but usually also the artist himself see in the development of an artist the search for the appropriate form.

From this viewpoint often arise several poisonous consequences.

The artist thinks that after he has finally "found his form" he can continue *calmly* to produce further works of art. Unfortunately, he himself does not even notice that from this moment (of "calm") he very soon begins to lose the form he has finally found.

The public (in part under the influence of the art theoreticians) does not notice this regression so quickly, and thrives on productions of a dying form. On the other hand, convinced of the possibility of an artist finally having achieved his personal form, they criticize sharply those artists who are still without form, who reject one form after another in order to find the "right" one. The works of such artists exist without the attention justly due them, and the public does not even try to glean from those works their obligatory content.

Thus arises a completely reversed relationship to art, in which the dead is taken for the living, and vice versa.

In reality, the progress of an artist consists not in the *external* development (a search for form for the unaltered state of the soul), but rather in the *inner* development (the reflection of spiritually attained desires in the form of painting).

The content of the artist's soul enlarges, it becomes more precise, and increases in inner dimensions, upward, downward, and in all directions. At the moment at which a certain *inner level* is reached, the outward form lends itself to being at the disposal of the inner value of this level.

And on the other hand: at the very moment when inner growth comes to a standstill and immediately falls prey to the decline of the inner dimensions, the "already achieved form" slips away from the artist. Thus we often see this dying off of the form, which is the dying off of the inner desire. Thus an artist loses mastery over his own form, which becomes fatigued, weak, poor. And hence is explained the wonder that suddenly an artist can no longer paint, for example, or that his earlier, living color lies on the canvas merely as a pale illusion, as an artistic carcass.

The decadence of form is the decadence of the soul, that is, of content. And the increase of form is the growth of content, that is, of the soul.

*   *
*

When we apply these standards to the paintings of Schoenberg, we see immediately that we are dealing here with *painting*, whether or not this painting may lie apart from the great movements of today.

We see that in every painting of Schoenberg, the inner wish of the artist speaks in the form that best befits it. Just as with his music (inasmuch as I, a layman, may affirm), so too in his painting does Schoenberg renounce the superfluous (therefore the harmful), and proceed along a direct path to the essential, (therefore to the necessary). He pays no attention to any embellishments and artistic detail.

His *Self Portrait* is painted with so-called "palette dirt." And what other painting materials should he have selected in order to achieve this strong, sober, precise and concise impression?

A portrait of a woman shows, in more or less accented color, *only* the sickly pink of the dress—otherwise no "colors."

A landscape is gray-green, *only* gray-green. The drawing is simple and truly "awkward."

A *Vision* is *only* a head on a very small canvas (or on a piece of cardboard wrapping). *Only* the red-rimmed eyes are extremely expressive.

I should most like to call Schoenberg's art *the painting of the "only"* [*Nurmalerei*].

Schoenberg reproaches himself for his lack of technique.

I would like to alter these reproaches according to the standards delineated above. Schoenberg is deceived—he is not dissatisfied with his technique of painting, but rather with his inner desire, with his soul, from which he demands more than it can give him today.

I would hope for this feeling of dissatisfaction for every artist—for all times.

It is not difficult to advance externally. It is not easy to progress inwardly.

May fate grant that we do not turn away the inner ear from the words of the soul.

W. KANDINSKY

PORTRAIT OF A LADY

SCHOENBERG THE PAINTER

[TRANSLATED WITH THE ASSISTANCE OF JEREMY BRETT]

A language that admits a listener to the work of a composer but fails when confronted by a painterly invention, that withholds the complement and even intends, in keeping with the noble indolence of an age-old incongruity, to close the door on the heated logic that opposes the viewer: this language has hidden, denunciatory capacities.

Since it is known that there are no coincidences in language, this moral universe of speech, and that laws and new tablets above us break through the horizontal line of resistance, which seems antisocial but is in reality aesthetic, and mix the denominator with a numerator that finally comprehends; since the most mature language has congealed into an authoritarian form: Therefore no hypothetical courage is necessary to find a judgment about painting and music themselves in the different ways we name those two representatives of art's most basic level. And to one who does not stop there, language, which in the highest sense could and ought to exist even without man, reveals something of its subtle drive to retaliation, which always expresses itself after periods that exhibit a scarcity of vocatives and whose need for complication has not been met by minds of equal caliber.

Thus it seems as if in this particular example, the proper language would recall innumerable ecstatic phenomena of the reception of good music. Thus Drama, caught in the act, surrenders to Fantasy brought up on the scenic: The concept Listener, attacked and overcome by Melos, convinced of the reality of earthly-musical values, foregoes the nobility of a deeper metaphysical meaning, and the serious might recognize that the sense organs at their origins did not receive impulses automatically, independent from the act of will, but that as consecrated places on the human being they were designated only for the perception of sudden, rare, and precious revelations.

Orpheus might have defiled the Patmos of the ear since he dared bring music unto the beasts—luckily, as reports a tradition not yet corrupted by higher humanity, which had perhaps already become aware of the parody in this affair.

But painting, of all the arts the one with the most unheroic origins, stable and unaggressive, has been inferior up to now in its struggle with the transcendent, and the viewer still bears the religious mask of the prophet, even though it has become a theatrical prop and is no longer seriously present.

If, astonished at the naïve legends that surround music, one were to measure the power of Melos to expand, and then turn with the same intention to painterly invention, one would get the impression that encounters with painting have never reached very deep. The excesses practiced in scholars' studies are artificially produced symptoms of critically engaged intellects, pretexts to enrich the language. Decisive, though, is the consumer, that most deceitful species: man, who, exposed in an honest moment, will admit that he views painting, as it has existed for him up to now, like word and tone, and that he has heard what the optical consciousness reproaches it for: it has won no victories over the metaphysical and has not increased the reality of the world.

This claim must sound strange, since in culture we believe we know that there is no art that is more naturalistic, none that better rises to the imitation of even the most idiomatic accents. This knowledge however is judgment. If for the sake of brevity I may be permitted a short metaphor: tone and word are like birds, which rise continually before my eyes from the invisible into the visible; which leave no trace of corporeal origins; which produce their effects precisely where they are farthest from the experience that provided the stimulus; which prefer to create anachronistically in the highest sense, and for that reason—because they are so misleading and they permit no inference from the artwork to the impulse—create the impression of a new and higher reality, which is accepted so unequivocally as real that one would laugh were one not also to accept as real the lower level of reality. Whereby the everyday world appears to be saved.

Perhaps painting was not psychically free enough from its material to be a match for such a moral process. In a panic-driven paralysis of the feet given him and him alone for running away when in place of the inside the outside asks to become plastic, the artist stood in reproductive patience before the object preying on his gaze, whose formal reflections he, by shifting the unities of time (his own and that of the object), in other words by counterpoint (Greco), turns from an uninteresting condition of virtue to an impression of the problematical, or by attempts like Cézanne's keeps them suspended above the objects through a disturbance of balance (slipping cloths, glasses in disarray) brought about by a simulated event beyond the canvas, which expresses itself for an eternity of seconds in a *suspension* of weight and stability, in a deep, liberated breath between two states.

Now comes along someone—and this someone is a musician—who already knows that a work of art expresses nothing but immeasurable distances. He possesses a cultivated terminology, is prepared to use it provisionally to underlay a palette poor in technical functions linguistically defined, and leads painting, which has grown soft through a dissipated life of the senses, first before an ice-cold eye of logic, and then, when the weaning from the objective has reached the arctic pole of its own reason, leads it back to the limits of the prehistoric, to that place pieced together by invisible diagonals, whence it might still be possible to achieve the indispensable connection to legend. Without costume, and in a completely unromantic manner, forms arise that no longer exist, which, were they to appear in the head of a painter, would be overlooked as incomprehensible atavisms, forms whose sole function is this: boundless mistrust of the man who, when he acts and perceives, thinks of himself as a machine; but who, when attacked, brims over with soul, pretends to be illogical and, as it were, manually active, and who at a cue from the mightier one begins to have doubts. According to universal human nature, doubt is no noble, early-morning, contemplative action, no inclination for theft, but rather an expression of slavish devotion, a doglike condition of humility in the face of a more powerful phenomenon: be it called God, Art, or Superman.

What are represented on Schoenberg's enigmatic canvases are neither sensuous feelings swarming hungrily in the darkened spheres of the brain, nor facts in physical light.

They are depictions, more colorful than one is accustomed to, of the moral man—in the Kantian sense. (Up to now, language alone was the material of the moral man.) It is beautiful how the morality of these pictures establishes itself: in order to translate these forms into something that is tangible and anecdotal—however inadequate this attempt may be—I would have to unite with all the observers in one focal viewpoint. But the paintings close themselves off to precisely this economy of optical powers, and begin to become incomprehensible in that moment when one person makes the step to another as a like member of the species.

Arnold Schoenberg, the thinker, attempts to recreate finally for painting that condition of psychological primitivism, that prehistoric kind of former life without which its present existence would not appear as truly legitimate. And he alone has been able patiently to create these forms that are so completely irrelevant for the one who enjoys them, since he, already protected by a progressive and comprehensible art—his music—appears almost immunized. Only those who already possess somewhere a boundless certainty are true discoverers; not those who have built their creations on nothing and have merely appropriated the universal gesture as their own. (With artists like Arnold Schoenberg, who are able to bring out the potential

VISIONS

of several media, the only question remaining is which medium projects the greatest assurance.)

The dangerous game interests the son: the forefathers construct.

That all paternity is uncertain was likely known by some esoterics among the Latins, who with a hopeless grimace toward women, raised this perception to the status of a law. But the really instructive and, in our case, tangential aspect of this perception does not serve the *man* in the *marriage*, but rather the *little man* in *science,* and it should ultimately occasion the explanation that the female in the cosmos is determined to leave the descent of the male entirely in the dark; that every development is the result of a general infidelity; that life will exist only so long as marriages with persons and spheres are broken.

But what has up to now been presupposed as the mythical age of painting, that primitiveness which referred merely to the physical appearance of the object, suddenly no longer appears to be the sole form of a still pretechnical productivity as manifested in children, barbarians, or decadents seeking to be archaic *in the place of* talent or genius; rather, beyond that primitiveness emerges a second origin that is truly spiritual and pure.

It is correct and should be stressed that the kind of primitiveness that employs the physical body and the objects of its plane as a language does not represent the beginning of a talent, the chaotic vortex of a crystal in the making, but is rather an attractive substitute for a talent, a *passive kind of ability*, and, for the cultivated, a handicraft-styled consolation for being merely the stimulus to genius.

Beginning, then talent and genius, and in man, finally, drive similar to other drives—such is Platonic primitiveness.

To the painter of such forms, any objective appearance is the obvious, and not at all desired or expected, peripheral reflex of the central process in the ideal, in the legend-circle of Platonic ideas.

The chain of causality, so thinks his eye, would better decorate the white neck of a lovely girl than would work of his own.

Since he may know no stable phenomenon, he may arrive at no stylistic mannerism, like the purely empirical primitive who is convinced of stasis; since he may know of nothing but the variable, and this knowledge articulates itself ever more inexplicably in technique the more often the uncertainty itself changes its molecular makeup, all comprehension of such forms remains relative, and some always obscure to any other than the creator himself, for the stage in which the variable finds itself when caught in any one of its projections cannot be maintained a second later, but is transformed into some other kind of condition by an extra-personal, higher insight, and so for the brain the only help would seem to be: to maintain something that was tenable in the hallucinatorily perceived *congruity* between *the probability of such a movement* and *the possibility of such an expression*. But as the moral person he has had to discover himself to be (perhaps at the expense of epic-sensual capabilities) since he elevated suspicion to a refined art (and thus vanquished psychology), he has kept watch on the intellectual functions, for inferior things and such pretexts of phenomena that served suppression and allowed their own misuse as symbols to be transformed into new organs beside the physical ones . . . into moral organs.

Someone who climbs from above to below in this way must be confronted by doubt, as mankind experiences it; this doubt is nothing more than a proof of the supernatural, and to the angel flying down to earth it would be the first proof of the earth's being inhabited.

But he took this doubt and set it above all his organs. An exceptional state, as none before! Not that he doubted the objects. Only the fanatically egocentric youth who overestimates the power of his skepticism avoids the dangers of such distances. But he who knows from the highest lyrical ideas of his art (ideas from the margins) that the real "I" begins where it is no longer expected and exists precisely in those areas of the sensitive cosmos that have until now withdrawn from conquest through memory: he discovered suddenly (one can only discover suddenly) that man is a sum of resistances.

Thus did a brilliant chaos of speculations (thieves of conscience) scatter into the light with its prey. The vertical frenzy of concluding thoughts befell a person inclined to every form of intellectualism (especially to the kind that makes its appearance geometrically and makes *that* artist who lets himself be seen next to a serious machine seem interesting). Words of the biologists associated with the terminology of the self-creator and concepts from the science of the poor and from compassionate sociology occur to this man who is passionately wedded to the hypothesis (the man whom conversance with the experimental sciences converted in favor of the doubtful): struggle for life, adaptation, natural selection, he himself in a thousand situations that show him still pensive when he retreated from the multitude, and that recall reproachfully those once so admired and much-thanked moments of conception, when from a brain numbed by ideas he could snatch away only a *single* one, could bring to a halt only *one* spoke from the wheel of motion.

Could? he asks, and thus falls victim to a rhyming, echo-like phonetics. He contemplated the vast powers of his will. And admitted: great, fantastically great, peripheral to all thoughts. And discovered and was not silent: my great power spans it, but many, many forces that express themselves posthumously, many thousand hereditary hands do the opposite on the same wood!

My will stands against the will of the species: the single man, wounded by divine impulse to leak for all seas of the earth, against his race, for whom he is only a creature that must be protected from being crushed by the fullness of figure, in which the ideal becomes plausible and whirls into the funnels of reason.

And through thousands of years, which seemed to this creature-turned-ornament to abound with developments and reflections of renaissances, this apodictic will of the species busied itself with nothing more energetically than pruning back the immense trees of the sense organs more and more, fashioning the canals of conception more and more narrowly, making the business of reception more and more difficult (*yet, in an act of tremendous dilettantism, accelerating the delivery*), so that today we already speak of a grace of inspiration, and, schooled on a glorious past, we recognize that nothing remains of the insatiable optical growths and tentacles of the first spirit-man except this hewn stump called the eye, and nothing remains from a sea of hearing except this last shell of an ear.

The sensitive organs, previously intended for reception, now serve only the fear of the unspiritual man: being crushed by the multitude, they have become organs of repulsion and defense, and "to look" means to choose, to reduce, to make less hideous, to paralyze, to undeify.

They have sunk to mere symptoms of being able to hear and see, and out of shame and contempt for the cowardliness of the external man, they have retreated completely within.

Sadly my painter saw in the sense-organs caves made comfortable by ornament; man has crawled inside to escape the multitude. There he experienced the possibility of his art. There he turned to that shattered man, preaching but not yet converting, and lured him out into the multiplying light of the multitude, and, himself standing before the cave of the intelligent troglodyte, raised Color, and thereby arrived at Line.

What arose from this sad, silent, almost hopeless tenderness brought forth his paintings.

The naked brain.

Very few trust these paintings. Most hate them instinctively at first sight.

Like the painters: for the fear of having perhaps to do likewise has scared the heathens to death.

PARIS VON GÜTERSLOH

THE TEACHER

(COLLECTED CONTRIBUTIONS BY HIS PUPILS)

What makes studying music with Schoenberg so fascinating is this enormous accumulation of energy contained in every word he speaks. Nothing ever becomes routine, formulaic, or rigid. It is characteristic that Schoenberg always walks back and forth when he develops something; because everything within him is in turmoil and motion. Lecturing for him always means developing, deflecting, making something fluid. Schoenberg never says what he knows, but rather what he thinks, what he thinks anew each time. Mere knowledge is a dead thing. It has been absorbed once, has been fixed in memory and slowly disintegrates there. Those who are weak thinkers live off knowledge. Their processes of renewal have stopped; they have shut themselves up like a snail that senses its end, with the one exception that the snail is a very delicate creature and *senses* its end; those people, however, whose development takes place in large part physically, go on living vacuously and let themselves be nurtured to a ripe old age by knowledge. If they have the misfortune to be involved with the next generation, for instance as teachers, they help create persons who always know where something can be "found," where "the same kind" is, and who "know those who." Wustmann[13] already made fun of those dime-a-dozen people twenty years ago, the kind who have an "opinion" everywhere because they have learned something everywhere. Learning is the thing. Most are proud of the thing learned, of that which someone else has drilled, pressed, and pounded into them, which is actually no learning at all, but rather mere addition. Facts are placed alongside facts; their functions and qualities are a part of other subjects, just as prescribed by a genuine theory of language. Oh, that kind of mind is great. Real learning would not be placing things next to each other, but things flowing in and out of each other, the capability of change and the capability of bringing new things to light. Learning is not addition, but multiplication.

Learning multiplication with Schoenberg is far more than one usually expects from the study of music. Because it shows us undeniably who has artistic merit. Every possibility of feigning music that did not originate multiplicatively, that did not flow together in the depths and become crystallized, is excluded. In the beginning those who study like to reject everything; they make everything more difficult than the material demands; they place artificial barriers around a simple melody so that it will at least seem interesting. They do not do this consciously or intentionally, but merely because they are not quite clear about a lot of things. But Schoenberg hears when a melody strays on purpose. He prefers honest banality to that.

Once I brought a song that I liked so much to a lesson, mainly because the song was so difficult. After Schoenberg had read it through, he said:

"Did you really conceive this so complicatedly?"

A pupil always answers yes to such a question, because it is flattering. But Schoenberg did not relent:

"I mean: Did your first inspiration so unambiguously include that complicated form of accompaniment?"

A pupil does not always answer that kind of a question in the affirmative. Because he feels how it cuts to the quick. I tried to recall the initial idea. But Schoenberg, strengthened by my uncertainty, continued:

"Didn't you add this figure onto it after the fact, in order to put clothes onto an harmonic skeleton? Like one sticks facades onto buildings?"

Now he had it, too. It turned out the idea was only harmonic, not a compelling generator of movement.

"Look, just accompany the song harmonically. It will seem primitive, but it will be more genuine than this. Because what you have here is ornament. These are three-part inventions decorated by a singing voice. Music is not supposed to decorate, it is just supposed to be true. Wait patiently for an idea that comes immediately into consciousness as a rhythm, in the horizontal dimension. You will be surprised how much driving force such an inspirational idea has. Look at Schubert's song "Auf dem Flusse," and how one movement creates the next. And then: nothing should present itself to you as difficult. What you compose should seem as obvious to you as your hands and your clothes. Until that happens, you should not even write it down. The simpler your things seem to you, the better they will be. Sometime bring me those works that you don't want to show me because they seem too simple and artless to you. I will prove to you that they are more genuine than these. Because I can only proceed from those things that are organic or seem obvious to you. If you find something that you have written to be very complicated, then immediately doubt its authenticity."

After being exposed like that a few times, the pupil becomes fanatically strict toward his own ideas. He hears his compositions through to the end with exactitude, which is the main point anyway. And sometimes—and this is the most wonderful part of these lessons—at some point or other of the compositional exercise, Schoenberg suddenly feels that something is forcing him away from the piece, that the path of the sound continues elsewhere, in order to flow together again further on. What is that? He listens for a while:

"Didn't you hear that part like *this*?" And he continues to play, differently of course, exactly what the pupil had been searching for but had not found—those measures where the logical sequence of the idea had gotten lost and could no longer be traced.

"Now let's think about why it has to continue like this!"

At this point the scientific work of the theoretician begins. Here a B♭ is discovered that forces the sound in another direction. This B♭ must have effects that were not complied with. Now it is important to listen up to the point where the piece would like to turn, to see how long it has the need to fall, and to find the moment that it pulls itself together in order to climb upward to its conclusion. Here Schoenberg speaks of an instinctive life of tones. Or it could be a slight displacement of the beat. If this turned out to be necessary, then it would appear more than once. Because then it would be organic and its possibility must lay hidden within each tone. The earlier occurrences must keep on vibrating in those that follow.

The pupils are made aware of this. This knowledge is the kind that seems as though it has come from someone else. The knowledge was merely hidden in them like an embryo and only needed the one who would rouse it from sleep. Schoenberg's manner of teaching is built upon the following: he has the pupil find things out. And only after someone has found out something by himself does it belong solely to him. What he has wrested from music in terms of serious work will never get lost, even if the composition has failed. Power has increased, even though it might not be victorious till the tenth or twentieth assault.

Composition pupils mature best through their work. Schoenberg recognizes early on those gifted for conducting—whose strength will lie in the reproductive sphere—by the way they take hold of things. Then he treats them differently. He aids their musical development through the works of the great masters themselves, through analyses. That is the second part of his instruction. Only on occasion does he lead to analysis those who produce things themselves, in order to show them how Brahms, for example, treats a harmonic problem or how Beethoven solves it in a quartet. Schoenberg never says the same thing twice, but he will come back to the same point ten times from different angles. The possibilities of explaining something are endless. Once someone told him that today he had explained the Beethoven sonata completely differently from the last time, to which Schoenberg responded:

"I am a different person today also, and I don't have the obligation to be consistent, but rather only this: to stay alive."

An explanation like "This is the main theme group, this is the secondary passage and within them there are these modulations" is too boring for him. He is looking for the instinctive in an artwork: he shows how everything proceeds from one seed and emanates in all directions, just like the most delicate intertwinings of a thematic arbor still have a relationship to the seed from which they were produced. Or he shows how at a seeming conclusion a tiny structure grows forth, still almost invisibly, as yet without meaning, how it wins over friends and becomes strong and mighty and finally takes up battle with the old one. I never had more respect for Beethoven than after the lesson when Schoenberg had analyzed a sonata in this manner. These analyses are no diagnoses of relationships; they are an illumination outward from within, a complete recreation of the work of art.

People have often told me that it is Schoenberg's amazing knowledge of musical literature that enables him to know so much about these things. I know many whose knowledge of the literature might be no less, but who still do not undertand how to arouse someone's interest with all that knowledge. Thus the reason cannot lie in the knowledge but rather in the person himself, in the way he examines, compares, and groups events; in the capability of immediately discovering similarities in different things; and of seeing immediately what is different in similar things. Only in this way will knowledge become fluid and fertile, and if at the beginning it seemed as if it were contemptible to have knowledge of something, by now it must be clear that what was meant was only the smell of decay that arose from dead knowledge. In the productive person everything becomes fertile, even history; for he will include it in the present.

It is remarkable that Schoenberg's way of teaching coincides with the kind that Scharrelmann[14] and other pedagogues actually demand for schools: to purge teaching of rigid formulae and deflect them from the person you have before you; because only in that way can learning become organic and fertile. Knowledge is a beautiful thing, but one ought not to be prouder of it than of a pretty face, for which one is not responsible. Because it was only acquired; at the very most it belongs to our brain and will get lost again. Comprehension, however, which has proceeded from within us, has a home in our blood and in our nerves, too, and is thoroughly our own possession. And if it seemed to have gone astray as a result of further development, it nevertheless built a step which we had to climb over and stride beyond. The step was necessary, however. The goal of education can only be knowledge that the pupil somehow has to acquire on his own. The distinct task of the teacher can be only to show each student his own path there and to remove those inhibitions that would merely delay rather than promote the process.

KARL LINKE

* *
*

Schoenberg has to an unusual degree the gift of revealing to the pupil the constructive element, the "logic" of music. Analyzing the classics, he uncovers in the most concealed places organic connections which shape the secret effect of some part or other. His main effort lies in training his pupils in the inventive power of rhythm, harmony and counterpoint. Above all, he demands mature technical skills as the foundation for composing. Without these, even the most talented artist will only be able to produce something incomplete. Schoenberg knows how to inspire the productive fantasy of the pupil during every stage of study by taking examples from the musical literature. Within the confines of a technically faultless manner of writing he allows the pupil every freedom and in no way does he ever put forth his own style as a prototype.

DR. EGON WELLESZ

* *
*

Truly everyone who has the good fortune of approaching Schoenberg marvels at the generosity, depth, and complete independence of his understanding in the most *varied* areas of artistic emotion and strictly serious thought, and understands that this man is not only the master of composition, but also a genuinely significant *human being*. And someone like that is always the best teacher of his subject, at least where it is not merely a question of developing someone's mechanical skills but more of enriching his capabilities, developing his individuality and furthering the whole personality of the pupil.

DR. ROBERT NEUMANN

* *
*

Schoenberg teaches you how to think. He guides the pupil toward seeing with his own eyes, as if he were the very first one to observe the phenomena. What has been thought of before should not be the norm. Even if our thoughts are no better than someone else's—it is not a matter of finding the absolute truth but rather a question of the search for the truth.

ERWIN STEIN

* *

*

Arnold Schoenberg possesses the two basic qualifications of every genius and thus of every brilliant teacher: on the one hand, the power of naive observation that can dispense with the crutch of tradition and force him to grasp and invigorate everything anew, from the most minute details of daily life to the highest human and artistic concerns, and, on the other hand, the power to impart convincingly a personal appreciation for all things. The miracle of his method of instruction and his unique influence on the pupil stems from these two basic powers of his being. In his lessons, all the long since dried-out artistic rules found in old textbooks or heard from the mouths of bad teachers seem rather to be born from the idea that is directly present; or they appear in an entirely new and exhilarating light, not to mention those utterly new vistas that are always opened up by his own personal way of looking at things. Thus, for the pupil, every step along the path of his instruction becomes an exciting experience that remains firmly anchored in his innermost being. With this completely independent treatment of the material, and with the utmost severity, Schoenberg insists on the observance of the most rigorous demands of artistic purity, so that the pupil learns to feel that an unmotivated progression is a spot of dirt. The pupil is nurtured by a musical sense of cleanliness that must ultimately make him understand, without rules, what is genuine and what is fake. Finally, Schoenberg, like any good teacher—and this is all the more remarkable for such a strong personality—has the gift of adjusting himself to the individuality of the least of his pupils in such a way that no two pupils are ever led down the same path in even remotely the same manner. The teacher does not "hold" to a particular method, rather it is continually arrived at by way of the pupil.

This is still a one-sided picture, for his effect on the pupil extends far beyond purely artistic parameters. When you are dealing with such a multidimensional and harmonious nature, a person who has been educated through and through, the relationship between teacher and pupil cannot be confined to instruction only.

Schoenberg *educates* the pupils in the fullest sense of the word and involuntarily establishes such compelling personal contact with each one that his pupils gather about him like disciples about their master. And if we call ourselves "Schoenberg pupils," this has a completely different emphasis from what it does for those who are inseparably linked to their teacher by virtue of a fingering that will make him happy, or the creation of a new figured bass. We know, rather, that all of us who call ourselves Schoenberg pupils are touched by his essence in everything that we think and feel and that we thereby feel in a kind of spiritual contact with everything. For anyone who was his pupil, his name is more than a mere recollection of student days; it is an artistic and personal conscience.

DR. HEINRICH JALOWETZ

*   *
*

"Don't strive to learn *anything* from this; rather try to learn from Mozart, Beethoven, and Brahms! Then perhaps some things here will seem worthy of note to you."

Arnold Schoenberg wrote me these words in my copy of his First String Quartet (D Minor, Op. 7). During my years of apprenticeship with him, I learned what he meant by that. I recall how often Schoenberg expressed himself energetically against superficialities that did not result organically from my style, how inexorably he inveighed against anything that was not deeply felt.

Only a short while ago—I was no longer his "pupil"—he warned me against being influenced externally by his style: "You do not have to write that way just because *I* write that way. Allow your personality to express what you feel driven to express with all your might. Each person goes through a different development on his way to the goal, which has to be an inevitable result.

Schoenberg's alpha and omega is precisely inner experience, warmth of emotion; expression and technique form themselves from these. He who has nothing to say should remain silent!

How much I have learned from Schoenberg can hardly be expressed; what I thank him for has no limits. I already knew the classics before I came to him; through him I lived them. I learned to see so much of what before had lain veiled in front of my eyes.

No less significantly must I grant that he never was just a "teacher." He was a relentless friend to me, always striving, working tirelessly to make me into a human being of high quality and above all self-critical.

DR. KARL HORWITZ

*   *

*

"Belief in technique as the only salvation had to be suppressed, and the urge for truthfulness encouraged."
—Schoenberg, "Problems in Teaching Art"[15]

The most brilliant refutation of all the ill-willed, envious hostility and slander that old-fashioned brains have plotted against Arnold Schoenberg has been offered by himself in his essay "Problems in Teaching Art."[16]

Never have more penetrating and truer words been said about those things.

And each of his pupils can and could experience for themselves what Schoenberg expresses in that essay. People are of the opinion that Schoenberg teaches his style and forces the pupil to adopt it. That is completely and utterly false.

Schoenberg teaches no style; he preaches the use of neither old nor new artistic means. He says: "So what is the point of teaching how to master everyday cases? The pupil learns how to use something he must not use if he wants to be an artist. But one cannot give him what matters most—the courage and the strength to find an attitude to things which will make everything he looks at an exceptional case, because of the way he looks at it."[17]

This "what matters most" is what a pupil of Schoenberg receives.

Schoenberg demands above all that the pupil not write any old notes he wants to just to fill out an academic form, but rather that he execute these works as a result of a need for expression.

Therefore, that he actually create something, even at the most primitive stages of constructing musical passages. What Schoenberg then explains to the pupil results organically from the work; he brings no external dogma to it.

Thus Schoenberg actually teaches as a part of the creative process.

With the greatest energy he follows the traces of the pupil's personality, attempts to deepen it, to enable it to achieve a breakthrough—in short, to give him "the courage and the strength to find an attitude to things which will make everything he looks at an exceptional case, because of the way he looks at it."

This is an education in extreme truthfulness toward oneself.

In addition to the purely musical, it touches upon all other areas of a person's life.

Yes, truly, one experiences more than artistic rules with Schoenberg. He who opens his heart will be shown the path of the good.

How can one explain that every one of his pupils, working independently today, composes in such a way as to make the style of his own composition seem extremely close to that of Schoenberg's works? This is certainly the main cause of the misunderstanding about Schoenberg's teaching alluded to earlier. There can be no explanation for it. This question really touches upon the secret of artistic creativity.

Who would like to explain it?

It is not a matter of merely appropriating these artistic means.

So what is it?

A necessity holds sway here, the causes of which we do not know but must believe in.

DR. ANTON VON WEBERN

*   *
*

There are those kinds of people who bestow clarity and strength on the things around them; people who illuminate everything with which they come into contact, in whose hands everything becomes original and spontaneous.

To study with Schoenberg is to receive continually. Everything that he gives comes from his depths, affects the innermost essence, and allows it to grow, like a tree grows out of inner necessity.

The person who might come to Schoenberg to acquire knowledge would go astray. What we are able to acquire is merely the knowledge of things about which we would be in error. The person who goes to Schoenberg to find out about himself would do right. Schoenberg can lead those who believe in him to that very path where they must find themselves. Experiences have to be lived. No system is handed the pupil because every acquisition of a perfect system is only a respite along the way and results from fatigue. It is always the weakest ones who speak of end results.

But the strong ones will create. Create values. Because all values are created by people and are placed above them. Schoenberg creates new values. And forces one to think anew and learn anew. Because it is impossible to set up new values and to determine new values without altering, reducing, or destroying the old ones. But having to learn anew is what many hold against him. For they are afraid and basically desire only that no one do anything to harm them. But he who creates new values has to be brave, has to have will, courage, and willfulness. He has to be able to surpass many and rise above them; the majority does not forgive that and declares his loneliness to be his fault.

The little and weak ones, who are wary and look to the right and left and try to guess what would be profitable in the marketplace, cannot abide to have the creative person above them; this witness who reminds them all too often of the very thing they distinctly assure one another of not being. But a lie is destined to be short-lived. And it is better to tell the truth, because: "Truth has a wide-range effect and is long-lived."

Schoenberg tells the truth. In everything that he creates, that he teaches, solely the truth.

It would be as difficult to give expression to what constitutes his influence, his personality, as to say in words what he teaches and how he gives of his wealth. The right words will be able to be found when, at the end of his life, his work will be spread out into a thousand things all over the world.

PAUL KÖNIGER

*   *

*

The genius is effective from the outset as a teacher. His words are instruction, his conduct is a model, his works are revelations. Hidden within him is the teacher, the prophet, the Messiah. And the spirit of language which understands the essence of the genius far better than those who abuse it, gives the creative artist the name "Master," and says of him that he has created a "school." This perception alone could convince a time of Arnold Schoenberg's predestination for the teaching profession if it had any idea about the importance of this artist and human being. That it has no such idea is natural, for had a time the capability of perceiving, of sensing something that is so contradictory to its essence as is everything immortal, it would not be the opposite of eternity. And yet, only if we first assume an artist's calling to the teaching profession in general can Schoenberg's particular method of teaching be properly judged. In addition to being inextricably linked to his artistry and his imposing humanity, his manner of teaching, which is the only justifiable kind, is supported by an express will to this profession. This will—whether it be involved with his own work, with reproduction, with criticism, or ultimately with the profession of teaching—must, like every great artistic will, produce at the highest level. To esteem highly enough such a miraculous achievement, which has come about under these presuppositions and conditions, would mean to solve the riddle of genius and to fathom the secrets of the Godhead, an effort that must of necessity fail by virtue of the impossibility of measuring the immeasurable, of fathoming the unfathomable. It can only remain an attempt, an attempt resembling the kind that would hope to describe the beauty, richness, and sublimity of the waves of the sea. Submitting himself to its constant currents, the lucky swimmer will be carried out toward eternity, easily and proudly taking leave of those who are shattered on the rocky crags of their intellectual and spiritual infertility or who remain behind in the secure harbor of their temporality.

ALBAN BERG

NOTES

1. In addition to the 1912 volume translated here, the most important tributes are: *Arnold Schönberg zum fünfzigsten Geburtstage: 13* September *1924*. Special issue of *Musikblätter des Anbruch* (Vienna, 1924); *Arnold Schönberg zum 60. Geburtstag: 13. September 1934* (Vienna: Universal, 1934); and *Schoenberg*, ed. Merle Armitage (New York: G. Schirmer, 1937; repr. Greenwood Press, 1977). A different kind of celebratory volume is *Dem Lehrer Arnold Schönberg: 13 September 1924*, a sort of scrapbook in which pupils provided photographs and short descriptions of when and where they studied with Schoenberg. The entries from this book are reproduced in facsimile in *Arnold Schönberg 1874–1951: Lebensgeschichte in Begegnungen*, ed. Nuria Nono-Schoenberg (Klagenfurt and Vienna, 1998), pp. 232–35.

2. On the history of Piper Verlag, see Ernst Piper and Bettina Raab, *90 Jahre Piper* (Munich, 1994); on the Schoenberg volume, see pp. 58–60, 69.

3. See Schoenberg, *Harmonielehre* (Vienna, 1911), pp. 24–25; *Theory of Harmony*, trans. Roy E. Carter (Berkeley and Los Angeles, 1978), pp. 423–25. I have not been able to identify Neumann definitively. Schoenberg describes him as "a young philosopher" (*Harmonielehre*, p. 431; *Theory of Harmony*, p. 384). He may be the Robert Neumann who completed a dissertation on Goethe and Fichte at the University of Jena in 1904, was teaching in Berlin at the Königstädtischen Real-Gymnasium, and in the same year as Schoenberg's *Harmonielehre* published a book on Herder.

4. Arnold Schoenberg, "Attempt at a Diary," trans. Anita Luginbühl, *Journal of the Arnold Schoenberg Institute* 9 (1986): 36. The context of these remarks is also significant. Schoenberg is writing about his complicated emotional and professional relationship with Alexander Zemlinsky, his brother-in-law, who (Schoenberg says) would probably be upset by the publication of the volume, because "he does not like to believe. Although he thinks much of me—I almost feel he would like it best if he alone thought highly of me! Strangely enough, he does not trust or believe in the enthusiasm of others. Despite the fact that he himself is capable of so much genuine enthusiasm! Why?" (p. 36).

5. Schoenberg, *Harmonielehre*, p. 462; cf., *Theory of Harmony*, p. 414. [Ed.]

6. Cited from Willi Reich, *Schoenberg: A Critical Biography*, trans. Leo Black (New York, 1971), pp. 48–49. This statement by Schoenberg appeared in the program notes for the concert of January 14, 1910, at which the *Hanging Gardens* cycle and the Three Piano Pieces, Op. 11, were premiered. [Ed.]

7. Schoenberg, *Harmonielehre*, pp. 466-67; *Theory of Harmony*, p. 417. [Ed.]

8. *Der Merker* 2/17 (1911): 718–21. [Ed.]

9. Schoenberg, *Harmonielehre*, p. 79; *Theory of Harmony*, p. 68. [Ed.]

10. Schoenberg, *Harmonielehre*, p. 360; *Theory of Harmony*, p. 321. [Ed.]

11. Schoenberg, *Harmonielehre*, p. 145; cf. *Theory of Harmony*, pp. 127–28. [Ed.]

12. Schoenberg, *Harmonielehre*, p. 364; *Theory of Harmony*, p. 325. [Ed.]

13. Gustav Wustmann (1844–1910), author of the popular book on German grammar and usage *Allerhand Sprachdummheiten* (1892, reprinted many times). This would seem to have been the Strunk and White, or Fowler, of its day in Germany. [Ed.]

14. Heinrich L. Scharrelmann (1871–1940), a renowned pedagogical reformer in Bremen. [Ed.]

15. Schoenberg, "Problems in Teaching Art" [1911], in *Style and Idea*, ed. Leonard Stein (New York, 1975), p. 368. [Ed.]

16. Appeared in *Musikalisches Taschenbuch* 2 (Vienna: Stern & Steiner, 1911). [Webern]

17. Schoenberg, "Problems in Teaching Art," p. 366. [Ed.]

PART III
ARNOLD SCHOENBERG SPEAKS

·

Arnold Schoenberg Speaks:

Newspaper Accounts of His Lectures and

Interviews, 1927–1933

SELECTED AND INTRODUCED BY JOSEPH H. AUNER
TRANSLATED BY IRENE ZEDLACHER

Introduction

Our access to Schoenberg's words today is limited for the most part to
the printed page. Often translated, and usually edited, his writings have
come down to us filtered through various sensibilities, polished,
grouped into collections, and presented with little indication of the
contexts in which his ideas were formulated. Yet many of the most
important writings were originally conceived as lectures for specific
occasions, with all that that entails in terms of the topics chosen,
organization, length, the manner in which ideas were presented, and a
consideration of how an audience might respond. Those interested in
recapturing "the grain of the voice" can turn to manuscript sources for
the writings to experience something of the flow and energy of
Schoenberg's thought by observing the vehemence of the hand as well
as the points of hesitation or revision. Schoenberg's careful annotations
of word emphasis and pacing in the reading copies of his lectures
similarly make it possible to reconstruct how a text might have been
delivered. Still more valuable in providing a sense of immediacy are the
few audio recordings that have survived, such as that for Schoenberg's
"My Evolution" lecture from 1949.[1] Yet none of these resources tells
us much about Schoenberg's physical presence as a speaker or the
rhetorical impact of his words and ideas on an audience.

The special significance of these seven newspaper accounts of his lectures and interviews is thus the evidence they provide about the contexts for his writings, the larger cultural and political implications and subtexts of the ideas and their formulations, and how specific audiences responded to the person behind the words. While studies of reception have focused primarily on musical compositions and performances, in the case of Schoenberg the concentration on works neglects many other facets of his role in the musical life of his time. This was particularly the case during the years covered by these articles, spanning the period from shortly after his arrival in Berlin in 1926 to teach at the Prussian Academy of the Arts, to a few months before his departure in May 1933. Schoenberg's prominent position, the long-standing controversies around his music, and the highly charged character of artistic politics in Weimar Germany, all figured in making his public appearances as a speaker just as newsworthy as his concerts.

Schoenberg gave many lectures throughout his career, but he was particularly active during his time in Berlin. This can be attributed in part to the considerable status of his position as professor at the Prussian Academy of the Arts, a level of recognition that brought with it both increased opportunities for speaking, as well as the responsibility to play a public role. As is evident from several of the articles below, Schoenberg was seen not only as the spokesman for his own compositional developments and the new directions in music, but— for supporters as well as critics—as a representative of the Republic and its cultural policies. This latter aspect was particularly important during his many travels outside of Germany, an issue raised directly in the second article (pp. 270–72) where his election to the Prussian Academy is interpreted as a challenge to the growing influence of French composers.

Many of Schoenberg's lectures during this period accompanied performances of his works, such as the 1928 Breslau lecture on *Die glückliche Hand* (pp. 272–74), which concentrated on preparing audiences to better understand his compositional intentions. Of particular significance for the Weimar context are the talks designed for radio broadcast, like the lecture on the Variations for Orchestra, Op. 31 (pp. 276–78). Schoenberg also lectured more generally about contemporary musical developments and his place in them, as in the case of "New Music, Outmoded Music, Style and Idea." In this talk and in the Problems of Harmony lecture, summarized in detail on pages 268–70, Schoenberg approached his own music only ellipitically, focusing instead on the underlying questions of the status of tonality as a natural law or a historically contingent compositional means, and the relationship between musical ideas and their presentation.

   The three very different accounts of the "New Music, Outmoded Music, Style and Idea" lecture, from Prague in 1930 (pp. 274–76) and those concerning a later reading in Cologne from 1933 (pp. 278–81), also make clear that these articles reveal a great deal about the reviewer as well. Readers of these and the other articles will no doubt note a level of technical detail in the musical discussion that is almost unthinkable today for the mainstream media. Also striking is the degree to which a basic knowledge of Schoenberg's works and writings could be assumed for the general reader. Indeed, in the case of the account of the lecture in Prague, Schoenberg's contemporary stance is challenged with detailed references to his own *Harmonielehre*, first published in 1911. Perhaps just as surprising is the implicitly and explicitly political nature of much music criticism in Weimar Germany, especially evident in the review from the *Völkischer Beobachter*, the primary organ of the Nazi party. While the ideological agenda is obvious in this example, we should be attuned to the cultural, racial, and national issues approached from all sides of the political spectrum that can be similarly traced in the other articles as well. To cite just one example, the anti-Semitic language used to describe Schoenberg that is so blatant in the *Völkischer Beobachter* review is evident in more subtle ways in the imagery used to describe his ideas and person even in the more sympathetic articles, such as the initial account of his first Berlin lecture (pp. 268–70).[2]

   The picture of Schoenberg as a public speaker that emerges from these newspaper accounts is in some cases a familiar one: harsh, severe, ironic, cerebral, an isolated figure supported by only a small circle of enthusiasts. But in other reviews we encounter quite a different image from what we have come to expect: a witty, self-deprecating, and playful celebrity, surrounded by admirers, and greeted with affection by audiences as one of the most famous and venerated composers of the time. Similarly, these commentaries can offer a new window on the meaning and significance of Schoenberg's words, some of which may have been dulled through familiarity and decontextualization over the years. The intensity and range of reactions to Schoenberg's adherence to the notion of *l'art pour l'art* or his statements about Gebrauchsmusik for example, underscore that more was involved in the debates around these ideas than just opposing aesthetic standpoints.[3]

   (Notes appear on p. 281.)

Schoenberg moved from Vienna to Berlin in January 1926 to take over Busoni's position as director of a master class in composition at the Prussian Academy of Arts, a position that along with other benefits brought with it the title of "Professor." This lecture, given on January 19, 1927, was followed the next day by his formal election to the Senate of the Academy, an honor that included the granting of Prussian nationality.[4] The painter Max Liebermann was president of the Academy until 1932, when he was succeeded by Max von Schillings, who presided at the time of Schoenberg's dismissal the following year. While Schoenberg did not respond here to the final question concerning the nationalistic implications of contemporary musical developments, he was to take up the idea, which was already anticipated in his remarks to his pupils about the twelve-tone method ensuring the dominance of German music, in the unpublished essay "National Music" of 1931.[5] The article "Problems of Harmony" was first published in an English translation by Adolph Weiss in *Modern Music* 9 (1934).[6]

Arnold Schoenberg Speaks—
Lecture at the Academy of Fine Arts in Berlin
Arno Huth (Berlin)
Allgemeine Zeitung Chemnitz
February 5, 1927

Prof. Arnold Schoenberg—Busoni's successor as teacher of the master class in composition at the Academy of Fine Arts—stepped behind a Berlin lecture lectern for the first time with a long lecture on "Problems of Harmony." Almost all members of the music section and nearly all professors of the Academy of Music, as well as a large number of important musicians, had accepted Max Liebermann's invitation to this internal event at the academy. Seen there were, among others, Schreker, Kahn, Kleiber, Horenstein, Schnabel, Jarnach, Weill, and Alban Berg, Schoenberg's most important pupil.

Schoenberg exudes something inexorable and severe. His irony is harsh, at times even very angry. One doesn't see his small figure, one sees only the eyes and mouth—and above them the extremely wide forehead which ends in an enormous baldness, as if the brow had not had enough space. His delivery is erratic, abrupt, and tied to the written word. But then again, it always draws things together, organizing and clarifying. Some things he stresses too much, others are mentioned only in passing, but what he says is always interesting, riveting, and is illustrated with vivid and mostly ironic examples and comparisons. The eyes are the strangest things about him. They continuously change their disposition. They gleam and then darken; there are flashes and flickers in them. And they observe, always examining the effect of each word and each sentence.

Modern music struggles with two problems, Schoenberg began, the familiar questions of tonality and dissonance. The term tonality (which to some degree is identical with the term key) refers to the relationship of a succession of sounds to one fundamental tone. This relationship is latent in every tone because each pitch consists, as is generally known, of a fundamental and its overtones. The overtones explain (according to Schoenberg) the major as well as the chromatic scale. The minor scale is an "emulation of the major scale under the influence of the church modes." Tonality is not a given but rather the result of an artistic practice. From the start, the basic triad belongs to at least three different keys. A succession of chords is not tonal in itself; it has to be made tonal (through emphasis, as for example through cadences). As a result, since tonality is only an artistic convention, tonality cannot be elevated to a status of being self-evident and natural. However, it may not be dropped if it is a necessary tool for the comprehensibility of the work, and if nothing else substitutes for it. The achievement of tonality is (1) its unifying and (2) its articulating function. Tonality unifies through the "relatedness of all musical events to a tonal center." It articulates through the distinct differentiation of individual tonal elements (e.g., C-major elements from G minor, etc.). However, a music using only the means of tonality is unthinkable. Quite apart from the unity of tonal relationships, music requires the unity of configurations and of ideas. If the same effect can be achieved with other means (form, motives) tonality may be relegated to the background!

The second issue is dissonance. Dissonances of any kind can be derived, just as are scales, from overtones. Dissonances are quite as natural as tonality. Like tonality they have to be accepted as artistic means. Modern music goes beyond Wagner in the use of dissonances because it has not limited itself to dissonances that tend toward a tonality. After a period of adjustment listeners will certainly be able to recognize the unity that governs the so-called "disturbing" dissonances. "It is to be hoped that in twenty years people will recognize the tonality of 'atonal' music." (Schoenberg is against the use of this term because atonal tones, i.e., tones completely without relation to one another, do not exist.) The difference between the past and today lies only in the emphasis or lack of emphasis on tonality. To modern music the other elements are more important than they are from the standpoint of tonality. The difference between old and modern music is not in kind but in degree!

This lecture, a defense of modern music against the criticism of unnaturalness, was followed by a lively discussion in which Schreker, Prof. Schünemann, and Arno Nadel, among others, participated.

• • •

Schoenberg and his second wife Gertrud, whom he married in 1924, traveled to Paris in December for two concerts of his works, which included along with *Pierrot lunaire* performed by Marya Freund, the premiere of the Suite, Op. 29, the Suite for Piano, Op. 25, and four songs from Op. 6. Schoenberg had studied French until he withdrew halfway through the 1890–91 school year, though not in Gymnasium as reported, but in Realschule. (Stuckenschmidt reproduces his final report cards, showing that he received high marks in French.[7]) The drama Schoenberg refers to could be either *Moses und Aron*, for which he wrote the bulk of the text the following fall, or more likely *Der biblische Weg*, the text of which was completed in July 1927 and for which a number of musical sketches are preserved.[8] The reference to a violin concerto relates to sketches for a twelve-tone violin concerto dating from November 1927, and possibly another work for a solo violin sketched in early January 1928, and not Schoenberg's Violin Concerto, Op. 36, written 1935–36. [9] Schoenberg had started the composition of the Variations for Orchestra, Op. 31, in 1926; it was completed in the fall of 1928 and performed in December by Furtwängler and the Berlin Philharmonic. The book he refers to is part of a series of projects left unfinished at his death, now published under the collective title, *The Musical Idea and the Logic, Technique, and Art of its Presentation*, ed. and trans. Patricia Carpenter and Severine Neff (New York, 1995).

Where is German Music Headed?—
An Interview with Schoenberg in Paris
Berliner Börsen Zeitung
December 16, 1927

Arnold Schoenberg, the representative of the newest musical trend whose melodrama *Pierrot lunaire* has just been performed in Paris with great success, was interviewed by an editor of the theater journal *Comoedia*:

I met Schoenberg, who was accompanied by his graceful blond wife and surrounded by a large number of male and female admirers, in the anteroom. In greeting me he told me that he had studied French in high school with the result that now he was not able to speak a single word of it. But even though he could not speak French, he still was able to understand it quite well. To my question regarding his new plans he replied: "I have been working on the incidental music [Bühnenmusik] for a drama for a long time. I have to keep its title a secret, however. I don't think it will be performed for some years. At present I am also writing the Variations for Orchestra, and finally I am thinking of composing a violin concerto which—I hope—will be introduced publicly by Kreisler. I want to provide new inspiration for music for the violin. And I use my leisure time for work on a book explaining my ideas about music. Its title will be *On the Structural Logic in Music* [*Von der Logik im Aufbau der Musik*]."

"Would you like to say something about German music, its development, and its relationship to French music?"

My question obviously embarrasses Schoenberg because he starts nervously playing with his wedding ring. A young woman helps him out of this embarrassment by handing him a plate of cake. The creator of *Pierrot lunaire* smiles ironically, takes a piece of torte from the plate, and answers me while lifting a cup of tea to his lips: "Let me think for a moment." The cake seems to be excellent, and apparently hinders Arnold Schoenberg from coming to a conclusion. At last he pushes back the plate, and turns to me with the words: "In my view the development of German and French music runs parallel. Both are against the 'pathos' that was in full bloom twenty years ago."—"Pathos and Romanticism," I interrupt. "No," was his answer. "Romanticism no longer exists. If one chooses to use that word, one does so without any justification, because there is nothing behind it. I want to emphasize 'pathos' once more—the grandiloquence of music of the past. It was music that didn't operate through the ideas it contained, but only through the composer's emotion, yes, sometimes only through his sentimentality. Today, be it France or Germany, we demand a music that lives through ideas and not through feeling."

To my objection that the younger generation, after all, had rediscovered a certain Gounod, Schoenberg quickly replied: "I am not speaking about the younger generation, I'm talking about myself. I have brought music a good deal forward. I can claim that without false modesty. I am quite conscious of this. There is a gap between the point to which I have led music and where it was before. It is a gap today's musicians must attempt to fill."

"You mean to say," I replied in my rebuttal, "Germany's entire musical movement has as its purpose and goal the discovery of a woman[10] who can convey to a large audience the understanding of a music that we want to triumph. It shall bring back the listeners after many artists and critics have spoken out against our music, which in its theoretical approach comes close to the formula of *l'art pour l'art*."

"That is right." replied Schoenberg. "In Germany we have a large number of individuals who can be mentioned alongside your most famous musicians. The styles may be different, but the tendencies are the same. These mainly concern form and the problems of modern harmony that have somewhat disrupted the permanence of forms. Hindemith is a kind of Darius Milhaud, and with his short musical aphorisms Webern reminds one of your Debussy."

"Do you believe then," I remarked, "that there is a return to the lyrical mode as a reaction to the directions you are taking?"

"I do not believe so," Schoenberg answered my question. "It only fills a gap. That is all. They only build the bridge which will permit the audience to come to me."

"But it is said," I continued, "that your election as a member of the Berlin Academy of Arts must be considered the expression of Germany's will to fight the influence of Debussy and French music in general. It is, on the other hand, therefore the expression of the wish to draw closer to the Austrian movement. I admit, the question is somewhat brutal, but it would be desirable for you either to refute or to correct this hypothesis."

At that moment the young lady again approaches Mr. Schoenberg to offer him a glass of port and a plate of delicious looking cake. Schoenberg again smiles ironically, takes the glass of port and prepares to eat the cake. "I will think about it further," he says as he sits down at the table. Since Schoenberg was still thinking about it half an hour later, I considered it high time to leave.

• • •

Schoenberg composed *Die glückliche Hand*, Op. 18, between 1910 and 1913. It was premiered in Vienna in 1924, and then presented for the first time in Germany with the Breslau performance on March 24, 1928. There the opera was performed twice, with a substantial lecture intervening in which Schoenberg discussed his attempt to integrate music, movement, and color, an idea he called "making music with the media of the stage." What has come to be called the

"Breslau Lecture on *Die glückliche Hand*," is published in *Arnold Schoenberg, Wassily Kandinsky: Letters, Pictures and Documents*, ed. Jelena Hahl-Koch, trans. John C. Crawford (London and Boston, 1984), pp. 102–07.

A. Schoenberg, *Die glückliche Hand* —German Premiere in Breslau

Dr. O. G.

Köngisberger Hartungsche Zeitung
April 24, 1928

Die glückliche Hand, written in 1912, belongs to a creative period for Schoenberg which no doubt peaked with *Pierrot lunaire*. The content of the play (luck smiles once more on an unhappy man; he achieves great things; everything proves a chimera; he breaks down again) is banal both in concept and in dramatic form. But that, ultimately, is not relevant.

The value and importance of the work lie in the music, in the *Melos*, which springs from the deep emotional world in which the heart of a musical genius expresses itself. The discomfort one doubtlessly experiences does not issue from the strangeness of this music, however, for the sounds correspond to our inner (and exterior) chaotic condition. Rather, it springs from the absence of balance between orchestra and stage. While the personality of the composer is represented in the music, expressed by sound symbols of the deepest feeling, the stage is dominated by the soulless technology of lighting and the material world of the sets, which cannot be internally assimilated emotionally. The human being on stage seeks to establish a connection between both, but he is torn between decor and gesture, i.e., emotional expression; he's disruptive more than helpful—at least as long as he is talking (and what he says!). If the dramatic events seemed necessary at all, then it should have been only a pantomime. Ultimately only sensation triumphs.

Schoenberg is no musical dramatist. He is, rather, a chamber musician. He belongs to those nonoperatic natures who do not need the stage. *Die glückliche Hand* is dramatized chamber music, just as *Fidelio*, for example, is a sung symphony. No theory or definition Schoenberg developed in his wonderful lecture—no matter how brilliant—can successfully obscure this fact even though he may speak of "making music with the means of the stage," or of "making music with inner concepts alone." "Abstract music" is a contradiction in itself.

Schoenberg's musical genius, however, rescues him from the cool arena of speculation to the beautiful green pastures of living music.

It was wonderful to see this genius groping around at first in his lecture till he found firm ground (and contact). He then continued, going higher and higher, until he lost himself finally in the distance in a spoken, but nevertheless almost musical fantasy on the obscure title of his work. These introductory words also were chamber music by one filled with and possessed by music.

Unexpectedly strong applause matched the perfect performance in that public stronghold of reactionary attitudes toward art, merrily accompanied as it was by the hissing of some charming old people.

• • •

The lecture discussed here, first delivered by Schoenberg in Prague on October 22, 1930, later became "New Music, Outmoded Music, Style and Idea." It was revised several times in the years following 1930, with variations on the title.[11] Readers familiar with the 1946 version of this lecture printed in *Style and Idea* will also note from the commentaries that there were significant differences in the early version. For example, passages concerning the frog that disguises itself by taking on the appearance of its surroundings, by which Schoenberg criticizes those who attempt to adopt other styles, was later omitted. The ascription of the Meyrink fable to Morgenstern was corrected in the 1933 version. The page references to the *Harmonielehre* are to the first edition, published by Universal Edition in Vienna, 1911.[12]

Arnold Schoenberg Holds Forth
M. B.
Prager Tagblatt
October 23, 1930

The great affection Schoenberg the innovator deserves was expressed by the strong applause that greeted him. Almost everybody in Prague who plays music or who considers music one of life's necessities had come to the lecture, which was presented by the "Literary-Artistic Society" in conjunction with the "Urania."

But the speaker was hard, very hard to understand in that large hall. The Viennese dialect, the habit of lowering the voice at the end of the sentence and simultaneously accelerating, the style of the lecture (which kept to the written manuscript, and only in some places acquired a rhetorical life of its own, as for example in the excursus on the art of the Netherlanders), all combined to make the lecture almost impossible to follow. The starting point was the thesis that all art had to be new. In his *Harmonielehre*, in the discussion of the fourth chord, Schoenberg defined in an unusually sensitively differentiated presentation the new as the essence of artistic life (p. 447ff.). At the same time, however, he pointed out the important role played by the unconscious in the breakthrough of the new. "He (the artist) does not break through, where there is a breakthrough, he does not know it." Even with that, the last word probably has not been said about this immensely complicated but commonplace dilemma regarding the work of conscious and unconscious elements in the creative process. But it seems that Schoenberg— irritated by unsympathetic criticism—stresses now somewhat stubbornly and defiantly the intellectual and constructive in his personality. In the *Harmonielehre*, however, he described the new with which every artist enters the creative world in much less intellectual terms. "Youthful sounds of that which is growing; pure feeling, with no trace of an awareness, still firmly attached to the germ cell, which is more intimately connected with the universe than is our awareness" [p. 488].

This time Schoenberg recounted the famous anecdote of Beethoven who received a letter from his brother signed "land owner." In response, Beethoven signed his own letter "brain owner." The conclusions Schoenberg draws from this (and other propositions) for the strictly intellectual in music seem too far-fetched. For Beethoven "brain" was a metaphor for "spirit" in general, for all the powers of the soul. Despite the importance of an organizing idea in art, it can not and must not be reduced to the purely intellectual. The many parallels Schoenberg found between music on the one hand, and mathematics and chess on the other, confuse more than they help to clarify.

Very attractive were his hypotheses on the new in Bach; on the full use of musical space as a principle underlying all invention. Equally fitting was the proud assertion—whose application to Schoenberg's art seems appropriate—that what once was new will always be new (i.e., it is experienced as a work of genius) and cannot go out of fashion or be refuted! Schoenberg was less fortunate in the caustic polemical part of his lecture, which was directed at Gebrauchsmusik and at the young who are only interested in "style" without, however, having an idea to be stylized in their art. Bitter irony and brilliant formulations were not lacking in the talk. However, neither this attack nor its literary character, such as the extensively drawn-out comparison with the mimicry-frog, was compelling. Those who consider Schoenberg infallible might have been surprised by his ascription of Meyrink's story of the centipede to Morgenstern, admittedly a minor error, but therefore also more noticeable.

The respect and veneration we owe Schoenberg interferes with a final verdict on the ideas he presented. After all, they did not achieve (maybe also for acoustic reasons) that glowing plasticity which characterizes his theoretical masterpiece, the *Harmonielehre*. The ideas he put forth in fragments today may soon gain definitive form. The *Harmonielehre* begins with the beautiful words: "This book I have learned from my pupils." Maybe the next work will reflect what he has learned from his audience.

• • •

Schoenberg's lecture on the Variations for Orchestra, Op. 31, was broadcast March 22, 1931, prior to its performance under Hans Rosbaud.[13] In his remarks Schoenberg no doubt had in mind the strong opposition the work faced at its premiere with the Berlin Philharmonic under Furtwängler. The innovative presentation combining detailed commentary, more general discussion of aesthetic issues, and musical excerpts performed on piano and by the orchestra reflect Schoenberg's interest in the medium of the radio for both the performance and promotion of his music and new music in general.

A Musician Offers a Glimpse into His Workshop
Karl Holl
Frankfurter Zeitung
March 23, 1931

On Sunday morning it was not just any musician—not even just one of the most famous composers—but Arnold Schoenberg who, in the Frankfurt station of Southeast Radio and South Radio, allowed us to take a deep look into his workshop, into the ways and principles of his work. The most influential stimulus in the new music movement, the first master of a compositional method emancipated from the tonal system and the principles of construction of the classic-romantic era, explained and analyzed in rough outlines his Variations on his own theme for orchestra, which will be premiered tonight at the 11th Monday concert of the Frankfurt Orchestra Society. As will always be the case with creative people of distinction, Schoenberg, by introducing us to one of his works, simultaneously opened up a view onto the whole of his situation, his goals, and his abilities. Schoenberg is no "lecturer." He lacks any rhetorical pathos, any desire to shine through words or a particular way of using them. When talking he is in the first place a thinker and a teacher. Over the years, in the course of his rise to prominence, he has liked to argue forcefully. Yet he has opened up to show much innate humor and has become an entertaining conversationalist as he teaches. He can teach and explain complicated things in a pleasant as well as a clear manner without us really noticing the complexity of the material. He is a master teacher and a teaching master. In addition, he is a person who as a creative artist has a broad perspective on his lonely situation as a pioneer, while having a full understanding of the headaches he causes to the majority. And he is content to have convinced his audience that he is no mere phantast or anarchist, but a responsible thinker who knows about the decisive questions concerning his art: a composer who understands his craft.

Schoenberg began the discourse with a simple defense of the rights of those seekers who stand on a lonely front and "are in the minority." He defended the right of this minority to use the radio. The radio allows them to interrupt the daily easy feasts for the ears of the "delirium of entertainment," with self-defensive explanations and the presentation of their exemplary works. He emphasized that no new music can be "beautiful" right from the start. Only "what one can remember" will please. He documented this with classical examples. He sketched out briefly and with astounding clarity the basics of his "nontonal"—not "atonal"!—concepts for music and the special structure of the idea of composition with twelve tones related to one another. Then he entered into an actual analysis. He explained (helped by Erich Itor Kahn at the piano) the structure of his variation theme, the logic behind the transformation of this theme, and the other "work" expressed in the character of the individual variations. The lecturer's words were interspersed with fragments and whole movements of the orchestral version of that intellectual edifice, presented by the Radio Symphony Orchestra under Hans Rosbaud. Schoenberg found particularly adroit and illustrative terms for the meaning and structure of the introduction and finale.

Gradually the image of the whole emerged, as did the outlines of a form that to some degree can be remembered, thus providing an excellent basis for the immediate appreciation of the entire work, even though the finer lines still might be difficult to comprehend. Many a listener, and particularly the group present in the station itself, may have been astonished by all that happens in a musical work both conceptually and technically, especially in this work by Schoenberg. During the hour and a half, they also may have learned how difficult it has been at any given time to understand new art, and thus to judge it. They also may have learned how irresponsible it is to strike it down with cheap arguments and thus to prejudice others against it. But for those who already knew something about new art, the most impressive aspect of the lecture lay in two things. First, that an artist equipped with the ability to communicate his ideas and goals in surprisingly simple verbal terms (and who not without humor and wit can distance himself from his work and its consequences) is still conscious that artistically he communicates only with difficulty. And finally, we see how much conviction and loyalty he nevertheless demonstrates as he searches for new values in this era of the inevitable reevaluation of old values.

• • •

Schoenberg revived the lecture "New Music, Outmoded Music, Style and Idea" to give in Cologne on February 10, 1933, and in Vienna five days later. The tone of the two following reviews of the Cologne event reflects the changed circumstances following Hitler's election as chancellor in January 1933. In the March parliamentary elections the National Socialists won a sizable majority; that same month Max von Schillings denounced the Jewish influence at the Prussian Academy. Schoenberg left Berlin in May, one month after the passage of the Law for the Restoration of the Professional Civil Service (Gesetz zur Wiederherstellung des Berufbeamtentums), which made it legal to terminate the contracts of those who could not prove Aryan descent. In the *Völkischer Beobachter* review Schoenberg is linked to the Frankfurt writer, conductor, and critic Paul Bekker, and to Otto Klemperer, who as conductor at the Kroll Opera and the State Opera in Berlin had been a long-time target of the extreme right.

Arnold Schoenberg's Idea
W. J.
Kölnische Zeitung
February 11, 1933

At the Society for New Music in Cologne, Arnold Schoenberg spoke on new and obsolete music, or style and idea, a topic no longer that relevant and thus essentially "obsolete," as he himself remarked at the beginning. Subsequent terminological definitions, however, did not match this joke. For if the ideas are correct in themselves (and even if they were not), they always have to be there and cannot "become obsolete." So much for Schoenberg on musical ideas. He started with a definition of homophonic-melodic music, in which the upper voice expresses all that is essential, and contrapuntal music, which distributes all its elements over several voices and uses the entire musical space. His ideal is: to fit the most content in the smallest space. New music is music that did not exist before. It is music that therefore will not be immediately understood, but it is also music that does not become obsolete. The fate of inauthentic music, of Gebrauchsmusik and Publikumsmusik, is that it becomes obsolete because it never was new. Schoenberg admitted to being a musical constructor and a cerebral person (with references to Beethoven's famous "brain owner" signature), a thinking musician who seeks to solve problems: how to create and work out thoughtfully the ideas that emerge. He confessed to share an adherence to the notion of *l'art pour l'art*.

His explanations were not always clear, despite fervent efforts to the contrary. They moved within the dialectic made familiar by Schoenberg's *Harmonielehre*, in a terminological realm intended only for the subsequent justification of the directions of "new music," which Schoenberg, as the spiritual father of an independent twelve-tone music, had determined. Schoenberg, the intellectual creator of a compositional method aiming to destroy occidental music as it becomes a part of history—the creator of a music whose style for the most part exists only on paper anyway—has withdrawn as a theoretician as well into the loneliness of an art for art's sake ideology untouched by a creative and functional life. The lecture found much approval among a small circle of listeners.

Music-Ideas from Yesterday—
A Lecture by Arnold Schoenberg
at the Society for New Music, Cologne
H.
Völkischer Beobachter
February 24, 1933

Schoenberg's introductory sentence, in which he pointed out that his lecture dated from two and a half years in the past, noted that some ideas therefore could be considered old or obsolete. This by all means provokes criticism. Even worse was a lack of a sense of obligation to the organizers who wanted to present to their community of listeners a relevant topic treated by its (seemingly) greatest prophet. For this year's engagement the lecturer deemed it unnecessary to update a lecture written years ago. Here are the signs of such mental poverty that it does not even allow him to "think up" something new, proving him to have become an absurdity to himself!

Schoenberg's sick and desperate efforts to believe himself important, to lull his listeners with witticisms of a typically Jewish manner, his striving to cover an inner emptiness and lack of restraint with a deluge of words, all has to repel any person with healthy feelings. His expatiations on the topic "new" music—interrupted along the way time and again by unconnected sophistries on other matters—and his notion that music can only be considered new if it expresses things never before said, mean nothing special in any case. An abysmal impertinence is revealed when he later attempts to ridicule composers endowed with the sure instinct to create with the greatest comprehensibility and with natural musicality, or when he considers himself happy to be a "brain owner" in contrast to their seeming lack of the ability to think. The content of his quote "What use is it to fall from the sky a master if one falls on one's head!" cannot be omitted here. On the one hand, he sides with Paul Bekker, who disparages the masters of the entire nineteenth century. On the other, only Beethoven—whose signature as "brain owner" had been induced by both anger and facetiousness—seems good enough to be in the limelight, modest as Schoenberg is, on one and the same level as himself. Have we not heard a similarly outrageous presumption before when Klemperer compared himself with Gluck, Weber, and Mozart?

His distorted notion that art music is not meant to be understood by everybody, clearly springs from his pride in being a "constructor," as he called himself. He thinks that Gebrauchsmusik can be dispatched with the ironic remark that its name derives from the fact "that one can make no use of it," but that again is not a valid explanation or opinion. Did not Haas, for example, with his Volks- and Gebrauchsmusik fully answer the expectations raised by their purpose? Finally, Schoenberg once more explicitly underscored his *l'art pour l'art* position, a position we decisively reject.

If it was possible for Schoenberg to add to the negative image of his personal and musical appearance, he succeeded with this lecture. The spiritual movement now underway and coming to the fore leaves us hope that today's generation of musicians will not have to remain under his destructive influence for long!

NOTES

1. This recording is the basis for a video production that accompanies the spoken lecture with visual materials drawn from various archival materials. *Arnold Schoenberg: My Evolution* (Films for the Humanities, n.d.)

2. It is instructive to compare the language used to describe Schoenberg's appearance with that used to characterize Mahler, which has been shown to be colored by stereotypical representations of the Jew. See, K. M. Knittel, "'*Ein hypermoderner Dirigent*': Mahler and Anti-Semitism in *Fin-de-siècle* Vienna," *19th-Century Music* 18 (1995): 257–76.

3. For the preservation of these reviews we are in debt to the efforts of Carl Steininger, a Jewish banker who lived in Dresden 1876–c.1945. Over his lifetime he assembled a massive collection of newspaper clippings on hundreds of figures from art, politics, science, etc.—with a special emphasis on Jews and Jewish issues—from a large number of publications from all the German-speaking areas and from England and the United States.

A large part of the collection is now housed at the Geheimes Staatsarchiv Preussicher Kulturbesitz in Berlin. A portion of the clippings concerning the visual arts have been published on microfiche (*Dokumentation zur jüdischen Kultur in Deutschland 1840–1940, die Zeitungsauschnittsammlung Steininger* [Munich, 1995]). The complete collection of Schoenberg reviews, numbering over 500 items, will be published in an edition edited by Joseph H. Auner and Klaus Kropfinger.

4. Hans Heinz Stuckenschmidt, *Schoenberg: His Life, World and Work*, trans. H. Searle (New York, 1978), p. 316.

5. Schoenberg, "National Music," in *Style and Idea*, ed. Leonard Stein (New York, 1975), p. 174.

6. Arnold Schönberg, *Stil und Gedanke: Aufsätze zur Musik*, ed. Ivan Vojtěch (Frankfurt, 1976), pp. 494–95. The English version is published in Schoenberg, *Style and Idea*, pp. 268–87.

7. Stuckenschmidt, *Schoenberg*, p. 536.

8. R. Wayne Shoaf, "*Der biblische Weg*: Principal and Related Manuscript Sources," *Journal of the Arnold Schoenberg Institute* 17 (1994): 151–61.

9. Jan Maegaard, *Studien zur Entwicklung des dodekaphonen Satzes bei Arnold Schönberg* (Copenhagen, 1972), vol. 1, pp. 126–27.

10. It is not clear whether the phrase "die Entdeckung einer Frau" is intended metaphorically to refer to the personification of a kind of music, as in "Frau Musik," or to the notion that the younger generation of composers could be viewed metaphorically as a wife serving as mediator between Schoenberg and the audience.

11. For the 1933 version and further details on the revisions see, Schönberg, *Stil und Gedanke*, pp. 466–77, 483, and 504–05.

12. The translations have been adjusted to follow Schoenberg, *Theory of Harmony*, trans. Roy E. Carter (Berkeley and Los Angeles, 1978), pp. 400–01. The passages cited were not substantially changed in the third edition of 1922 on which the translation is based.

13. The lecture is published in Schönberg, *Stil und Gedanke*, pp. 255–71, and in *Arnold Schoenberg Self-Portrait*, ed. Nuria Schoenberg Nono (Pacific Palisades, 1988), pp. 41–53.

PART IV
SCHOENBERG AND AMERICA

·

Schoenberg and America

SELECTED AND INTRODUCED
BY SABINE FEISST

The premise of the following selection of excerpts is to present, in their original language, unpublished or little known published writings by and about Schoenberg, all centering on his relationship to the United States. Obvious typographical errors have been tacitly corrected and the formatting has mostly been accommodated to the layout of the present publication. Small changes have been introduced in those selections which are not translations in order to standardize punctuation and Schoenberg's grammatically peculiar English. Editorial additions are indicated by brackets.

Schoenberg on America: Articles, Speeches, Commentary

America seemed to hold a great attraction for Schoenberg from relatively early in his career. Already in the 1910s he made several attempts—all in vain—to tour the United States and conduct the American premieres of *Gurrelieder* and *Pierrot lunaire*. In the 1920s he contributed to American music periodicals and newspapers, where he answered questions about the future of music ("Arnold Schönberg: Foremost Representative of Modernistic School in Europe") and the influence of jazz on "German" music ("Comment on Jazz"). In 1931 Schoenberg expressed his concern that a kind of fast-moving and stereotyped music production—what he called "Americanism in art"—would spoil the public's taste ("Crisis of Taste"). His remarks undoubtedly reflect the very limited knowledge in Germany at that time about American music. In fact, Schoenberg enjoyed listening to jazz recordings available in Germany in the twenties, and later he made no secret of his appreciation of music by George Gershwin, Artie Shaw, and others.

At the age of almost sixty Schoenberg had to flee the Nazis. In October 1933 he came to the United States, where he had been offered a position at the newly established Malkin Conservatory of Music in Boston. On November 11, 1933, he was warmly welcomed in New York City with an all-Schoenberg concert and a reception by the League of Composers, at which occasion he gave one of his first speeches written and delivered in English ("For New York"). Grateful for, but somewhat overwhelmed by, the attention with which he was showered, Schoenberg expressed some concern about being overestimated at the moment, but insufficiently appreciated later on. He would rather be valued like "daily and basic food" than "rare and refined delicacies." In his "First American Radio Broadcast," on November 19, 1933, he spoke not only about the process of composition and the difficulties for listeners in understanding and appreciating his music, but also about his teaching conditions and goals with regard to his American pupils. Numerous interviews were to follow in which Schoenberg was questioned about his teaching experience in America.

Although he had good prospects for teaching positions in Chicago and in New York, health problems forced Schoenberg to move to the West Coast in autumn 1934. The favorable climate, the picturesque landscapes, the friendly atmosphere, and relative prosperity in California lifted Schoenberg's spirits. In a speech given in October 1934, he gratefully and enthusiastically stated, "I was driven into Paradise!" Nor did Schoenberg seem to yearn for the Old World when a few years later, in an exuberant mood, he substituted a pitiless satirical text for the refrain of one of the most popular Viennese songs, "Wien, du Stadt meiner Träume" (Vienna, you city of my dreams).

Soon after his arrival in California, he became one of the most sought-after teachers of composition in the Los Angeles area. He first taught privately and at the University of Southern California. In 1936 he joined the faculty of the University of California at Los Angeles and was later also engaged as a guest lecturer at the Music Academy of the West in Santa Barbara and at the University of Chicago. Schoenberg became very involved in developing and improving music education in America; he drafted numerous proposals and critical essays on issues of music pedagogy. In his "First California Broadcast" in 1934, Schoenberg, in comparing conditions for music students in America and Europe, acknowledged the commitment, ambition, and talent of young Americans, but regretted their lack of acquaintance with the important works of the past. He emphasized that all students should hear and own the scores of all the important compositions of the past, and in his lessons he focused on the thorough study and analysis of such works.

As a teacher, Schoenberg was also much in demand by composers working in the Hollywood film industry. Among them was Alfred Newman, who invited Schoenberg in 1938 to present the Oscar for the best film score of 1937, given to Charles Previn (a second cousin of André Previn) for *One Hundred Men and a Girl*.[1] Because he was ill, Schoenberg could not attend the awards ceremony, but wrote a speech that was delivered on his behalf. In it, Schoenberg expressed hope for the future acceptance of uncompromising modern music within the film industry. Making concessions in order to please mass audiences meant to him artistic immorality, which he saw in many stage works, radio productions, music, and movies, as well as in novels, and which he condemned in such essays as "Art and the Moving Pictures" (1940)[2] and "Music and Morality" (1948).

After the mid-twenties, when his Serenade and Wind Quintet were premiered in the United States, Schoenberg became categorized more frequently in this country as the leading twelve-tone composer and atonalist. Although a whole young generation of American composers started to embrace dodecaphonic methods enthusiastically, in a contribution to the *New York Times* ("Protest on Trademark") toward the end of his life Schoenberg objected to this label, which he viewed as a stigma. The emphasis on "twelve-tone" often encouraged people to focus on counting notes and rows rather than on studying many other features of a composition.

In the same year, 1950, in a survey entitled "The Transplanted Composer," Albert Goldberg asked Schoenberg whether living and working in America had influenced or changed his artistic output. The composer answered in the negative, admitting that he at least was not aware of any changes. Schoenberg certainly remained faithful to his self-imposed moral principles as an artist and never gave up composing with twelve tones. Yet banishment from Germany, with whose musical traditions and musical progress he had identified so strongly, must have been a bitter experience for him. Once "transplanted" to America, he never returned to Europe, despite numerous opportunities and invitations. In 1939, he was elected to active ASCAP membership and in 1941 he acquired United States citizenship. In a sense he became an American composer writing works for Americans—works inspired and commissioned by Americans, works that bear America's influence. Yet one somehow hesitates to consider Schoenberg an "American" composer, like Ernest Bloch or Edgard Varèse.[3] His influence and legacy were too powerful and too far-reaching to be contained by either his native country or adopted land alone. Unlike many other émigré composers, Schoenberg was a truly international figure.

(Notes appear on p. 309.)

• • •

On the occasion of the fortieth anniversary of *The Etude*, a widely distributed music magazine mainly intended for music teachers and students, its editor asked Schoenberg and other prominent musicians of the world to send salutations, and to answer the following questions: "Have we reached the pinnacle of musical activity, or will the people of the earth in four decades witness a still greater utilization of music in life? Is it possible for the art itself to progress materially beyond the high achievements of 1923, or may we expect in 1963 new phases of musical accomplishment?" (James F. Cooke to Schoenberg, letter of May 16, 1923, Library of Congress.) The manuscript of this reply is entitled "Satirische Antwort auf eine Rundfrage der *Etude*" (Satirical Reply to a Survey by the *Etude*). This was the first text of Schoenberg published in the American press.

Arnold Schönberg: Foremost Representative of Modernistic School in Europe
The Etude 41
October 1923

On the occasion of the fortieth anniversary of your journal, I take pleasure in sending you herewith as a greeting, my answer to the questions that you have asked. Prophesying is a very difficult matter, especially if one stresses the fact that the prophecy must be made in advance and that it ought to come true. The task is made easier, however, by the fact that the prophet is not without honor, save in his own country (and that beforehand), so that he does not risk losing much.

In spite of this, I do not venture to answer your question directly, as you put it; but, adopt a slight variation in which I do not ask if we have attained the greatest perfection and method of development, but if one is likely to believe or question it independent of the circumstances, and to this my answer is: In another forty years some persons will rejoice in the fact that the climax of perfection has been reached, while others will lament over the decline and the decadence. Of the first group, some will maintain that we may rest content, while others will seek new laurels in further progress. Among the advocates of decadence only a small number will admit, just as to-day, that their own lack of talent and distinctive character is the only indication of that decadence; and even that minority will take good care not to admit this openly. The larger and more fanatical number of those who support the idea of decline will, on the other hand, exclude themselves from the general and complete decadence and will undertake to appear as the only ones who recall the splendor of bygone days. Moreover, most persons are also likely to believe them, although all can see that the latter only remember the greatness of earlier times, because in those days there were also such persons to whom the incompetence in creative ability left but one possible expression and one possible thought: The lamentation over the creative incompetence of the others.

(At the special request of Mr. Schönberg, we reprint his original letter in the German language.)

Zum 40-ten Jahrestag der Begründung Ihrer Zeitschrift sende ich Ihnen gerne als Gruss hier meine Antwort auf die gestellten Fragen: Prophezeien ist eine sehr schwere Sache, insbesondere wenn darauf Gewicht gelegt wird, dass die Prophezeiung im voraus erfolgt und dass sie eintreffen soll.

Erleichtert wird diese Aufgabe jedoch dadurch, dass der Prophet ohnedies im Vaterland nichts gilt und das schon im vorhinein, so dass er also dabei nicht viel zu verlieren riskiert. Trotzdem mag ich es nicht wagen, Ihre Frage direkt so zu beantworten, wie Sie sie stellen, sondern nehme eine kleine Abänderung vor, indem ich nicht frage, ob man die grössere Betriebsamkeit und Vollendung *erreicht* haben wird, sondern ob man das unabhängig von den Tatsachen *glauben oder bezweifeln* wird. Und darauf lautet meine Antwort: Auch in 40 Jahren wird ein Teil der Menschheit darüber jubeln, dass der Gipfel der Vollendung erreicht ist, während ein anderer Teil den Niedergang, die Dekadenz bejammern wird. Von den ersteren werden einige meinen, dass man nun ausruhen könne, während andere neuen Lorbeer in weiterem Fortschreiten werden suchen wollen. Von den Anhängern des Niedergangs wird genau wie heute ein nur kleiner Teil annehmen, dass ihre eigene Talent- und Charakterlosigkeit das einzige Merkmal dieses Niedergangs ist; und selbst dieser Teil wird sich wohl hüten, das öffentlich zu bekennen. Der grössere und fanatischere Teil der Niedergangsanbeter hingegen wird es verstehen, sich selbst aus der sonst allgemeinen und vollkommenen Dekadenz auszuschliessen und im Gegenteil als die Einzigen zu scheinen, die an den Glanz verschwundener Zeiten erinnern: und das werden ihnen die meisten auch glauben, obwohl alle sehen könnten, dass jene an die Grösse früherer Zeiten nur dadurch erinnern, dass es auch damals eben solche gegeben hat, denen die Unfähigkeit in schöpferischer Hinsicht nur eine einzige Ausdrucksmöglichkeit und nur einen einzigen Gedanken gelassen hat: das Jammern über die schöpferische Unfähigkeit der Anderen!

—Mödling, den 12. Juni 1923, Arnold Schönberg.

• • •

Since it was cabled from Berlin, we can assume that the following text was written between 1925 and 1932. It has also been published in *Arnold Schönberg: Gedenkausstellung 1974*, ed. Ernst Hilmar (Vienna, 1974), pp. 332–33. The text and its translation into English are based on Schoenberg's typescript and handwritten note at the Arnold Schönberg Center, Vienna.

Comment on Jazz
Midwest Chicago Daily News

I was asked by telegraph whether I think that jazz has exerted an influence on German music.

As long as there is German music and one rightly understands what that has meant up to now, jazz will never have a greater influence on it than did Gypsy music in its time. The occasional use of several themes and the addition of foreign color to several phrases has never changed the essential: the body of ideas and the technique of its presentation. Such impulses can be compared to a disguise. Whoever dresses up as an Arab or a Tyrolean intends to appear this way only externally and temporarily, and as soon as the fun of the masquerade is over, he wants once again to be the person he was before.

•

Ich wurde telegraphisch gefragt, ob ich glaube, dass die *Jazz Musik* auf die deutsche einen Einfluss ausgeübt habe.

Solange es deutsche Musik gibt und man mit Recht dasselbe darunter versteht wie bisher, wird der Jazz auf sie nie grösseren Einfluss ausüben als seinerzeit die Zigeunermusik: die gelegentliche Verwendung einzelner Themen und die Verleihung fremdländischen Kolorits an einzelne Sätze hat niemals das Wesentliche: den Gedankenkreis und die Darstellungstechnik verändert. Solche Anwandlungen sind einer Maskierung zu vergleichen. Wer sich aber als Araber oder als Tiroler verkleidet, will das doch nur äusserlich und vorübergehend scheinen und sobald der Maskenscherz zuende ist, wieder der sein, der er vorher war.

Berlin

Arnold Schönberg

• • •

Schoenberg wrote the following brief contribution for a survey on modern music, "Das Heute in der Musik. Prominente Komponisten, Dirigenten und Sänger über die moderne Musik" (The present in music. Prominent composers, conductors and singers on modern music). Besides the *Berliner Börsen-Zeitung*, it was published in *Die Musik* 25 (1932): 149–50. When he was criticized for what he said against America, he tried in an unpublished text, "Mein Stil" (My style) of January 31, 1931, both to justify himself and to be more precise: "I think and could have said, that the Americans, who in a few decades have consumed our entire European culture of many centuries, now will have soon, and without interruption, used up the modern music too: In the way they have brought things to such a state, that every year, once or several times, they not only wear clothes of the very latest fashion, but also own a new car and a new quill for their fountain pen, they apparently want one to two new fashions per year in art too." (Handwritten manuscript, Arnold Schönberg Center, Vienna.)

Crisis of Taste
Berliner Börsen-Zeitung
January 1, 1931

Today musical taste, as well as the public's ability to absorb musical works, is considerably hampered by Americanism in art, which to art's detriment, imposes upon it a mechanical cliché. The result is the public's acclimation to inferior musical production so that it is no longer able to distinguish between music of value and inferior kitsch. With a shrug, all masterpieces are declared outdated. That is the effect of the present on music. One cannot even claim that music is in a crisis. It is rather a crisis of public taste that we can observe today.

•

Sowohl der musikalische Geschmack als auch die Aufnahmefähigkeit des Publikums für Musikwerke ist heute schwer beeinträchtigt durch den Amerikanismus in der Kunst, der ihr zu ihrem Schaden ein mechanisches Klischee aufdrückt. Das Resultat ist eine Gewöhnung des Publikums an minderwertige musikalische Produktion, so daß es oft wertvolle Musik von minderwertigem Kitsch nicht mehr zu unterscheiden imstande ist. Alle Meisterwerke werden achselzuckend für überholt erklärt. Das ist die Wirkung des Heute auf die Musik, von der man nicht einmal behaupten kann, daß sie sich in einer Krise befindet. Es ist vielmehr eine Krise des Publikumgeschmacks, die wir heute beobachten können.

• • •

The following speech was prepared for the League of Composers' All-Schoenberg Welcome Concert and reception, at Town Hall in November 1933. Works presented at the concert included Schoenberg's Second and Third String Quartets, four songs from Op. 6, and the Piano Pieces, Opp. 11 and 33. Schoenberg gave this speech after the performance of the Third Quartet. Olin Downes considered it "one of the shortest and most sincere speeches in recent musical history" ("League of Composers Opens Season at the Town Hall With Schoenberg Concert," *New York Times*, November 12, 1933). This version is drawn from an unpublished typescript in English at the Arnold Schönberg Center, Vienna.

For New York
November 11, 1933

Ladies and gentlemen!

At first, let me say, that I am charmed and honored in the highest degree of the reception I have found by *you* and wherever I have been in America till now.

Please, let me express the thanks to *you*, which I wish to direct to you and to those, who had honored me in these days. But allow me to say, that I am not only charmed, but also astonished, by this reception, which is in quantity and quality very different from those, I am knowing of the old continent.

And allow me to say: in the same measure, as your acknowledgement enjoys me, in the same measure I am apprehensive.

I fear now to be overestimated by you! Don't think, that I am saying that only for *modesty*! For, in reality: I *know* my value; and I know also, which is my *work* and my merit. And, on the contrary, as I am knowing all that, I must consequently fear that, one day, you will have enough of such an appreciation, so as one has enough of certain foods of an extraordinary or extravagant character; so as human beings get enough of all that, what seems out of order, out of the daily regularity. And then, you shall *depreciate* me, and that without that my work had changed his character; just as little, as the extraordinary foods has changed their character.

Human being has an affection to his bread; to his *simple* and *daily* bread; and this affection is the only passion to which he is remaining faithfully. All the other "higher" and "more differentiated" and more "refined" pleasures, these "caviar," and "creams," these colors and forms, these sonorities and harmonies—all these are depending from the change of fancy and fashion. But the simple bread is *always* true to human beings, so as, vice versa, these are true to him.

You will be astonished, that a composer as I am, is speaking in such a manner. But don't believe, that somebody, whose work has disturbed the whole world, that such one now could *ask*, that other composers may write in the manner of "daily bread." This is not my opinion. But, by this parallel I wish to express the following:

An artist, who has *not* created his work, for, that the *master* may be praised by the work; but one, which, on the contrary, has always and exclusively intended: to concentrate *all praise* to the *work*, such an author must fear to be overestimated as "caviar" and "creams"; and he must fear, that, one day, he could be depreciated, even as "caviar" and "creams." And therefore it is a burning desire of such authors, to get a place in the valuation of men, not as an extravagant, but as a *daily* food; to grow: *daily bread* of friends and art!

• • •

The following inteview with Schoenberg by William Lundell was broadcast by NBC on November 19, 1933. The version given here is based on a transcript at the Arnold Schönberg Center, Vienna. A German translation has appeared in Arnold Schönberg, *Stil und Gedanke: Aufsätze zur Musik*, ed. Ivan Vojtěch (Frankfurt, 1976), pp. 301–03.

First American Radio Broadcast
November 19, 1933, 11:00–11:30 A.M.

ANNOUNCEMENT: (*Verklärte Nacht*: Kroll Sextet)
LUNDELL: This work of yours, Mr. Schoenberg, we have just heard, is very interesting to me, because it has such close relationship to the great classical tradition. In that respect it is very different from your more recent compositions. It prompts me to ask if it is true, as some have said, that you demand as an essential requirement that any

pupil who wishes to study with you must have a thorough training in the classical tradition?

SCHOENBERG: Well, I prefer to instruct pupils which have learned something before coming to me. The degree of instruction he has before he comes to me is not always significant, for there is much instruction, and many teachers. It is not that I wish to criticize the teachers, or any method that they employ, for each teacher is a good teacher if he has a good pupil. And he is a bad teacher very often if he has a bad pupil.

LUNDELL: Mr. Schoenberg, you are a superb diplomat.

SCHOENBERG: (laughs) I have had bad pupils, and I have had good pupils. And I have always been the same teacher to both.

LUNDELL: But we are getting away from the point. What I mean is this. Do you demand a training in Bach, Beethoven and Brahms? Must any pupil coming to you know these classics?

SCHOENBERG: No, Mr. Lundell, it is not absolutely necessary. But I would prefer if the pupil knew Bach and Beethoven and Brahms, and Mozart. Even if he has not this classical training, but has musical ability and talent, I can sense it—*ich kann es bemerken*—yes, how you say it—in English—I can see it.

LUNDELL: Well now, about yourself, Mr. Schoenberg. We have just heard the Kroll String Sextet play this *Verklärte Nacht* Suite. But Mr. Bela Rózsa, whom I have heard playing your music all the past week, and who will play some of your piano music following this interview at the close of the program, shows with this piano music a totally different style from the *Verklärte Nacht* Suite. He tells me that there is a great difference between your Opus 10, for instance, with its classical tone, and this later style of Opus 11 and the succeeding works. Why did you make a change?

SCHOENBERG: Why? Well I was forced to.

LUNDELL: What do you mean, forced to?

SCHOENBERG: My fancy, my imagination. The musical pictures I had before me. I have always had musical visions before me, all the time I was writing still in the more classic mode, in the earlier days. Then finally, one day, I had courage to put on paper these pictures I had seen in music. Many times before I have written my music in this new style—what you call a new style—I have seen this music in my mind. And so, for me it was not such a great *Sprung*—as you say in English jump—for me it was a gradual development.

LUNDELL: But, Mr. Schoenberg, these pictures you saw in your mind, and which you finally had the courage to put down in music on paper, they were not pictures of flowers and brooks and thunderstorms, or landscapes?

SCHOENBERG: No, it was music and tones—it is not a transcription of natural scenery. Musical figures and themes and melodies I call pictures. It is my idea that it is a musical story with musical pictures—Not a real story, and not real pictures—quasi pictures.

LUNDELL: Would you call it absolute—pure music?

SCHOENBERG: No, I do not prefer to call it that. Fancy is the dominant force which drives the artist, and it is not of great difference to me, whether it is a poetical idea or a musical idea. A musician can always only see music, and the cause is of no importance. I am not against what you call "program music."

LUNDELL: If a composer can write music describing a storm at sea or a skyscraper, you would agree that that may be thoroughly good music?

SCHOENBERG: Yes, if a composer can describe a skyscraper, a sunrise, or springtime in the country, that is all right, the cause and the source of it is irrelevant. It is the result that is always important.

LUNDELL: A number of the critics and students of music in discussing your music refer to this change from your earlier to your later style as a change from the classical to the atonal.

SCHOENBERG: Ah, no, don't say atonal. I do not like the word "atonal."

LUNDELL: But there is distinct difference in your styles. Have you developed any theory of composition based upon your later style?

SCHOENBERG: Not in this sense, I am never after a theory; and for the general public there is no difference between my present manner to compose and my earlier manner to compose. I am always writing that, what my fancy gives me, and always I can only write if I have seen a musical idea.

LUNDELL: When you have seen that musical idea, how do you seek to express it?

SCHOENBERG: Well, it is hard to explain. With the musical idea I get an impression of musical form and extension, and of the whole and of the parts. By and by I am seeing this form more exactly, and I begin to hear themes and sonorities, and then I begin with the writing with the pen. Sometimes with sketches, and sometimes I write the music directly. And then, there the music is.

LUNDELL: About the appreciation and understanding of your music, Mr. Schoenberg, as we know, it took people generally many years to understand and appreciate Wagner and Berlioz, Ravel, Stravinsky—but they are all now so well accepted as to be performed in movie theatres, and in one instance, in a musical comedy. Have you any anticipation as to the length of time that will be needed for an understanding of your compositions?

SCHOENBERG: Ach, I only hope it will not be so long, but I am not sure. The difficulty for the public to understand my music is the conciseness and the shortness.

LUNDELL: You mean that you speak musically in a kind of aphorism, epigrams—I almost said enigmas, Mr. Schoenberg.

SCHOENBERG: Yes, my works are apparently enigmas to many people, but there is an answer to all of them. What I mean is, I never repeat. I say an idea only once.

LUNDELL: But even saying it once, Mr. Schoenberg, was too much for some people twenty-five years ago. Did those riots among the critics and the audience during that celebrated concert in Vienna when the public was so excited about your music as to let fists fly and shout and scream—did all that uproar discourage you? And does the present day failure to understand your work trouble you?

SCHOENBERG: Yes, my feelings are always offended by trouble and misunderstanding. For I think the public could know that I have worked with the greatest sincerity and I think I have the right to demand the respect of the public for my work.

LUNDELL: Now that you have come to America from Europe, Mr. Schoenberg, to be at the Malkin Conservatory of Music in Boston and New York, and from your knowledge of modern music—what would you say is the greatest need in contemporary music?

SCHOENBERG: I think what we need in music today is not so much new methods of music, as men of character. Not talents. Talents are here. What we need are men who will have the courage to express what they feel and think.

LUNDELL: Are there any men like that on the musical horizon today?

SCHOENBERG: Oh yes, I have seen some of them. For instance, I have some of them among my pupils. Alban Berg, Anton von Webern, and others. For it is my important intention to fortify the morale of my pupils. The chief thing I demand of my pupils, with their basic technical knowledge of music taken for granted, of course, is the courage to express what they have to say.

• • •

The following speech was written and delivered in English at a reception in Los Angeles in October 1934. A heavily edited version has appeared in Schoenberg, *Style and Idea*, pp. 501–02, as the first of what are called (by the editor, Leonard Stein) "Two Speeches on the Jewish Situation." A German translation of the text was published in Schoenberg, *Stil und Gedanke*, p. 326, and republished in *Arnold Schönberg 1874–1951: Lebensgeschichte in Begegnungen*, ed. Nuria Nono Schoenberg (Klagenfurt and Vienna, 1998), pp. 310–11. The present text is based closely on the original typescript at the Arnold Schönberg Center, Vienna.

Driven into Paradise
October 9, 1934

Ladies and Gentlemen:

There are among you certainly many, who know about my person only the fact of my so called expatriation and probably some know this fact not much longer than for a few minutes.

They fear—I can understand it—they fear to hear now those nightmare-tales which cause an agreeable kind of shuddering and give the speaker the feeling to have deeply affected his hearers and which, indeed in as far, are very satisfactory. But unfortunately they are not in the slightest degree as satisfactory if you regard their influence on the state of German Jewry or on World Jewry.

I must disappoint this part of my hearers, for from the very first beginning it was my opinion, that the state of the Jewry can not be bettered by such nightmare-tales or by fighting against Germany. But I want to abstain from politics and, preferring other subjects, I must disappoint also another group of my hearers. Namely those, who know a little more about me: who have learned from all the musical misdeeds, attributed to my person, that I am the so-called "father of modern music," and that I have broken the eternal rules of musical art and aesthetic, that I have spoiled not only my own music, but also that of the classics, and that of the past, present and future times—that I am a sort of musical gangster—and that men who know how to distinguish between Beethoven and Gershwin have to protect themselves only by being conservatives against the terror of *atonality*, of this terrible atonality.

I must disappoint them.

It is not at all my intention to speak about terror: neither about such one which made suffer myself, nor about such one by which—as stated—I made suffer others.

I did not come in this marvelous country to speak from terrors, but only to forget them.

Let us leave them!

As the snake was expatriated, as it was driven out of the paradise, as it was sentenced to go on its belly and to eat dust all the days of its life—this was another kind of expatriation.

For the snake came out of the paradise and—going on its belly, I fear, this was symbolizing a certain lack of freedom. And I fear further, the dust it wanted to eat, this poor food was rationed out as in wartime and the animal could not get enough to appease the hunger and was forced to get *dust-e*rsatz, dust-surrogate . . .

I, on the contrary, I came from the one country into another country where neither dust nor better food is rationed and where I am allowed to go on my feet, where my head can be erect, where kindness and cheerfulness is dominating and where to live is a joy where to be an expatriated of another country is the grace of *God*. I was driven into the paradise!

• • •

The following is a transcript of an interview Schoenberg gave in the fall of 1934 (no more precise date can be established) to Max van Leuwen Swarthout of the University of Southern California. It was published in German translation in Schoenberg, *Stil und Gedanke*, pp. 320–23. The text is based on a typsecript at the Arnold Schönberg Center, Vienna.

First California Broadcast
Fall 1934

SWARTHOUT: Mr. Schoenberg: You have taught at the University of Southern California during the recent summer session and I am happy in the knowledge that you are to be associated with us at the School of Music during the coming year. Doubtless you had a number of interesting experiences during the past six weeks that you have been with us; as well as during the past two [sic] years that you have been in America, and in all probability you have formed a number of conclusions concerning American schools of music and American music students.

I would like to ask you, if you can tell me why the American student of music goes to Europe to further his education. Is there, in your opinion, any great difference between the American and European school of music, which would justify an American student going abroad for study? Please state your opinion as fully as you care to do so.

SCHOENBERG: In general, Mr. Swarthout, I find the organization of the schools here not very much different from that of the European schools. The standard of the American schools of music is the highest I know. There is an astonishing[ly] great number of renowned teachers, many of them of international fame. But concerning pedagogy I found out a difference for your credit. Whilst old Europe is resting somewhat on her tradition, America advances and develops pedagogy through very scientific means and with the ardent ambition of her happy youth. And the same I find among pupils: Their eagerness to learn is of the same youthful ardor and I feel young with them, when I feel the touch of their power.

Thus, to answer your question, I have therefore to speak from some other differences, whose influence is perhaps explaining the fact that American pupils go to Europe. These differences concern neither pedagogy, nor the talent of pupils, nor the efforts of the teachers. But their influence is fundamental.

At first: In every country in Europe, where the musical standard is as high as in America, you will find cities with one or more opera houses and with one or more symphony orchestras, which give performances during at least eight to nine months, even in summer in the larger cities. By this circumstance already the musician or music lover has the possibility to hear as much music as he likes. But there is also another important circumstance: Almost everywhere in these musical centers these institutions are enabled to be nearly independent in building up their programs, because they do not pay so much attention to the returns of the box office. Many of these institutions are supported by public means and can fulfill artistic necessities. Certainly they can not perform only such works, as have had no success at all. But if the artistic necessity is evident, you will always find the possibility of a performance. By this way, you will find in these places a repertoire of a much more extended compass than in America, where it has partly to be built of popular pieces and where the box office often forbids the performance of valuable works. As an example I want to mention one of my works, whose performance requires not only a number of about six hundred people as performers, but involves also a very great financial support. This work, the *Gurrelieder*, has been only *once* performed in America: by Mr. Stokowski in Philadelphia. But in Europe I have counted nearly one hundred performances. This number could only be achieved by the circumstance, that even cities of less than two hundred thousand inhabitants had the ambition to perform such a work.

But the independence of the box office is also shown by the very low prices of admission, which enable the less rich people and the students to attend the concerts and the opera performances.

For musicians the knowledge of the important works is as necessary as it is for a technician to be acquainted with the achievements of his predecessors. This knowledge is offered to a musician in Europe by the number of performances and by the nature of their programs which are built always according to artistic requirements.

But there is also another circumstance which helps the students to get the necessary background:

Nearly every young music student in Europe possesses a small library of a few hundred copies of the most important musical works. This is possible because of the very low prices of printed music. A musician has not only to listen very often to the works of the masters, but he has also to study them, to analyze, to memorize, to acknowledge the innumerable variety of artistic means. And for that purpose he has to *possess* the copies.

I find there is in America so much talent for music and so much love for it, that America will certainly in a short time be the first as regards to musical culture, if only the interest of the public could be concentrated on these two facts, and if it would change this circumstance with such a speed, which fulfills us Europeans with astonishment and admiration:

Firstly to give the music lover and the music students the possibility to hear the works of the masters at low prices and as often as it [is] done in Europe.

Secondly to provide the music students with the necessary music and scores. But that means: to publish music at low prices.

SWARTHOUT: What do you think would be the influence of such an achievement on musical education?

SCHOENBERG: I find that the education of not only composers, teachers of harmony, counterpoint and composition, but also of conductors and other performers and of teachers of the different instruments *must* be based on an acquaintance with the works of the masters.

By some circumstance the musical teaching has become a little abstract, a little mechanical. It seems to me as if the teaching is by this way too technical, but not enough essential. Certainly the pupil is enabled by such a manner of training to conquer every technical difficulty he encounters. I understand that a boxer can be trained this way. If he is taught to counter every attack known by experts, he will quickly learn to fight correctly in each instance, because, if he did not, he would feel it not only on his body, but on his record. But there is no similar possibility for a musician or for a composer. He may know every possible trick, but *he* will *not* feel it when he composes or performs poorly.

To know how to make a modulation is of no use if the pupil does not know how to employ this in a composition. But even if he knows, he may perhaps be able to harmonize a given theme, but will *not* know how to invent themes on a basis, from which you can look forward to the further development and which guarantees the constructive purpose of harmony. The same is true in counterpoint: you have to write a canon or a fugue when you are a pupil. But in free composition you would write a canon or fugue only if you did not understand how to develop contrapuntal ideas according to their true nature and according to constructive purposes. And the same things happens with the knowledge of musical forms, if the student does not know the true meaning of musical formation, that is, to arrange and to build up one's ideas in such a manner that the pictures produced show one's ideas in an understandable and sound manner. In such a way the listener may be convinced, that one has spoken only of his ideas and has carried them out thoughtfully and fancifully.

I think this can not be brought about without a profound knowledge of the achievements of the great thinkers of music. You will admit that I do not ask a pupil to write like Bach, or Beethoven, or Mozart or Brahms. But I *do* ask that he realizes how profoundly they carried out their ideas and how manifold the means were, by which these great masters did their work.

And therefore my teaching is based on the knowledge of the works of the masters. And therefore I find it so necessary to strive that the students may have enough opportunity to hear these works and to possess a small library of the most important compositions.

And now, Mr. Swarthout, let me tell you that I am very, very happy not only to live in this marvelous country, but also to be associated with you and the University of Southern California, and to take advantage of your experience and your knowledge. And let me thank you for giving me the opportunity to work together with you for the education and the future of young American musicians.

SWARTHOUT: Thank you, Mr. Schoenberg, for your most interesting comparison of the American and European school of music. As one who felt the necessity himself, some thirty years ago, to go abroad for advanced music study, I feel that your analysis of present day conditions as regards music study is well considered. However, may I not, in conclusion, state that in my opinion America has made splendid progress in musical appreciation during the past quarter of a century, and may it not be hoped, that such help for the music student as you have suggested—inexpensive concerts and opera, and inexpensive music—may shortly come to stimulate still further American music schools for American music students!

• • •

The letter reproduced here, taken from an unpublished type-script at the Arnold Schönberg Center, Vienna, contains the text of a speech Schoenberg intended to deliver at the ceremony for the Oscars given by the Academy of Motion Picture Arts and Sciences in March 1938. The speech was delivered on his behalf.

Oscar Speech
March 1938

Mr. Donald Gledhill, Executive Secretary
Academy of Motion Picture Arts and Sciences
1680 North Vine Street
Hollywood, California

I deeply regret that illness during the past two nights will prevent me from attending the banquet tonight. Please express my disappointment and offer my apologies to your board and the guests. I add the remarks, which I had planned to deliver and which I should like to have represent me on this important occasion.

It seems to me one of the most estimable traits of mankind, that men like to find out, who are their best. And, that mankind always is ready to venerate outstanding persons in every field, symbolizes to me the tendency of mankind toward progress, toward development, toward improvement, toward a better future.

As almost my whole life as an artist has been devoted—scarcely to the present—but distinctly to the future, I use with pleasure this occasion to express the hope, there will soon come a time, when the severe conditions and laws of modernistic music will be no hindrance any more toward a reconciliation with the necessities of the moving picture industry.

By its use of music as a means of stimulation, the movie industry has already succeeded in making the people music conscious. Step by step it will educate them also to ideas and ways of expression, which they cannot appreciate today.

Because of this effect, in time to come, every outstanding man in this field will deserve the title of pioneer of culture.

Therefore I congratulate most heartily the Universal Pictures, whose picture *100 Men and a Girl* has been chosen as this year's best musical score.

Arnold Schoenberg

• • •

The following excerpts, from unpublished manuscripts at the Arnold Schönberg Center, Vienna, show Schoenberg's attempt to satirize Rudolf Sieczyński's song "Wien, du Stadt meiner Träume" (Wienerlied), Op. 1 (©1914). Schoenberg reworded only the refrain. He then wrote out two settings, which differ slightly from each other in key and certain details of melody and rhythm.

"Wien, Wien, nur du allein"
November 1939

Vienna, Vienna, you alone have to be despised by everyone! Others may possibly be forgiven, but you will never be free from guilt. You must perish, only your shame shall endure. You are stigmatized for all eternity by falseness and hypocrisy.

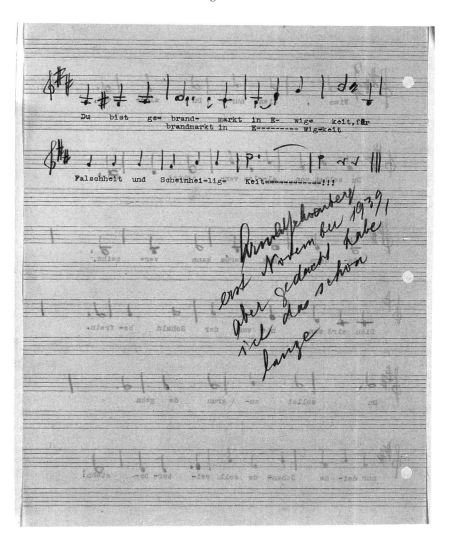

• • •

The following was written for the newsletter of the League of Composers. Schoenberg seems to be responding to an article, "Over the Air" by Gail Kubik, that had appeared in the previous issue. Kubik had criticized music written for the radio, faulting its lack of creativity and its tendency toward simplification and standardization. Readers were invited to present their reaction to Schoenberg's provocative statement, but the *News-Record* ceased publication after one further issue, without printing any responses.

Music and Morality
The Composer's News-Record 7/8
Fall–Winter 1948–49

One can understand that a young composer, at the beginning of his twenties, is influenced by a ten- or fifteen-year-older composer, whose style and technique are already established distinctly. But after having acquired a certain ability himself, everybody must start producing something that has not been said before him.

This is perhaps why Mozart had said: "Lernt's was, Buben, damit ihr was koennt!" (Study, boys, in order to know something!) and Wagner: "Macht etwas Neues!" (Produce something new!)

How then can one explain today's aim of most composers, artists, writers, etc., to produce something similar to the last success on the stage, the movies, the radio, novels and music? Has originality lost its appreciation? Does it interfere too much with the commercial success?

One can understand that fear for one's life may cause a man to bow to dictatorship, though, however, there have been men who did not hesitate to die for their conviction. Tolerate Shostakovitch's bow to the pressure of ignorant politicians. But must one tolerate the moral and mental baseness of people who bow to the mere temptation of profits?

There arise the following problems:

1) Is it esthetically and morally admissible to accommodate to the listener's mentality and preference?

2) If so, is there not a limit how far such accommodation is allowed to go?

3) Does such accommodation promote the artistic culture of a nation?

4) Does it promote morality?

5) Is it not more healthy to give a nation a chance to admire its heroes than to applaud the fleeting success of an ephemeron?

December 1948
Arnold Schoenberg

• • •

The following text was originally written as part of program notes commissioned by Dean Mark Schubart for the Juilliard Quartet's performance of Schoenberg's Four String Quartets at Times Hall, New York, in January–February, 1950. The *Times* article bore the subhead "Schoenberg Asks Stress on What He Has to Say."

Protest on Trademark
New York Times
January 15, 1950

It looks as if the time has come when audiences will listen to my music with more favor and kindness. This seems to me the given moment to do also something in my favor.

For years, instead of studying my scores and trying to find out who I am, for years one has tried to get rid of the problems I possibly might offer, by stamping me with a trade-mark—the twelve-tone composer, the atonalist. Whatever I might have to present, good or bad, beautiful or ugly, soft or harsh, true or false, was of no concern.

I have often enough explained that the method of composing with twelve tones is only a matter of organization and what displeases many listeners are the dissonances and the absence of a constantly present tonality. It looks as if today's listeners are not enough afraid of such evils and are ready to accept meaningless noises such as what murder mystery stories on the radio use for background illustration. That such nonsense is possible is the result of the audiences failing to question "What did he say." Instead they are satisfied with recognizing a style, a mannerism, "How-did-he-say-it" atonality.

Today atonality is tolerated by all radio listeners, on condition that it will not try to say anything sensible, anything to move your soul, to touch your feelings.

I could not have foreseen that in 1921 when I showed my former pupil, Erwin Stein (now at Boosey & Hawkes) the means I had invented to provide profoundly for a musical organization granting logic, coherence and unity. I then asked him to keep this a secret and to consider it as my private method with which to do the best for my artistic purposes.

But in the meantime, Josef Hauer had tried similar procedures, and if I were to escape the danger of being his imitator, I had to unveil my secret. I called a meeting of friends and pupils, to which I also invited Hauer, and gave a lecture on this new method, illustrating it by examples of some finished compositions of mine. Everybody recognized that my method was quite different from that of the others.

The fact of the use of the twelve tones was now made public by pupils and friends of mine. When in 1933 I came to America I could not change my trade-mark: I was the man with "the system of the chromatic scale."

Laymen, musicians, newspapermen and critics whom I met wanted me to explain briefly what I had in mind. Thus against my "free" will, I had to write a lecture and give it in several places, though I was sure of the immaturity of attempts to explain at this time properly the problems involved in this method. I was, of course, only capable of delivering a superficial explanation of the methods of distribution of the twelve tones.

I was always aware of this imperfection and this is why I gave to the lecture the title, "Method of Composing with Twelve Tones." I was convinced that in emphasizing composing—method of composing—I had created a splendid isolation between my inquisitive tormentors and myself.

Composing—in my opinion—is something which, if one knows what it means, would lead one to avoid such silly questions.

• • •

The following three paragraphs, written by Schoenberg on April 19, 1950, were published a month later in Albert Goldberg's column "The Sounding Board."

The Transplanted Composer
Los Angeles Times
May 14, 1950

When for eight months I lived in Barcelona, finishing the second act of my opera, "Moses and Aron," a Spanish musician wondered whether climate and character of this country might not refresh my mind to replace the somber aspect of my music by lively, gay and light colors.

I asked whether he would expect me to write another style as often as live in a different country: extremely cold in Alaska and Siberia, very hot near the equator, damp in the jungles and so forth.

If immigration to America has changed me—I am not aware of it. Maybe I would have finished the third act of "Moses and Aron" earlier. Maybe I would have written more when remaining in Europe, but I think: nothing comes out, what was not in. And two times two equals four in every climate. Maybe I had four times four times harder to work for a living. But I made no concessions to the market.

NOTES

1. *One Hundred Men and a Girl*, directed by Henry Koster, starred Deanna Durbin and the conductor Leopold Stokowski, one of Schoenberg's greatest champions. This comedy alludes to the programs of the Federal Music Project of the Works Progress Administration established in 1935 under Roosevelt to improve the situation of unemployed musicians during the Depression era.

2. "Art and the Moving Pictures," *Style and Idea*, ed. Leonard Stein (New York, 1975), pp. 153–57.

3. Slonimsky consistently called Schoenberg an "Austrian born American composer." See "Schoenberg (originally Schönberg), Arnold (Franz Walter)," in *Baker's Biographical Dictionary of Musicians*, 8th edition, ed. Nicolas Slonimsky (New York, 1992). Oliver Neighbour, on the other hand, called him an "Austro-Hungarian composer." See Neighbour, "Schoenberg [Schönberg], Arnold (Franz Walter)," in *The New Grove Dictionary of Music and Musicians*, ed. Stanley Sadie (London, 1980). In the adaptation of Neighbour's article for *The New Grove Dictionary of American Music*, ed. H. Wiley Hitchcock (London and New York, 1986), Schoenberg is called an "Austrian composer, naturalized American." Such contradictions are symptomatic of how difficult it can be to categorize the national identity of émigré composers and the nationality of musical works.

American Composers on Schoenberg

Reports about Schoenberg performances reached the American public before the 1910s, thanks to America's close ties to the European musical tradition and strong interest in imports of music from Germany and Austria. When Schoenberg's music was performed in the United States for the first time in 1913, the public was relatively polite, while most music critics reacted with a sense of outrage and sensational reviews. But a great number of budding American composers, among them Philip Clapp, Edward Burlingame Hill, Walter Kramer, and Roger Sessions, did not take the critics' opinions for granted and came forward with their own open-minded views. Kramer, who became better known as a publisher, editor, and critic, was one of Schoenberg's earliest champions. In 1915, at a time when World War I had triggered strong anti-German feelings, and when music from Germany was disappearing from American programs, Kramer wrote an offbeat and ardent essay for the *Musical Observer* ("This Man Schoenberg! A Warning to the Unwise").

In the 1920s Schoenberg's cause was taken up and discussed by composers such as Marion Bauer, Louis Gruenberg, Edgard Varèse, and Adolph Weiss—the latter being one of the first Americans to study with Schoenberg in Vienna and Berlin and to make use of the newly developed method of composing with twelve tones. Among contemporary composers Henry Cowell seemed to be the most committed to Schoenberg's works and ideas.[1] Cowell programmed many Schoenberg works with the New Music Society in California, founded in 1925. Cowell not only wrote and lectured about Schoenberg, but also published the Klavierstück, Op. 33b, in his *New Music Quarterly* in 1932. Shortly after he had met and made friends with Schoenberg in Berlin, Cowell, at the instigation of his friend, the composer John Becker, wrote an enthusiastic essay on Schoenberg for the *Northwest Musical Herald* ("Who Is the Greatest Living Composer?"). Cowell could not know that he had smoothed the way for Schoenberg's imminent entrance onto the American musical scene.

Nicolas Slonimsky, who had just performed Schoenberg's *Accompaniment to a Film Scene* in Havana and Hollywood, looked forward to the composer's arrival in Boston in autumn 1933. Slonimsky refreshed the Bostonians' memory of Schoenberg's music and career with a detailed article for the *Boston Evening Transcript* ("Welcome for the Incoming Modern Master"). Slonimsky and Schoenberg, both living and working in Boston, became good friends, exchanged ideas, and continued to correspond when Schoenberg moved away.

At the Malkin Conservatory Schoenberg taught only a limited number of composition students, about whom little is known. Some of his California pupils, on the other hand, became esteemed and prolific composers. Among them was Lou Harrison, whom Schoenberg listed in a letter to Roy Harris (May 17, 1945) as one of the most promising young American composers. Harrison, ever appreciative of what he learned in Schoenberg's lessons, used dodecaphonic methods occasionally, for instance in the Suite for Piano (1943) and the opera *Rapunzel* (1952). But perhaps the best reflection of what Harrison owes him is apparent in the essay he wrote on the occasion of Schoenberg's seventieth birthday ("Homage to Schoenberg: The Late Works"). Harrison even seems to have kept in mind Schoenberg's emphasis on principles such as "clarity" and "simplicity" when composing a melody for gamelan.[2]

As his own birthday greeting in 1944, Roger Sessions, briefly a colleague of Schoenberg's at the Malkin Conservatory and since the early 1940s a friend and correspondent, wrote a lengthy article for *Tempo* ("Schoenberg in the United States"). Very pleased about Sessions's essay, Schoenberg gave him as a sign of friendship autographed copies of the first page of *Die Jakobsleiter* and the Birthday Canons for Carl Engel.[3] As a "source of energy and impulse" (see p. 335) Schoenberg had a great impact on his many American pupils who set out to explore not only serial, but also microtonal, electronic, experimental, and film composition. He also influenced an equally broad range of American composers who never studied with him, but used and developed his compositional methods. Innumerable American composers, however, considered Schoenberg an example in challenging their artistic and moral concepts and drew from him "renewed faith in the relevance of their own efforts, as well as renewed courage to go on making them."[4]

NOTES

1. See Sabine Feisst, "Henry Cowell und Arnold Schönberg—eine unbekannte Freundschaft," *Archiv für Musikwissenschaft* 55 (1998): 57–71.
2. Harrison quoted by Mark Levine, "Annals of Composing. The Outside. Lou Harrison Comes from the Fringe," *The New Yorker* (August 26, 1990): 155.
3. Andrea Olmstead, "The Correspondence between Arnold Schoenberg and Roger Sessions," *Journal of the Arnold Schoenberg Institute* 13 (1990): 48.
4. Ibid., p. 50.

This Man Schönberg!
A Word of Warning to the Unwise
A. Walter Kramer

Musical Observer

February 12, 1915

As civilization advances in its steady march, treading measures anew and adding to its vocabulary innovations and reforms, there comes a halting place where the appearance on the horizon of a figure new and individual must either be a cause for joy or sorrow. None will deny that it is meet and just to consider every phase of human development without prejudice; yet it is truly difficult to do so.

New personalities, those that arrest the attention, that make for such halting places in mankind's onward march, are rarely realized until they have accomplished some act that calls forth the disapproval of some person or group. Invidious minds proceed all too quickly to assail them. They refrain quite voluntarily from either acquainting themselves thoroughly with the matter in hand and count their applying themselves to a serious study thereof as unnecessary and quite beneath their dignity.

Every decade, however, reveals figures who stand out because of their unlikeness to other men of the age. In the arts these men, with a message fresh and different, have invariably been ridiculed, maligned and held up to scorn. With few exceptions they have survived it and have gone down to posterity as leaders in their respective fields of activity.

The age in which we live is often spoken of as one of but slight productivity in the fine arts. Some affect calling it a transitional age; others deny it any place at all in the vast scheme of artistic development. Yet in music we live contemporaneous with Richard Strauss, Max Reger, Claude Debussy, Maurice Ravel, Sergei Rachmaninoff, Jan Sibelius, Edward Elgar, George Whitefield Chadwick, Horatio Parker, in literature with Maurice Maeterlinck, Bernard Shaw, Hermann Sudermann, Gerhart Hauptmann, Arthur Schnitzler, William Butler Yeats, Stephen Philips, Gabriele d'Annunzio, Sem Benelli, Pierre Loti, Romain Rolland, Bliss Carman, Selma Lagerlöf; while in painting and sculpture Auguste Rodin, Franz von Stuck, Michetti and numerous others are figures of distinction. These are names, all of them, of spirits in the world of art who have made contributions that have received recognition and have been stamped with approval.

Out of Austria comes the new voice. In roughly hewn accents, strong, muscular, unmindful of whether they please the masses or not, speaks Arnold Schönberg. This man—Schönberg! Madman, they have called him! Charlatan, sensationalist, fakir—these are some of the charmingly graceful epithets which he has been given. And why?

Arnold Schönberg is breaking new paths—he is working into the future in a manner not understood by the many. There are already those who would scourge him! They would insist that his iconoclastic proceedings can work no good. Many of them actually live in the hope that he will not be performed in America. But their hope is vain. Already the Flonzaley Quartet has played his String Quartet in D minor, Op. 7, in New York and Boston, after producing it on the Continent and in London. The Kneisel Quartet will produce his Sextet this winter. Reinald Werrenrath, the distinguished young American baritone, has sung some of his songs not only in New York, but in many other American cities as well. Herr Schönberg is a personality and his music demands serious consideration. Leo Ornstein will play his piano compositions this month. His *Gurrelieder* will eventually be heard here, while, of his orchestral works, the *Five Pieces* have just been played in Boston.

It is, to be sure, easy enough to brand him sensationalist and put him aside. But is it fair? Already the Futurist movement in music is gaining ground and things far more radical than Schönberg have been created. Whether they are imitations—and consequently bad, as are the majority of imitations—it is difficult to say. One thing is certain, namely, that what seems unreasonable to-day to a trained musical ear will in a decade be simple enough. Those of us who remember the premiere American performances of the Strauss symphonic works have a case in point to guide us.

The String Quartet, Op. 7—a work which dates from the composer's second period—must win him admirers wherever it is heard, for it is the most colossal conception for two violins, viola and violoncello which any composer has set down. Kurt Schindler, apostle of ultra-modernity, who spoke on the composer and his work at the private hearing which the Flonzaley Quartet gave last winter, very aptly stated that it impressed him as being the natural outgrowth of Beethoven's last quartets. He pointed out the type of theme which Schönberg employs and his scheme in developing. And here is the crux of the matter. Schönberg takes a theme (call it motif or anything else that you will) and builds on it a work that lasts full fifty minutes; the thematic ideas which occur within that period are all subservient to the main subject, which is *the* thing. Nowhere in musical literature has a composer handled a theme in just this way. Pregnant in line is his subject and he has treated it with a mastery at once apparent to the student of his score.

One big movement—the doing away with divisions in a string quartet is new, but natural enough when one considers that with the coming of the symphonic poem the same thing in orchestral music occurred years ago—a movement that carries the listener through all the rhythmic, harmonic and melodic combinations which our modern musical art knows, occupies the work. What Arnold Schönberg says in the space of an hour many musicians try to utter in a life-time. Yet his message is not programmatic; it illustrates no story, it narrates no tale. There is philosophic thought in his music, if you will; clear, healthy thought that all, who desire, may understand. If Mr. Schindler calls the score "early" he does so with reason. It is surely not the Schönberg of 1914. That Schönberg is another individual.

For a taste of this look at the *Klavierstücke*, Op. 11 (Piano Pieces, Op. 11), three impressionistic *Stimmungsbilder* that repel you as you play them. You will be lucky if you can force yourself to go through them at a single sitting. You will say "ugly,"—you will wonder "why?" Then you will put them aside. You will, however, return to them and, if you are honest with the composer and yourself, you will eventually begin to find in them a message, the like of which tonal art has never before conveyed. Ernesto Consolo, the eminent Italian pianist, told the writer that it was fully eight months before he found the pieces comprehensible. And he, sane and intelligent artist, had applied himself to their perusal daily. On the other hand, Rafael Joseffy remarked, "They are not even bad. The case is pathologic." Opus 11 reveals the impressionistic master, seeking new piano colors, undisclosed moods. He delves into the matter of overtones, produced by pressing down the keys of the instrument with one hand without striking them and playing a certain passage with the other hand. The effect, once accomplished, is entrancing. Only a master could have conceived it!

As for the early songs, Op. 1, 2, 3, etc., which America heard first last fall from Mr. Werrenrath: They are real *Lieder*, some of them individual, others not, *Lieder* that are not more modern in texture than the music of the Wagner *Ring*. But examine them closely, minutely, and you will see peering through the curtains of pure diatonics a face that, once observed, must always be remembered. Already are the germs of iconoclasm sown! Look at the setting of Richard Dehmel's curiously thought-out poem "Warning." Do ordinary composers set such poems to music?

Of the *Pierrot lunaire*, the *Five Orchestral Pieces* and the *Gurrelieder* cannot, with justice to the composer, be spoken. He who dares speak of them adversely from a mere examination of the printed page is foolhardy. All three works are colossal in their originality of thought; they lean on nothing, as it were. They blaze a path. We, in America, need Schönberg champions—we must not allow time to pass without hearing these monumental works. If our conductors refuse us the opportunity we must protest.

Arnold Schönberg is the man of the hour. With uncompromising frankness has he hurled his hat into the arena; he has asked to be tested. His music must be heard. A whole army of men and women will cry to suppress it, shortsightedly will they beg that their ears be spared. *They are the persons for whom the development of musical art came to a close with the death of one Richard Wagner.* They will charge Herr Schönberg with all kinds of malicious things. But they dare not claim that he is not a master of his art. Apart from his compositions he has written and published a *Harmonielehre* (Study of harmony) in which he shows his superlative erudition in an unmistakable manner. He is even strict about progressions and does not allow students any more freedom than do other theorists. This work he has dedicated to the memory of Gustav Mahler, a musician who championed him years ago in Vienna, long before his name had gone round the world as "musical madman."

Richard Strauss's work seems almost to be completed. He is now fifty years old and has achieved an enviable place. Schönberg advances with his new message. Let us receive his work, not foolishly as we did ten years ago the now accepted music of Strauss—but with a generous, open mind, with that attitude which makes for progress in all life as well as in the arts. This man—SCHÖNBERG!!!

Who is the Greatest Living Composer?
Henry Cowell
Northwest Musical Herald
January 7, 1933

Who is the greatest living composer? Perhaps none of us are great enough to answer the question! It is said that only time can decide. Yet we may make some observations on the side; perhaps we can say with fair certainty who the greatest living composer isn't! On mature reflection, we must admit that he will probably not be an imitator; all great ones in the past have had their own message, and have said it in their own way. We must therefore look for him among those who say something of their own. This limits the field greatly, as 99 per cent of those who pass for composers only make a weak rehashing of what has already been better said by others. And in the search among the composers of originality, we must discount those who are charlatans, and who seek newness for the sake of notoriety; those who do not write with seriousness but to be amusing; and those who have developed no form or craft in the handling of their new materials and ideas. There are many sincere writers who feel they have done enough when they have written a new chord or rhythm, and never trouble themselves about how this chord or rhythm is to develop into perfectly formed music. Every old master was in regal command over the materials he employed. So must the new master also.

If we sift through the well-known European modern composers with these ideas in mind, only a few remain for consideration. Schoenberg, Stravinsky (in his older style), Webern, Berg, Bartók, and possibly a few others. Perhaps it is impossible to say, now, which of these will prove to be the most lasting in value. Yet Schoenberg stands out very decidedly for several reasons: he was the first to inaugurate, in Europe at any rate, the complete change of materials harmonically and melodically which have become recognized as the basis of the "modern" style. Practically every living composer makes use of the type of new materials, which were first brought into use by Schoenberg, in Europe, and by Ives, in America. Schoenberg has developed the most complete control of his new materials. Schoenberg has developed and mastered a new orchestration which fits his new harmonic and melodic innovations. Lastly, and very important, is the fact that the line of development taken by Schoenberg is a direct furthering of the line of progress outlined by the greatest Teutonic masters—Bach, Beethoven, Haydn, Mozart, Brahms. Their greatness lay, at least in part, in constructing large forms built out of a smaller thematic germ, which was developed. Schoenberg not only applies this mode of development to his new materials, but also has found new ways of developing a theme, which are in direct line with the ways used by Mozart and other classical masters. A thematic analysis will show Schoenberg's works to be more closely knit in thematic development than those of any other living composer.

I have not spoken of the content. The value of the expressive or emotional side of new music is very difficult to judge. Very fine music may seem at first to be ugly, unclear, formless, etc., only because its medium is not familiar. Music which has no lasting worth may please greatly, because every melodic fragment and harmony it uses, as well as what it expresses, is already familiar through other work. The clew, however, lies in the examination of materials which I have outlined. Fine handling of materials and valuable musical expression always go together. One's emotional judgement of a new work is to be distrusted, but the materials may be analyzed with value.

What Arnold Schoenberg says in his music I believe to be as important as his developments in musical resources. The pedant is one who sticks to the letter of the rule, never questioning its source. It takes a real composer to take the known rules of procedure and carry them a step further, and to apply them to newly found materials. Schoenberg has done this. Few others have. Therefore I nominate him as a most likely candidate for the post of the world's most significant composer.

Welcome for the Incoming Modern Master: Roundabout with Schoenberg Who Should Arrive in Boston Next Week
Nicolas Slonimsky
Boston Evening Transcript
October 28, 1933

"What others count as beauty matters nothing to the artist. He is concerned only with what he needs."
(Arnold Schoenberg in *Harmonielehre*)

When, on September 13, 1924, Arnold Schönberg reached his fiftieth birthday he was greeted by the mayor of his native city of Vienna in an official reception at the steps of the City Hall. Schönbergian choruses, hitherto considered unperformable, joyously rent the air. There was an admiring populace, consisting not only of his atonal disciples.

When Schönberg was forty, the critical contumely was at its peak. He had just completed a European tour with *Pierrot lunaire*, "the last word in cacophony and musical anarchy," as the Berlin correspondent of the *Musical Courier* characterized it at the time of its first performance. And, in bidding him a sincere farewell to Berlin, a Vienna musician summarized his impressions of the Three Piano Pieces, Opus 11, as follows: "First, a child bangs aimlessly on the piano, then a drunk pounds like a madman on the keys, and finally somebody sits full weight on the keyboard." In London, after the performance of the Five Orchestral Pieces, the merriment in the press was general. In a letter to the editor of the *Daily Telegraph*, that early champion of freedom of musical expression, Dr. Leigh Henry objected to the vulgarity of a writer's remark that "the long hair which used to be indispensable has now been superseded by the bald head"—an obvious and disgraceful attack on the appearance of Herr Schönberg, who conducted the performance, Dr. Henry adds indignantly.

At twenty-seven Schönberg had to eke out his meager wages by conducting at a cabaret in Berlin, and also scoring operettas for successful composers. It is said that he had thus orchestrated six thousand pages of other people's music—and what music! At that time, at the turn of our century, Schönberg already had the *Gurrelieder* and the *Verklärte Nacht* to his credit—works of magnificence and poesy well within the respectable code of esthetics. In fact, Richard Strauss, having looked over the first pages of the *Gurrelieder,* suggested Schönberg's name for a conservatory position and a Liszt Prize. Biographers still shudder at the thought that Schönberg had to interrupt the composition of *Gurrelieder* because of pecuniary stringency. There are many budding Schönbergs in our own time, seeking musical amanuensis work in order to squeeze as many devaluated pennies, marks, shillings or zlotys as possible to keep the body and soul together.

Where are their future biographers, and whence can come the urgent aid?

There is something biblical in Schönberg's spectacular martyrdom. Shuttling between Vienna and Berlin, revered by disciples, derided by scurrilous critics, he is the very picture of a prophet of the faith. Not content with music alone, he pursues literature and poetry, in the most esoteric form of expression. Not an open adherent to theosophical doctrines, he is none the less attracted to the metaphysical lore which relieves him of stressing reality. His poetry, such as the book to *Jacob's Ladder*, an oratorio begun during the war days, is abstruse and, to the uninitiated, irritatingly tangential. His choice of words to his monodramas, operas, songs and song cycles is of the same tantalizing sort, when you seem to grasp the meaning at one moment only to see it fade into distressing nonsense at another. Often, coarse matter succeeds evanescent symbolism—thus, an early song of Schönberg, as yet not out of Wagnerian indentures, ends with the words "I think of my dog." In one song Schönberg "feels the air of other planets," yet, in his monodramas, he is earthly, too earthly. A metaphysical woman with a child, a strangely unjealous Lover-To-Be, these visions of his operas are as difficult to grasp as a stranger's dream. They are certainly excellent material for easy burlesque, as newspaper critics of both hemispheres have discovered to their advantage.

Schönberg is also an autodidactic painter. His paintings, cognate with Blake and Goya, but perhaps more directly influenced by impressionists of the pre-war era, are subjective visions. If the observation is correct, that one's weaknesses in art are often revealed more patently in the artist's avocation, then subjectivism and adumbration should be Schönberg's great failings. Much has been said and written about Schönberg's presentiment of a personal and general catastrophe, as evidenced by his paintings, his writings and his music. The subsequent events must have strengthened this morbid faith, for no sooner had Schönberg settled down in Berlin as a professor of the Prussian Academy of Arts than the Hitlerian cataclysm burst over his non-Aryan and modernistic head. Under the stress of a double stigma, he had to leave Germany for France. The shock of a new discrimination led him, probably in the spirit of an emphatic demonstration, to return to the religion of his youth which he had relinquished some years before. Momentarily in Paris, he responded to a call from America; the last country that still offers a refuge to European undesirables regardless of creed or race.

What is the essence of Schönberg's music that makes him the object of veneration to some, an odious figure to many? Obviously, we must draw a line of demarcation between the early, acceptable Schönberg and the later true Schönberg. Although the evolution from the *Verklärte Nacht* of 1899 to the *Accompaniment to a Cinema Scene* of 1932 can be traced as one continuous line, the difference between these two works compasses the whole of transition from tonality to atonality. The latter term is usually connected with Schönberg's name. Atonalists themselves reject the label as inadequate. Atonality, i.e., tonality prefixed with a privative particle, is as unjust a definition as that of the sans-culotte of the French Revolution. After all, the sans-culottes had not entirely renounced the integument for the nether limbs, and the nickname tended to convey a wrong picture. However, both the sans-culottes and the atonalists reconciled themselves to their respective appellations. The works of Josef Matthias Hauer are even advertised as atonal, and the publisher, realizing that Hauer's "Twelve-tone Music" is hard to sell, adds in pleading tones: "Let us send you these works for perusal that you may delve into their singular art. It is not at all difficult to penetrate into these problems." Incidentally, Hauer, a theoretician and a die-hard twelve-tonalist, author of the treatise on the twelve-tone technique and an essay, "From Melody to the Kettle Drums," has calculated that there are

479,001,600 possible combinations derivable from the forty-four Hauer tropes, all within the twelve-tone scale. This number will supply a motive a day to 220 atonalists for 6000 years.

Roughly, atonality is the system in which all twelve tones of the chromatic scale are used on equal terms; it is a democracy of sharps and flats; there are no "dominants," for no tone dominates another tone; there is no keynote to prevent a semblance of one, it is strongly recommended not to repeat a note before the eleven other notes have been made use of, it is indeed a raffle of chromatics, a system of integral chromaticism. It makes new demands on the ear; small wonder, then, that atonality enjoys such a hearty unpopularity among middle-class musicians. As to critics, their ears close up like sensitive pieces of mimosa at the first contact with atonality. The best of them seek refuge in a melancholy resignation: "If this be the music of the future, may I never live to see that future."

Serge Taneiev, the eminent Russian composer and academic savant of music, wrote twenty years ago to a friend: "The scale is no longer confined to its seven tones, but compasses all twelve, and this not only in the melody, but in harmony as well. There is no tonality." In our own day, a member of the Russian Association of Proletarian Musicians, writing in the *Sovietskaya Musika*, repeats unknowingly almost word for word what the pre-revolutionary Taneiev said in the spirit of justifiable distress. "Atonality destroys all conceptions of tonality, concord or discord, destroys the functional connection among the twelve tones of our scale, defacing and equalizing them. Small wonder that a special society such as the Schönberg Verein had to be organized to listen to such music."

The "special society" referred to is the Society for Private Performances, which Schönberg founded in Vienna in order to secure serious listening to new music, sans the newspaper critics. The attitude of the Communist party towards atonality as a product of disintegration of Western music resulted in a "bolt" from atonality by one of Schönberg's disciples, Hanns Eisler, who changed his style abruptly in the direction of the simplest diatonic writing in four-four time, mostly for the use of mass singing. In a collection of valedictory essays on the occasion of Schönberg's fiftieth birthday, he wrote an article entitled "Schönberg, the Reactionary." To be sure, the meaning was inoffensive—merely that Schönberg, having established a school and striving to preserve its tenets, has ipso facto become a conservative.

Schönberg is celebrated as the founder of a new school of musical expression, but performers prefer compositions of his youthful consonant days. The titanic *Gurrelieder*, scored for a very expensive [*sic*] orchestra with eight flutes, four harps and everything else in proportion, has enjoyed several performances during the third of a century of its existence. The *Verklärte Nacht*, scored for a string sextet, is much better known. But these two works belong chronologically as well as substantially to another century. They have arisen as a magnificent aftermath of Wagnerian splendor. The symphonic poem to Maeterlinck's play, *Pelléas and Mélisande*, written at the same time with Debussy, reveled in post-Wagnerian harmonies. Of course, the Wagner in either of these scores was greatly modified, and some Schönbergians would not admit it was Wagner at all. Some Wagnerians, among them Ernest Newman, agree with this analysis—from different motives, perhaps. Schönberg's Chamber Symphony, originally scored for fifteen instruments, has some elements of the new style, notably in the melody and chord building through a progression of fourths.

With the Quartet in F♯ Minor, Schönberg says good-bye to tonality, not without a practical joke, in the form of a quotation from "Oh, mein lieber Augustin, alles ist hin!" introduced in the second violin against a fully matured atonal quip in the first. But it remained for the "Thrice Seven Poems," originally known under the title of one of them, the Lunar Pierrot, to catapult Schönberg into fame and make him a target of facile witticisms and dire threats ever since. The craziest paradox of the situation consists in the fact that while critics dubbed Schönberg a wild anarchist who discards all law and order and substitutes noise for sound, the atonal savants explain for your benefit the extreme rationality of these seemingly impressionistic tableaux. In one of the thrice seven, a three-note figure is threaded into every musical phrase, figuration and ornament so that the whole thing is made a mathematical function of those three variants. Through the devices of crab and inversion, or both combined, with transposition not hampered by the late regretted major-minor complex, the thing is created like a homunculus out of an alchemist's retort.

But this is not all. Schönberg, the author of the astonishing book on harmony, brings all music within the bounds of pure reason. Every old scale and progression finds its place in this sunlit expanse of integral harmony. The timbres go into the pot along with the scales. Thus, in the "Altered Chord," from his Five Orchestral Pieces, the conductor is instructed to let nature take its course, and not to bring out any seeming themes, for the dynamics indicated in each instrumental part make the very tone color thematic. A marvelous subject for newspaper jokesters. One of them (unidentified) fell a victim of the linotype when, about to burst in a shower of vituperation, an intrusive letter made him say fine instead of five orchestral pieces. Was the linotypist a secret Schönbergian?

The Variations for Orchestra, coming after a long period of silence (Schönberg composed little after the war) were in turn accused of excessive cerebration. At least, this reproach has the advantage of plausibility. We deal with a composer, founder of a new school, based on theoretical deductions from a rational scheme. We are told that melody and harmony are the same inasmuch as harmony may be dismembered into melody through placing its components in spatial succession, after which the resultant melodic ripple can be again gathered into a harmonic column, much in the manner of a retrogressive film reel, which makes a splash in the water integrate back into homogeneous surface. Von Webern, in his *Sinfonietta* [Symphonie, Op. 21] (famous in the atonal circles), decomposes a timbre-chord into a succession of timbre-notes. Each instrument plays only one note of the motive, the next overtaking the line the moment the first ceases to vibrate. Atonal lore is richer in surprises than we imagine, and one cannot summarize it briefly without doing a great injustice to it.

Schönberg's latest composition to date, an *Accompaniment to a Cinematic Scene*, with its subdivisions, "Danger, Fear, Catastrophe," is not likely to be taken up by Hollywood. But what a marvelous background it would supply to a surrealistic film of images and geometric designs! The score, for small orchestra, is the acme of mastery. Here is the twelve-tone system brought into full life. It is simple as atonality goes, and it is immediately impressive. The visionary of *Pierrot lunaire* and the rationalist of the *Harmonielehre* have here arrived at a synthesis.

Schönberg's "influence" on contemporary composition? It is undeniable. Ravel attests the power of Schönberg's logical scheme animated by impressionistic imagination. Honegger's Symphony is obviously atonal in its use of the chromatic scale spaced in contiguous octaves. (This "registering" is one of the traits of the Three Piano Pieces, which sounded to the ear of a Vienna musician like a child's aimless roving or a drunkard's vicious banging.) There are atonal daubs in Stravinsky's *Rossignol*. There are several composers in America who independently use the system of twelve tones. And, of course, there is Alban Berg. There are talented composers writing atonally, and there are unhappy drudges that have no power of selective genius. As in old music of the seven tones, genius, ability, and—horribile dictu—inspiration play a great part in the domain of twelve equal, interdependent, liberated tones.

Homage to Schoenberg: The Late Works
Lou Harrison
Modern Music, vol. 21
March/April 1944

Before discussing Arnold Schönberg's late works, I should say first that I know them chiefly from a study of the available scores. The NBC performance of the Piano Concerto, Opus 42, early in February, was the first orchestral piece of the period that I have actually heard. Of that production it should be set down for the record that the solo part was beautifully played by Edward Steuermann under the leadership of Leopold Stokowski. I now wonder why Schönberg isn't more often presented. I would certainly travel a distance and pay a price to hear his other big works.

Part of the excitement of this occasion was a pleasant surprise in the beauty of sound made by the orchestra. Schönberg's use of the orchestra is like no other composer's, saving, perhaps, Bach's. The instruments are treated almost always as in chamber music, and though the score contains much of doubling and strengthening of individual lines, the general effect is still one of differentiation among the sounds. Particularly striking is the use of brass which plays muted more often than not, and makes lovely, reedy sounds. The use of the piano throughout is in the best of taste, never relaxing into arpeggiated accompaniments nor, on the other hand, challenging the orchestra to the conventional virtuoso battle. In this way the work bears a noticeable relation to the concerto-grosso style.

The experience of examining the score (published by G. Schirmer) and further hearings of recordings made at the broadcast only confirm the profound impression of the performance. In form the concerto is divided into four sections, but it is played as one movement. This four-in-one form harks directly back to the First Quartet and the Chamber Symphony. It is an arrangement of which Schönberg seems particularly fond. The opening andante in $\frac{3}{8}$ is a long and undulating cantilena for the piano. The orchestra gradually joins in and there is a development out of which emerges the second movement—a kind of scherzo, rapid and brilliant. This section is marked by every sort of instrumental amusement—percussion, tremolandos, sul ponticello, harmonics and the like—taken directly out of the early expressionist style but here used in a genuinely classic piece and without suggesting a program. The adagio which follows is more contrapuntal and symphonic in nature, and very moving. A short cadenza leads directly into the last movement, an invigorating rondo. In character, this is of a piece with the finales of his Third and Fourth Quartets and that of the Wind Quintet, and is in one of his most captivating styles. There follows an exciting stretto, and with a few chords the concerto is ended.

The concerto was completed December 30, 1942 and is inscribed to Henry Clay Shriver, who commissioned the work. In contrast to Schönberg's other late pieces this one seems to revert to the more ingratiating manner of the Third Quartet and the Variations for Orchestra. There is a less broken quality about the continuity. The sudden stops and violent motives of the Fourth Quartet are not nearly so evident here, rather, there is a feeling of clarity and consistency from beginning to end. In comparison with the Violin Concerto one notices a more concertante manner of treating the solo and a more informal sequence of ideas. The bitter brilliance of style in the Violin Concerto and the rigidity of its three conventional movements help make it far less accessible to the average listener than the Piano Concerto.

One of the major joys in this piece, as in many others of his absolute compositions, is in the structure of the phrases. You know when you are hearing a theme, a building or answering phrase, a development or a coda. There is no swerving from the form-building nature of these classical phrases. The pleasure to be had from listening to them is the same that one has from hearing the large forms of Mozart and the other Viennese masters. This is a feeling too seldom communicated in contemporary music, in much of which the most obvious formal considerations are not evident at all. The definiteness of Schönberg's ideas about phrase and form he has himself expressed many times, and that he practices what he preaches, is evident even without the score, from one hearing of the Concerto. The nature of his knowledge in this respect, perhaps more than anything else, places him in the position of torch-bearer to tradition in the vital and developing sense.

The Piano Concerto is a twelve-tone piece on the series E♭–B♭–D–F–E–C–F♯–G♯–C♯–A–B–G, and introduces many new devices for expanding the technic [*sic*]. It is not my intention here to enter into a discussion of twelve-tone problems. The nature of this technic should by now be a matter of common knowledge. However, one must note the inclusion in the present work of ideas similar to those in the late music of Berg. New devices of doubling, classical chordal figurations and octave skips are all in evidence. I believe that the full expansion necessary to make the twelve-tone technic as useful as the classic tonal organization has been achieved in this Concerto.

Since Schönberg's arrival in America his music has undergone a distinct change. Whether this has been due to the influence of his new environment or to the natural advent of a third period is not certain. His first work here was the Suite for String Orchestra. Since it was written as a useful piece for schools and colleges it displays but few of the characteristics of the new style. However, the next two works, the Violin Concerto, Opus 36, and the Fourth Quartet, Opus 37, are marked by a style so arrestingly different from the preceding one that the beginning of a new period is evident.

Since the whole texture and effect of a twelve-tone piece is to a large extent determined by the structure of the original series, it might be interesting to show the vital difference between typical rows of the middle period and the rows of the Violin Concerto and the Fourth Quartet.

MIDDLE PERIOD
Wind Quintet: E♭–G–A–B–C♯–C♮–B♭–D–E–F♯–A♭–F♮
Variations for Orchestra: B♭–E–F♯–E♭–F♮–A–D–C♯–G♮–G♯–B–C

LATE PERIOD
Violin Concerto: A–B♭–E♭–B♮–E♮–F♯–C♮–C♯–G–A♭–D–F
Fourth Quartet: D–C♯–A–B♭–F–E♭–E♮–C–A♭–G–F♯–B

It will be seen at once by this comparison that in the late period a distinct preference is shown for the fifth and minor second as opposed to the major second and third of the middle period. In the music itself the stress is laid on these new intervals, which makes for a different sound and accounts for the steely brilliance of some passages and the tonally-rooted Hebraic quality of others. The series of the Piano Concerto is so made that all kinds of parallel fourth and fifth chords are possible; however, various other factors in the composition cut down the hardness of sound.

In the musical structure of Schönberg's works from Opus 26 to Opus 36, every effort is made to achieve stylistic unity by close imitation and a general tendency to maintain a single dominant rate of rhythmic flow. In the Violin Concerto and the Fourth Quartet this is not the case, but the clarity and simplicity of form he attained in, for instance, the Third Quartet is not sacrificed, though much of the method is abandoned. In these works a more delicate and occult balance of forms is maintained, which allows for greater differentiation of musical idea and intense dramatic contrast. It is the kind of structural difference that exists between, say, the structure of Schubert's music and that of Brahms. This essential freedom within a sensitive over-all balance has made it possible for Schönberg to reintroduce the special expressive features of his early expressionist style without inferring either an esthetic regression or an upset in the solidity of his works. Both in length and conception the late period has seen a continuation and establishment of the high classic values which Schönberg began to assume shortly after his extraordinary creation of the twelve-tone technic.

Besides the Violin Concerto, the Fourth Quartet, and the Piano Concerto, which must be included among the major works of the late period, there are also the Second Chamber Symphony begun in 1906 but completed only recently, the Variations for Band, and the *Ode to Napoleon* which is discussed elsewhere in this issue. Among didactic writings penned in America are the Faculty Research Lecture, U.C.L.A., 1942, his only treatise on twelve-tone composition, the *Models for Beginners* and the large work on counterpoint which is nearing completion.

Schönberg is, at the time of this writing, temporarily retired from teaching and one looks forward to the works of his leisure. Already he has written much in the United States and has contributed generously to our musical life. As an American citizen he is singularly well adjusted, amiable, inquisitive. He has enough energy today to supply several twenty-year olds. He seems in much better health and much younger than when he arrived in this country. Limping into the classroom, one day last spring, he explained that his toe had been injured in an accident at his workshop. He had been building furniture. His hobby-habit, perhaps, contributes much to his excellent vigor and helps appease an insatiable curiosity. That curiosity is, of course, proverbial. It has made him the most reliable compendium of musical knowledge in existence. He said one day that many accused him of being a mathematician. There was a moment's silence; then he mock-maliciously remarked that he couldn't help it if he could think better than others. One must agree. May his seventieth birthday find him as vigorous and adventurous as ever.

Schoenberg in the United States
Roger Sessions
Tempo, vol. 9
December 1944

In any survey of Schoenberg's work one fact must be emphasized above all: that no younger composer writes quite the same music as he would have written, had Schoenberg's music not existed. The influence of an artist is not, even during his life-time, confined to his disciples or even to those who have felt the direct impact of his work. It is filtered through to the humblest participant, first in the work of other original artists who have absorbed and re-interpreted it for their own purposes; then through the work of hundreds of lesser individuals, who unconsciously reflect the new tendencies even when they are opposed to them. For genuinely new ideas determine the battlegrounds on which their opponents are forced to attack. In the very process of combat the latter undergo decisive experiences which help to carry the new ideas forward.

In Schoenberg's case this process is clear. The appearance, around 1911, of his first completely characteristic works, and of his *Harmonielehre*, mark the approximate beginning of the years that were decisive in the formation of contemporary music. True, these works—both, music and book—only carried to more radical conclusions tendencies already present in the music of the time; these manifestations, then hailed as revolutionary, seem to us now more like footnotes and queries to established modes of thought than integral and challenging steps towards new ones. What was new in Debussy and Ravel and Scriabin seemed more fundamental and far-reaching than it does to-day.

But in the Three Piano Pieces, Op. 11, and the Five Orchestral Pieces, Op. 16, a much more thorough-going challenge became evident. What led in Wagner to an enlargement of musical resources, in Debussy and Scriabin to the cultivation of special and restricted corners, here openly insists that new resources, having multiplied to an overwhelming extent, demand a logic of their own, depriving the earlier principles of their validity even in music of a relatively conventional type. The *Harmonielehre*, which exerted its influence on some of the least likely persons, raised the same questions in the realm of theory, deducing them from the very logic of previous practice. The musical *status quo* has never completely recovered from the blow.

In 1933 Schoenberg came to the United States and ten years later became an American citizen. In the country to which he came, musical activity is intense on many levels, and despite many necessary reservations the development within the last generation has been phenomenal. Musical education has penetrated everywhere; both the general level and the quality of instruction available on the highest level of all have risen to a degree amazing to all who confronted the musical conditions of thirty-five years ago. American composers of serious intent have begun to appear in considerable numbers, and to achieve an influence and recognition undreamed by their predecessors; moreover, they have become aware of themselves, of their inner and outer problems, and better equipped to face these. Above all it has become evident that musical talent, the raw material from which musical culture grows, is strikingly abundant.

It is however clear that the institutional structure of music in the United States has not yet been established in definitive outlines. The relationship between the art and the business of music, and of both of these with the "public"; the role and direction of musical education; the influence of radio, gramophone, and amateur musical activities—these are questions which in the United States are still fundamentally unsettled. There is similar confusion as to what we may call the structure of musical effort: the respective roles in musical culture and production of the composer, performer, critic, and scholar.

These latter observations are true of course not only of the United States, but of modern civilization in general. But conditions here differ from those elsewhere in the fact that whereas elsewhere the forces of opposition are those of an established cultural tradition, here there is a perceptible undertow in the growing musical consciousness of a culture still in the making. It is this which keeps the musical life of the country in a state of constant change and flux, and which makes the situation chaotic but far from hopeless.

It is not surprising therefore, that Schoenberg should have found himself in a quite new relationship to his environment and that his impact should have taken on a new significance. I do not mean to minimize the importance of either the revolutionary or the specifically Viennese Schoenberg. The former has already affected the course of music in a profound sense, and though possibly the first full impact of a composer's work is the most immediately powerful one—think of the *Eroica*, of *Tristan*, in contrast to the last quartets or *Parsifal*—nevertheless with the constant ripening of his art, the latter imposes itself in another, more gradual and more definitely constructive, sense. But that is a task for the composer's successors, and is even independent of his purely historical importance.

As for Vienna, Schoenberg has outlived it as he has outlived Alban Berg. Had he not done so his position might be to-day less evident than it is. There are other musicians from Central, also from Western and Eastern Europe whose impact has been purely provincial; they have conceived their mission as that of winning spheres of influence for their own native background; and have found—by an inexorable law of human polarization—the most sympathetic acclaim often in circles most tenacious in the pursuit of an American "national" style. Undeniably Schoenberg is a product of Vienna, and of a Viennese tradition with which he is as deeply imbued as anyone living. But it is characteristic of the man, the situation, and possibly of the Viennese tradition itself that his impact on the United States has been that of a third Schoenberg—one by no means unknown in Europe nor difficult to find for those who sought him, but one often obscured in the heat of controversy and the battle positions which his followers were led to assume in his behalf. For in coming to the United States he left the scene of his most bitter struggles; he came with the prestige of a fighter of distant and only dimly understood battles; with the respect and admiration of a few to whom the battles were neither so distant nor so dimly understood. Others recognized the achievement of the composer of *Verklärte Nacht* and other early works, and were, ready to acclaim him as at least an asset to American musical life.

He taught and lectured in Boston and New York and finally was appointed Professor of Music, first at the University of Southern California, later at the University of California in Los Angeles. His music received sporadic performances; he found himself frequently quoted, frequently in demand as a writer and lecturer. His main influence, however, has been exerted through his teaching, the musicians with whom he has come in contact, and finally the series of works composed in the years since he has lived in the United States—works which in my opinion represent a separate phase and a new level in his music as a whole.

These works include a Suite for Strings, written in 1934; the Fourth String Quartet written in 1936 and performed by the Kolisch Quartet in 1937; the Violin Concerto, performed in 1940 by Louis Krasner with the Philadelphia Orchestra; a Second Chamber Symphony; a setting of the *Kol Nidre* for chorus and orchestra; Variations on a Recitative for Organ, first performed by Carl Weinrich for the United States section of the I.S.C.M. in March 1944; the Concerto for Piano first performed by Edward Steuermann and the

Philadelphia Orchestra in the spring of this year; finally two works shortly to be performed, the *Ode to Napoleon*, after Byron, for *sprech-stimme*, piano and strings, and a Theme and Variations, written originally for band and later arranged for orchestra.

Of these works, the Suite is consciously in an "old style," and the Second Chamber Symphony is the completion of a work left unfinished some forty years earlier. With the latter, the Organ Variations have given rise to rumors of a "conservative" trend in Schoenberg's music—a "return" at least to "tonality" and to a more "consonant" style. No doubt, the new Variations and possibly the *Ode*, both shortly to receive their world premieres, will add to these rumors which purport to herald a "capitulation" on Schoenberg's part. The Organ Variations are extremely freely but none the less unmistakably, in the key of D minor, though also in the twelve-tone system; the Orchestral Variations are in G minor, signature and all, and definitely in a simpler style. The *Ode to Napoleon*, though still in the twelve-tone system, is superficially more "consonant" than many of Schoenberg's earlier works in that, to a very large extent, its style is characterized by the superimposition of triads and their derivatives. It is however doubtful if either the *Ode* or the Organ Variations will prove comforting to those who pretend to see any reversal on Schoenberg's part. They are presumably quite as "forbidding" as any of his reputedly "atonal" works.

"Atonality," in fact, is a conception which Schoenberg has never accepted and which has certainly no relationship to the experience of a practiced listener to his music. If "tonality" means anything in other than academic terms it must certainly denote the *sensation* of relationships between tones, and of functional differences arising from these relationships. The tonic, the leading-tone, and so on are sensations habitual in all listeners. In no sense are they mere theoretical abstractions; they are not inextricably bound up with any systematic formula yet established nor are they in the last analysis definable in terms of any such formula alone. The prevailing harmonic concepts or definitions of "tonality" are inadequate not only to the music of contemporary composers, but to many elusive problems in classic music. It should however be clear that these inadequacies are in no manner to be conjured away through the adoption of the essentially meaningless term "atonal," any more than the presence or absence of an occasional triad or six chord is of more than incidental significance in determining the characteristics of a style such as Schoenberg's.

I believe that in these works written since 1936 Schoenberg has achieved a freedom and resourcefulness which carries them in this respect far beyond his earlier works, especially those in the twelve-tone technique. Regarding that technique itself much misleading nonsense has been written. I am in no sense a spokesman for it; I have never been attracted to it as a principle of composition. But one must distinguish carefully between technical principles in the abstract, and the works in which they become embodied; even a great work does not validate a dubious principle, nor does a valid principle produce in itself good or even technically convincing work. It would for example be easy, though basically irrelevant, to show that Beethoven's "Heiliger Dankgesang" in the Lydian mode, like most other modern "modal" works, is based on a technically specious conception of the nature and function of the modes. Similarly, assuming the fugue or the sonata to have been valid as principles of musical structure, how many grievous sins have been committed in their names!

One cannot too often insist that in music it is the composer's inner world of tone and rhythm which matter, and that whatever technical means he chooses in order to give it structure and coherence are subject to no *a priori* judgment whatever. The essential is that structure and coherence be present; and the demand which art makes on its creator is simply that his technique be sufficiently mastered to become an obedient and flexible instrument in his hands. True, the twelve-tone technique became at one time a fighting slogan; this happened under the stress of combat, the inevitable result of bitter opposition met by Schoenberg and his disciples. To-day however it is no longer invoked as a universal principle; it is recognized for what it is as a mode of technical procedure, a principle which evolves and becomes modified by practice. Once more—the significance of music springs solely from the composer's imagination and not from ideas about technique. The latter are merely tools which he forges for himself, for his own purposes. They gain what validity they possess from the results, in music, to which they make their imponderable contribution.

In regard to Schoenberg's work it may also be stressed that the twelve-tone technique is a part of the *process* rather than an essential element of the form. It is not essential or even possible for the listener to apprehend it in all its various transformations. He must listen to Schoenberg's music in exactly the same spirit as he listens to any music whatever, and bring to it the same kind of response. If he is fortunate he will from the first discover moments of profound and intense beauty which will tempt him further. He will always find that the music makes the utmost demands on his ear and his musical understanding, and he will probably find that with a little familiarity it begins to impose itself. In any case, esoteric notions or strained efforts will, as in the case of all music, serve as a barrier rather than as an aid to his understanding.

So if in some works of the twenties one feels a certain tenseness and dogmatic insistence, one must regard that as a necessary phase in Schoenberg's development. At that time he was exploring and mastering the resources of the new technique. In the works of the last ten years one feels no such limitation. The technique is used with the ease of virtuosity, with complete resourcefulness, and with such freedom that it is sometimes difficult to discover. The Fourth Quartet, the Violin and the Piano Concertos are, as far as I can see, his finest achievements of these years, perhaps of his whole work. They are larger in scope, if not in gesture, than the *Ode to Napoleon* or the *Organ Variations*; like these they are in no conceivable wise more "conservative" than the earlier works even though they differ from these in several essential respects.

They differ first of all in their longer and broader lines. This is not simply a question of "continuity;" Schoenberg has always been in this respect a master of form, and in no work known to me can he be accused of a lack of logic. But—with those qualifications and exceptions—the individual details are underlined to a degree that they, rather than the larger lines, seem to bear the main expressive burden. It is a question of emphasis; the "fragmentary" impression that disturbs many listeners results from the fact that every sensation is intensified to the utmost degree. All contrasts are of the sharpest kind, and it is not surprising that they strike the hearer most forcibly, even after familiarity with the work has brought their essential continuity more to the fore. In the later works, above all in the Piano Concerto, the expressive emphasis shifts strikingly to the line as a whole. A sustained melodic line becomes the rule rather than the exception. The melodic style itself has become more concentrated, less extravagant and diffuse in detail. I am tempted to cite examples: the graceful melody which opens the Piano Concerto; the declamatory opening phrase of the slow movement of the Quartet; or the haunting and tender Andante of the Violin Concerto.

The very adoption of the concerto form, with the predominance of one instrument, underlines this tendency. Through Schoenberg's uncompromising polyphony results in a large measure of obbligato treatment of the solo parts, especially in the Piano Concerto, this treatment is nevertheless on the broadest lines, the constant tone quality contributing unmistakably to the architectonics of the works. Equally consistent is the orchestral dress. Though certainly as vivid as in the earlier works, it contrasts strikingly with these in that it, too, is laid out on broader lines. The constant and kaleidoscopic change so characteristic of the *Five Orchestral Pieces* or the Bach transcriptions, has been super-seded by style in which tone colors, in all their characteristic boldness, remain constant over longer stretches, and are opposed to each other in sharply defined and large-scale contrasts. Needless to say, the instruments are employed with complete freedom from preconceived ideas and with full awareness of the relationship between ends and means. While it makes extreme demands, technical and otherwise, on the performers—the solo parts of both concertos are truly formidable—it does so always with full awareness; the demands lie in the musical ideas themselves and are in no way superimposed on them. They pose new problems for the performers—but they have this in common with much of the best music of every generation.

These works possess other and more elusive characteristics, at some of which I have already hinted in connection with the *Ode to Napoleon*. It is not easy concretely to demonstrate, in the two concertos and the quartet, a still wider range of harmonic effect—one which includes all the simplest as well as the most complex relationships—or a much vaster harmonic line, at the least suggesting a new tonal principle, powerfully binding like the *Ode* but embracing all possible relationships within the chromatic scale. As far as I know, no adequate study has yet been made of Schoenberg's work in its harmonic and tonal aspects—aspects which lie deeper than the twelve-tone system or the individual sonority, and guide the ear of the listener in his real apprehension of the music. The above-mentioned qualities seem to me however strikingly present in all of this later music and a most important element in the effect of unity, sweeping movement, and concentration which the works produce. If I express myself cautiously in this regard it is because they raise questions of capital importance, for which nothing less than a painstaking effort of research, and a totally new theoretical formulation, would be necessary. Meanwhile the works are there, with a new challenge, different in kind but perhaps not in importance from that embodied in the Three Piano Pieces and the Five Orchestral Pieces thirty-odd years ago.

The above remarks are at best cursory and convey all too little idea of the works themselves. It goes without saying that performances have been very few, and their real impact limited. The scores are available, however, through the foresight of G. Schirmer, Inc. The enthusiasm of many of the most gifted among young musicians as well as the gradually deepening interest of their elders is one of the striking phenomena of a period in which the prevailing trend seems superficially to be all in the direction of a not entirely genuine "mass appeal," facile and standardized effect, and a kind of hasty shabbiness of conception and workmanship.

As a teacher Schoenberg has fought against these latter tendencies with undiminished energy. Here, too, his influence has been both direct and indirect. In New York and especially in California considerable numbers of Americans have passed under his instruction. At one time he even was in demand among the composers of film music in Hollywood; his demands however proved too high, and composers in search of easy formulas of effect withdrew in disappointment. The same thing has happened to those who have gone to Schoenberg in the hopes of learning to compose in the twelve-tone system or in the "modern idiom." Nothing is farther from Schoenberg's ideas than that sort of instruction. He does not, in fact, preoccupy himself with "style" at all, in the usual sense of the word. What concerns him is the musical development, in the most integral sense, of the pupil. He insists on the most rigorous training in harmony and counterpoint; those familiar with his *Harmonielehre* must needs appreciate the extent to which this is true. For one who has never been his pupil, the striking feature of his teaching is precisely that it is systematic without ever becoming a "system" in any closed sense; that it is almost fanatically rigorous in its ceaseless striving after mastery of resource; logical and clear in its presentation of materials, but as free as teaching can be from any essential dogmatic bias. It is based on constant experiment and observation; theoretical comment is offered always in the most pragmatic spirit—as an aid to the clarification of technical problems and not as abstract principle. They are literally, as with many such features in the *Harmonielehre*, the observations of a keen and experienced mind with reference to a specific matter in hand, to which they are completely subordinate.

Musical experience, and development through experience, is Schoenberg's watchword as a teacher. His pupils speak of his boundless love for music—the energy of his enthusiasm for a classic work as he analyses it in his classes, or of the demands on which he insists in its performance by them. They speak of his tireless energy in asking of them—above all the gifted ones—that they bring into their work the last degree of resourcefulness of which they are capable. It is not surprising that under such instruction they learn to make the greatest demands on themselves, or that their love of music and sense for music is developed both in depth and intensity as a result. It is this which distinguishes Schoenberg's pupils above all—their training is not merely in "craftsmanship" but an integral training of their musicality, of ear and of response. The conceptions which they have gained are rounded and definite; they have not only gained tools of composition, but have developed also their own individual sense of the purposes for which these tools are to be used.

In complete agreement they testify to the fact that nothing has been taught them of the twelve-tone system or of "modern" composition as such. Schoenberg's attitude is that musicians must come to these things, too, through development and necessity or not come to them at all. Having given them a basis on which they can develop further, and a sense of the demands of art, he insists that they must find for themselves their path in the contemporary world. He is fond of telling them that there is still much good music to be written in C major, and offering them no encouragement to follow the paths he himself has chosen.

Perhaps it will be seen from this what I meant in speaking at the beginning of this paper of a "third Schoenberg." In his educational tenets he has not, of course, changed through living in the United States. But he has brought these tenets from the principal stronghold of a great and old tradition to a fresh land which is beginning slowly and even cautiously to feel its musical strength. He has given to many young musicians by direct influence, and to others through his disciples, a renewed sense of all that music is and has been, and it is hardly over-bold to foresee that this is going to play its role, perhaps a mighty one, in the musical development of the United States. A small testimony to what this new contact may produce may be seen in a very valuable little book—*Models for Beginners in Composition*—which Schoenberg prepared for students in a six-weeks' summer course in California. Certainly the eagerly awaited treatise on counterpoint, and the one also planned on the principles of composition, based on Beethoven's practice, will furnish deeper insights; they cannot fail to prove to be works of capital value. But the little book has for me a special significance as a moving testimony to Schoenberg's relationship to the American musical scene, and his brilliantly successful efforts to come to grips with certain of its problems.

In this essay I have purposely avoided dwelling on the more problematical aspects of Schoenberg and his work; I have made no attempt at an exact or careful estimate. No doubt, Schoenberg is still in many respects a problematical figure, as is every other living composer. But it seems more relevant to regard him as a source of energy and impulse; final estimates may well be left to posterity, and the habit of attempting them at every turn is one of the dangerously sterile features of our contemporary culture. It is a symptom of a rather nervous self-consciousness and above all of self-distrust.

What is essential now is to recognize the need our world has for the qualities that Schoenberg possesses, and how admirably he supplies our need. In a worldwide condition in which the rewards of facile mediocrity and of compromise are greater than ever, and in which one hears an ever insistent demand that music and the other arts devote themselves to the task of furnishing bread and circuses to an economically or politically pliable multitude, the musical world yet celebrates in sincere homage the seventieth birthday of an artist who not only, in the face of the most bitter and persistent opposition, scorn and neglect, has always gone his own way in uncompromising integrity and independence, but who has been and is still the most dangerous enemy of the musical *status quo*. This takes place in spite of the fact that his work is all too seldom performed, that it is exacting in the extreme, and is virtually unknown except to a very few who have made the attempt really to penetrate its secrets. It is in the last analysis an act of gratitude to one who has, so much more than any other individual, been one of the masculine forces that have shaped the music of our time, even that music which seems farthest from his own. It is not only a tribute to a truly great musician, but a hopeful sign that art on the highest level may still survive the bewilderments and the terrors of a mighty world crisis, of which so much is still ahead of us, and which contains so many imponderables.

Index

Index of Musical Works

Subject Index

13er-Quartett of the
Arbeitergesangverein Vorwärts
(Hanau), 88, 89, 98, 121n14
Thomson, William J., 49n4
tonality
abandonment of, 27, 35
achievement of, 269
of "atonal" music, 269–70
defenders of, 22–23
functional relationships in, 57–59
functions of, 58, 59
monotonality, 57–58
"natural" music and, 22–23
nature of, 269
in Schoenberg's music, 168–70, 320–21
see also twelve-tone approach
tonal problem, 60–67
tone, compression of, 153–59
tone-color melody (*Klangfarbenmelodie*),
132
tonic, 57
centrifugal forces, 58–59, 60
centripital forces, 58–59
Tudor, Anthony, 13
twelve-tone approach
analogy with Zionism, 38–39, 46–47,
52n42
choral music and, 104–15
chromatic completion in, 172–74
circulation of twelve chromatic notes
in, 174–80
combinatoriality in, 191n35, 191n37
connection between counterpoint and,
79–80, 81, 126–39
as fresh approach to old problem,
42–47, 162–74, 180–88, 316
integration of melody and harmony in,
167–74
interaction of tonal elements with,
104–15
as mode of technical procedure,
331–32
modernism and, 22–23, 42–47, 53n53
nationalism and, 268
nonrepetition principle in, 35, 164–66,
172–73, 175, 187
origins of, 25, 28, 41, 170, 307–8
pitch classes in, 124n58
principles of, 176–77
radical implications of, 36

as reaction, 174–80, 187–88
row structure in, 107–9, 176–80
set theory and, 189–90
traditional forms in, 175, 180–81, 185
twelve-tone area and, 191n36
vertical/horizontal dimensions in, 25,
48, 49, 58, 145, 146

United States, Schoenberg moves to
(1933), 285, 286, 328
Universal Editions, 4
University of California at Los Angeles,
11–13, 286, 329
University of Chicago, 10, 14, 286
University of Southern California (Los
Angeles), 11, 286, 298, 301, 329

Varèse, Edgard, 7, 20, 287, 310
variation
in counterpoint, 74–78
motive and, 56, 57–67, 164–66, 187
Verdi, Giuseppe, "La donna è mobile,"
71, 72
Verein für muskalische
Privataufführungen (Society for private musical performances), 6, 43,
67, 86, 142, 320
Vereinigung schaffender Tonkünstler
(Society of creative composers), 3,
216
vertical dimension of music, horizontal
dimension versus, 25, 48, 49, 58,
145, 146
Vienna
anti-Semitism in, 29, 39, 40, 44
Arnold Schönberg Center, 23 50n14
audience reception of Schoenberg's
music in, 4, 29, 32, 34, 35, 39–41, 44,
296
critical reception of Schoenberg's
works in, 39–40, 51n28
Imperial Opera House, 29–32, 35
Jewish community in, 39–41
modernism of art and architecture in,
32
Musikverein, 51n26
Royal Academy of Music, 4, 202
Schoenberg's return to (1903), 3, 202
Schoenberg's return to (1921), 7

Notes on the Contributors

Joseph Auner, associate professor of music at SUNY–Stony Brook, is preparing *The Schoenberg Reader* for Yale University Press. His articles and reviews have appeared in the *Journal of the American Musicological Society, Music Theory Spectrum,* and other journals. He serves as General Editor for the series Studies in Contemporary Music and Culture for Garland Press.

Leon Botstein is president of Bard College, where he also serves as professor of history and music history. He is the author of *Judentum und Modernität* (Vienna, 1991) and of a forthcoming study, *Music and Its Public: Habits of Listening and the Crisis of Modernism in Vienna, 1870–1914,* and editor of *The Compleat Brahms* (New York, 1999) and of *The Musical Quarterly.*

Reinhold Brinkmann, the James Edward Ditson Professor of Music at Harvard University, has prepared editions of Schoenberg's piano works and *Pierrot lunaire* for the *Sämtliche Werke.* He is the author of *Late Idyll: The Second Symphony of Johannes Brahms* (Cambridge, Mass., 1995) and *Schumann und Eichendorff: Studien zum Liederkreis Opus 39* (Munich, 1997).

J. Peter Burkholder, professor of music and associate dean of the faculties at Indiana University, is the author of *Charles Ives: The Ideas Behind the Music* (New Haven, 1985) and *All Made of Tunes: Charles Ives and the Uses of Musical Borrowing* (New Haven, 1995). He served as editor of a previous volume in the Bard Festival Series, *Charles Ives and His World* (1996).

Sabine Feisst, who holds a fellowship from the Deutsche Forschungsgemeinschaft, is working on a book about Schoenberg and the United States. The author of *Der Begriff "Improvisation" in der neuen Musik* (Sinzig, 1997), she is an associate researcher for the Busoni Edition at the Musicology Department of the Free University, Berlin.

Walter Frisch, professor of music at Columbia University, is the author of *The Early Works of Arnold Schoenberg, 1893–1908* (Berkeley and Los Angeles, 1993) and of *Brahms: The Four Symphonies* (New York, 1996). He has served as editor of the journal *19th-Century Music* and of the inaugural volume in the Bard Festival Series, *Brahms and His World* (1990).

Marilyn L. McCoy works as a freelance musicologist in the Boston area. Though primarily a Mahler specialist, she worked at the Arnold Schoenberg Institute in Los Angeles for the last three years of its existence, serving as assistant archivist and co-author of *A Preliminary Inventory of Schoenberg Correspondence.*

Severine Neff, professor of music at the University of North Carolina at Chapel Hill, has edited two books of Schoenberg's theoretical writings: *The Musical Idea and the Logic, Technique, and Art of its Presentation* (with Patricia Carpenter) (New York, 1995) and *Coherence, Counterpoint, Instrumentation, Instruction in Form* (Lincoln and London, 1994).

Barbara Zeisl Schoenberg is adjunct associate professor of German at Pomona College. She has published articles on the Viennese fin de siècle and exile studies. Recent translations, for Ariadne Press, include *Hollywood Haven, Homes and Haunts of the European Émigrés and Exiles in Los Angeles*, by Cornelius Schnauber (1997), and *The Morning Before the Journey*, by Julian Schutting (forthcoming).

Rudolf Stephan, professor emeritus at the Free University in Berlin, is the general editor of the Schoenberg *Sämtliche Werke* and the author of many studies on twentieth-century music. Two collections of his essays and lectures have appeared as *Vom musikalischen Denken* (Mainz, 1985) and *Musiker der Moderne* (Laaber, 1996).